QUR'AN TRANSLATIONS IN THE EASTERN BLOC AND BEYOND

Qur'an Translations in the Eastern Bloc and Beyond

Edited by Elvira Kulieva, with Johanna Pink and Mykhaylo Yakubovych

https://www.openbookpublishers.com

©2025 Elvira Kulieva, Johanna Pink and Mykhaylo Yakubovych.
Copyright of individual chapters is maintained by the chapter's authors

This work is licensed under a Creative Commons Attribution-ShareAlike 4.0 International (CC BY-SA 4.0). This license allows you to share and adapt the text providing that: if you remix, transform, or build upon the material, you must distribute your contributions under the same license as the original; attribution is made to the authors (but not in any way that suggests that they endorse you or your use of the work). Attribution should include the following information:

Elvira Kulieva, Johanna Pink and Mykhaylo Yakubovych (eds), *Qur'an Translations in the Eastern Bloc and Beyond*. Cambridge, UK: Open Book Publishers, 2025, https://doi.org/10.11647/OBP.0444

Copyright and permissions for the reuse of many of the images included in this publication differ from the above. This information is provided in the captions and in the list of illustrations. Every effort has been made to identify and contact copyright holders and any omission or error will be corrected if notification is made to the publisher.

Further details about CC BY-SA 4.0 licenses are available at
https://creativecommons.org/licenses/by-sa/4.0/deed.en

All external links were active at the time of publication unless otherwise stated and have been archived via the Internet Archive Wayback Machine at https://archive.org/web

Digital material and resources associated with this volume are available at
https://doi.org/10.11647/OBP.0444#resources

The Global Qur'an Series Vol. 3
ISSN Print: 2753-8036 | ISSN Digital: 2753-8044SSN

ISBN Paperback: 978-1-80511-487-1
ISBN Hardback: 978-1-80511-488-8
ISBN Digital (PDF): 978-1-80511-489-5
ISBN Digital ebook (epub): 978-1-80511-490-1
ISBN HTML: 978-1-80511-491-8
DOI: 10.11647/OBP.0444

Cover photo by Elvira Kulieva and Johanna Pink
Cover design by Jeevanjot Kaur Nagpal

This book was generously supported by a grant from Albert-Ludwigs-Universität, Freiburg.

Table of Contents

Acknowledgements ix

Transliteration Notes xi

Contributors xiii

List of Illustrations xvii

Introduction 1
Elvira Kulieva and Johanna Pink

Part I: Qur'an Translations Across National Boundaries **27**

1. Hybrid Subjectivity in a Translation of the Qur'an: al-Ramzī's Farewell to Sufism 29
Alfrid Bustanov

2. 'Vernacular Qur'anic Space' within Post-Soviet Uzbekistan: A Qur'an Translation by a Leader of the Turkestani Émigré Community, and its Uzbek Competition 69
Filipp Khusnutdinov

3. 'I Quenched the Thirst of Seventy Million': Sumayya ʿAfīfī, an Egyptian Qur'an Translator for a Post-Soviet Readership 109
Elvira Kulieva

Part II: State Policies and Qur'an Translations **157**

4. The State, 'Official' ʿUlamāʾ and Tatar Qur'an Commentary-Translations in Russia 159
Elmira Akhmetova

5. A 'Qur'an Race' in the Cold War: Max Henning's Qur'an Translation in the German Democratic Republic 197
Johanna Pink

6. Constructing a Qur'an-Based *sīra* in Post-Soviet Azerbaijan: Denominational Approaches to the Prophet's Biography in Azerbaijani Qur'an Translations   239
Elnura Azizova

7. Implications of Theological Diversity in Shii-Authored Translations of the Qur'an and *tafsīrs* into Russian   279
Akif Tahiiev

Index   309

About the Team   319

Acknowledgements

This book is a result of the research project 'The Global Qur'an: Shared Traditions, Imperial Languages, and Transnational Actors' (GloQur), funded by the European Research Council (ERC) under the European Union's Horizon 2020 programme.[1] The editors are immensely grateful to the ERC for providing funding. We also wish to thank the University of Freiburg and its university library, whose logistic and financial support made this publication possible. The University also facilitated the workshop 'Nation-states and the Qur'an: translators, narratives and debates in the post-Soviet space' that took place in Freiburg on 14–15 October 2022, from which this book ultimately emerged. The help of these institutions allowed us to pursue our goal of bringing more attention to a region that has long been neglected in Islamic studies and linking it to global debates.

We extend our sincere thanks to all colleagues who participated in the above-mentioned workshop for their valuable insights and contributions to discussions, which have greatly inspired the development of this book. Our special thanks go to our student assistant, Christoph Langer, for his invaluable help in organising the event and welcoming our guests. Appreciation is also due to all the GloQur team members, especially Yulianingsih Riswan, who captured memorable photographs of the event, and Kamran Khan, who skillfully moderated a session.

We are also deeply grateful to Dr Helen Blatherwick for her meticulous editorial work for GloQur. Her contribution has significantly improved the language and overall quality of this volume, and all our other English-language publications. We furthermore thank our student

---

1   Grant agreement n° 863650.

assistants, Amadeus Tkocz and Edmée Maeder, for their efforts in compiling the index.

In addition, we are grateful to Dr Alessandra Tosi at Open Book Publishers as well as to the two anonymous reviewers whose valuable feedback helped improve this book.

Last but not least, we would like to express our sincere appreciation to the international team of contributors who wrote chapters for this edited volume. Your patience, expertise, and dedication have made this book possible.

Funding

The research leading to these results has been funded by the European Research Council (ERC) under the European Union's Horizon 2020 research and innovation programme, grant agreement n° 863650, project GloQur: 'The Global Qur'an. Shared Traditions, Imperial Languages and Transnational Actors'.

Transliteration Notes

For Arabic text, the chapters in this volume follow the transliteration scheme of the *International Journal of Middle East Studies* (IJMES). For transliterations from Russian sources, a simplified version of the Library of Congress transliteration system is applied, except where a widely accepted English spelling exists. Beyond these two languages, several chapters incorporate transliterations from regional languages:

Chapter 1 deals with a Turkic manuscript written in the Arabic script, incorporating Turkic elements. To reflect these features, the transliteration includes the vowel markers [ä], [ï], [ö], and [ü]. Chapter 2 uses Uzbek sources and follows the Uzbek Latin alphabet, which is the official state script in Uzbekistan. No additional transliteration system was applied. Chapter 4 relies on Tatar sources, and when these are written in Cyrillic, the transliteration system developed by Edward Allworth is used. Chapter 6 applies two different Azerbaijani transliteration systems: the main text uses simplified Latin spelling (e.g. Mammadaliyev), and the footnotes use Azerbaijani-specific Latin characters such as [ə] that reflect the modern Azerbaijani Latin alphabet (e.g. Məmmədəliyev). Chapter 7 engages with the Russian translations of Iranian authors. To facilitate online searches for these texts, Russian transliteration has been used consistently.

Contributors

Elmira Akhmetova (PhD) is the Director of Research and Grants at the Institute of Knowledge Integration, Georgia. She was previously employed as a Senior Fellow at the Freiburg Institute for Advanced Studies (FRIAS) at the Albert-Ludwigs-University Freiburg, Germany, to conduct a research project, 'Tatar Translations and Commentaries of the Qur'an in Imperial Russia', funded by the Alexander von Humboldt Foundation (2021–2023). Her most recent publications are *Muslim Women in Science, Past and Present* (Cambridge: Cambridge University Press, 2025), 'Russia' in *Yearbooks of Muslims in Europe* (Leiden: Brill, 2024), and 'Tradition of the Qur'an Commentaries and Translations among Kazan Tatars' (Azerbaijan Institute of Theology, 2024).

Associate Professor **Elnura Azizova** is a faculty member at the Department of Religious Studies of Azerbaijan Institute of Theology (AIT) and Khazar University. Dr. Azizova currently holds the position of the dean of the Faculty of Theology at the AIT. Dr. Azizova graduated with a PhD in Islamic history from the Marmara University, Istanbul, Turkey in 2007. Her PhD dissertation is on the socio-economic history of early Muslims. She is the author and coauthor of several academic books and articles on Islamic history, Qur'an and *ḥadīth* studies.

Alfrid Bustanov (PhD) is an independent researcher who has published on topics of Islam in Russia, Central Asia, and the Caucasus.

Filipp Khusnutdinov is a research fellow at the al-Biruni Institute of Oriental Studies at the Uzbekistan Academy of Sciences (Tashkent, Uzbekistan). From 2012 to 2018, he studied at the Tashkent Islamic University under the Cabinet of Ministers of the Republic of Uzbekistan (now the International Islamic Academy of Uzbekistan), specialising in the history and source studies of Islam. His main research interests include the intellectual history of Central Asian Muslim communities in Soviet and early post-Soviet times, both within Central Asia and in the process of their emigration to the Near East. Filipp has participated in a number of international conferences, internships, and summer schools in Leiden, Freiburg, Rabat, Vienna, Kazan, and St. Petersburg, among other venues. He is the author of about ten articles.

Elvira Kulieva is a PhD candidate involved in the Global Qur'an Project at the University of Freiburg, where she is focusing on her dissertation about modern Qur'an translations produced by diverse Muslim communities following the dissolution of the USSR. Previously, she conducted research on contemporary Sufism and published several papers.

Johanna Pink is a Professor of Islamic Studies at the University of Freiburg in Germany. Her primary research focus is the transregional history of *tafsīr* and Qur'an translation. She serves as the general editor of the *Encyclopaedia of the Qurʾān Online* and was the Principal Investigator of the ERC-funded project GloQur. Her publications include *Muslim Qur'ānic Interpretation Today: Media, Genealogies, and Interpretive Communities* (Sheffield: Equinox, 2019) and *Qur'an Translation in Indonesia: Scriptural Politics in a Multilingual State* (London: Routledge, 2024). She has worked and published extensively on the study of the global history of modern Muslim Qur'an translation.

Akif Tahiiev is a postdoctoral research fellow at Goethe University Frankfurt and the Max Planck Institute for the Study of Religious and Ethnic Diversity in Göttingen, Germany. Previously, he served as a research and teaching assistant in the Department of Human Rights and Legal Methodology at Yaroslav Mudryi National Law University in Kharkiv, Ukraine, and held research positions at the University of Vienna and the Institute for Human Sciences (IWM) in Vienna, Austria. He has authored numerous articles and chapters on Shii Islam, Islam in post-Soviet countries, digital religion, minorities, legal history, and Islamic law.

Mykhaylo Yakubovych obtained his PhD in 2011 from The National University of Ostroh Academy with a study on interreligous relations in medieval Sunni traditionalism. Currently a member of the research team on the ERC-funded project GloQur (University of Freiburg, Germany), he studies Qur'an translations produced by international institutions and publishers, with a focus on Central Asian and Eastern European languages. He is the author of an annotated translation of the Qur'an into Ukrainian (first published in 2013), along with several books and translations from Arabic, and many research articles published in academic journals from the UK, Turkey, Saudi Arabia, and Australia. Yakubovych has conducted several academic projects on the heritage of Islamic manuscripts, including the post-classical intellectual history of the Crimean Khanate (at the Institute for Advanced Study, Princeton University, USA) and sixteenth- to seventeenth-century Qur'an interpretations produced by Lithuanian Tatars (at Nicolaus Copernicus University, Poland). His most recent monograph is entitled *The Kingdom and the Qur'an: Translating the Holy Book of Islam in Saudi Arabia* (Cambridge: Open Book Publishers, 2024, https://doi.org/10.11647/OBP.0381).

The Eastern Bloc (Communist Bloc). States with communist governments are marked with a star pattern, states that the USSR once considered as 'moving toward socialism' are striped, and other socialist nations are marked with squares. However, not all star-patterned states remained allied with the Soviet Union. Wikipedia, CC BY-SA 4.0.

List of Illustrations

1.1 & 1.2	Colophons in al-Ramzī's work: intermediary (1.1) and final (1.2). ©Alfrid Bustanov, Creative Commons license CC BY.	p. 37
1.3	The text, commentary, and glosses in al-Ramzī's work. ©Alfrid Bustanov, Creative Commons license CC BY.	p. 41
2.1	Undated photograph of al-Sayyid Maḥmūd al-Ṭarāzī. The identity of the photographer is unknown. ©Filipp Khusnutdinov, Creative Commons license CC BY.	p. 73
2.2	The first edition of al-Ṭarāzī's Qur'an translation and exegesis, published in six volumes in Bombay (1956), vol. I, al-Biruni Institute of Oriental Studies, Tashkent. ©al-Biruni Institute of Oriental Studies, Creative Commons license CC BY.	p. 82
2.3	The fragmentary publication of al-Ṭarāzī's Qur'an translation in Cyrillic by Ismatulla Abdullayev in *Fan va turmush*, 8 (1989), pp. 20–21. ©*Fan va turmush*, Creative Commons license CC BY.	p. 88
2.4	Al-Ṭarāzī's writings, preserved in the library of the Mir-i ʿArab Madrasa (2021). ©Filipp Khusnutdinov, Creative Commons license CC BY.	p. 91
2.5	The front cover of the first Tashkent edition of al-Ṭarāzī's Qur'an translation (1994). ©*Al-Qur'on ul-karim (o'zbek tilida izohli tarjima)*, Creative Commons license CC BY.	p. 94
2.6	The front cover of the second Tashkent edition of al-Ṭarāzī's Qur'an translation (2002). ©*Al-Qur'on al-karim ma'nolarining tarjimasi va sharhlar*, Creative Commons license CC BY.	p. 96
3.1	Sumayya ʿAfīfī (1935–2005). ©Elvira Kulieva, Creative Commons license CC BY.	p. 125

Introduction

Elvira Kulieva and Johanna Pink

Why Qur'an Translations in the Former Eastern Bloc?[1]

The first Qur'an translation into Kazakh to be printed and distributed in Kazakhstan was written by a man born in East Turkestan, or Xinjiang. Halifa Altay (1917–2003) was one of a number of ethnic Kazakhs who fled China in the early 1950s, when the Chinese Communist Party was asserting its control over the province. He went on to live in Turkey until 1991 and remained active in the Kazakh diaspora movement throughout his time there. His Qur'an translation, which was first published in Turkey in 1989,[2] was, however, largely inaccessible to people in the Kazakh Soviet Socialist Republic, not only because the publisher's distribution networks were mostly confined to diaspora groups in Turkey and Iran, but also because it was written in Arabic script, which limited its potential for a Kazakh readership as the Soviets had imposed the Cyrillic script on the region in 1940. This soon changed when, only one year later, in 1990, a Cyrillic-script edition of Altay's Qur'an translation was published in Kazakhstan; a year after that, the King Fahd Glorious Qur'an Printing Complex (KFGQPC) in Medina,

---

1 This publication is a product of the project 'GloQur—The Global Qur'an' that has received funding from the European Research Council (ERC) under the European Union's Horizon 2020 research and innovation programme (Grant agreement No 863650).

2 Halifa Altay, *Kälam- Şarïf: tüzetip, tolıqtırıp bastırwsı X. Altay* (Istanbul: Elïf-ofset baspası, 1989).

Saudi Arabia, published another edition, thereby giving literate Kazakh Muslims the opportunity to learn about the meaning of the Qur'an in their own language for the first time in many decades.³ Furthermore, as a result of his years in exile, during which he had been disconnected from linguistic developments in the Kazakh SSR, Altay's version of Kazakh came across sometimes as archaic and difficult to understand.

After the collapse of the USSR, many Kazakh Muslims were eager to use their new-found freedom to learn about their religion. However, due to the restrictions on religious freedom during the Soviet era—in which all *madrasa*s had been closed—there was a lack of trained Islamic scholars.⁴ Unlike many other members of the Kazakh diaspora, when the Kazakh SSR ended and the country gained its independence in 1991, Altay moved back to Kazakhstan, where he made a major contribution to filling the gap in Islamic scholarship. His role in the country's national and religious revival earned his translation lasting prestige despite its linguistic archaism, as did the fact that the King Fahd Complex continued to distribute it.⁵ At the same time, it soon faced competition as other Kazakh actors entered the field and produced translations into modern, more accessible Kazakh. For instance, a number of Kazakh muftis who were closely associated with the Kazakh Muftiate, as well as others working outside the muftiate but whose translations were officially certified by it, authored translations during various periods after Kazakhstan's independence.⁶ Scholars who had received their religious training in Egypt, a destination that became accessible after

---

3   Halifa Altay, *Quran Şarïf* (Almatı: Jazwşı: Sözstan, 1991); Halifa Altay, *Quran Kärim: qazaqs̲a mağına jäne tüsinigi* (Medina: King Fahd Glorious Qur'an Printing Complex, 1991).

4   In the USSR, the only two officially recognised *madrasa*s were located in Bukhara and Tashkent, which were both in the Uzbek SSR. For an extensive account of Soviet history of Islamic education, including the moderate possibilities it had prior to the 1930s and information about 'unofficial' or 'illegal' Islamic education, such as private learned circles (*ḥujra*s), see *Islamic Education in the Soviet Union and its Successor States*, ed. by Michael Kemper, Raoul Motika, and Stefan Reichmuth (London–New York: Routledge, 2009).

5   This account is based on Mykhaylo Yakubovych, *The Kingdom and the Qur'an: Translating the Holy Book of Islam in Saudi Arabia* (Cambridge: Open Book Publishers, 2024), pp. 106–09, https://doi.org/10.11647/OBP.0381

6   Such as the translation by Ra'tbek Nysanbai'uly, who held this position from 1990–2000; and the recent translation in 2020 by the current deputy (*naib*) mufti of the Kazakh Muftiate, Dr Ers'at On'g'arov. See: Ratbek Nysanbai'uly and Y'ahap Qydyrhanuly (trans.), *Quran Ka'rim* (Almaty: Jazy's'y, 1991); Ers'at

the fall of the USSR, also played a significant role in shaping the field of Kazakh Qur'an translations.⁷

The case of Halifa Altay is in many ways emblematic of developments in the Eastern Bloc and the countries that broke free from it in the years around 1990. It is the story of a Qur'an translation whose fate was profoundly shaped by the mobility of its author and readers, both forced and voluntary. And it was intimately tied to the nation-state whose language it used, even though its author had not actually been born on the territory of that state. It demonstrates the speed of the transformation that occurred around 1990 and the impact of the religious revival that started around that time. And it also shows the extent to which international actors entered the field at an early stage after the fall of the Soviet Union.

Much like earlier Qur'an translations—such as the famous English translation by Abdullah Yusuf Ali (1872–1953) or the French rendition by Muhammad Hamidullah (1908–2002), both of whom hailed from India—Altay's project tells a story of empire, exile, and migration.⁸ And much like many other Qur'an translations from the second half of the twentieth century onwards, whether they be in Hausa or Indonesian, it also tells a story of nation building and the assertion of linguistic and religious identity. It is, in addition, the story of a Muslim scholar who tried to maintain the legacy of the *tafsīr* tradition, just as other scholars were trying to do from British India to Mali.

On'g'arov and Nurjan Murata'li, *Qasi'etti Quran:mag'ynasy men tu'siniktemeler* (Nur-Sultan: Baspa, 2020).

7   See, for example, the recent work of Asqar Bolatbekuly A'kimhanov and Nurlan Sai'lay'uly Anarbaev, two graduates of ʿAyn al-Shams and al-Azhar universities in Egypt, who also received their PhDs from the Kazakh-Egyptian University Nur-Mubarak: Asqar B. A'kimhanov and Nurlan Sai'lay'uly Anarbaev, *Quran Ka'rim qazaqs'a oqyly'y ja'ne ay'darmasy* (Almaty: Samg'a, 2022). This is also evident in the above mentioned translation of Ers'at Ag'ybai'uly On'g'arov who, in addition to his post-graduate degrees and muftiat position, also studied in Egypt with the Azhari scholars.

8   ʿAbdullah Yūsuf ʿAlī, *The Holy Qur-ān: English Translation & Commentary. Parts I–XV* (Lahore: Muḥammad Ashraf, 1934); ʿAbdullāh Yūsuf ʿAlī, *The Holy Qur-ān: Arabic Text with an English Translation and Commentary. Vol. II, Containing Sūras IX to XXIX* (Lahore: Muḥammad Ashraf, 1937); ʿAbdullāh Yūsuf ʿAlī, *The Holy Qur-an: Text Translation & Commentary. Vol. III, Containing Suras XXIX to CXIV* (Lahore: Muḥammad Ashraf, n.d.); Muḥammad Hamidullah, *Le Saint Coran* (Paris: Hadj Mohamed Noureddine Ben Mahmoud, 1963).

And yet, stories such as that of Halifa Altay are rarely treated as part of the wider narrative of the global modern history of Islam. They are hardly ever brought into conversation with stories of scholars working within other empires, or other independent nation-states, or the melting pot that was the United States. This book tries to lay the groundwork for starting such conversations by exploring the field of Qur'an translation in the Eastern Bloc during the Soviet era and in its aftermath, concentrating first on mobilities enforced by the transformations that took place at the beginning of the Soviet Union, and those that were facilitated throughout the existence of the Eastern Bloc, or encouraged after it fell apart; and second, on the impact of states and their institutions, from the Tsarist Empire that first started to 'govern Islam', throughout the duration of the socialist satellite states of the Soviet Union, until the independent nation-states of the contemporary period.

Qur'an translations might not be an obvious subject to use as a focal point for studying these developments but, as the case of Altay shows, they are born from a specific dialectic that allows for unique insights: the dialectic between innovation and continuities that is inherent in many modern forms of Islamic expression. On the one hand, the dividing line between translation and the premodern genre of *tafsīr*, or the Qur'an commentary, is very narrow. On the other hand, the form and style of the modern genre of Qur'an translation and its target audience are radically different from the elite scholarly tradition of *tafsīr*.[9] Paradigms of modernisation can hardly do justice to this dialectic, which involved continuities and discontinuities, and the interplay between these as well as various shifts from 'classical' styles of Islam to its transformed contemporary representations—and back.

Qur'an translations are useful to study this dynamic not only because of their intimate relationship with premodern exegetical practices but also because they play such a significant role in modern Muslim publishing activities. The momentum they gained in the twentieth and twenty-first centuries can be attributed to several factors, including the

---

9   This does not mean that the phenomenon of Qur'an translation did not exist in the past; rather, contemporary forms and conditions have made it uniquely different from previous practices. The contemporary trend is traceable from the early twentieth century, when Muslims began translating the Qur'an into European languages.

global post-colonial situation and the ensuing movement of people, as well as the enormous increase in literacy facilitated by secular mass education through public school and modern university systems that operate within the framework of nation-states, not to mention the rise in access to printing and the internet. In non-Arab Muslim-majority contexts, the shift from the Arabic script to Cyrillic or Latin scripts was also an important factor that contributed to the rising popularity of, and interest in, Qur'an translations, as an increasing number of Muslims were unable to read the script in which both the Qur'an and traditional exegetical texts were written. There were also changes in the ways that people engaged with Muslim scripture, as previously dominant, traditional forms of engagement were challenged by technical and educational innovations. In many contexts, priority was given to newly emerging national languages, and secular education gained primacy over the traditional *madrasas*.[10] Moreover, the status of the ʿulamāʾ as the main custodians and mediators of sacred knowledge who had privileged status in interpreting the Qur'an drastically changed.[11] This was reflected in the emergence of 'new spokesmen for Islam'[12] who also began translating the Qur'an into various languages for various reasons, ranging from *daʿwa* to personal piety projects. The unprecedented interest in the Qur'an's meanings as a 'source of guidance' in the modern world for the Muslim masses, a phenomenon described as a 'shift to the centre',[13] was possible because an increasing number of Muslims had access to the Qur'an or its meanings—for example, in the medium of translation—through the press and, later, the internet. This, however, does not mean that the ʿulamāʾ have fully lost their authority. They continue to play an important role by adapting to and accommodating the demands of modernity, in part through their active participation in the production of Qur'an translations, either on their own authority or at an institutional level. In this regard, the role played by influential

---

10 Johanna Pink, 'Editor's Preface', *Journal of Qur'anic Studies*, 17:3 (2015), 1–9.
11 More on the role of ʿulamāʾ in modernity, see Muhammad Qasim Zaman, *The Ulama in Contemporary Islam: Custodians of Change* (Princeton: Princeton University Press, 2002).
12 Suha Taji-Farouki and Basheer M. Nafi (eds), *Islamic Thought in the Twentieth Century* (London: I. B. Tauris, 2004), p. 5.
13 Johanna Pink, *Muslim Qur'ānic Interpretation Today: Media, Genealogies and Interpretive Communities* (Bristol: Equinox, 2019), p. 17.

Islamic institutions such as Egypt's al-Azhar, the Turkish Diyanet, and the KFGQPC in Saudi Arabia, all of which exert a strong influence in shaping global Islamic discourses, should also be emphasised. For them, Qur'an translations are a way of propagating and spreading a distinctive ideology, and attaining global Islamic influence. The KFGQPC, for example, is the largest producer of Qur'an translations globally today.[14]

Thus, Qur'an translations are a site of constant contestation in which diverse stakeholders are involved: the nation-state, local and global Islamic authorities, individual Muslims, publishers, and so on. The questions of who has the right to translate, which exegetical basis should be used or shunned, and what kind of theologically and politically correct translational choices should be made, form part of the ongoing debates currently taking place in various Muslim societies in non-Arab Muslim majority or minority contexts. Each Qur'an translation is ultimately a normative vision of how the Qur'anic meanings are understood by a particular actor, be it an author (or authors), editor, publisher, or the particular religious group they represent.

Increasingly, the field of Qur'an translations attracts more scholarly attention, allowing us to take a comparative look at global trends and relate them to particular historical developments in various regions. Recent studies have greatly enhanced our understanding of *tafsīr* and Qur'an translation in the premodern period, from the beginning of the Middle Period to the nineteenth century.[15] Given the sheer number

---

14 On this topic, see Yakubovych, *The Kingdom and the Qur'an*.

15 For example, see: Travis Zadeh, *The Vernacular Qur'an: Translation and the Rise of Persian Exegesis* (Oxford: Oxford University Press, 2012); M. Brett Wilson, *Translating the Qur'an in an Age of Nationalism: Print Culture and Modern Islam in Turkey* (Oxford: Oxford University Press, 2014); Kristian Petersen, *Interpreting Islam in China. Pilgrimage, Scripture, and Language in the Han Kitab* (Oxford: Oxford University Press, 2017); Peter G. Riddell, *Malay Court Religion, Culture and Language: Interpreting the Qur'an in 17th Century Aceh* (Leiden and Boston: Brill, 2017); Susan Gunasti, *The Qur'an between the Ottoman Empire and the Turkish Republic: An Exegetical Tradition* (London and New York: Routledge, 2019); Simon Leese, 'Arabic Utterances in a Multilingual World: Shāh Walī-Allāh and Qur'anic Translatability in North India', *Translation Studies*, 14:2 (2021), 242–61; Kamran Bashir, *The Qur'an in South Asia: Hermeneutics, Qur'an Projects, and Imaginings of Islamic Tradition in British India* (New York: Routledge, 2022); Gulnaz Sibgatullina, 'On Translating the Qur'an into Turkic Vernaculars: Texts, Ties, and Traditions', in *European Muslims and the Qur'an: Practices of Translation, Interpretation, and Commodification*, ed. by Gulnaz Sibgatullina and Gerard Wiegers (Berlin: De Gruyter, 2024), pp. 219–58.

of Qur'an translations that exist in the contemporary Islamic textual tradition, they should constitute a central source for understanding modern Islam, but so far few attempts at approaching them in a historically situated, comparative manner have been made.

This lacuna is even more obvious in regards to translations produced in countries from the former Soviet region, which shared a common communist history in the twentieth century. Oft overlooked, they have not yet been incorporated into the narrative of the global rise of Qur'an translation. Islam in the region has long been a subject of scholarly investigation, with research drawing on various sources, such as archives, personal manuscript collections of religious texts, egodocuments like diaries, anthropological, and sociological approaches, and media discourses. However, it is clear that modern Qur'an translations have rarely been seen as a useful analytical tool for understanding intellectual discourses, state policies, and religious practices in these countries.[16] Our aim in this volume is to begin to fill this gap and to put the region into productive conversation with developments in other regions. This will connect the history of the former Eastern Bloc with the broader history of the Muslim world, and tell the story of the Qur'an and those who translated it from a new perspective.

This perspective is informed by the stories of those countries in which religious activity was disrupted under Soviet rule, beginning in the 1920s and later extending to other parts of the Eastern Bloc after World War II. Many religious scholars went into exile, becoming part of diasporas that were largely, although not entirely, disconnected from local developments in their respective homelands—in contrast to, for example, South Asian diasporas in the English-speaking world. Religious expression and publishing were severely restricted, if they were at all possible; and due to script reforms and the closure of religious institutions, indigenous Muslims' connection to their own traditions and heritage was severed. Needless to say, there was no possibility of

---

16 There are a few exceptions. For example: Alfrid K. Bustanov, 'Beyond the Ethnic Traditions: Shamil' Aliautdinov's Muslim Guide to Success', in *Islamic Authority and the Russian Language: Studies on Texts from European Russia, the North Caucasus and West Siberia*, ed. by Alfrid K. Bustanov and Michael Kemper (Amsterdam: Pegasus, 2012), pp. 143–66; Mykhaylo Yakubovych, 'Qur'an Translations into Central Asian Languages: Exegetical Standards and Translation Processes', *Journal of Qur'anic Studies*, 21:1 (2022), 89–115.

revival in terms of Islamic publishing in the 1970s in these countries—if anything, it was Orientalists who were able to publish Qur'an translations, which were geared towards non-Muslim readers. However, while there was a notable decrease in Islamic practices and literature production, the USSR did not manage to eliminate them completely.[17] The late 1980s, with the weakening of the Soviet Union and the arrival of *perestroika*, saw an Islamic revival. This strengthened and grew with the emergence of new nation-states from the ruins of the USSR, and a wide range of Islamic publishing activities began to flourish during the 1990s. This included the production of Qur'an translations into many languages, especially in those countries that had a large Muslim population. From the outset, this localised religious revival was part of a wider, international scene in which actors ranging from government institutions to missionary societies of various religious persuasions were competing for influence and saw the former Eastern Bloc as fertile ground.

However, the history of Muslim Qur'an translation publishing in Russia, other former republics of the Soviet Union, and, more broadly, the Eastern Bloc, is very diverse and it would be overly simplistic to propose a 'universal (post-communist) pattern' through which we can approach the topic. Instead, there is a need to recognise the nuances of each case, as well as the historical particularities of each Muslim community and their respective interactions with the state, local non-Muslim populations, and international networks.[18] That said, the shadow of the Soviet Union looms large and it is possible to emphasise certain region-specific trends that influenced the modern Qur'an translations. In fact, the communist past shaped the specific Soviet 'Weltanschauung of Muslim individuals' who lived behind the Iron Curtain,[19] which is

---

17 For case studies on the production, preservation, and transmission of Islamic knowledge in the post-Stalinist period, see: Al'frid K. Bustanov, 'Koran dlia sovetskikh grazhdan: ritorika progressa v bogoslovskikh trudakh Gabdelbari Isaeva', *Antropologicheskii forum*, 37 (2018), 92–114; Alfrid K. Bustanov, 'Muslim Literature in the Atheist State: Zainap Maksudova between Soviet Modernity and Tradition', *Journal of Islamic Manuscripts*, 9:1 (2018), 1–31.
18 Egdūnas Račius, *Islam in Post-Communist Eastern Europe: Between Churchification and Securitization* (Leiden: Brill, 2020), p. 214.
19 Alfrid Bustanov, *Muslim Subjectivity in Soviet Russia: The Memoirs of 'Abd al-Majid al-Qadiri* (Leiden: Brill, 2022), p. 1; see also Paolo Sartori, 'Towards a History of the Muslims' Soviet Union: A View from Central Asia', *Die Welt des Islams* 50:3–4

crucially important for understanding and locating the genealogies of contemporary Muslim subjectivities. To understand the origins of Soviet Islam, one must also acknowledge its connection to the imperial past.

This brings us to the Muslim intellectuals of that time such as Ismail Gasprinskii (1851–1914), who lived at the turn of the nineteenth and twentieth centuries and whose ideas on the Qur'an as a repositorium of 'universal values' embodied a specific 'hybrid' kind of Muslim leadership. Having been shaped by Islamic *mekteb* settings as well as Russian and European educational systems, individuals like Gasprinskii were recurrent examples of culturally 'hybrid' intellectuals across various empires, challenging the clear-cut distinction between the cultural categories of the coloniser and the colonised.[20] For sure, hybridity, is not exclusive to particular individuals but intrinsic to human nature in general. However, the task of scholars lies in uncovering certain historical trends such as 'imperial hybridities' and their regional specificities, identifying the recurring forms that emerge across different contexts.

The hybridity of the Russian imperial context was particularly distinctive and exemplary among Russian Muslim intellectuals, as it also intersected with Russia's own identity struggles, such as the domestic debates between Slavophiles and Westernisers. These debates reflected the complex and ambivalent relationship between Russia and Western Europe, ideas from days long gone by, yet apparently relevant again today. In regards to Muslim imperial identities, Sibgatullina noted that 'many of the social categories imposed on Russia's Muslims were in themselves already "hybrid", having emerged from the "encounter" between Russian and European cultural codes.'[21] This hybridity did not disappear with the advent of communism as despite the Stalinist purges, we find cases of pre-revolutionary Islamic discourses seeping into this new Soviet Muslim *Weltanschauung*. For example, the case of Tatar Soviet mufti Gabdelbari (ʿAbd al-Bārī) Isaev (1907–1983) and his Qur'an translation, as studied by Alfrid Bustanov, illustrates

---

(2010), 315–34; Paolo Sartori, 'Why Soviet Islam Matters', *Anzeiger*, 157:1–2 (2022), 5–24; Paolo Sartori, *A Soviet Sultanat: Islam in the Socialist Uzbekistan (1943–1991)* (Vienna: Austrian Academy of Science Press, 2024).

20   Gulnaz Sibgatullina, 'When the Other Speaks: Ismāʿīl Gasprinskii and the Concept of Islamic Reformation', *Journal of the Economic and Social History of the Orient*, 65 (2022), 214–47 (p. 216).

21   Ibid., p. 217.

the complex and multilayered nature of Soviet Muslim 'hybridity'. In Isaev's work, pre-revolutionary Muslim reformist discourses combined with the Soviet cult of labour and a fascination with Soviet science and cosmonautics, all of which found expression in his Qur'an translation.[22] Although this Qur'an translation was never made public during the Soviet era, it demonstrates the ways of interpreting the Qur'an that were practised by Muslims during the Brezhnev era.

On the other hand, it is equally important to understand the subjectivities of 'resistance', namely the exiled groups and other indigenous intellectuals who found communist and post-communist dictatorial regimes incompatible with their religious beliefs.[23] Subjectivities of 'resistance' can manifest through specific modes of translation, particularly in post-colonial contexts or amid ongoing cultural repression by foreign authorities. Modern translation studies highlight historical instances where translators acted as agents of social change, turning translation into a 'resistance' tool. In the broader communist context beyond Islamic studies, Soviet authors, for example, used paratextual spaces—such as footnotes and commentaries in state-approved translations—as sites of subtle opposition to Soviet values and Marxist dogma. Brian James Baer observes that through text selection, translation choices, and paratextual commentary, literary translators in the Soviet era encoded resistance for a select intelligentsia audience.[24] In the search for translations that can be conceptualised as 'resistant', the most obvious example is perhaps *samizdat* a form of literature aimed at challenging censorship and cultural repression. In contrast to more widespread *samizdat* literature, *islamizdat* literature does not easily fit into the clear 'resistance' paradigm. Compared to the variety of *samizdat* literature, *islamizdat* (lit. 'Islamic self-publishing') complicates the notion of resistance. While some texts, such as translations of works by Sayyid Quṭb or Abū l-Aʿlā Mawdūdī, were clearly political, many others

---

22 Alfrid Bustanov, 'The Qur'an for Soviet Citizens: The Rhetoric of Progress in the Theological Works of 'Abd al-Bari Isaev', *Forum for Anthropology and Culture*, 14 (2018), 169–84 (p. 176).

23 Botakoz Kassymbekova and Aminat Chokobaeva, 'On Writing Soviet History of Central Asia: Frameworks, Challenges, Prospects', *Central Asian Survey*, 40:4 (2021), 483–503 (p. 486).

24 Brian James Baer, 'Literary Translation and the Construction of a Soviet Intelligentsia', in *Translation, Resistance, Activism*, ed. by Maria Tymoczko (Amherst and Boston: University of Massachusetts Press, 2010), pp. 149–67 (p. 149).

were not, making it difficult to situate them within a straightforward resistance paradigm.²⁵ Sophie Roche in her analyses of Tajikistan's *islamizdat* literature since the era of *perestroika* argued that this literature represented the 'imagination of a Muslim world' where the guiding rationale of these *islamizdat* pamphlets was the 'notion of shared Islamic culture, which finds its very existence in the interface of local and global relationships.'²⁶

In translation studies, the idea of 'resistance' if understood conceptually is perceived to be problematic due to its semantically reactive rather than proactive nature. Tymoczko notes that if 'resistance' is taken as 'the foundation for conceptualising political and ideological agency and activism in translation in general: it is unnecessarily restrictive with regard to initiative, limiting translators to a more passive role than is required or desirable.'²⁷ This resonates with much of the contemporary academic scholarship as it understands Soviet Islam through the lens of compromise, challenging the classical assumption of Cold War paradigm studies that resilience and moral rearmament are inherently tied to resistance.²⁸ However, so far much of this scholarship

---

25   The dissemination of these authors in the 1980s can be traced to students from the Near and Middle East who came to the study in the USSR, and to increased possibilities for ḥajj pilgrimage. See: B. M. Babajanov, A. K. Muminov, and A. von Kügelgen, 'Introduction: Religious Texts of the Soviet Era', in *Disputes on Muslim Authority in Central Asia (20th Century): Critical Editions and Source Studies. Disputy musul'manskikh religioznykh avtoritetov v Tsentral'noi Azii v XX veke*, ed. by Bakhtiyor M. Babajanov, Ashirbek K. Muminov, and Anke von Kügelgen (Almaty: Daik-Press, 2007), pp. 32–54.

26   Sophie Roche, *The Faceless Terrorist: A Study of Critical Events in Tajikistan*, 1st edn, Transcultural Research: Heidelberg Studies on Asia and Europe in a Global Context (Cham: Springer, 2019), p. 128, https://doi.org/10.1007/978-3-030-03843-4

27   Maria Tymoczko, 'Translation, Resistance, Activism: An Overview', in *Translation, Resistance, Activism*, ed. by Maria Tymoczko (Amherst and Boston: University of Massachusetts Press, 2010), pp. 1–22 (p. 10).

28   For example, the studies on Soviet *kolkhozes* and *sovkhozes* in Muslim majority settings, together with various resettlement policies, were marked by dynamic interactions between Muslim unofficial authorities and the Soviet system. This arose from the polarising standards and 'rules of the game' of colonisers, with many returned Gulag prisoners seeking compromises with those in power. Quite often there was also an awareness of clandestine teaching or dissemination of Islamic literature, which in some periods was tolerated if it did not have a political message. See, for example, Stéphane A. Dudoignon and Christian Noack (eds), *Allah's Kolkhozes: Migration, de-Stalinisation, Privatisation and the New Muslim Congregations in the Soviet Realm (1950s-2000s)*, Islamkundliche Untersuchungen, Band 314 (Berlin: K. Schwarz, 2014).

focuses on Muslims within the Iron Curtain, rarely situating the perspectives and legacies of exile groups within the broader context of communist influences and formations.[29]

Another perspective is to understand the approaches and specific frameworks that Marxist Orientalist scholars developed towards the publication of religious literature under communist regimes,[30] as the influence of these scholars extended far beyond academia and thus should be taken into account, especially when discussing the successor states of the Soviet Union or larger post-communist prospects. These approaches closely linked to Qur'an translations produced during the communist era, as well as later works by scholars trained in Oriental studies through a Marxist lens, who either authored their own translations or contributed to shaping specific Qur'an-centric discourses. For instance, the Russian academic Taufik Ibragim exemplifies this trend, with his work reflecting distinct approaches shaped by historical and ideological contexts.[31]

Another important factor to consider, especially in countries that were part of the Soviet Union, is the influence of the administrative structures known as Muslim spiritual administrations or 'muftiates'. Their activities have had a significant impact on the production of Qur'an

---

29   A rare example of a study exploring the connection between post-Soviet Uzbeks and the exiled diaspora emigrated to Hijaz after the arrival of the Soviets to Central Asia is offered by Bayram Balci, *Islam in Central Asia and the Caucasus since the Fall of the Soviet Union* (Oxford: Oxford University Press, 2018). However, as this study does not focus primarily on religious literature, this area remains an important avenue for the future research.

30   On Mirasism—a trend developed among Tatar academics in the post-Stalinist periods—see, for example: Alfrid K. Bustanov and Michel Kemper, 'From Mirasism to Euro-Islam: The Translation of Islamic Legal Debates into Tatar Secular Cultural Heritage', in *Islamic Authority and the Russian Language: Studies on Texts from European Russia, the North Caucasus and West Siberia*, ed. by Alfrid K. Bustanov and Michael Kemper (Amsterdam: Pegasus, 2012), pp. 29–52; Danis Garaev, 'Post-Secular Mirasism and Reforming Islam in Russia: From Euro-Islam to Confessional Scholarship', *Islam and Christian–Muslim Relations*, 34:1 (2023), 1–29; Elvira Kulieva, 'In the Shadow of Orientalism: Tracing the Legacy of Ignatiĭ Krachkovskiĭ in Russian Salafi Qur'an Translations', in *Retranslating the Bible and the Qur'an: Historical Approaches and Current Debates*, ed. by Pieter Boulogne, Marijke de Lang, and Joseph Verheyden (Leuven: Leuven University Press, 2024), pp. 109–141.

31   Michael Kemper and Gulnaz Sibgatullina, 'Liberal Islamic Theology in Conservative Russia: Taufik Ibragim's 'Qurʾānic Humanism'', *Die Welt des Islams*, 61:3 (2021), 279–307, https://doi.org/10.1163/15700607-61020002

translations in the post-communist era.³² In many countries of the former Eastern Bloc, the roots of this contemporary institution can be traced back through both the communist and pre-communist periods. Their pervasiveness has resulted in a specific form of governance of Islam in the region which finds many parallels in a number of Eastern European countries. Račius refers to the operations of these institutions as 'the churchification of Islam',³³ a term that resonates with Sibgatullina's notion of a 'Church for Islam' with reference to the specific intertwinement of Islamic and Orthodox Christian languages that has occurred in the Russian context.³⁴ In the production of Qur'an translations, her concept of 'the double-rootedness of religious language'³⁵ plays an important role in understanding these dynamics. When it comes to Central Asian religious institutions, the presence of muftiates can be dated to the Soviet period, during which this 'monopolist religious bureaucracy that had no precedent in the region' was established.³⁶ The Soviet legacy also manifests in the Azerbaijani religious bureaucratic institutions that prioritise Qur'an-centrism in their 'state-hermeneutics' as one of the ways of handling diverse Sunni and Shii Muslim populations.³⁷ At the same time, looking at the publishing activities of individuals who worked outside of the muftiate structures is an enriching avenue that complicates the existing narratives.

Overall, looking at the history of Qur'an translations in the region sheds light on both the particular connections and similarities of the post-communist era and the networks that transcend established patterns of the Russian Empire and the Eastern Bloc, revealing new

---

32 See, for example, a study dedicated to the Muftiate institution in Russia: Renat Bekkin, 'People of Reliable Loyalty ...: Muftiates and the State in Modern Russia.' (unpublished doctoral dissertation, Södertörns högskola, 2020).

33 Egdūnas Račius primarily focused on Bosnia, Lithuania, Bulgaria, North Macedonia, Poland, Czechia, and Hungary (Račius, *Islam in Post-Communist Eastern Europe*, p. 214).

34 Gulnaz Sibgatullina, 'The Muftis and the Myths: Constructing the Russian "Church for Islam"', *Problems of Post-Communism* (2023), 1–12; Gulnaz Sibgatullina, *Languages of Islam and Christianity in Post-Soviet Russia* (Leiden: Brill Rodopi, 2020).

35 Sibgatullina, *Languages of Islam and Christianity*, p. 177.

36 Michael Kemper, 'Soviet and Muslim: The Institutionalization of Islam in Central Asia, 1943-1991, written by Eren Tasar, 2017', *Die Welt des Islams*, 59:1 (2019), 124–26.

37 Kamal Gasimov, 'The Bureaucratization of Islam in Azerbaijan: State as the Principal Regulator and Interpreter of Religion', *Central Asian Affairs*, 7:1 (2020), 1–37 (pp. 21–24).

connections and relationships that have emerged from old historical contexts and extended into unconventional geographies. Although the issues addressed in each chapter of this book uncover many parallels, it is not a foregone conclusion that these factors are conceptually related, especially given the politicised nature of the geographical framing and context from which this book emerged. Work on this volume has coincided with Russia's war against Ukraine, a factor which has prompted a general reconsideration of both the entrenched language used to describe the region and the established framing of regional histories. However, even prior to Russia's invasion of Ukraine, some of the localities under consideration here were the subject of ongoing terminological dilemmas. For instance, Svetlana Gorshenina has demonstrated how terms in use today such as 'Inner Asia', 'Central Asia', and 'Middle Asia', among others, relate to various geopolitical projects that date back to the nineteenth century.[38] Those countries that are located in Europe and were part of the communist space were labelled in the political terminology of the Cold War as 'Eastern Europe', a label that many countries prefer not to use any more.[39] Azerbaijan's location at a crossroad between Europe and Asia is also bound up in geopolitical narratives which are subject to complex and ongoing processes.[40] In the following chapters, we have aimed to decentre the scholarly focus from Russia (which is often prioritised in the Western perspective), without neglecting its significance in the region. However, current political instabilities in the region mean that speaking about the cartography of the so-called 'post-Soviet space'—although this term has received much criticism for continuing to inscribe a colonial history into the independent states of the region—is increasingly complex.[41]

---

38 Svetlana M. Gorshenina, *Izobretenie kontsepta Srednei / Tsentral'noi Azii: mezhdu naukoi i geopolitikoi*, trans. by M. R. Maizul (Washington: Central Asia Program, The George Washington University, 2019).
39 Račius, *Islam in Post-Communist Eastern Europe*, p. 6.
40 Joshua Kucera, '"Between Europe and Asia": Geography and Identity in Post-Soviet Nation-Building Narratives', *Central Asian Affairs*, 4:4 (2017), 331–57.
41 For example, see some recent public debates: Paula Erizanu, 'Thirty Years After the Collapse of the Soviet Union, is it Time to Finally Stop Using the Term "Post-Soviet"?', *New East Digital Archive*, 31 August 2021, https://www.new-east-archive.org/features/show/13044/30-years-independence-ussr-term-post-soviet-use; Claudia Eggart, 'The End of the Post Soviet', *Zentrum für Osteuropa- und internationale Studien*, 1 June 2022, https://www.zois-berlin.de/en/publications/zois-spotlight/the-end-of-the-post-soviet; Latvian Public Broadcasting,

Given these complexities, we have aimed to decentre and look beyond established geo-political framings in this book, rather than confine the discussion solely to the area and era of the Soviet Union.[42] As we reflected on the boundaries of our scholarly focus and the influence of the Soviet empire, both became increasingly elusive while the boundaries of our imaginary simultaneously expanded.

For example, Western Chinese towns such as Chuguchak (Tacheng, Chawchak) were part of the Russian imperial trade network in the nineteenth century, within which Tatar merchants and educators operated.[43] Subsequently, following Bolshevik Russia's takeover in the early twentieth century, these spaces became a retreat and safe haven for a number of Muslim scholars. Nowadays, Muslim families seek 'reverse' refuge from these areas back to Russia in the post-communist era, bringing with them unknown histories.

Another perspective involves Soviet policies towards and diplomatic connections with countries of the Non-Aligned Movement (NAM): an organisation that emerged in the context of the Cold War, whose constituent countries technically were not part of the Soviet universe.[44] However, close, cooperative Soviet ties with states such as Nasserist Egypt, for example, yielded unexpected outcomes following the dissolution of the USSR, including in the religious domain. Additionally, the stories of the communist German Democratic Republic (GDR) and 'capitalist' Federal Republic of Germany (FRG) had a particular influence on the publication of Islamic texts both prior to and following German reunification.

Taking all of these avenues into account, the chapters in this volume demonstrate the broader legacy of post-communism and the former

---

'UPDATED: Baltic States Please Stop Calling Us Former Soviet Countries', *Eng. LSM.lv*, 6 January 2017, https://eng.lsm.lv/article/politics/politics/updated-baltic-states-please-stop-calling-us-former-soviet-countries.a217911/; For academic scholarship, see also Diana Ibañez Tirado, '"How Can I be Post-Soviet if I was Never Soviet?" Rethinking Categories of Time and Social Change—a Perspective from Kulob, Southern Tajikistan', *Central Asian Survey*, 34:2 (2015), 190–203.

42 Botakoz Kassymbekova, 'On Decentering Soviet Studies and Launching New Conversations', *Ab Imperio*, 23:1 (2022), 115–20.

43 Danielle Ross, *Tatar Empire: Kazan's Muslims and the Making of Imperial Russia* (Bloomington: Indiana University Press, 2020).

44 For more on NAM, see Lorenz M. Lüthi, 'The Non-Aligned Movement and the Cold War, 1961–1973', *Journal of Cold War Studies*, 18:4 (2016), 98–147.

Eastern Bloc in both Muslim and non-Muslim engagement with the Qur'an, encompassing a complex entanglement of geographical spaces either within or connected to the Eastern Bloc, ideologically, culturally, or militarily. They cover the entire period from the late Tsarist and early Soviet (Bolshevik) era up to the modern day.

A Survey of the Contributions to this Volume

The idea for this volume emerged from an international research workshop entitled 'Nation States and Qur'an Translators: Narratives and Debates in the Post-Soviet Space', organised by the ERC-funded project 'GloQur—The Global Qur'an' at the University of Freiburg in October 2022. The workshop brought together diverse perspectives on the dynamics of Qur'an translation and, more generally, engagement with the Qur'an in the Soviet Union, its successor states, and countries that were under its control. It was conceived as an important space of 'horizontal cooperation' with and among scholars from different parts of the region, and it inspired us to produce a volume that will introduce English-speaking audiences to some important trends and histories related to the modern phenomenon of Qur'an translation in geographical areas that are often overlooked from the perspective of global Islamic studies.[45]

Several overarching questions are addressed in this book: was there a space for Qur'an translation before the end of communism, and if so, what purpose did it serve? What implications arise from the circulation of various Qur'an translations in regions formerly dominated by communist ideology? What were the multi-layered subjectivities and life trajectories of the translators that led to the production of these works? What role did nation-states play in their production? By aiming to integrate areas that have received limited attention in the growing body of scholarship on Qur'an translation, this collection of essays seeks to contribute to the literature, and especially the English-language literature, on these areas, and to highlight the significant role that Qur'an translations play in contemporary Islam.

---

45 Kassymbekova, 'On Decentering Soviet Studies', p. 118.

The book is divided into two parts, each of which is devoted to a theme that conceptually links the chapters.

The first part is devoted to the mobility of Qur'an translations. It consists of three chapters exploring the concept of mobility in relation to both Qur'an translators and their translations. Translation is a cross-cultural phenomenon often associated with a semantic movement across different cultural and linguistic universes. Translators, thus, are cross-cultural agents of this semantic movement, whose lives and experiences matter because of the particular embeddedness they represent. Semantic mobility is typically connected to physical mobility, which is fundamental to human experience of the world and, as Tim Cresswell notes, may be associated with a wide range of meanings, from supposedly positive experiences relating to progress and freedom to experiences of forced displacement and exile.[46] The mobility of people and things can also be a form of resistance. Both translators and their translations are thus deeply involved in broader power dynamics pertaining to their historical and geographical contexts.

In the first chapter of this section Alfrid Bustanov elucidates the fate of a surviving manuscript containing the complete Turkic Qur'an translation by the Tatar Muslim scholar Muḥammad Murād al-Ramzī (1855–1935). Al-Ramzī, renowned for his historical works on Muslim scholars in his region and his Arabic translation of Aḥmad Sirhindī's (1564–1624) *Maktūbāt*, found refuge in Chuguchak (West China, presently part of Xinjiang) after the Bolshevik revolution, where he penned his Qur'an translation. This manuscript was finally, recently found in Russia, where it is currently being prepared for publication. Bustanov's study provides a nuanced portrayal of al-Ramzī's hybrid subjectivity, which diverges notably from his Sufi background, a facet downplayed by al-Ramzī himself in the Qur'an translation and described by Bustanov as a 'farewell to Sufism'. Bustanov's chapter not only offers insights into the manuscript but also situates al-Ramzī within the contemporary Tatarstani debates surrounding his persona, in which his text and persona are subject to reappropriation within the discourse of the post-secular Sufi revival. The emigration of al-Ramzī's family from modern China to Russia, fleeing ongoing repression, and

---

46 Tim Cresswell, *On the Move: Mobility in the Modern Western World* (London and New York: Routledge, 2006), pp. 1–24.

the subsequent discovery of the manuscript, signify another layer of mobility which is related to the histories of exile.

The second chapter provides another story of migration and exile. In it, Filipp Khusnutdinov explores the dynamics and trends of the 'vernacular Qur'anic space' in Uzbekistan from the 1950s to the present day, focusing on the case of al-Sayyid Maḥmūd al-Ṭarāzī's Qur'an translation, which is written in Central Asian Turki. Unlike al-Ramzī's translation, which until recently remained unknown to both scholars and the wider public, this translation—by a prominent figure in the Turkestani émigré community in Saudi Arabia—managed to reach Soviet Uzbekistan despite the Iron Curtain, albeit with limited circulation due to the anti-religious policies of the Uzbek SSR. Khusnutdinov provides a history of the circulation and reception of al-Ṭarāzī's translation and argues that it was primarily 'popular' and recognised during the Soviet era, while its post-Soviet reception highlights the challenges of competing with locally produced works. Al-Ṭarāzī's ability to disseminate his translation in a land walled in by communist dogma not only demonstrates the mobility of Qur'an translations, but also shows how translation can be an act of resistance in itself.

In the third chapter of this section, Elvira Kulieva explores the story of Sumayya ʿAfīfī, an Egyptian translator who translated the concise Qur'an commentary *al-Muntakhab* into Russian. Kulieva traces the trajectory of ʿAfīfī's life against the backdrop of the Cold War era Egyptian-Soviet collaboration and the subsequent Islamic revival in Egypt. ʿAfīfī's journey serves as a demonstrative case of a professional woman with a career spanning Nasserist socialism and Hosni Mubarak's alliance with Islamic institutions. During the former period, ʿAfīfī was among the first cohort of Egyptian students who travelled to study in the USSR, seeking educational opportunities to aid Egypt's post-colonial development. Her educational mobility here provides a lived example of the Nasserist vision of progress in which women balanced career and home life, manifesting the state's progress towards modernisation. During the period of Hosni Mubarak's alliance with Islamic institutions, ʿAfīfī gained public recognition as a prominent and celebrated Qur'an translator. The secular mobility of her past became key to enabling and legitimising her activities in religious translation and *da'wa* activism—spreading Egyptian Islam to the lands of post-Soviet Russia through the dissemination of her translations of the *tafsīr al-Muntakhab*. The chapter contextualises ʿAfīfī's life within these diverse political and cultural landscapes, charting her evolution from 'Nasser's translator' to a *dāʿiya* during Egypt's Islamic revival. In doing so, Kulieva explores the dynamics of female engagement in conservative Egyptian religious initiatives and the implications of such inclusion.

The second part of the book, consisting of four chapters, addresses the varying level of influence (or lack thereof) of nation-state authorities on Qur'an translations, on the basis that nation-states can play a crucial role in defining and shaping the interpretative strategies of Qur'an translations.[47] In the case of formerly Soviet countries, the ideological shift to the new era created conditions in which the post-independence governments constitutionally adopted secular state-identities which became a defining principle for the newly formed nation-states.[48] However, the course of the past thirty-four years has demonstrated that this declared secularity coexists with various state engagements with religion through numerous assertive policies.[49] These de-facto 'post-secular' tendencies demonstrate the fusion of secular and religious elements in various spheres through state regulations.[50] In the particular case of Qur'an translations, the influence of the state is evident in several areas, from large-scale policies such as language reforms, debates about teaching religion in schools and establishing theological faculties,

---

47 Pink, *Muslim Qurʾānic Interpretation Today*, p. 210.
48 Alexander Agadjanian, 'Vulnerable Post-Soviet Secularities: Patterns and Dynamics in Russia and Beyond', in *Multiple Secularities Beyond the West*, ed. by M. Burchardt, M. Wohlrab-Sahr, and M. Middell (Boston: De Gruyter, 2015), p. 243.
49 Robia Charles, 'Secular Regimes and State Engagement with Religion in Post-Soviet Eurasia' (unpublished doctoral thesis, University of California, 2013), p. 5.
50 'Post-secular tendencies' here do not imply societies becoming uniformly more religious (although this can occur in certain contexts), nor do they suggest a shift toward theocratic governance or similar systems. Instead, the term refers to the contemporary condition of Western countries that once were emblematic of the classical secularisation thesis, which predicted religion's decline in the face of modernisation. The condition is primarily manifested through the renewed preoccupation with religion, particularly in the public sphere. This development is shaped by globalisation, post-colonial migration patterns, and growing dissatisfaction with the secular order's inability to fulfil its promises of a safe world or to holistically address fundamental questions about the meaning of life. José Casanova, 'Exploring the postsecular: Three meanings of 'the secular' and their possible transcendence', in *Habermas and Religion*, ed. by Craig Calhoun, Eduardo Mendieta, and Jonathan VanAntwerpen (Cambridge: Polity Press, 2013), pp. 27–48.

to censorship and specific localised practices such as the financial sponsorship of certain Qur'an translations or the demonstrative public use of particular translations by state leaders. For example, the policing of the Qur'an and its interpretations by the state—as described by Aguilar and Ahmad in relation to Germany—applies to many countries of the former Eastern Bloc where the state's concern with religion is particularly high.[51] While the state's interest in 'policing the Qur'an' can be observed across various countries in the region, the approach varies significantly. For instance, in Germany, the focus lies on concerns for gender justice and equality, where 'Muslims in contemporary Germany are problematised as deficient and archaic readers.'[52] In contrast, in Russia and Uzbekistan, the primary concern centres on Salafi interpretations, which are deemed inherently problematic from a securitisation perspective.

Often, it is the state, through its centralised religious institutions (or competing institutions), that defines the incorporation of a certain vision of Islam into the nation-state narrative. This incorporation is significantly influenced by subjective interpretations of historical pasts and the promotion of particular religious practices and beliefs, which in turn often define the translatorial strategies used by individual translators or state-related local Islamic institutions and publishers.

The section opens with a chapter by Elmira Akhmetova, in which she traces the history and contemporary issues of Qur'anic commentary (*tafsīr*) and translation (*tarjama*) among the Kazan Tatars in Russia, from the nineteenth century to the present day. Akhmetova emphasises the interaction between the institution of the muftiate, which emerged during the Russian colonial period in the eighteenth century, and Russian state authorities. This interaction manifests as a central theme and remains discernible in contemporary Qur'an translations such as that associated with the Spiritual Administration of Muslims of Tatarstan (Muftiate DUMRT). The muftiate's dominant role in determining normative religious interpretations and translations has been shaped against the backdrop of existing political agendas. Akhmetova emphasises shifts in

---

51 Luis Manuel Hernández Aguilar and Zubair Ahmad, 'A Dangerous Text: Disciplining Deficient Readers and the Policing of the Qur'an in the German Islam Conference', *ReOrient*, 6:1 (2020), p. 89.

52 Ibid., p. 86.

Tatar Qur'an commentary over time, especially noting the emergence of modernist and anti-colonial interpretations in the early twentieth century and the ongoing influence of the Russian state in the post-Soviet era.

In the following chapter, Johanna Pink explores the publishing history and ideological framing of Max Henning's revised editions of his Qur'an translation, one of which was produced in the socialist German Democratic Republic (GDR), which was part of the Eastern Bloc, and the other in the 'capitalist' Federal Republic of Germany (FRG), which was not. The competitive nature of the Cold War context extended even to Qur'an translations, since the two branches of the publisher Reclam—situated in East and West Germany, respectively—produced different editions, in what Pink calls a 'Qur'an race'. In this intriguing story of debates on and obstacles to the publication of a religious text in an ideologically fraught, bureaucratic, and academically complex environment, we learn about the impact of censorship and ways to circumvent it, as well as the particular image of Islam and Muhammad that transpires from the GDR edition. Pink concludes her chapter by describing the fate of Henning's Qur'an translation in reunified Germany, against the backdrop of new political dynamics and demographic shifts.

In the third chapter of this section, Elnura Azizova introduces the Qur'an translations that have been produced in Azerbaijan in the Azerbaijani language since 1991. The country's religious, cultural, and geographic heterogeneity, which has been influenced by Russia, Turkey, and Iran, as well as its Soviet heritage (notably in terms of the Soviet Orientalist tradition), is reflected in various translatorial strategies. Azizova focuses on the biography of the Prophet (*sīra*) to demonstrate the differing treatments of a number of verses connected to the Prophet's biography, depending on whether the translators were Sunni or Twelver Shii Muslims. She argues that Qur'an translations in post-Soviet Azerbaijan provide readers with examples of Prophetic *sīras* that offer similar general chronologies but have different focal points when it comes to the image they convey of the Prophet and his Companions, as well as the episodes of his life that they reference. These divergences stem from differences in the individual translators' religio-cultural backgrounds, the official perception of Islam espoused in state-supporting institutional translations, and the need to meet the expectations of the target audience.

In the final chapter, Akif Tahiiev explores a variety of existing Shii *tafsīr* and Qur'an translations in Russian—an area of study that is often overlooked. Tahiiev introduces these texts and relates them to the diverse actors who produced these works, such as local individuals and foreign institutions. He demonstrates that while Shii texts sometimes face similar problems to other religious texts in Russia in terms of state censorship, the absence of instruments of governance and institutionalisation of Russian Shii Islam (such as muftiates), in contrast to Sunni Islam, has ensured relative freedom for Shii scholars in terms of their choices regarding what to write, translate, and publish in the Russian language. This is the main reason, according to Tahiiev, for the comparative diversity of Shii literature in the Russian-speaking context, both in print and online.

It is our hope that this book will initiate dialogue among scholars of Islam in the region and beyond, integrating the ideas and stories discussed in this volume into a larger conversation about contemporary Islam and the role of the Qur'an for contemporary Muslims, and that this dialogue will flourish, enriching both the Muslim communities themselves and the scholars who study them.

Bibliography

A'kimhanov, Asqar B., and Nurlan N. Anarbaev (trans.), *Quran Ka'rim qazaqs'a oqyly'y ja'ne ay'darmasy* (Almaty: Samg'a, 2022).

Agadjanian, Alexander, 'Vulnerable Post-Soviet Secularities: Patterns and Dynamics in Russia and Beyond', in *Multiple Secularities Beyond the West*, ed. by M. Burchardt, M. Wohlrab-Sahr, and M. Middell (Boston: De Gruyter, 2015), pp. 241–60.

Aguilar, Luis Manuel Hernández, and Zubair Ahmad, 'A Dangerous Text: Disciplining Deficient Readers and the Policing of the Qur'an in the German Islam Conference'. *ReOrient*, 6:1 (2020), 86–107.

Altay, Halifa (trans.), *Kälam- Şarif: tüzetip, tolıqtırıp bastırwsı X. Altay* (Istanbul: Elïf-ofset baspası, 1989).

—— (trans.), *Quran Kärim: qazaqșa mağına jäne tüsinigi* (Medina: King Fahd Glorious Qur'an Printing Complex, 1991).

—— (trans.), *Quran Şarïf* (Almatı: Jazwşı: Sözstan, 1991).

Babajanov B. M., A. K. Muminov, and A. von Kügelgen, 'Introduction: Religious Texts of the Soviet Era', in *Disputes on Muslim Authority in*

Central Asia (20th Century): Critical Editions and Source Studies. Disputy musul'manskikh religioznykh avtoritetov v Tsentral'noi Azii v XX veke, ed. by Bakhtiyor M. Babajanov, Ashirbek K. Muminov, and Anke von Kügelgen, (Almaty: Daik-Press, 2007), pp. 32–54.

Baer, Brian James, 'Literary Translation and the Construction of a Soviet Intelligentsia', in *Translation, Resistance, Activism*, ed. by Maria Tymoczko (Amherst and Boston: University of Massachusetts Press, 2010), pp. 537–560.

Balci, Bayram, *Islam in Central Asia and the Caucasus since the Fall of the Soviet Union* (Oxford: Oxford University Press, 2018).

Bashir, Kamran, *The Qur'an in South Asia: Hermeneutics, Qur'an Projects, and Imaginings of Islamic Tradition in British India* (New York: Routledge, 2022).

Bekkin, Renat, 'People of Reliable Loyalty ...: Muftiates and the State in Modern Russia' (unpublished doctoral thesis, Södertörns högskola, 2020).

Bustanov, Al'frid K. [Alfrid K.], 'Koran dlia sovetskikh grazhdan: ritorika progressa v bogoslovskikh trudakh Gabdelbari Isaeva', *Antropologicheskii forum*, 37 (2018).

——, 'Beyond the Ethnic Traditions: Shamil' Aliautdinov's Muslim Guide to Success', in *Islamic Authority and the Russian Language: Studies on Texts from European Russia, the North Caucasus and West Siberia*, ed. by Alfrid K. Bustanov and Michael Kemper (Amsterdam: Pegasus, 2012), pp. 143–66.

——, and Michel Kemper, 'From Mirasism to Euro-Islam: The Translation of Islamic Legal Debates into Tatar Secular Cultural Heritage', in *Islamic Authority and the Russian Language: Studies on Texts from European Russia, the North Caucasus and West Siberia*, ed. by Alfrid K. Bustanov and Michael Kemper (Amsterdam: Pegasus, 2012), pp. 29–52.

——, 'Muslim Literature in the Atheist State: Zainap Maksudova between Soviet Modernity and Tradition', *Journal of Islamic Manuscripts*, 9:1 (2018), https://doi.org/10.1163/1878464X-00901001

——, 'The Qur'an for Soviet Citizens: The Rhetoric of Progress in the Theological Works of 'Abd al-Bari Isaev', *Forum for Anthropology and Culture*, 14 (2018), 106.

——, *Muslim Subjectivity in Soviet Russia: The Memoirs of 'Abd al-Majid al-Qadiri* (Leiden: Brill, 2022), https://doi.org/10.30965/9783657793778

Casanova, José, 'Exploring the postsecular: Three meanings of "the secular" and their possible transcendence', in *Habermas and Religion*, ed. by Craig Calhoun, Eduardo Mendieta, and Jonathan VanAntwerpen (Cambridge: Polity Press, 2013), pp. 27–48.

Charles, Robia, 'Secular Regimes and State Engagement with Religion in Post-Soviet Eurasia' (unpublished doctoral thesis, University of California, 2013).

Cresswell, Tim, *On the Move: Mobility in the Modern Western World* (London and New York: Routledge, 2006).

Dudoignon Stéphane A. and Christian Noack (eds), *Allah's Kolkhozes: Migration, de-Stalinisation, Privatisation and the New Muslim Congregations in the Soviet Realm (1950s-2000s), Islamkundliche Untersuchungen, Band 314* (Berlin: K. Schwarz, 2014).

Eggart, Claudia, 'The End of the Post-Soviet', *Zentrum für Osteuropa- und internationale Studien*, 1 June 2022, https://www.zois-berlin.de/en/publications/zois-spotlight/the-end-of-the-post-soviet

Erizanu, Paula, 'Thirty Years After the Collapse of the Soviet Union, is it Time to Finally Stop Using the Term "Post-Soviet"?', *New East Digital Archive*, 31 August 2021, https://www.new-east-archive.org/features/show/13044/30-years-independence-ussr-term-post-soviet-use

Garaev, Danis, 'Post-Secular Mirasism and Reforming Islam in Russia: From Euro-Islam to Confessional Scholarship', *Islam and Christian–Muslim Relations*, 34:1 (2023), https://doi.org/10.1080/09596410.2023.2193498

Gasimov, Kamal, 'The Bureaucratization of Islam in Azerbaijan: State as the Principal Regulator and Interpreter of Religion', *Central Asian Affairs*, 7:1 (2020), https://doi.org/10.30965/22142290-0701001

Gorshenina, Svetlana M., *Izobretenie kontsepta Srednei / Tsentral'noi Azii: mezhdu naukoi i geopolitikoi*, trans. by M. R. Maizul (Washington: Central Asia Program, The George Washington University, 2019).

Gunasti, Susan, *The Qur'an between the Ottoman Empire and the Turkish Republic: An Exegetical Tradition* (London and New York: Routledge, 2019).

Hamidullah, Muhammad (trans.), *Le Saint Coran* (Paris: Hadj Mohamed Noureddine Ben Mahmoud, 1963).

Kassymbekova, Botakoz, and Aminat Chokobaeva, 'On Writing Soviet History of Central Asia: Frameworks, Challenges, Prospects', *Central Asian Survey*, 40:4 (2021), https://doi.org/10.1080/02634937.2021.1976728

——, 'On Decentering Soviet Studies and Launching New Conversations', *Ab Imperio*, 23:1 (2022), https://doi.org/10.1353/imp.2022.0011

Kemper, Michael, Raoul Motika, and Stefan Reichmuth (eds), *Islamic Education in the Soviet Union and its Successor States* (London–New York: Routledge, 2009).

——, 'Soviet and Muslim. The Institutionalization of Islam in Central Asia, 1943–1991, written by Eren Tasar, 2017', *Die Welt des Islams*, 59:1 (2019), https://doi.org/10.1163/15700607-00591P11

Kemper, Michael, and Gulnaz Sibgatullina, 'Liberal Islamic Theology in Conservative Russia: Taufik Ibragim's "Qurʾānic Humanism"', *Die Welt des Islams*, 61:3 (2021), 279–307, https://doi.org/10.1163/15700607-61020002

Kucera, Joshua, '"Between Europe and Asia": Geography and Identity in Post-Soviet Nation-Building Narratives', *Central Asian Affairs*, 4:4 (2017), https://doi.org/10.1163/22142290-00404002

Kulieva, Elvira, 'In the Shadow of Orientalism: Tracing the Legacy of Ignatiĭ Krachkovskiĭ in Russian Salafi Qur'an Translations', in *Retranslating the Bible and the Qur'an: Historical Approaches and Current Debates*, ed. by Pieter Boulogne, Marijke de Lang, and Joseph Verheyden (Leuven: Leuven University Press, 2024), pp. 109–141.

Latvian Public Broadcasting, 'UPDATED: Baltic States Please Stop Calling Us Former Soviet Countries', *Eng.LSM.lv*, 6 January 2017, https://eng.lsm.lv/article/politics/politics/updated-baltic-states-please-stop-calling-us-former-soviet-countries.a217911/

Leese, Simon, 'Arabic Utterances in a Multilingual World: Shāh Walī-Allāh and Qur'anic Translatability in North India', *Translation Studies*, 14:2 (2021), https://doi.org/10.1080/14781700.2021.1919192

Lüthi, Lorenz M., 'The Non-Aligned Movement and the Cold War, 1961–1973', *Journal of Cold War Studies*, 18:4 (2016), https://doi.org/10.1162/JCWS_a_00682

Nysanbai'uly, Ratbek, and Y'ahap Qydyrhanuly (trans.), *Quran Ka'rim* (Almaty: Jazy's'y, 1991).

On'g'arov, Ers'at, and Nurjan Murata'li (trans.), *Qasi'etti Quran:mag'ynasy men tu'siniktemeler* (Nur-Sultan: Baspa, 2020).

Petersen, Kristian, *Interpreting Islam in China: Pilgrimage, Scripture, and Language in the Han Kitab* (Oxford: Oxford University Press, 2017).

Pi-nk, Johanna, 'Editor's Preface', *Journal of Qur'anic Studies*, 17:3 (2015).

——, *Muslim Qur'ānic Interpretation Today: Media, Genealogies and Interpretive Communities* (Bristol: Equinox, 2019), https://doi.org/10.3366/jqs.2015.0209

Račius, Egdūnas, *Islam in Post-Communist Eastern Europe: Between Churchification and Securitization* (Leiden: Brill, 2020).

Riddell, Peter G., *Malay Court Religion, Culture and Language: Interpreting the Qur'an in 17th Century Aceh* (Leiden and Boston: Brill, 2017).

Roche, Sophie, *The Faceless Terrorist: A Study of Critical Events in Tajikistan*, 1st edn, Transcultural Research: Heidelberg Studies on Asia and Europe in a Global Context (Cham: Springer, 2019), https://doi.org/10.1007/978-3-030-03843-4

Ross, Danielle, *Tatar Empire: Kazan's Muslims and the Making of Imperial Russia* (Bloomington: Indiana University Press, 2020).

Sartori, Paolo, 'Towards a History of the Muslims' Soviet Union: A View from Central Asia', *Die Welt Des Islams*, 50:3–4 (2010), https://doi.org/10.2307/41105358

——, 'Why Soviet Islam Matters', *Anzeiger*, 157:1–2 (2022), https://doi.org/10.1553/anzeiger157-1s5.

——, *A Soviet Sultanat: Islam in the Socialist Uzbekistan (1943–1991)* (Vienna: Austrian Academy of Science Press, 2024).

Sibgatullina, Gulnaz, *Languages of Islam and Christianity in Post-Soviet Russia* (Leiden: Brill, 2020).

——, 'When the Other Speaks: Ismāʿīl Gasprinskii and the Concept of Islamic Reformation', *Journal of the Economic and Social History of the Orient*, 65 (2022).

——, 'The Muftis and the Myths: Constructing the Russian "Church for Islam"', *Problems of Post-Communism* (2023), https://doi.org/10.1080/10758216.2023.2185899

——, 'On Translating the Qur'an into Turkic Vernaculars: Texts, Ties, and Traditions', in *European Muslims and the Qur'an: Practices of Translation, Interpretation, and Commodification*, ed. by Gulnaz Sibgatullina and Gerard Wiegers (Berlin: De Gruyter, 2024), pp. 219–58.

Taji-Farouki, S., and Basheer M. Nafi (eds), *Islamic Thought in the Twentieth Century* (London: I. B. Tauris, 2004).

Tymoczko, Maria, 'Translation, Resistance, Activism: An Overview', in *Translation, Resistance, Activism*, ed. by Maria Tymoczko (Amherst and Boston: University of Massachusetts Press, 2010), pp. 1–22.

Tirado, Diana Ibañez, '"How Can I Be Post-Soviet if I Was Never Soviet?" Rethinking Categories of Time and Social Change—A Perspective from Kulob, Southern Tajikistan', *Central Asian Survey*, 34:2 (2015), https://doi.org/10.1080/02634937.2014.983705

Wilson, M. Brett, *Translating the Qur'an in an Age of Nationalism: Print Culture and Modern Islam in Turkey* (Oxford: Oxford University Press, 2014).

Yakubovych, Mykhaylo, 'Qur'an Translations into Central Asian Languages: Exegetical Standards and Translation Processes', *Journal of Qur'anic Studies*, 21:1 (2022), https://doi.org/10.3366/jqs.2022.0491

——, *The Kingdom and the Qur'an: Translating the Holy Book of Islam in Saudi Arabia* (Cambridge: Open Book Publishers, 2024), https://doi.org/10.11647/OBP.0381

Yūsuf ʿAlī, ʿAbdullāh (trans.), *The Holy Qur-ān: Arabic Text with an English Translation and Commentary. Vol. II, Containing Sūras IX to XXIX* (Lahore: Muḥammad Ashraf, 1937).

—— (trans.), *The Holy Qur-ān: English Translation & Commentary. Parts I–XV* (Lahore: Muḥammad Ashraf, 1934),

—— (trans.), *The Holy Qur-an: Text Translation & Commentary. Vol. III, Containing Suras XXIX to CXIV* (Lahore: Muḥammad Ashraf, n.d.).

Zadeh, Travis, *The Vernacular Qur'an: Translation and the Rise of Persian Exegesis* (Oxford: Oxford University Press, 2012).

Zaman, Muhammad Qasim, *The Ulama in Contemporary Islam: Custodians of Change* (Princeton: Princeton University Press, 2002).

PART I

QUR'AN TRANSLATIONS ACROSS NATIONAL BOUNDARIES

1. Hybrid Subjectivity in a Translation of the Qur'an: al-Ramzī's Farewell to Sufism

Alfrid Bustanov

Introduction[1]

Sceptical of sensational claims, I did not believe it at first when I heard of the existence of a manuscript containing the full Turkic translation of the Qur'an by Muḥammad Murād al-Ramzī (1855–1935).[2] Previously, rumours had circulated that the translation kept by the author's daughter Ṣiddiqa had perished together with al-Ramzī's library during the Chinese cultural revolution of the 1960s and 1970s.[3] However, the manuscript had, in fact, survived in the family ownership of the shaykh's direct descendants in Chuguchak, West China—the exact

---

1 The project 'MIND: The Muslim Individual in Imperial and Soviet Russia' (2019–2024) has received funding from the European Research Council (ERC) under the European Union's Horizon 2020 research and innovation programme (grant agreement No. 804083). I am indebted to Shamil Shikhaliev and Michael Kemper, with whom I discussed al-Ramzī's translation of the Qur'an at length.
2 Al-Ramzī's work was first mentioned by one of his students among the shaykh's unpublished manuscripts: Abdulsait Aykut, 'The Intellectual Struggle of Murād Ramzī (1855–1935) An Early 20th Century Eurasian Muslim Author' (unpublished doctoral thesis, University of Wisconsin-Madison, 2015), p. 29.
3 Diliara Usmanova, 'Murad Ramzi (1853–1934): biografiia islamskogo uchenogo v svete novykh svidetel'stv', *Gasyrlar avazy—Ekho vekov*, 2 (2019), 93–114 (p. 102).

place where it was first composed and copied in the late 1920s. It is a massive codex of 372 folios with several colophons by the translator and his assistant. With the intensification of state persecution of Muslims in the region in the 2010s, it became dangerous for the family to remain in Chuguchak and, with the support of the World Congress of Tatars, they moved to Kazan, the Republic of Tatarstan. As it turns out, this escape was facilitated by the exchange of part of al-Ramzī's personal archive, which consisted of his private belongings, such as his glasses and his writings. A member of the Tatar Congress, a state-run organisation dedicated to the support of Tatar culture worldwide, has found the manuscript after hunting through their archives for some time, with the goal of celebrating al-Ramzī in the locality where the shaykh was born—the village of Almat in eastern Tatarstan. There are currently plans to establish a museum which will house these original artefacts, among other things. As a result of these new developments, I was lucky to be able to access the manuscript *de visu* and obtain a full digital copy, which the following account is based on.

At the current time, the Tatarstani Muftiate intends to publish a Cyrillic adaptation of al-Ramzī's work, and a translation into modern Sovietised Tatar[4]—an understandable project given al-Ramzī's iconic significance for the post-secular Sufi revival in Kazan,[5] but, as will be demonstrated below, one that is completely alien to al-Ramzī's own political project and his sense of self.

---

[4] The project has been announced on the Tatar Congress' official website: 'The DUM RT started translating the famous *tafsīr* by Murad Ramzi into literary modern Tatar', https://tatar-congress.org/en/news/the-dum-rt-started-translating-the-famous-tafsir-murad-ramzi-into-the-modern-tatar-literary-language/. At the time of writing, one portion of the text has been published (the last *juz'* of the Qur'an): Shäikh Mulla Morad Rämzi äl-Kazani, *Kor''än gazyimu-sh-shannyng törkichä tärjemäse häm bu tärjemäneng khäzerge tatar telenä iaraklashtyrylgan variant. 30nchy parä* (Kazan: Tynychlyk näshriiat iorty, 2023). The publisher has introduced the original verses of the Qur'an into the volume in the style of the famous Kazan print (*qazan basmasï*), but the Arabic text is not present in the manuscript itself. There are also plans to publish a Cyrillic transliteration of the text in parallel to its translation into present-day Tatar, because the language of the original would be completely incomprehensible for non-specialists. As far as I have been informed, the full edition of the manuscript is now under way.

[5] For present-day practices of urban Naqshbandiyya in Kazan see Alfrid Bustanov, 'Postsekuliarnyi sufizm v Rossii', in *Sufizm posle SSSR*, ed. by Igor' Pankov and Sergei Abashin (Moscow: Izdatel'skii dom Mardzhani, 2022), pp. 28–51.

In my contribution here, I look closely at the material and textual aspects of al-Ramzī's impressive work. I aim to show that his translation of the Qur'an was intended as a weapon against the enemies of Islam, as al-Ramzī understood them—namely Islamic reformism and Western colonialism. To construct his translation this way, al-Ramzī employed linguistic and scholarly tools that allowed him to maintain intellectual autonomy within the breadth of the Islamic discourse. The work showcases an interplay of Chaghatay and literary Tatar, and is devoid of any influences from the Soviet language experiments that took place during the 1920s, namely the change of alphabet from Arabic to Latin and the secularisation of the vocabulary. At least on the surface, al-Ramzī's project in Qur'anic exegesis purposefully avoided any links with the Soviet state. Even after his death, unlike many of their compatriots, Ramzī's children did not relocate to eastern parts of the Kazakh SSR[6] and remained in Xinjiang until recently.

In the following section, I will first briefly describe what we know about al-Ramzī and how he has been portrayed in scholarship. This will set the backdrop for a close reading of the manuscript of his Qur'an translation, with a focus on its paleographical features. Here I attempt to explain why the work remained in the dark for so long, unpublished despite the fame of its author. After discussing the physical characteristics of the book, we move on to analyse hybridity as the key method employed by the author, both in his approach to language choice and his take on the structure of the translation, which is organised in the style of the post-classical *taqlīd*-triad: the main text (*matn*), the commentary (*sharḥ*), and the gloss (*ḥāshiya*). Reading the glosses takes us on a journey through the landscape of al-Ramzī's worldview, as he criticises the wrongdoers of Islam at length. The theme of holy war brings multiple elements of the project together, culminating in a seven-page-long treatise on *jihad* that al-Ramzī appended to his translation. Given the crucial role of this appendix in casting light on the author's approach to the Qur'an and

---

6   On the history of Tatar diaspora in Eastern Turkestan, see: Malik Chanyshev, *Kytaida tatar megarife tarikhy* (Kazan: Zhyen, 2007); Mirkasim Gosmanov, *Iabylmagan kitap iaki chechelgen orlyklar* (Kazan: Tatarstan kitap nashriiaty, 1996); Mirkasim Gosmanov, 'Tatar Settlers in Western China (Second Half of the 19th Century to the First Half of the 20th Century)', in *Muslim Culture in Russia and Central Asia from the 18th to the Early 20th Centuries*, ed. by Anke von Kügelgen, Michael Kemper, and Allen J. Frank (Berlin: Schwarz Verlag, 1998), pp. 243–69.

the fact that this portion of the manuscript is unlikely to appear in the forthcoming publication of al-Ramzī's Qur'an translation, I provide a translation of this treatise at the end of my contribution. My reading of al-Ramzī's text suggests that, faced with the realities of modernity, in this final work, the shaykh silently bids farewell to Sufi cosmology.[7]

Yet Another Male Biography

Muḥammad Murād was born in a village in the Menzelinsk district of Kazan governorate, hence his *nisba* al-Manzalawī, in 1854–55. At that time, this area—unlike the booming cities of Kazan and Orenburg—still valorised Persianate scholarship, a tradition that had been cultivated through long-standing ties with Central Asian centres of learning.[8] After receiving a basic education in his home village, al-Ramzī travelled to the *madrasa* of the prominent Tatar theologian al-Marjānī (1818–89)[9] in Kazan, then to Troitsk, Tashkent, and Bukhara. In 1875, he went on a pilgrimage to Mecca, and stayed there for several decades. He returned to Russia in 1914, only to emigrate soon after the Bolshevik revolution to Chuguchak in Eastern Turkestan, the meeting place of many migrant Muslim intellectuals of the time. At first he planned to collect money and resettle in Mecca and spend the rest of his life there, but al-Ramzī's financial situation and personal attachments to Chuguchak residents prevented these plans from coming to fruition. Al-Ramzī passed away there in 1934 or 1935.[10]

---

7   By Sufi cosmology I mean 'the imaginative and theoretical underpinnings of the Sufi universe' expressed in a respective vocabulary associated with Sufi ideas and practices. For more details, see *Sufi Cosmology*, ed. by Christian Lange and Alexander Knysh (Leiden and Boston: Brill, 2023), here I quote from p. 3.

8   Allen Frank, *Bukhara and the Muslims of Russia: Sufism, Education, and the Paradox of Islamic Prestige* (Leiden: Brill, 2012).

9   Years later, al-Ramzī would speak highly of Shihāb al-Dīn al-Marjānī: see his 'Muḥaqqiq wa ʿallāma dāmullah Shihāb al-Dīn al-Marjānī al-Qazānī häzrätlereneng ... dar-khatir itmäk ichin ber-ike jumlä', in *Märjānī: Shihāb al-Dīn al-Märjānī häzrätlereneng wiladätenä yuz yil tulu mönasäbätlä näsher itelde*, ed. by Ṣālih b. Thābit ʿUbaydullin (Kazan: Maʿārif, 1333), pp. 513–16.

10 For a detailed treatment of al-Ramzi's lifepath, see: Abdulsait Aykut, 'Muhammad Murad Ramzi (1855–1935) and his Works', *Krymskoe istoricheskoe obozrenie*, 2 (2016), 8–26; Salavat Akhmadullin, *Murad Ramzi kak istorik tiurkskikh narodov Rossii* (Moscow: Institut rossiiskoi istorii, 2022); Murad Ramzi, *Talfik al'-akhbar va talkikh al'-asar fi vakai' Kazan va Bulgar va muluk at-tatar*, vol. I, ed. by S. I. Khamidullin (Ufa: Bashkirskii gosudarstvennyi universitet, 2017).

Al-Ramzī attracted scholarly attention thanks to his *Talfīq al-akhbār*, a historical work on the Muslim peoples in Inner Russia[11]—a reference source for the biographies of *ʿulamāʾ* in the Volga-Ural region—and the journal articles that he published in Tatar periodicals in the early twentieth century.[12] In his treatment of history, al-Ramzī maintained a critical attitude towards the Russian Empire, and this caused controversy around the publication of *Talfīq al-akhbār*.[13] While later scholars would emphasise this side of the author's legacy, the role of al-Ramzī as a mediator between the Persianate Central Asian and the Ottoman Arab intellectual worlds was of greater value in the wider religious circles that continued to celebrate key Naqshbandiyya texts through al-Ramzī's Arabic renditions of these works. While in Russia and Central Asia the Persian texts of the classical *Rashaḥāt ʿayn al-ḥayāt* by ʿAlī b. Ḥusayn al-Kāshifī (1463–c.1532) and the *Maktūbāt* by Aḥmad Sirhindī (1564–1624) have been in circulation in the original language for centuries, al-Ramzī introduced them to an Arabic readership. These translations enjoyed great popularity among the Naqshbandī Sufis, especially in Turkey where the books were continuously reprinted throughout the second half of the twentieth century.[14] Al-Ramzī also authored a detailed description of Naqshbandī ideas and practices, which is preserved in the work of his Daghestani initiate Shuʿayb al-Baghinī (1857–1912), who maintained the scholarly persona of a Sufi shaykh in Daghestan.[15] As a scholar well-versed in Central Asian traditions of mysticism and scholarship—and someone who spent almost forty years of his life teaching multiple subjects in the holy cities—by the time of his escape to Eastern Turkestan, al-Ramzī was an unquestionable authority in Islamic

---

11 Muḥammad Murād Ramzī, *Talfīq al-akhbār wa-talqīḥ al-athār fī waqāʾiʿ Qazān wa-Bulghār wa-mulūk al-Tātār*, 2 vols (Orenburg: Karimov, Khusainov i Ko, 1908).

12 Rozaliya Garipova, 'The Protectors of Religion and Community: Traditionalist Muslim Scholars of the Volga-Ural Region at the Beginning of the Twentieth Century', *Journal of the Economic and Social History of the Orient*, 59 (2016), 126–65.

13 Nuriia Garaeva, 'Kem ul Morad Ramzi', *Kazan utlary*, 2 (1990), 171–74. Muslim scholars in Russia often had their own opinions on al-Ramzī's treatment of history, but not all of these reactions were published. In particular, ʿArīfullāh Ṣāliḥī penned a very critical review of al-Ramzī's historical work that never saw the light of the day: Institute of Oriental Manuscripts, D 481.IV.

14 Muḥammad Murād Ramzī, *Dhayl Rashaḥāt ʿayn al-ḥayāt* (Mecca: n.p., 1890); Muḥammad Murād Ramzī, *Muʿarrab al-maktūbāt* (Istanbul: Ihlas Vakfi, 2002).

15 Shuʿayb al-Bagini, *Ṭabaqāt al-khwājagān al-Naqshbandiyya wa-sādāt al-mashāʾikh al-khālidiyya al-maḥmūdiyya* (Makhachkala: Dār al-Risāla, 2016), pp. 600–32.

scholarship and truly a translator-*mutarjim* who was able to employ the inner richness of Islamic literatures to establish an intellectual autonomy from European modernity.

The numerous writings left by al-Ramzī leave us with a picture of someone with multiple scholarly personas, each of which were intentionally constructed to provide a specific public image.[16] We know of al-Ramzī the historian, who put together the fragmented pasts of Muslim Eurasia.[17] Similarly, we learn about al-Ramzī the shaykh, who mastered the mystical path and articulated Sufi models of self-fashioning, with their peculiar language of *ijāzas*, veneration of shrines, and purification of the soul.[18] We also hear of al-Ramzī the ʿ*ālim*, or traditionalist scholar, who staunchly defended the established norms of creed and practice against reformist innovators who, he believed, distort religion.[19] One might expect that an elderly scholar at the end of his career would be willing to construct his Qur'an translation, possibly the highest point of his intellectual path, in a way that reflects one of the types of scholarly persona he had embraced in his earlier life. However, in the following section it will become apparent that this Qur'an translation project proved too ambitious for a single form of self-fashioning, and instead revealed the hybrid character of al-Ramzī's true sense of the self.

---

16   For the concept of the scholarly persona, see Herman Paul, 'What is a Scholarly Persona? Ten Theses on Virtues, Skills, and Desires', *History & Theory*, 53:3 (2014), 348–71. For its application to Muslim ego-documents from Russia, see *Muslim Subjectivity in Soviet Russia: The Memoirs of 'Abd al-Majid al-Qadiri*, ed. by Alfrid Bustanov and Vener Usmanov (Leiden: Brill, 2022), pp. 5–11, 36–50.

17   Salavat Akhmadullin, *Murad Ramzi kak istorik tiurkskikh narodov Rossii*; Il'shat Nasyrov, 'O nauke istorii i proshlom i nastoiashchem narodov Evrazii. Fragmenty iz sochineniia "Talfik al-akhbar". Vvodnaia stat'ia, perevod i kommentarii', in *Ishrak: Ezhegodnik islamskoi filosofii*, vol. IX (Moscow: Sadra, 2019), pp. 375–412.

18   Shamil Shikhaliev and Michael Kemper, 'Sayfallāh-Qāḍī Bashlarov: Sufi Networks between the North Caucasus and the Volga-Urals', in *The Piety of Learning: Islamic Studies in Honor of Stefan Reichmuth*, ed. by Michael Kemper and Ralf Elger (Leiden: Brill, 2017), pp. 189–90.

19   Il'shat Nasyrov, 'Murat Ramzi i ego vzgliady na dzhadidizm', in *Religioznye aspekty globalizatsii: faktor islama*, vol. III (Ufa: Villi Oksler, 2006), pp. 138–140; Il'shat Nasyrov, 'Vzgliady Murada Ramzi po voprosam reformirovaniia i modernizatsii islama', in *Arabskie issledovaniia* (Moscow: RUDN, 2012), pp. 27–34.

The Production of the Manuscript

The only manuscript of Muḥammad Murād al-Ramzī's Qur'an translation constitutes an impressive physical object. Its dimensions are 28 x 23 x 5cm, and the binding is pasteboard with leather on the endband. The paper is lineated and bears neither stamps nor watermarks. In fact, there are no immediate material features that would suggest its Eastern Turkestani origin.[20] There are multiple signs of restoration, and the first folio has been glued onto a xeroxed page with the handwritten title 'The Turkic Translation of the Qur'an. The Work of the Poor[21] Muḥammad Murād Ramzī Manzalawī Makkī' (*Qurʾān ʿaẓīm al-shaʾnining türk[i]chä[22] tärjemäse. Athār-i faqīr Muḥammad Murād Ramzī Menzelewī Makkī*). The main text is written within a demarcated box (15 x 22cm) with occasional glosses on the margins. No carry-over words are present, and the Arabic pagination is placed on each side of the folio.

The manuscript features two colophons—one, unusually, in the middle of the translation, right before Q 18, and another after Q 114. The first colophon (Fig. 1.1) runs as follows:

> Praise be to God, the first half of the Qur'an translation has been finished at the house of the most distinguished Mīr 'Ābid Bāy, where I was hosted with my family, in Chuguchak near the Tarbughatay mountains at the time of ʿaṣr, on Thursday 24 Ṣafar al-khayr 1348 of the Muslim calendar, 1 August of the European and 19 Temmūz of the Eastern calendar, in the Christian year of 1929. May God ease the task of completing the second half. Amen. This has been written by the poor Muḥammad Murād Ramzī al-Naqshbandī.

---

20 Unlike, for example, the paper of an early seventeenth-century manuscript of the *Abwāb al-jinān* by Dawlat Shāh al-Ispijābī composed in Yarkand (Kazan University Library, Ms. 6764 T), in which case the material exposes its local origin. For the importance of paper in manuscript studies, see Jan Just Witkam, *Values of Old Paper* (Leiden: Ter Lugt Press, 2022).

21 *Faqīr* is a traditional polite self-reference in Tatar text of the early twentieth century.

22 If read directly, the title says 'Turkish' (*törekchä*) and not 'Turkic' (*türkichä*). I reason that for those who had access to the manuscript there was no need to emphasise the distinction between the western and eastern forms of Turkic language. For our purposes, however, the difference is important, hence my interpretation.

> Praise be to God, the final copying (*bayāḍ*) of the first half of this translation has been accomplished in my house on Friday night, 8 Rabīʿ al-Ākhīr 1348 of the Muslim calendar [12 September 1929]. My boy ʿAbd al-ʿAzīz had a stomach disease at the time. May God grant him a cure. This has been written by the poor ʿImād al-Dīn b. Muḥammad ʿArīf al-Chochakī.[23]

According to a note in the manuscript, al-Ramzī continued his work a few days later, on 4 August, and al-Chochakī began copying the second half on 14 September. The final colophon (Fig. 1.2) provides more details on the way these two proceeded with their task:

> Thanks God, this has been completed on Monday morning, 27 Dhū-l-Ḥijja 1348, or 13/ 26 May, 1930.[24] The work began on 13/28 October 1927 corresponding to Sunday 2 Jumāda al-Ākhīr 1346. This means that the work has been accomplished in nearly two years and seven months of the lunar calendar. During this time, only four months after the death of the former governor, between early July and early November 1928, no work related to the translation was done. Hence the period of engagement was two years and three months.
>
> In my home in Chuguchak, I, ʿImād al-Dīn b. Muḥammad ʿArīf Abū Bakrī al-Chochakī, have copied and completed this translation on 1 Muḥarram 1349 [28 May 1930]. May God make it of use to my family, who will remember me in their prayers. May God grant me endless reward and allow me to Paradise. Completed on 7 Jawza 1308 of the solar Muslim calendar and on Thursday 16/29 May 1930 of the Christian calendar.[25]

---

23   Muḥammad Murād al-Ramzī, *Qurʾān ʿazīm al-shaʾnīnïng türk[i]chä tärjemäse*, p. 374.
24   This double form of date reflects the difference in Julian and Gregorian calendars.
25   al-Ramzī, *Qurʾān tärjemase*, p. 738. This mix of multiple calendars, including the solar and lunar Muslim calendars, the Julian and Gregorian calendars, reflects the peculiarity of the region in which al-Ramzi found himself: between empires, on the fridges of Central Asia and the Islamicate world, at the intersection of Turkic, Persian, and Chinese cultures.

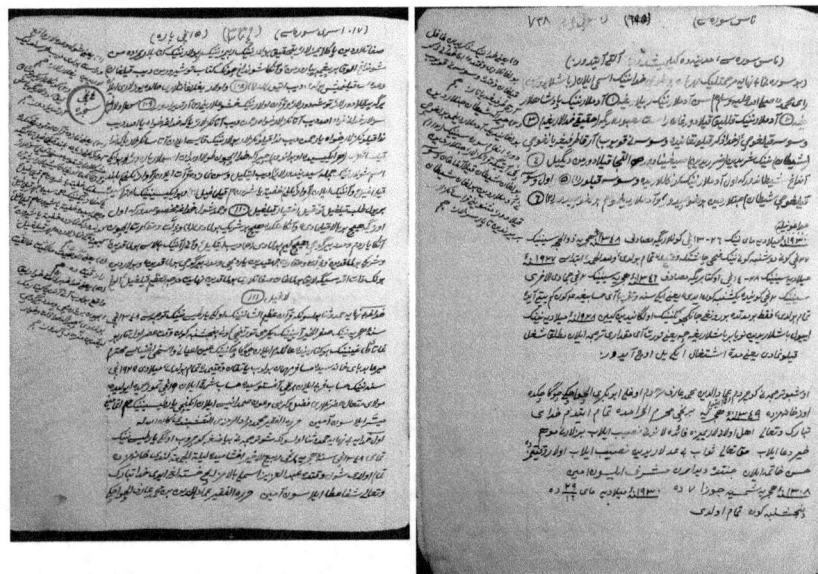

Figs 1.1. and 1.2. Colophons in al-Ramzī's work: intermediary (on the left) and final (on the right). ©Alfrid Bustanov, Creative Commons license CC BY.

These colophons thus provide informative details about the composition process. Even though the manuscript is no autograph, there can be no doubt as to authenticity of the text and its attribution to al-Ramzī. It is not only in the colophons that the author reveals his identity. On several occasions he refers to himself as 'I the poor' (*faqirimiz*).[26] In another place he calls himself 'Murād efendi', for example when warning his readers from erroneous understanding of his translation of Q 10:24.[27]

Even though ʿImād al-Dīn the copyist had aimed to produce a final copy (*bayāḍ*), the manuscript, while clearer in the first pages, contained just enough omissions and mistakes—possibly caused by the illness of his son mentioned in the first colophon—that someone had to go through the entire text once more and leave corrections with a traditional abbreviation of approval (*ṣad* and *ḥāʾ* for *ṣaḥḥ*).[28] A break in pagination after p. 207, the next page left blank with the page after paginated as 165 and then corrected to 208, suggests that the part

---

26 al-Ramzī, *Qurʾān tärjemase*, pp. 41, 157, 173.
27 Ibid., p. 281.
28 Ibid., p. 211 especially is full of corrections.

running before this was rewritten due to an abundance of mistakes and later attached to the remaining body of the manuscript. The copyist was in a hurry, as this rewriting must have taken place after already copying the book, and he allowed himself wider handwriting. Thus, the copyist ended up taking up more space than was previously planned, i.e. more than 165 pages of initial pagination. This oddity is not reflected in the colophons but is attested by the double pagination starting from p. 207—the new numbers were written in pen next to the old ones. In fact, there are very few omissions in the text before this break.[29] The task of copying such a text was clearly difficult for this person, who failed to do justice to the idea of the final copy announced in the colophons. This could be the reason the manuscript remained unpublished: there was still more work to be done with the text, and no resources to continue the project, especially after al-Ramzī's passing and/or the disappearance of his patron. Given that the manuscript survived in the ownership of al-Ramzī's direct descendants, one might speculate that any earlier versions of the text, namely al-Ramzī's autograph, have been destroyed. According to Dilyara Usmanova, in the 1960s a portion of the manuscript was acquired by the Public Academy in Xinjiang and another copy of the translation has been lost.[30] However, I suggest that rumours of its destruction may owe much to the widespread trope of the Bolsheviks' intended destruction of Muslim libraries in Soviet Russia—a trope which downplays the inner logic of manuscript production and circulation.[31] Autographs usually bear a great deal of editorial work and, despite their appreciation in Orientalist scholarship, often lose their practical function after the appearance of a better copy, as was the case with the manuscript in question.

This eagerness to have as clean a copy as possible can be explained by the desire to eventually publish this text, for example in a lithographed form, for which a manuscript would be suitable.[32] The organisation

---

29 On page 28 the copyist unnecessarily repeated the phrase *hammä päygambärlärgä*, and on p. 84 he first omitted a word *birgüche* but later added it on the top. Similar edits were made throughout the text, clearly upon comparison with the original.

30 Diliara Usmanova, 'Murad Ramzi (1853–1934)', p. 103.

31 For a critique of this trope, see Alfrid Bustanov and Shamil Shikhaliev, 'Archives of Discrimination: The Evolution of Muslim Book Collections in Daghestan', *Journal of Islamic Manuscripts*, 15:1 (2023), 82–109.

32 On the impact of printing on Sufism, see *Sufism, Literary Production, and Printing in the Nineteenth Century*, ed. by Rachida Chih, Catherine Mayeur-Jaouen, and

of the manuscript supports this hypothesis: the book has Arabic pagination on each side of the folio, every Qur'anic verse bears a number to facilitate consultation, there are indications in the margins for the divisions into parts (*para*) and chapters (*sūra*). These notes have been applied systematically throughout the text, which would be unusual for a manuscript for private use. Similarly, the presence of European punctuation—i.e. inverted commas, brackets, dots, and even quotes—suggests that the author aims to address a broader audience than just readers of the manuscript itself.

According to the obituary for al-Ramzī published in the journal *Yanga Yapon Mökhbire* in Tokyo in 1935, the local governor in Chuguchak wanted to get rid of al-Ramzī, using his Turkish passport as a pretext. As the population in Chuguchak did not want to lose al-Ramzī, the governor stipulated a condition for his remaining in the area: al-Ramzī had to produce a translation of the Qur'an in the regional form of the Turkic language (*mämläkät türkichäse*). If he failed to prove his status as a great scholar of Islam by doing so, he would have to leave the country. Reportedly, al-Ramzī promised to present the governor a copy of the translation for his library.[33] If I understand the second colophon correctly, this is the governor who passed away in 1928, which caused a break in the project. However, work on the translation soon recommenced and was completed by May 1930.

Based on paleographic evidence, I reconstruct the manuscript history of al-Ramzī's work as follows. The project was backed by Mīr ʿĀbid Bāy, a wealthy local, who seized the opportunity to have the famous Sufi shaykh and scholar at his premises. He sponsored the endeavour, provided enough paper and ink, and hired an assistant named ʿImād al-Dīn who would produce a clean final copy of the text for a lithograph publication. The shaykh took his time and produced approximately one page of the translation every day—his glosses suggest that he had to experiment with the phrasing and consult the opinions of classical scholars of *tafsīr*. Al-Ramzī and ʿImād al-Dīn worked in parallel, the latter regularly taking portions of the text from the translator, with a time lag of only one month between the production of the original and its copy. Once the job was done, the copy was compared with the

---

Rudiger Seesemann (Würzburg: Ergon Verlag, 2015).
33 Ibid., pp. 108–09.

autograph and the numerous errors became apparent. To fix these mistakes, ʿImād al-Dīn produced the first 207 pages anew, leaving the rest intact. Despite all these efforts, the quality of the manuscript remains far from perfect. I reason that the failure of the copyist to accomplish the task to a sufficiently high standard is one reason that the work did not enjoy wider circulation. The old age of the translator could have played a part in this: he went through eye surgery in 1923 and possibly did not recover completely enough to perform the endeavour. ʿImād al-Dīn's copy was transferred to the mosque in Urumchi on its completion, but soon after al-Ramzī's passing away it was returned to his family.[34]

Al-Ramzī the Scholar

Despite the utterly modern appearance of the manuscript, which could easily serve as a basis for a printed edition, the book maintains the tradition of providing glosses in the margins, directly labelled as *ḥāshiya* at one instance.[35] While the additions in brackets within the main body of text helped al-Ramzī to establish a clearer narrative in his translation, he used glosses to explain subtle matters, to prevent people from misunderstanding the translation or to further highlight the meaning (*mafhūm*) of the Qurʾanic verses. Interestingly, each gloss is accompanied by his signature—at the beginning in full as 'translator' (*mutarjim*), and later on only with two letters *jīm* and *mīm*. The latter feature resembles the system of shortcuts used in Arabic premodern legal and grammatical works for quotes from established authorities in the field.[36] By applying this system to his engagement with the Qurʾan (Fig. 1.3), al-Ramzī developed a hybrid intellectual approach that would combine the tools of translation, commentary within the text (akin to *sharḥ* in legal compendia), and glosses on the margins. Indeed, on many occasions al-Ramzī refers in his glosses to the legal tradition (*fiqh kitaplarïda*) to further elucidate this or that notion in the text.[37]

---

34 Ibid., p. 103.
35 Ibid., p. 100, on the margin.
36 For example: Diana Gadzhieva, '"Al-Kafiia fi-n-nakhv" Ibn al-Khadzhiba s ierarkhiei kommentariev v Dagestane', *Vestnik instituta istorii, arkheologii i etnografii*, 1:37 (2014), 40–55.
37 For example, al-Ramzī, *Qurʾan tärjemase*, on p. 39 and 129 in the margin.

1. Hybrid Subjectivity in a Translation of the Qur'an

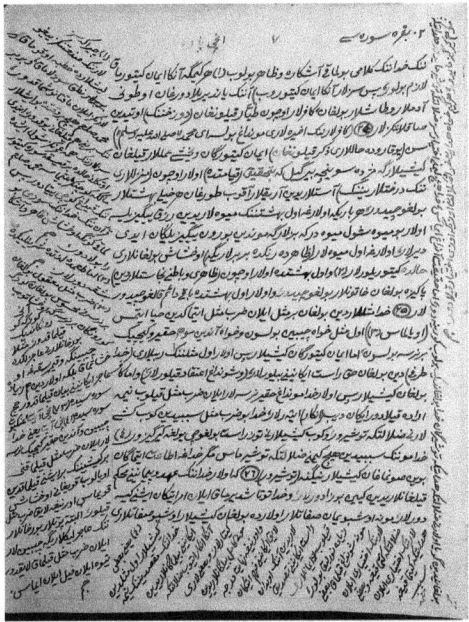

Fig. 1.3. The text, commentary, and glosses in al-Ramzī's work. ©Alfrid Bustanov, Creative Commons license CC BY.

Al-Ramzī's Qur'an translation is also notable for the fact that in it he continues his decades-long fight with a particular faction of Islamic reformists within Russia. This is how al-Ramzī introduces his commentary on Q 6:111:

> In our times in Russia (*rusiyya yortïnda*) have appeared those who have moved towards atheism, and fallen away from the right path and true religion. They are ignorant of the meaning of the Qur'anic verses and reject the miracle descending to the Prophet from God. They make fun of and ridicule the prophetic miracle (*mu'jiza*). Mūsā Bīgī and Diyyā Kamālī[38] are the leaders of these reckless people. Stay far away from reading and accepting their books, and from listening and accepting the words of their unfortunate supporters. Otherwise you will join them in hell.[39]

---

38 Musa Bigeev (1873–1949) and Diyyā al-Dīn al-Kamālī (1873–1942) were prominent Muslim intellectuals and public figures in early twentieth-century Russia who advocated for Islamic reform.

39 Al-Ramzi, *Qur'an tärjemase*, p. 201.

As he did in his early writings,[40] al-Ramzī does not hold back on the use of negative epithets for Musa Bigeev and his followers, accusing them of heresy (*zindiq*).[41] One of the main points of disagreement he had with them related to the eternal nature of hell. According to al-Ramzī, the unbelievers 'will stay in hell forever. This is the creed of all Muslims, except for Jāhiz—the worst of the Mutazilites, Abū al-Ḥusayn al-Baṣrī the Rafidite, and Mūsā Bīgī and his stupid followers.'[42] As is well known, Musa Bigeev was indeed of a different opinion on this subject and wrote that all humankind at some point will enjoy Paradise thanks to God's all-encompassing mercy.[43] In several places in the translation, al-Ramzī warns his readers that such assistants of Satan (*shayṭān vakīllerī*) were also present in his current place of residence.[44] Al-Ramzī was right in saying that Chuguchak and, we should add, the entire region of Eastern Turkestan, was home to Islamic reformists of various sorts,[45] and even scholars of Wahhabi tendencies, such as Shāmī Dāmullāh.[46]

To remain true to the tradition of Qur'anic exegesis, al-Ramzī consulted numerous sources as part of his translation methodology. His approach to *tafsīr* as a field of knowledge is hybrid too. In glosses, he references a wide range of more conventional, classical *tafsīr*s by authors such as al-Nasafī,[47] al-Bayḍāwī,[48] Ḥasan al-Baṣrī,[49] Ibn Mujāhid,[50] and

---

40 Muḥammad Murād al-Ramzī, *Mushāyaʿat ḥizb al-raḥmān wa-mudāfaʿat ḥizb al-shayṭān* (Orenburg: n.p., 1911).
41 Al-Ramzi, *Qur'an tärjemase*, p. 191. Here al-Ramzi translates Q 6:71 as promising hell to those with incorrect beliefs (*nachar i'tiqadlarï*).
42 Ibid., p. 394.
43 Musa Bigeev, *Rähmät ilahiya burhannarï* (Orenburg: Waqït, 1911).
44 Al-Ramzi, *Qur'an tärjemase*, pp. 39, 507.
45 David Brophy, *Uyghur Nation: Reform and Revolution on the Russia-China Frontier* (Cambridge: Harvard University Press, 2016); Alexandre Papas, 'Muslim Reformism in Xinjiang: Reading the Newspaper Yengī Ḥayāt (1934–1937)', in *Kashgar Revisited: Uyghur Studies in Memory of Ambassador Gunnar Jarring*, ed. by Ildikó Bellér-Hann, Birgit N. Schlyter, and Jun Sugawara (Leiden and Boston: Brill, 2017), pp. 161–83; Eric Schluessel, 'History, Identity, and Mother-Tongue Education in Xinjiang', *Central Asian Survey*, 28:4 (2009), 383–402.
46 David Brophy, '"He Causes a Ruckus Wherever He Goes": Saʿid Muḥammad al-'Asali as a Missionary of Modernism in North-West China', *Modern Asian Studies*, 54:4 (2020), 1192–224.
47 Al-Ramzī, *Qur'ān tärjemase*, p. 376.
48 Ibid., p. 161.
49 Ibid., p. 153.
50 Ibid., p. 173.

al-Ṭabarī,⁵¹ to al-Zamakhsharī,⁵² Fakhr al-Dīn al-Rāzī,⁵³ and Abū Muslim al-Isbahānī.⁵⁴ In addition to these references, al-Ramzī turned to the *Bustān al-ᶜārifīn* by Abū-l-Layth al-Samarqandī, a legal treatise that was very popular in Russia and Central Asia in the nineteenth century.⁵⁵ In one instance he does not shy away from quoting Ibn Taymiyya on the longevity of the seven sleepers' stay in the cave.⁵⁶ Such recourse to Ibn Taymiyya in a text by a conservative Sufi shaykh may be surprising, but it seems that al-Ramzī shared the respectful attitude towards Ibn Taymiyya that was prevalent among the Tatar ᶜ*ulamāʾ* of the early twentieth century.⁵⁷ This is despite the terrible losses caused to the Sufi heritage in Saudi Arabia by the newly enthroned dynasty of Wahhabis who also celebrated Ibn Taymiyya.⁵⁸ In addition to Islamic literature, al-Ramzī writes of consulting the Pentateuch for his commentaries.⁵⁹ However, he was not interested in engaging in anti-Christian polemics when doing so: when he writes about the theological views held by Christians, he does not go beyond mere description or brief refutation.⁶⁰ Thanks to the Bolshevik anti-religious struggle, by the late 1920s the Orthodox mission had ceased to present a challenge to Muslim thinkers.⁶¹

Although he used a wide range of sources, al-Ramzī was very critical of the opinions translated in the premodern *tafsīr* tradition, claiming at times that 'everything that is written about this [the story of Yūsuf and Zulaikha] in *tafsīr*s is baseless and false superstition (*khurafāt*)',⁶² which cannot but remind us of reformist anti-Sufi rhetoric. In other cases he refrained from narrating the opinion of commentors, instead referring the readers to consult those works directly.⁶³ When it came to views that

---

51   Ibid., pp. 157, 310.
52   Ibid., p. 362.
53   Ibid., pp. 376, 419, 553.
54   Ibid., p. 59.
55   Ibid., p. 377.
56   Ibid., p. 378.
57   Ibn Fakhr al-Dīn, Riḍā al-Dīn, *Ibn Taymiyya* (Orenburg: n.p., 1911).
58   Rosie Bsheer, *Archive Wars: The Politics of History in Saudi Arabia* (Stanford: Stanford University Press, 2020), ch. 1.
59   Al-Ramzī, *Qurʾān tärjemase*, p. 173.
60   Ibid., p. 145, 377, 391.
61   Things were different throughout the nineteenth and early twentieth centuries when a series of anti-missionary treatises were composed by Tatar ᶜ*ulamāʾ*.
62   Al-Ramzī, *Qurʾān tärjemase*, p. 312.
63   'Tafsir igeleri bu tugrida kub nerseler ziker qilgandurlar. Khokhlagan keshe anda qarasun' (ibid., p. 319).

he found intolerable, al-Ramzī harshly criticised the hagiographic style of Qur'anic commentary. In particular, in his note on the identity of Dhū l-Qarnayn in Q 18:84, the translator did not hide his emotions:

> God did not inform us of Dhū l-Qarnayn's lifetime, his location, or identity. People ask who he really was, but in fact there is a lot of uncertainty about him. Most of the authors in *tafsīr*, *ḥadīth* and history have been mistaken in this issue. Only a few have escaped grave mistakes [...] To say that he was Iskander Rūmī Yūnānī Makidonī is faulty, I swear to God. This is a fault by all the names of God. He was a worshipper of idols who claimed to be a deity.[64]

We find a similar note of criticism on the premodern style of interpreting Islamic history in his commentary on the passage of the Qur'an that deals with the wall erected by the same Dhū l-Qarnayn to protect the world from the evil Yājūj and Mājūj:

> The authors in *tafsīr*, *ḥadīth* and history claimed that this is the wall built between the Turks and Chinese people. This is a mistake, as the Chinese erected the wall themselves. According to al-Bayḍāwī, what is meant here is Darband or Timer Qapu [which is] located between the Armenians and Daghistanis in the Caucasus.[65]

These quotes reveal the complex profile of al-Ramzī as a scholar. While he was a famed Sufi shaykh, he developed a rational method of verification of facts and sources, in the same vein as did the reformists[66] he so terribly disliked. His Qur'an translation reveals instances in which al-Ramzī's scholarly personas contradicted each other. On the one hand, he promised hell to the unbelievers, who have discovered the telegraph system, the phone, the gramophone, and cars and airplanes.[67] On the other hand, he observed that all these technical discoveries are part

---

64 Ibid., p. 385.
65 Ibid., p. 386.
66 For example, Ḥasan al-Alkadarī (1834–1910), a Daghestani intellectual, made sure to carefully distinguish between the historical Alexander the Great and the distinguished person of Islamic tradition. See Ḥasan-afandī al-Alkadarī ad-Dagistānī, *Jirāb al-Mamnūn* (Temir-Khān-Shūrā: al-Maṭbaʿa al-Islāmiyya li-Muḥammad-Mirzā Mavraev, 1912). I would like to thank Dr. Shamil Shikhaliev for bringing this similarity to my attention.
67 Al-Ramzī, *Qur'ān tärjemase*, p. 17.

of God's creation,⁶⁸ and referenced Aḥmad Midhat Pāshā's (1822–83) book on zoology⁶⁹ and proudly claimed that modern botanical science has proved observations made in the Qur'an.⁷⁰ Al-Ramzī speaks of modernity (*hazirda*) as the time when material objects have become extremely efficient.⁷¹ Judged from this perspective, al-Ramzī's translation of the Qur'an can be seen to lie at the intersection of the author's lifelong professional engagement with history, translation, and theology. This mix of approaches explains a lot when it comes to the hybrid character of the book.

Al-Ramzī the Sufi

What does the hybrid style of al-Ramzī's translation conceal? In fact, there is not much trace of Sufism, hagiography, and story-telling left in the text.⁷² From the text, one would not guess that the translation was authored by someone who had in previous years written extensively on *murāqaba* (a Sufi's concentration on the self) and *tawassul* (turning to God's help via one's master). There are very few Sufi terms throughout the book,⁷³ but when they do occur their usage does not suggest a specific mystical dimension and does not make it a Sufi commentary on the Qur'an, as one might expect given al-Ramzī's famous Sufi persona. For example, this is how al-Ramzī translates Q 2:152, a verse that is central to Sufi cosmology and practice: 'Therefore, remember me (*ziker qilingizlar*) [in the margin: "by following God's orders, respecting and abiding Him"] and I will remember you [in the margin: "by expressing

---

68 'Bu kungeche parakhutlar, ut arbalar, tramvaylar, avtomobiller, tayyara (aeroplanlar), telegraflar, telefonnar, kitab basmalari, yazu mashinalari, tikesh mashinalari wa har qism mashinalar [Khuda] yaratdi. Mondin kiyin yana nimeler yaratir.' (Ibid., p. 345, commenting on Q 16:8, saying that until the Day of Judgement God will create for you things previously unknown).
69 Ibid., p. 183.
70 'Bu 'asïrïmizda fän ilän thabitder.' (Ibid., p. 340).
71 Ibid., p. 198.
72 It is remarkable, however, that at one point al-Ramzī uses Fuzūlī's poem to comment on a Qur'anic verse.
73 Clearly under the influence of my public lecture (see the discussion below), the publishers commented on the lack of Sufi terminology in al-Ramzī's work: 'this is a translation and it needs to be brief, otherwise it would turn into an extensive commentary (*tafsīr*), and one would not read a huge book' (äl-Kazani, *Kor''än gazyimu-sh-shannyng törkichä tärjemäse*, p. 5).

mercy and rewarding you"].'[74] Neither here, nor elsewhere, is the reader to find engagement with an explicitly Sufi interpretation.

The only element that reminds the reader of the author's grounding in *taṣawwuf* is his very detailed treatment of *küngel* as a metaphysical concept denoting the space of emotions and knowledge within human body. This is a Turkic word that al-Ramzī uses throughout the text as an equivalent for the Qur'anic *qalb* (heart), and in so doing establishes an intertextual link with the rich tradition of *küngel* as a theme in Tatar poetry and autobiographical writing. In close relation with *küngel*, the author occasionally speaks of love towards God (*ʿishq, maḥabba*),[75] purification of the soul (*tazkiyyat al-nafs*),[76] establishing a bond with God (*tawassul*),[77] and the ethics of God's remembrance—apparently in defence of the silent forms of *dhikr*,[78] but these separate notions never formed a system. Thus, al-Ramzī the shaykh is almost absent from his Qur'anic commentary.

When it comes to the veneration of shrines—one of the key practices in Naqshbandiyya Sufism—al-Ramzī expresses his negative attitude towards Sufi shrines of questionable, in his opinion, origin. For example, he says that the shrine of the Seven Sleepers (*aṣḥāb al-kahf*) in Turfan is 'undoubtedly a lie and something that has been created recently to collect money from people.'[79] In addition, he writes negatively of the occult (*siher jadu*).[80] Topics relating to sex are dealt with in a legalist fashion, which is completely alien to the usual explicit descriptions in the early-nineteenth century of same-sex relationships.[81] The story of Yūsuf and Zulaikha that was paradigmatic for generations of Tatar *madrasa* graduates in the Volga-Ural region[82] is not even mentioned

---

74 Al-Ramzī, *Qurʾān tärjemase*, p. 32.
75 Ibid., pp. 20, 34, 37, 73.
76 Ibid., p. 75.
77 Ibid., p. 19.
78 Ibid., a gloss for Q 2:198 on p. 43: 'That is, remember God appropriately (*adab ilän*), not like the ignorant innovators who have no respect and make a lot of noise (*hay-huy dib*).'
79 Ibid., p. 376.
80 Ibid., pp. 21–22, 401.
81 Ibid., pp. 40, 43 (*jimāʿ*), 302 (*liwāṭa*).
82 Agnes Kefeli, 'The Tale of Joseph and Zulaykha on the Volga Frontier: The Struggle for Gender, Religious, and National Identity in Imperial and Post-Revolutionary Russia', *Slavic Review*, 70:2 (2011), 373–98.

in al-Ramzī's dry translation.⁸³ Again, these aspects make al-Ramzī look very much like the reformists he criticised and suggest a rational approach towards the Qur'an and a rejection of literary takes on the holy text that is characteristic of the Persianate cultural sphere. For a Sufi shaykh, al-Ramzī has written a very rationalist translation that does not allow space for even a bit of the Sufi cosmology that is so richly present in the premodern Tatar tradition of Qur'an commentaries.⁸⁴ Even the very genre of al-Ramzī's work suggests engagement with reformist and colonial discourses: the Qur'an was turning into the sacred book of Islam, like the Bible has for Christianity, at the beginning of the twentieth century.⁸⁵

Al-Ramzī the Translator

When writing the final colophon to the translation, ʿImād al-Dīn added that he had not only copied the work, but also completed it (*tämam ittem*). This hints at a prominent role that the copyist felt the need to articulate in the work's final stage. If I am correct in my reading of the production process, the project's sponsors wanted to have a translation of the Qur'an that would bear the blessing of the Sufi shaykh, but that was written in a vernacular familiar to the people of Chuguchak. Without denying al-Ramzī's linguistic talents as a translator (he apparently knew Arabic, Persian, and Ottoman well, in addition to Tatar and Russian), it is plausible that ʿImād al-Dīn's role went beyond the mechanical reproduction and ordering of al-Ramzī's original writing, and that he helped to make the language colloquial and idiomatic.⁸⁶

---

83 Al-Ramzī, *Qur'ān tärjemase*, p. 311.
84 A good case in comparison is the *Sidrat al-muntahā* by Tāj al-Dīn al-Bulghārī (1768–1838), which is full of Sufi cosmology in a Persianate style. See Tadzh ad-Din b. Ialchygul al-Bulgari, *Sidrat al-muntakha* (*Lotos krainego predella*), 2 vols, ed. by Alfrid Bustanov (Kazan: Tatarskoe knizhnoe izdatel'stvo, 2022).
85 Gulnaz Sibgatullina, 'The Ecology of a Vernacular Qur'an: Rethinking Mūsā Bīgī's Translation into Türki-Tatar', *Journal of Qur'anic Studies*, 24:3 (2022), 46–69.
86 The contrast in language is especially striking when compared with the Turkic texts penned by al-Ramzi—there he preferred forms closer to Ottoman. See, for example, Shaykh Muḥammad Murād [al-Ramzī], *Inṣāf* (Kazan: Tipografiia Karimovykh, 1900).

The question of translating the Qur'an into vernaculars was a hot topic during al-Ramzī's youth,[87] but in the last years of his life he clearly had no doubt about his take on the issue. Throughout the manuscript his approach to the text is consistently termed as 'translation' (*tarjama*), sometimes accompanied by explanations as to why a certain way of rendering a given verse was found preferable in comparison with previous, classical commentaries.[88] However, what we are dealing with is not simply a word-by-word translation, but an elaborated narrative that includes extensive additional remarks from the translator, all presented in parenthesis so that they are discernable from the actual translation of the Qur'anic passages.

The hybridity of al-Ramzī's approach mirrors the hybridity of the language used in the translation. The linguistic choices in the book struck me the most while reading it. Most of the text is written in Chaghatay, clearly bearing in mind the immediate linguistic environment of Chuguchak where the work was composed and where al-Ramzī spent his last years.[89] Moving beyond grammar, the choice of vocabulary is also very indicative. For example, the translator uses *gap* for 'speech',[90] *nan* for 'bread',[91] *tilla* and *pul* for 'money',[92] and never uses their Tatar equivalents.[93] There are, however, many instances throughout the text when the language changes to Tatar and even uses its spoken variant, as with the use of the vernacular expression *falan-tugan*—i.e.

---

87 Al-Ramzi's eternal rival Musa Bigeev was also engaged in these debates and prepared a Qur'anic translation on his own: see Gulnaz Sibgatullina, 'The Ecology of a Vernacular Qur'an'.
88 Al-Ramzī, *Qur'ān tärjemase*, pp. 125, 307, 367.
89 Interestingly, Dilyara Usmanova managed to guess the language of the work without consulting the manuscript: see Usmanova, 'Murad Ramzi (1853–1934)', p. 102. The publishers of the manuscript claim that the language used in al-Ramzī's translation was the language customarily used by prerevolutionary Tatar ʿulamāʾ (which is simply not true) and that it only 'slightly' diverges from the contemporary Tatar language and appears close to Uyghur(!) and Chaghatay language: see äl-Kazani, *Kor''än gazyimu-sh-shannyng törkichä tärjemäse*, p. 8.
90 Al-Ramzī, *Qur'ān tärjemase*, pp. 4, 22, and throughout the text.
91 Ibid., p. 13.
92 Ibid., p. 81.
93 In al-Ramzi's youth it was customary and fashionable to use Ottoman phrases. See *Muslim Subjectivity in Soviet Russia*, pp. 102–5; Alfrid Bustanov, 'On Emotional Grounds: Private Communication of Muslims in Late Imperial Russia', *Asiatische Studien*, 73:4 (2019), 655–82 (p. 673).

'such-and-such'—in one of the glosses.[94] In another place, al-Ramzī refers the reader to his commentary on various other verses of the Qur'an using the Tatar formula *shunda baq* ('look there').[95] Sometimes Tatar forms are used interchangeably with Chaghatay ones: for example, while he usually uses *yagach* for 'tree', it is sometimes *agach*.[96] Al-Ramzī also refers to Russian Muslims as *nūghāy*, which was a customary terminology current in Central Asia.[97]

There is also a very prominent Persian influence in the text, which gives it a peculiar flavour.[98] For example, al-Ramzī extensively uses the words *āsmān-u zamīn* in his translation of Qur'anic passages on *al-samāwāt wa-l-arḍ* (the skies and earth).[99] Another word pair is very productively used for the term *farḥ* (happiness): in al-Ramzī's translation, it becomes the poetic *khursand-u shād*.[100] *Kaʿba* is rendered as *khāna-yi khudā* (the house of God),[101] and the worshippers of idols as *pot-parāst*.[102] When reading al-Ramzī's translation I expected to find an elaborate treatment of garden culture, full of Persianate imagery and descriptions. However, al-Ramzī clearly decided to refrain from the more traditional (for Tatar literature) concept of *bāgh(cha)*, or garden, in the description of Paradise. For 'heavenly gardens', al-Ramzī uses the Persian word *behesht* with *arïqs*, or irrigation canals (and not springs, *chishmälär!*) flowing beneath.[103] Even though the Qur'anic text uses the term *janna* consistently when speaking of both heavenly and earthly

---

94 Al-Ramzī, *Qur'ān tärjemase*, p. 60.
95 Ibid., p. 120.
96 Ibid., p. 229.
97 See ibid., p. 353 (where he explains the word *umarta* and provides its Arabic equivalent *khaliyya*), and p. 363 (where he quotes a Tatar colloquial expression *uh tuydïm* to comment on Q 17:5). Needless to say, Soviet-style ethno-nationalism was completely alien to al-Ramzī's sense of self.
98 On the role of Persian in Eastern Turkestan, see David Brophy, 'A Lingua Franca in Decline? The Place of Persian in Qing China', in *The Persianate World The Frontiers of a Eurasian Lingua Franca*, ed. by Nile Green (Oakland: University of California Press, 2019), pp. 175–91; Alexandre Papas, 'Lingua Franca or Lingua Magica? Talismanic Scrolls from Eastern Turkestan', in *The Persianate World*, pp. 208–12.
99 Al-Ramzī, *Qur'ān tärjemase*, pp. 25, 34, 57, 64, and elsewhere.
100 Ibid., p. 101 (Q 3:169–71).
101 Ibid., pp. 26, 33.
102 Ibid., p. 104.
103 For example, the translation of Q 3:195: 'Saraylarï wa darakhtlarïnïng astlarïnnan arïqlar aqïb yatqan beheshtlärgä kirgezermen' (ibid., p. 106). A similar phrase is repeated for Q 2:25, Q 3:136, Q 3:198, and elsewhere.

gardens, al-Ramzī prefers to distinguish between the two, using *behesht* for Paradisical gardens and the term *bāgh* for orchards in the translation of Q 18:32–34 and his commentary on Q 17:1.[104] By doing so, al-Ramzī, in a rationalist fashion, establishes the difference between the sacred and the profane, thereby ignoring the centuries-old concept of physical gardens serving as an earthly metaphor of Paradise.[105] In doing this he goes even further than the Tatar translators of the Soviet era, who preserved the garden imagery in the translations they produced during the 1950s and 1970s.

A big absentee from Ramzī's impressive translation work is the Russian language. Strikingly, not a single word of Russian has slipped into the translation[106]—in sharp contrast to many Tatar commentaries and translations of the Qur'an in the nineteenth and twentieth centuries, where the occasional use of Russian loanwords was a norm. It is safe to assume that for al-Ramzī, this rejection was a personal choice that emphasised his intellectual struggle against colonialism.

Al-Ramzī the Warrior

In the obituary published by the Tatar press in Tokyo, al-Ramzī was portrayed as a staunch enemy of Russia who would take up a weapon if needed.[107] This aspect of al-Ramzī's personality certainly informed his reputation as a scholar, and we can find it spectacularly manifested in his Qur'anic translation. As far as I can judge, the work in question is the only case of a Russian Muslim's detailed engagement with the Qur'an that takes the question of *jihad* seriously. In no other work can we find such eagerness to discuss the matter as part of the contemporaneous political

---

104 Ibid., p. 360 (here: *bāgh-bustānlar*), and pp. 379–80.
105 Alfrid Bustanov, 'A Space for the Subject: Tracing Garden Culture in Muslim Russia', *Journal of the Economic and Social History of the Orient*, 65 (2023), 74–125; Nicolas Roth, 'Poppies and Peacocks, Jasmine and Jackfruit: Garden Images and Horticultural Knowledge in the Literatures of Mughal India, 1600–1800', *Journal of South Asian Intellectual History*, 1 (2018), 48–78. For a comparison with the medieval European context, see Thomas Hinton, 'Conceptualizing Medieval Book Collections', *French Studies*, 70:2 (2016), 171–86.
106 After the first portion of the translation was published, I was shown one instance using a Russian word: *kravat* (bed). See äl-Kazani, *Kor"än gazyimu-sh-shannyng törkichä tärjemäse*, p. 41.
107 Usmanova, 'Murad Ramzi (1853–1934)', pp. 106, 109. I am surprised to see these fragments uncensored.

situation, as Eastern Turkestan was an arena of competition between the Russians and the Chinese. Al-Ramzī brings the reader's attention to *jihad* at the first mention of the topic in Q 2:190. In various glosses on the page, the author makes his point of view clear: war with infidels is only permissible when there is discrimination, especially religious discrimination. The only legitimate goal for war, he claims, is to eliminate the trouble that has led to conflict, not the conversion of unbelievers to Islam. Here he promises to attach a detailed treatment of the topic either at the start or the end of the manuscript,[108] and indeed, the copyist has placed al-Ramzī's treatise on *jihad*—the language of which is plain Tatar, unlike the rest of the book—after the final colophon. This detail suggests that this discussion was important to al-Ramzī personally, such that he did not risk it being translated inaccurately into Chaghatay.

In his anti-imperialist treatment of *jihad*,[109] al-Ramzī criticised European colonialists and ignorant Muslims who viciously accuse Islam of promoting war for the sake of spreading religion among the unbelievers. In his opinion, this political rhetoric is intended to defame the religion in the eyes of Europeans as well as those Muslim elites who have distanced themselves from the bearers of true Islamic values, i.e. Sufis. The irony here is that although he was a Sufi shaykh, al-Ramzī himself had unwittingly joined the ranks of those among whom European colonialists 'had planted the seeds of trouble.'[110] In his treatise on *jihad*, al-Ramzī effectively adopted the language of European modernity and adapted this to Islamic discourse, thus adopting the early twentieth-century debates around Ernest Renan.[111] To prove his argument of the defensive nature of *jihad*, al-Ramzī turned to the works of a number of Orientalists, one of them being Thomas Walker Arnold (1864–1930),

---

108 Al-Ramzī, *Qur'ān tärjemase*, p. 41. Later on (pp. 125, 266), he returns to explaining the reasons for *jihad*.

109 See my translation of the text in the attachment to this contribution.

110 Al-Ramzī, *Qur'ān tärjemase*, pp. 739–40.

111 *Moderne Muslime: Ernest Renan und die Geschichte der ersten Islamdebate 1883*, ed. by Birgit Schäbler (Leiden: Brill, 2017), esp. pp. 205–30 with a German translation of Ataullah Bayazitov's reply to Renan. On the latter, see: Anke von Kügelgen, '"Progressiver Islam" im ausgehenden Zarenreich: Das Plädoyer des St. Petersburger Imams und Regierungsbeamten Ataulla Bajazitov (1846–1911) für die Partizipation der Muslime an der modernen Zivilisation', *Asiatische Studien / Etudes asiatiques*, 67:3 (2013), 927–64; Ol'ga Bessmertnaia, 'Ponimanie istorii i identichnost' avtora v vozrazheniiakh Ataully Baiazitova Ernestu Renanu', *Islamology*, 9:1–2 (2019), 54–82.

who had spent many years teaching in British India and was a friend of Sayyid Ahmad Khan (1817–98), a key figure in the Islamic reformist movement in South Asia.[112] Remaining true to Orientalist tropes, Arnold promoted the idea of the golden age of Islam, and as a historian of art he celebrated the great achievements of premodern Muslim civilisation.[113] For al-Ramzī, the well-intentioned Orientalists knew Islam well and their discourse and ideas served his goal of proving the defensive nature of *jihad* and consequently the civilised (as opposed to 'savage') nature of Islam, the best of all religions. 'The seeds of trouble' were indeed implanted quite literally: al-Ramzī Arnold's *The Preaching of Islam* held a cherished spot in his private library.[114] Al-Ramzī's silence on Sufi topics throughout his engagement with the Qur'anic text, combined with his position on the question of *jihad*, moved al-Ramzī dangerously close to alignment with the Islamic reformers he so tirelessly condemned in his theological works.

What al-Ramzī did with the concept of *jihad* is very similar to his novel approach to creating a distinction between the heavenly gardens (*behesht*) and the earthly—almost secular!—orchards (*bāgh*) discussed earlier. He broke away from the established semantic tradition that had been preserved and transmitted by Sufis, and started to speak in the language of modernity. This becomes especially apparent when al-Ramzī turns to the issue of the defence of human rights, dignity, and justice—this entire discourse was borrowed from European sources via Ottoman intermediaries (in this context, it is important that he accessed the ideas of European Orientalists through Arabic and Ottoman Turkish translations). It is bitterly ironic that when speaking of his 'defensive *jihad*', al-Ramzī still used the term *jang*, a paradigmatic term known in conversion narratives in Central Asia and Western Siberia between

---

112 See Margrit Pernau, 'Fluid Temporalities: Saiyid Ahmad Khan and the Concept of Modernity', *History & Theory*, 58:4 (2019), 107–31.

113 Thomas Walker Arnold, *The Preaching of Islam: A History of the Propagation of the Muslim Faith* (Westminster: A. Constable & Co., 1896); Thomas Walker Arnold, *The Court Painters of the Grand Moghuls* (Oxford: Oxford University Press, 1921). See also Roy Bar Sadeh, 'Islamic Modernism between Colonialism and Orientalism: Al-Manar's Intellectual Circles and Aligarh's Mohammedan Anglo-Oriental College, 1898–1914', in *The Muslim Reception of European Orientalism: Reversing the Gaze*, ed. by Susannah Heschel and Amr Ryad (Oxon and New York: Routledge, 2019), pp. 103–28.

114 Al-Ramzī, *Qur'ān tärjemase*, p. 741.

the fourteenth and the twentieth centuries.[115] Hagiographic works associated with the Yasawī and Naqshbandī traditions insisted on the crucial role of warrior heroes who spread religion by the sword, and fought the infidels with precisely the goal of military proselytism so fiercely denied by al-Ramzī.[116] The topic of *jihad* in modern Qur'anic exegesis was so important for al-Ramzī that he elevated it to the level of a personal duty, saying 'Even if there is no one [else] willing to fight the infidels, do it alone. Do not harm those [who did not join you], but encourage them. God will help you.'[117]

Discussion

Muḥammad Murād al-Ramzī had no monopoly on hybrid subjectivity, as many other intellectuals of his era shared a similar profile, defined by complexity and uncertainty.[118] The main challenge for scholarship so far has been identifying an analytic framework that would explain how such

---

115 *Islamizatsiia i sakral'nye rodoslovnye v Tsentral'noi Azii: nasledie Iskhak Baba v narrativnoi i genealogicheskoi traditsiiakh*, vol. I, ed. by Ashirbek Muminov, Anke von Kügelgen, Devin DeWeese, and Michael Kemper (Almaty: Daik-Press, 2008); vol. II, ed. by Ashirbek Muminov and Devin DeWeese with an appendix by Alfrid Bustanov (Almaty: Daik-Press, 2013); Devin DeWeese, 'Khwaja Ahmad Yasavi as an Islamising Saint: Rethinking the Role of Sufis in the Islamisation of the Turks of Central Asia', in *Islamisation: Comparative Perspectives from History*, ed. by A. C. S. Peacock (Edinburgh: Edinburgh University Press, 2017), pp. 336–52. *Jihad* as part of conversion narratives was quite a common thing in the premodern Islamicate world. See: Alfrid Bustanov, 'Sufiiskie legendy ob islamizatsii Sibiri', in *Tiurkologicheskii sbornik, 2009–2010: Tiurkskie narody Evrazii v drevnosti i srednevekov'e*, ed. by Sergei Kliashtornyi, Tursun Sultanov, and Vadim Trepavlov (Moscow: Vostochnaia literatura, 2011), pp. 33–78; Ahmed Manan, *A Book of Conquest: The Chachnama and Muslim Origins in South Asia* (Cambridge: Harvard University Press, 2016); A. C. S. Peacock, *Islam, Literature and Society in Mongol Anatolia* (Cambridge: Cambridge University Press, 2019), pp. 188–217.
116 Several Eastern Turkestani hagiographies have been published recently. See: Jeff Eden, *The Life of Muhammad Sharif: A Central Asian Sufi Hagiography in Chaghatay*, with an appendix by Rian Thum and David Brothy (Vienna: OAW, 2015); Muḥammad Ṣadiq Kashghari, *In Remembrance of the Saints: The Rise and Fall of an Inner Asian Sufi Dynasty*, trans. by David Brothy (New York: Columbia University Press, 2021).
117 Al-Ramzī, *Qur'ān tärjemase*, p. 127.
118 Cf., for example: Michael Kemper, 'Sufi Saint or Salafī Reformer? ʿAlī Tūntārī in Fakhreddinov's Tatar Lineage of *Kalām* Critique', in *From the Khan's Oven: Studies on the History of Central Asian Religions in Honor of Devin DeWeese*, ed. by Eren Tasar, Allen J. Frank, and Jeff Eden (Leiden: Brill, 2022), pp. 258–83; Danielle Ross, 'The Age of the "Socialist-Wahhabi-Nationalist Revolutionary": The Fusion of

hybrid subjectivities were performed socially and textually. As I hope to have demonstrated above, different segments of al-Ramzī's written oeuvre were associated with distinct types of scholarly persona. In his earlier writings he adopted the persona of a Sufi shaykh, a sociolinguistic mediator between Central Asian and Ottoman Sufi trends, a historian of Muslim Turks in Russia, and a polemicist well-grounded in questions of theology and Islamic law. In some texts these distinct personas could be present together. In other cases, only a single persona can be located in his text. Moreover, one can also speculate about al-Ramzī's personal transformation and his unwillingness at a later stage of life to build his archival self around imagery from the past. The marginal gloss format al-Ramzī chose to use in his Qur'an translation allowed the author make exegetical comments freestyle, without caring much about constructing one coherent version of the self, leaving the task of interpretation to future readers and historians.

For al-Ramzī, his Qur'an translation was a project initially set in motion by a bureaucratic request, but it subsequently evolved into a wide discursive platform in which he made discrete claims that reflected the complexity of his thought and personality in the later years of his life, and is impossible to categorise under a single type of scholarly persona. Significantly, the Sufi persona that brought al-Ramzī so much fame is almost entirely absent from his final intellectual achievement. The Qur'an translation reads as if the elderly shaykh had tired of Sufi cosmology by the late 1920s, and simply did not want to produce a work full of specialised terminology and intertextual references to the great Sufi thinkers of the past. He was undoubtedly able to take this approach if he had so wished, but it is clear that he consciously refrained from doing so. Were we not familiar with al-Ramzī's outstanding contribution to Sufism, his translation of the Qur'an would make an impression similar to the science-inspired and strictly rational commentaries and translations produced by Tatar Muslim reformists in Soviet Russia.[119] An ambiguous attitude towards modernity and colonialism, even in his

---

Islamic Fundamentalism and Socialism in Tatar Nationalist Thought, 1898–1917', *Genealogy*, 3:4 (2019), 1–18.

119 Alfrid Bustanov, 'The Qur'an for Soviet Citizens: The Rhetoric of Progress in the Theological Works of 'Abd al-Bari Isaev', *Forum for Anthropology and Culture*, 14 (2018), 169–84.

treatment of the topic of holy war, brought al-Ramzī very close to his lifelong intellectual opponents and led him to bid farewell to hagiographies, metaphoric exegesis, the drive to convert, the blessings of holy places, and the symbolism of spatial terminology. In the competition between Sufis—the self-proclaimed guardians of the Islamic tradition—and Orientalists—the vanguard of European colonialism—al-Ramzī seems to have silently taken the side of the latter. Of his entire written oeuvre, it is in his translation of the Qur'an that al-Ramzī's hybrid subjectivity found its most vivid manifestation.

Appendix

Muḥammad Murād al-Ramzī, *An Explanation of Holy War in Islam*[120]

/739/ Opponents [of Islam] claim: if the Islamic religion is true and sacred, why does God prescribe war (*jang*) and the killing of His slaves for the followers of this religion? They say that this call constitutes the correct religion and comes God.

This forms, in fact, the biggest and strongest criticism of Islam and the Qur'an, therefore I found it my biggest duty (*farḍ*) to react to this critique here and to highlight the issue. The critique is articulated by two groups of individuals. The first group is ignorant fools who are unaware of the Qur'anic meanings and secrets, Islamic prescriptions and grace, [and] human nature, who have no idea about the goal of the ruling [of *jihad*] as well as the difficulties experienced at that time and place by the Prophet and his companions from the unbelievers. They say that the Qur'an orders [Muslims] to kill unbelievers everywhere [they] find them. They believe that Islam consists of stealing property, humiliation of human dignity (*namūs-abrūy*), discrimination against women, failure to implement Qur'anic rules, the rejection of all human rights in political, personal, social and religious dimensions, and in slavish submissiveness to any will like a donkey, without defending one's rights and defaming God's predestination, by saying 'You can do whatever you please, it was destined by God for us.' This group is not just the opponents [of Islam].

---

120 In the margin: 'These seven pages are to explain the regulations in regards of *jihad* in Islam in the third line of p. 41 [of the manuscript].' Interestingly, this is the only part of the manuscript that has carry-over words at the end of each folio.

Unfortunately, many people who claim to be Muslims these days also fall into this group.

The second group is the unfortunate cursed people. They are like Pharaoh and Abū Jahl, who were cognizant of the Qur'an being the word of God, its content being true, and Islam being the best religion. They know who was the object of the verses of war (*jang ayatlarï*) and with whom war is legally allowed and not. Out of enmity towards the Islamic religion and Muslims they have tried to find flaws in the Qur'an and Islamic religion, but after they failed to discover the smallest bit of error, they started to slander Islam with the goal of placing enmity towards Islam in [the hearts and minds of] God's slaves and making them leave it by saying that the Qur'an is full of verses that call for the killing of non-Muslims without leaving them in peace, that such religion cannot be from God, [and that] this is a savage and cruel religion. Europeans, who are known among the Chinese as *fan qu'i* or 'the red savages,' have spread like locusts throughout Africa, the Arabian deserts, Hindustan and China. They have preached among the ignorant people their belief that 'God slept with Maryam and she gave birth to ʿIsā. Maryam is God's wife and ʿIsā is God's son.' In every place they have planted the seeds of trouble. The missionaries who have propagated their religion are people of outrage. They are mainly present in China. Many of them are Christian (*ruslar dindä*) and some of them have even reached the rank of general. They convinced not only the lay people /740/ but also the Muslim elites that the Qur'an has such verses [of war] and warned them about it. They have established friendships with the elites and spread the seeds of trouble among the Sufis (*Ṣidāqat fuqarasï*, literally: the poor [speaking] the truth),[121] and in this way they have caused coldness [towards Islam]. Some true-hearted rulers have trusted these claims and started to look with suspicion at Sufis, and distance [themselves] from them. They would also perform deeds that are not appropriate to their status. They harmed their hearts (*küngel*) and polluted their consciences (*wijdān*), causing inner struggle. Sometimes this also led to wars, as is known from history. Among [such leaders] is Kuyuk Khan, the son of Ugedey Khan and the grandson of Chingis Khan. Those who want to find a detailed discussion [of this] can look [it] up [in] the *Rawḍāt al-ṣafā* and the first volume of my Arab-language historical book the *Talfīq al-akhbār*, pages 389, 392–399.

Some thirty to thirty-five years ago, the first European, named Mr. Gladstone, the British prime minister who claimed first-rank intelligence

---

121 *Ṣidāqat fuqarasï* is the kind of epithet that I expected to find in abundance in al-Ramzi's translation of the Qur'an but, as I have shown above, he rarely used Sufi vocabulary in the text.

and culture, referred to the Qur'an during a speech in the Parliament and exclaimed to its members: 'With this Qur'an in existence, our Christian folk will not be in peace.' With this idea in mind, they intend to discredit the religion by claiming that Islam was spread by force. The falseness of this claim is apparent from Q 2:256, Q 18:29 and Q 41:40, as well as from history books. If their claims were true, no people (*millāt*) except Muslims would have been left on earth at the time when Muslim rule was strong and had spread to China, Africa and Europe. Historical records bear witness [to the fact] that all peoples lived in freedom and peace under Muslim rule. Did five of the six Muslim travellers who called Almas Khan, the ruler of Bulghar, with all his folk to convert to Islam exercise any violence? Who managed to force Berke Khan, among Chingis Khan's descendants, Uzbek Khan, Sultan Ahmad Khan, Ghazan Khan and Tughluq Timur Khan to accept Islam? Nobody did, as they all consciously recognised the supremacy of this religion and chose to become Muslims with free will. Therefore today the first-rank European scholars of Islam who have mastered the true meaning of Islam, the Qur'an and Islamic history, have produced books debunking the proofs formulated by the second group of liars. They serve not the cause of conflict, but truth. /741/ I have in my library (*kitabkhāna-yi ʿajīzī*) the Turkish translation of a [work by a] British professor from London University and a teacher of Arabic, T.W. Arnold, the *Intishār-i Islām tarikhi*,[122] and an Arabic translation of [work by] a French Professor Sadon, the *ʿArab tarikhī*. Such true scholars and good persons recognise the enmity of Islam's opponents and spread the word by compiling books. This is a divine support (*ʿināya ilāhiyya*) from God for Islam and Muslims.

And now, as we are done with this subject, let us proceed to explaining the true reason for God's call for war. Anyone with a basic understanding of the world and humankind knows that people were initially created ignorant, with a tendency to do evil and disrespect each other's rights. God says in the Qur'an: 'Humans will be exceedingly cruel and ignorant.' Arabs have a saying to the effect that 'If people were just, the judge would rest.' From the creation of the world up to now this enmity of people towards one another has been the main reason for all wars. If one person does, or intends to do, an injustice to another, or one community to another, the will of the oppressed to defend [themselves] against the oppressor is a natural and moral thing. There is no one in the world who would welcome and support anyone who wants to kill them. This is why the Prophet, his Companions and [all] Muslims until the present day have survived, because they had to defend themselves against the enmity of other peoples. To create balance God, allowed and

---

122 In the margin: 'The original English title is *The Preaching of Islam*.'

prescribed for Muslims to fight [their] enemies for self-defence under certain conditions. This is the war meant by God in the Qur'an, nothing else.

Let me provide details on the matter. For 530 years after ʿĪsā there was no Prophet and humankind drowned in the darkness of ignorance and idolatry without knowing God. Some of them worshipped idols, [while] others preferred cows, snakes, the sun or the moon. To save humankind in general, and Arabs in particular, God (*khodāwand-i jahān*) sent the final Prophet from the Quraysh tribe and descendants of Hashim—Muhammad b. ʿAbdallah. He supported his prophethood by multiple miracles and granted him his Word in the form of the Qur'an. At that time, the Arabs made sacrifices and worshipped self-made idols of stone and wood, and they filled the Kaaba meant for God with these idols. When people saw how the Prophet destroyed these self-made meaningless idols, some of them /742/ became Muslim, however many— especially the elites—knew the truth but, due to their arrogance, became the Prophet's enemies: 'He threatens our idols and blames our ancestors in stupidity.' They caused much trouble to him and his Companions. They even killed some of them cruelly, as the latter had no one to help. When the Muslims asked the Prophet permission to fight back, he refused by saying: 'God has not instructed me to go to war. You have to be patient as He will help soon.' The Prophet ordered the migration to Ethiopia. More than a hundred people migrated in two instances. [The Arab unbelievers] sent two persons after them with countless presents for the Ethiopian ruler, asking [him] to return their people. He replied: 'How would I give away the oppressed to their enemy?,' and these two messengers were beaten up and sent back. [The Arabs] attempted to bribe Ibn Hashim with a great sum to kill the Prophet, but he naturally rejected the offer, for which he was imprisoned in the mountains near Mecca. He spent three years there in terror until the people of Medina converted to Islam and invited the Prophet and his companions to resettle [with them]. Even though [his opponents'] forces tried to prevent the Prophet, with God's protection all his community moved to Medina and it became a Muslim city. Even though the Muslims left their belongings and their children in Mecca and went with simple luggage, their resettlement was akin to a move from hell to Paradise. The unbelievers of Mecca started to be even harsher with the weakest [believers] who remained in Mecca, i.e. women, children and elderly people. They put them in chains and imprisoned them without food or drink. That time the poor Muslims prayed to God crying: 'Let us leave Mecca, the city of evil people and be our helper in our affairs.' Look up Q 4:74. They fought with Muslim Bedouins near Medina, who were called to invade the city regularly. In short, the unbelievers tried everything to harm the Muslims.

1. Hybrid Subjectivity in a Translation of the Qur'an

And now, given this was the situation, what would those liars who find war problematic and call it a cruelty say? Would they say that the Prophet and Muslim should have submitted themselves to these godless and ignorant idol-worshippers who knew no mercy and humanity? /743/ Of course not. As mentioned above, Islam is not about submitting like a donkey while having all the chances to resist the enemy. Islam consists of peace and mercy towards all the slaves of God, and commanding right and forbidding evil. At the same time Islam entails full possession of human rights and dignity (ᶜizzat-i nafs) to an extent allowed by law (ᶜurf wa-ᶜadat wa-sharīᶜat jihhetleri), especially in regards of religious identity. And if one has to sacrifice oneself to preserve the religion, Islam consists of sacrifice (fidā qīlmaq). Islam is not about capitulation, showing weakness or consent to injustice and shame, especially turning a blind eye to religious oppression while one has resources to fight. Maybe Judaism is about submission, but when someone disregards the rights of Muslims and other Muslims support each other in defence, the issue is not with Islam and Muslims. This enemy is akin to the Meccan unbelievers. Those who blame Islam for the call for *jihad* have no idea what Islam is and what difficulties the Prophet and Muslims had to go through. Only hypocrites would pronounce such lies that the verses on *jihad* deal not with the infidels of Mecca, but with all unbelievers in the world. Only they would be the enemies of Islam willing to show the religion in a false light while knowing the truth. Others would surely not utter such words.

In short, the Muslims resettled in Medina and mixed with the locals and the city became the centre of Muslim government. For many years they were forced to tolerate the terror caused by their enemies, and subsequently God showed them mercy by sending down Q 22:38–41. He allowed the Muslims to fight the infidels of Mecca after so many years of injustice [at their hands]. He helped them, promising to defend [them] against the evil of [their] enemies (truly, God has enough power to lift the trouble from Muslims), and allowed them to go to war with the words 'Allah is our God' against those who had harmed Muslims unjustly and deprived them of their homes. The Qur'an says that God is capable of helping them. The words 'Fight those who are fighting you' /744/ has a similar meaning of allowing defensive action against aggressive unbelievers. They do not allow war against all unbelievers in the world. [The Qur'an] orders that war should not go beyond the rules [set down by] God, namely leaving women, children, and the elderly and weak in peace, as well as religious personnel engaged in praying in their places of worship. It is forbidden to fight those who have good relations with Muslims and those who did not join in the war on the side of the opponent, simply on the grounds of them being unbelievers. It is forbidden to kill unbelievers living peacefully under Muslim rule without any sign of rebellion. It is forbidden for Muslims living under non-Muslim rule to fight a government that does not suppress religion. It is forbidden for a Muslim peacefully entering the lands of unbelievers to cause injury to their property or safety without experiencing any injury themselves. Similar things go beyond the divine limits in performing *jihad* and are strictly forbidden (*ḥarām*). God does not like those who transgress the limits of what is permitted. If someone caused you trouble, do the same to them, anything beyond that would be against the law. Fear God in this regard, He who addressed the God-fearing this way in Q 5:3–9: 'Be severe with unbelievers who forced you from the Sacred Mosque. Do not exceed beyond what is just in regards of their rights and do not harm them unjustly. Justice is closer to piety.' In Q 60:8–9, it says: 'God does not prescribe you to break justice and peace with those who do not harm your religion and do not force you from your homes, simply on grounds of being infidel. God loves those who respects justice towards everyone. God only calls you to break friendship with those who struggle against your religion, who force you from home, or help in doing so.'[123] This is God's approach towards the infidels of Mecca who had terrorised Muslims for so many years. However, /745/ the unfortunate liars and enemies of Islam do not see these verses and do not want to see them, may their eyes become blind. The following are the verses that they do see [and use] to criticise Islam and Muslims. In Q 9:6, it says: 'Upon the end of holy months, kill infidels wherever you find them and break their ways.' And Q 9:37 says: 'All of you fight with infidels. Do not stay aloof when one community is in fight,' because the infidels are fighting against all of you. These unfortunate liars understand the word 'infidel' in both verses as pertaining to all unbelievers in the world. They attach a faulty meaning to the latter verse by saying that you have to fight with all unbelievers and kill them all without leaving a single person [living]. This way, they manage to cheat ignorant and simple-hearted people. In fact, the meaning of the verse is as I have explained. The meaning of 'infidel' here is not all unbelievers, but the aforementioned infidels of Mecca who had been terrorising the Prophet and Muslims for so many years, and those Arab infidels who had had bad relations with them. This is because, except for one or two verses, all the rest relate to the Arab infidels in Mecca. The matter concerns them and the word 'infidel' refers to them. The definite article *al-* at the beginning [of the word] suggests this meaning. Another meaning is also possible: since the Prophet was an Arab and the Qur'an is in Arabic, the Arab infidels had

---

123 In the margin: 'Note that He warns against being friends with them, but does not preclude from doing good towards them. Can there be a better and merciful religion?'

no excuse to reject Islam and it was expected that they convert. In any case, these two verses are not about all unbelievers. How could they be? Fighting against those who do not harm Muslims is strictly forbidden [in other verses], as we have demonstrated. In short, the war verses in the Qur'an all relate to the Arab infidels of Mecca. As for other [unbelievers], if they behave similarly towards Muslims, Muslims have the right to defend themselves.[124] [However,] war in Islam cannot be aggressive, it is always a defence. This means [it can only be undertaken with the intent] to defend against harming property and dignity, especially when it comes to enmity towards the holy religion. This verse and Q 8:39, which says 'Fight them until disorder caused by the infidels is over and until they fulfil their religious duties to their ability,' are clear arguments that support my case. The verse Q 47:4 says that 'You have to fight them until the war lays down its burdens' with the word 'burden' referring to the cause of war. The goal is not, as the enemies of Islam and ignorant Muslims would have it, to fight infidels for their infidelity and to convert them to Islam. The former are enemies, and the latter are idiots and their words should not be taken seriously. I have explained here the goals and regulations of war in Islam because of the terrible damage caused by these two groups. Other verses coming later in the Qur'anic text build on this explanation with some specific provisions. What is the problem with these goals and regulations? What other religion allows as much justice and grace? The true problem is probably in the savage wars of Europeans.

Post Scriptum[125]

Upon completing my preliminary investigation of al-Ramzī's translation of the Qur'an, I ventured to make my findings publicly available to Muslim audiences that might be interested in the project for pious reasons.[126] Unexpectedly, my lecture on the subject found some currency among Sufi circles in the Republic of Tatarstan. As a result, I received substantial feedback from the mufti, Kamil Samigullin, who has proposed an alternative reading of the manuscript. Among a number of technicalities, contrary to my statement in the article above, he has

---

124 Explained in the margin as follows: 'If Muslims defend themselves against trouble, the problem is not with Muslims or Islam, but with those who perform injustice, like the infidels of Mecca.'

125 I would like to thank Waleed Ziad and Igor' Pankov for their insightful comments on the developments described here.

126 https://www.youtube.com/watch?v=YTHYhpEfoGI&t=3283s

pointed out the presence of Russian loanwords in al-Ramzī's work—this does not, however, change my conviction that al-Ramzī was critical of the Russian state. The mufti and his group of Sufi disciples are especially critical of my argument that the absence of Sufi terminology in the manuscript testifies to the fact that the author had drifted away from Sufism towards the modernist platform. In our interviews, which took place at a street café in the Fatih neighbourhood of Istanbul, I was repeatedly questioned by the mufti's associates: 'how come you claim al-Ramzi broke with Sufism?', 'what is your definition of Sufism?', and even 'does the work you do make you closer to God?' In this debate, I was seen by my opponents as a Muslim historian who 'studies Sufism from outside as a medical scientist would inspect a frog'. Moreover, I received some half-joking comments on my assumed sympathies towards Salafis—indeed, why else would anyone dare to say that al-Ramzī experienced an intellectual transformation? However, the attitude towards the camp of Orientalist scholarship supposedly embodied in my person remained ambivalent in the debate. My opponents insisted that I have to consult specialists in Sufism, e.g. Kamil Samigullin, before formulating ideas of doubt, and read the *Maktūbāt* in al-Ramzī's translation to get what Sufism is really about. While my critics claimed that, in fact, the opinions of secular scholars can safely be disregarded and cannot serve as a guide in matters of religion, they still made sure to communicate their opinions on al-Ramzī, in some cases without having read the actual manuscript, insisting that Sufism is not about reading books, being rather a matter of emotional experience.

According to Samigullin, one should not expect any particularly Sufi language in a Qur'anic commentary, especially one written in the *mujaddidī* spirit. In the final years of his life, he said, al-Ramzī entered the highest stage of his spiritual path and did not need the technical language of Sufism to convey his messages. At the stage of *sayr fī l-ashyā* (a path in the created world)—here Samigullin used the kind of terminology I failed to locate in the manuscript—al-Ramzī made it clear that Sufism cannot be decoupled from *sharīʿa* and ethics, and this is the reason for his language choices. This concept forms the main doctrine promoted by Samigullin and his followers. Himself a *mujaddidī* shaykh, Samigullin celebrates al-Sirhindī's pious letters, the systematic reading of which evidently forms an essential part of their Sufi group's practice.

For al-Sirhindī, so the narrative goes, the Sufi path was about the strict following of legal rules and the rejection of religious innovations introduced by mystics. It is thus no surprise that al-Ramzī would take the approach he did in his Qur'an translation. Here, Samigullin and his followers fail to note that his translation of the *Maktūbāt* might have had a different purpose from al-Sirhindī's original: the defence of Sufism against modernist critique. In the present day, Samigullin and his associates instrumentalise the *mujaddidī* legacy to counter, as I read it, the challenge presented by Salafis who undermine the significance of Sufi ideas on the basis of the legalist streams in Islam.

It would be all too easy to dismiss Samigullin's discursive constructions as merely ahistorical, and failing to situate al-Ramzī's work in its place and time. However, this debate reminds us that secular scholarship's pretence to authoritative interpretation of Islamic past can be challenged by well-informed non-academic discourses in the field. As an anthropologist, I can only praise the Tatarstani Sufis' insistence on intellectual autonomy, in sharp contrast to their predecessor al-Ramzī who, at least in matters of *jihad*, gave in to the opinions of European Orientalists and turned his back on the centuries-old literary tradition nurtured in Sufi hagiographies of the type that he had translated in his early years. It is probable that the anti-Orientalist and anti-Western convictions of Samigullin and his followers have their roots in the self-defensive writings of Muslim authors popular in the second half of the twentieth century.[127] Al-Ramzī's oeuvre, of course, predates these developments and, as I maintain, has proved to be closer to the reformist writings of his era than his Sufi roots.

Bibliography

Akhmadullin, Salavat, *Murad Ramzi kak istorik tiurkskikh narodov Rossii* (Moscow: Institut rossiiskoi istorii, 2022).

al-Alkadarī ad-Dagistānī, Ḥasan-afandī, *Jirāb al-Mamnūn* (Temir-Khān-Shūrā: al-Maṭbaʿa al-Islāmiyya li-Muḥammad-Mirzā Mavraev, 1912).

Arnold, Thomas Walker, *The Preaching of Islam: A History of the Propagation of the Muslim Faith* (Westminster: A. Constable & Co., 1896).

---

127 One good example is the scandalous work by al-Nadwi.

———, *The Court Painters of the Grand Moghuls* (Oxford: Oxford University Press, 1921).

Aykut, Abdulsait, 'The Intellectual Struggle of Murād Ramzī (1855–1935) An Early 20th Century Eurasian Muslim Author' (unpublished doctoral thesis, University of Wisconsin-Madison, 2015).

———, 'Muhammad Murad Ramzi (1855–1935) and his Works', *Krymskoe istoricheskoe obozrenie*, 2 (2016).

al-Bagini, Shuʿayb, *Tabaqāt al-khwājagān al-Naqshbandiyya wa-sādāt al-mashāʾikh al-khālidiyya al-maḥmūdiyya* (Makhachkala: Dār al-Risāla, 2016), pp. 600–32.

Bar Sadeh, Roy, 'Islamic Modernism between Colonialism and Orientalism: Al-Manar's Intellectual Circles and Aligarh's Mohammedan Anglo-Oriental College, 1898–1914', in *The Muslim Reception of European Orientalism: Reversing the Gaze*, ed. by Susannah Heschel and Amr Ryad (Oxon and New York: Routledge, 2019), pp. 103–28.

Bessmertnaia, Ol'ga, 'Ponimanie istorii i identichnost' avtora v vozrazheniiakh Ataully Baiazitova Ernestu Renanu', *Islamology*, 9:1–2 (2019).

Bigeev, Musa, *Rähmät ilahiya burhannarï* (Orenburg: Waqït, 1911).

Brophy, David, *Uyghur Nation: Reform and Revolution on the Russia-China Frontier* (Cambridge, MA: Harvard University Press, 2016).

———, 'A Lingua Franca in Decline? The Place of Persian in Qing China', in *The Persianate World The Frontiers of a Eurasian Lingua Franca*, ed. by Nile Green (Oakland: University of California Press, 2019), pp. 175–91.

———, '"He Causes a Ruckus Wherever He Goes": Saʿid Muḥammad al-ʿAsali as a Missionary of Modernism in North-West China', *Modern Asian Studies*, 54:4 (2020), https://doi.org/10.1017/S0026749X18000264

Bsheer, Rosie, *Archive Wars: The Politics of History in Saudi Arabia* (Stanford, CA: Stanford University Press, 2020).

al-Bulgari, Tadzh ad-Din b. Ialchygul, *Sidrat al-muntakha* (*Lotos krainego predella*), 2 vols, ed. by Alfrid Bustanov, (Kazan: Tatarskoe knizhnoe izdatel'stvo, 2022).

Bustanov, Alfrid, 'Sufiiskie legendy ob islamizatsii Sibiri', in *Tiurkologicheskii sbornik, 2009–2010: Tiurkskie narody Evrazii v drevnosti i srednevekov'e*, ed. by Sergei Kliashtornyi, Tursun Sultanov, Vadim Trepavlov (Moscow: Vostochnaia literatura, 2011), pp. 33–78.

———, 'The Qur'an for Soviet Citizens: The Rhetoric of Progress in the Theological Works of 'Abd al-Bari Isaev', *Forum for Anthropology and Culture*, 14 (2018), https://doi.org/10.31250/1815-8927-2018-14-14-169-184

———, 'On Emotional Grounds: Private Communication of Muslims in Late Imperial Russia', *Asiatische Studien*, 73:4 (2019), https://doi.org/10.1515/asia-2019-0026

——, and V. Usmanov (eds), *Muslim Subjectivity in Soviet Russia: The Memoirs of 'Abd al-Majid al-Qadiri* (Leiden: Brill, 2022).

——, 'Postsekuliarnyi sufizm v Rossii', in *Sufizm posle SSSR*, ed. by Igor' Pankov and Sergei Abashin (Moscow: Izdatel'skii dom Mardzhani, 2022), pp. 28–51.

——, 'A Space for the Subject: Tracing Garden Culture in Muslim Russia', *Journal of the Economic and Social History of the Orient*, 65 (2023), https://doi.org/10.1163/15685209-12341563

——, and Shamil Shikhaliev, 'Archives of Discrimination: The Evolution of Muslim Book Collections in Daghestan', *Journal of Islamic Manuscripts*, 15:1 (2023), 82–109, https://doi.org/10.1163/1878464X-01501008

Chanyshev, Malik, *Kytaida tatar megarife tarikhy* (Kazan: Zhyen, 2007).

Chih, Rachida, Catherine Mayeur-Jaouen, and Rudiger Seesemann (eds), *Sufism, Literary Production, and Printing in the Nineteenth Century* (Würzburg: Ergon Verlag, 2015).

DeWeese, Devin, 'Khwaja Ahmad Yasavi as an Islamising Saint: Rethinking the Role of Sufis in the Islamisation of the Turks of Central Asia', in *Islamisation: Comparative Perspectives from History*, ed. by A. C. S. Peacock (Edinburgh: Edinburgh University Press, 2017), pp. 336–52.

Eden, Jeff, *The Life of Muhammad Sharif: A Central Asian Sufi Hagiography in Chaghatay*, with an appendix by Rian Thum and David Brothy (Vienna: OAW, 2015).

Frank, Allen, *Bukhara and the Muslims of Russia: Sufism, Education, and the Paradox of Islamic Prestige* (Leiden: Brill, 2012).

Gadzhieva, Diana, '"Al-Kafiia fi-n-nakhv" Ibn al-Khadzhiba s ierarkhiei kommentariev v Dagestane', *Vestnik instituta istorii, arkheologii i etnografii*, 1:37 (2014).

Garaeva, Nuriia, 'Kem ul Morad Ramzi', *Kazan utlary*, 2 (1990).

Garipova, Rozaliya, 'The Protectors of Religion and Community: Traditionalist Muslim Scholars of the Volga-Ural Region at the Beginning of the Twentieth Century', *Journal of the Economic and Social History of the Orient*, 59 (2016), https://doi.org/10.1163/15685209-12341395

——, 'From Kolkhoz to Pulpit: Rashida Abïstay and Female Religious Authority in Soviet and Post-Soviet Russia', *Journal of Islamic Studies*, 33:1 (2022), https://doi.org/10.1093/jis/etab064

Gosmanov, Mirkasim, *Iabylmagan kitap iaki chechelgen orlyklar* (Kazan: Tatarstan kitap nashriiaty, 1996).

——, 'Tatar Settlers in Western China (Second Half of the 19th Century to the First Half of the 20th Century)', in *Muslim Culture in Russia and Central Asia from the 18th to the Early 20th Centuries*, ed. by Anke von Kügelgen, Michael Kemper, and Allen J. Frank (Berlin: Schwarz Verlag, 1998), pp. 243–69.

Hinton, Thomas, 'Conceptualizing Medieval Book Collections', *French Studies*, 70:2 (2016), https://doi.org/10.1093/fs/knw005

al-Ispijābī, Dawlat Shāh, *Abwāb al-jinān*. Kazan University Library, Ms. 6764 T.

Kashghari, Muḥammad Ṣadiq, *In Remembrance of the Saints: The Rise and Fall of an Inner Asian Sufi Dynasty*, trans. by David Brophy (New York: Columbia University Press, 2021).

Kefeli, Agnes, 'The Tale of Joseph and Zulaykha on the Volga Frontier: The Struggle for Gender, Religious, and National Identity in Imperial and Post-Revolutionary Russia', *Slavic Review*, 70:2 (2011), https://doi.org/10.5612/slavicreview.70.2.0373

Kemper, Michael, 'Sufi Saint or Salafī Reformer? ʿAlī Tūntārī in Fakhreddinov's Tatar Lineage of Kalām Critique', in *From the Khan's Oven: Studies on the History of Central Asian Religions in Honor of Devin DeWeese*, ed. by Eren Tasar, Allen J. Frank, and Jeff Eden (Leiden: Brill, 2022), pp. 258–83.

Khamidov, Evgenii, 'Trud istorika Murata Ramzi "Zainulla bin Khabibulla" i ego znachenie dlia izucheniia biografii Zainully Rasuleva', in *Islam v sovremennom mire*, ed. by Denis Brilev et al. (Kazan: KFU, 2012), pp. 291–97.

Lange, Christian, and Alexander Knysh (eds), *Sufi Cosmology* (Leiden, Boston: Brill, 2023).

Manan, Ahmed, A Book of Conquest: The Chachnama and Muslim Origins in South Asia (Cambridge: Harvard University Press, 2016).

Muminov, Ashirbek, Anke von Kügelgen, Devin DeWeese, and Michael Kemper (eds), *Islamizatsiia i sakral'nye rodoslovnye v Tsentral'noi Azii: nasledie Iskhak Baba v narrativnoi i genealogicheskoi traditsiiakh*, vol. II (Almaty: Daik-Press, 2008).

——, and Devin DeWeese (eds), *Islamizatsiia i sakral'nye rodoslovnye v Tsentral'noi Azii: nasledie Iskhak Baba v narrativnoi i genealogicheskoi traditsiiakh*, vol. I, with an appendix by Alfrid Bustanov (Almaty: Daik-Press, 2013).

Nasyrov, Il'shat, 'Murat Ramzi i ego vzgliady na dzhadidizm', in *Religioznye aspekty globalizatsii: faktor islama*, vol. III (Ufa: Villi Oksler, 2006), pp. 138–40.

——, 'Vzgliady Murada Ramzi po voprosam reformirovaniia i modernizatsii islama', *Arabskie issledovaniia* (2012).

——, 'O nauke istorii i proshlom i nastoiashchem narodov Evrazii. Fragmenty iz sochineniia "Talfik al-akhbar." Vvodnaia stat'ia, perevod i kommentarii', *Ishrak: Ezhegodnik islamskoi filosofii*, 9 (2019).

Papas, Alexandre, 'Muslim Reformism in Xinjiang: Reading the Newspaper Yengī Ḥayāt (1934–1937)', in *Kashgar Revisited: Uyghur Studies in Memory of Ambassador Gunnar Jarring*, ed. by Ildikó Bellér-Hann, Birgit N. Schlyter, and Jun Sugawara (Leiden and Boston: Brill, 2017), pp. 161–83.

——, 'Lingua Franca or Lingua Magica? Talismanic Scrolls from Eastern Turkistan', in *The Persianate World: The Frontiers of a Eurasian Lingua Franca*, ed. by Nile Green (Oakland: University of California Press, 2019), pp. 208–12.

Paul, Herman, 'What is a Scholarly Persona? Ten Theses on Virtues, Skills, and Desires', *History & Theory*, 53:3 (2014).

Peacock, A. C. S., *Islam, Literature and Society in Mongol Anatolia* (Cambridge University Press, 2019).

Pernau, Margrit, 'Fluid Temporalities: Saiyid Ahmad Khan and the Concept of Modernity', *History & Theory*, 58:4 (2019), https://doi.org/10.1111/hith.12138.

al-Ramzī, Muḥammad Murād, *Qur'ān 'azīm al-sha'nīnīng türk[i]chä tärjemäse*. A manuscript in private possession. Kazan, Republic of Tatarstan.

——, *Dhayl Rashaḥāt ʿayn al-ḥayāt* (Mecca: n.p., 1890).

——, *Inṣāf* (Kazan: Tipografiia Karimovykh, 1900).

——, *Talfīq al-akhbār wa-talqīh al-athār fī waqāʾīʿ Qazān wa-Bulghār wa-mulūk al-Tātār*, 2 vols (Orenburg: Karimov, Khusainov i Ko, 1908).

——, Mushāyaʿat ḥizb al-raḥmān wa-mudāfaʿat ḥizb al-shayṭān (Orenburg: n.p., 1911).

——, 'Muḥaqqiq wa 'allāma dāmullah Shihāb al-Dīn al-Marjānī al-Qazānī häzrätlereneng ... dar-khatir itmäk ichin ber-ike jumlä', in *Märjānī: Shihāb al-Dīn al-Märjānī häzrätlereneng wiladätenä yuz yil tulu mönasäbätlä näsher itelde*, ed. by Ṣāliḥ b. Thābit ʿUbaydullin (Kazan: Maʿārif, 1333 AH), pp. 513–16.

——, *Muʿarrab al-maktūbāt* (Istanbul: Ihlas Vakfi, 2002).

——, *Talfik al'-akhbar va talkikh al'-asar fi vakai' Kazan va Bulgar va muluk at-tatar*, vol. I, ed. by S. I. Khamidullin (Ufa: Bashkirskii gosudarstvennyi universitet, 2017).

Ibn Fakhr al-Dīn, Riḍā al-Dīn, *Ibn Taymiyya* (Orenburg: n.p., 1911).

Ross, Danielle, 'The Age of the "Socialist-Wahhabi-Nationalist Revolutionary": The Fusion of Islamic Fundamentalism and Socialism in Tatar Nationalist Thought, 1898–1917', *Genealogy*, 3.4 (2019), https://doi.org/10.3390/genealogy3040058.

——, 'Debunking the "Unfortunate Girl" Paradigm: Volga-Ural Muslim Women's Knowledge Culture and its Transformation across the Long Nineteenth Century', in *Shari'a in the Russian Empire: The Reach and Limits of Islamic Law in Central Eurasia, 1550–1900*, ed. by Danielle Ross and Paolo Sartori (Edinburgh: Edinburgh University Press, 2020), pp. 120–55.

Roth, Nicolas, 'Poppies and Peacocks, Jasmine and Jackfruit: Garden Images and Horticultural Knowledge in the Literatures of Mughal India, 1600–1800', *Journal of South Asian Intellectual History*, 1 (2018), https://doi.org/10.1163/25425552-12340003

Ṣāliḥī, ʿArīfullāh, 'A Review of al-Ramzī's *Talfīq al-akhbār*', Institute of Oriental Manuscripts, D 481.IV.

Schäbler, Birgit (ed.), *Moderne Muslime: Ernest Renan und die Geschichte der ersten Islamdebate 1883* (Leiden: Brill, 2017).

Schluessel, Eric, 'History, Identity, and Mother-Tongue Education in Xinjiang', *Central Asian Survey*, 28:4 (2009), https://doi.org/10.1080/02634930903577144

Shäikh Mulla Morad Rämzi äl-Kazani, *Kor"än gazyimu-sh-shannyng törkichä tärjemäse häm bu tärjemäneng khäzerge tatar telenä iaraklashtyrylgan variant. 30nchy parä* (Kazan: Tynychlyk näshriiat iorty, 2023).

Shikhaliev, Shamil, and Michael Kemper, 'Sayfallāh-Qāḍī Bashlarov: Sufi Networks between the North Caucasus and the Volga-Urals', in *The Piety of Learning: Islamic Studies in Honor of Stefan Reichmuth*, ed. by Michael Kemper and Ralf Elger (Leiden: Brill, 2017), pp. 189–90.

Sibgatullina, Gulnaz, 'The Ecology of a Vernacular Qur'an: Rethinking Mūsā Bīgī's Translation into Türki-Tatar', *Journal of Qur'anic Studies*, 24:3 (2022), https://doi.org/10.3366/jqs.2022.0515

'The DUM RT started translating the famous tafsir Murad Ramzi into the modern Tatar literary language', *World Congress of the Tatars*, August 27, 2022, https://tatar-congress.org/en/news/the-dum-rt-started-translating-the-famous-tafsir-murad-ramzi-into-the-modern-tatar-literary-language/

Usmanova, Diliara, 'Murad Ramzi (1853–1934): biografiia islamskogo uchenogo v svete novykh svidetel'stv', *Gasyrlar avazy—Ekho vekov*, 2 (2019).

von Kügelgen, Anke, '"Progressiver Islam" im ausgehenden Zarenreich: Das Plädoyer des St. Petersburger Imams und Regierungsbeamten Ataulla Bajazitov (1846-1911) für die Partizipation der Muslime an der modernen Zivilisation', *Asiatische Studien / Etudes asiatiques*, 67:3 (2013), https://doi.org/10.5167/uzh-85105

Witkam, Jan Just, *Values of Old Paper* (Leiden: Ter Lugt Press, 2022).

2. 'Vernacular Qur'anic Space' within Post-Soviet Uzbekistan: A Qur'an Translation by a Leader of the Turkestani Émigré Community, and its Uzbek Competition

Filipp Khusnutdinov

Introduction

The widespread Bolshevisation of Soviet Central Asia and the anti-religious policies of the Soviet authorities during the 1920s and 1930s triggered a wave of emigration from the region.[1] Many emigrants from Central Asia, which they preferred to call Turkestan (Persian for 'Land of the Turks'), ended up settling in Afghanistan, Xinjiang,

---

[1] I would like to express my sincere gratitude to Alfrid Bustanov, Shamil Shikhaliev, the editors of this book, the copyeditor Helen Blatherwick, and Alexander Maier for their valuable advice, thoughtful questions, and kind support during the writing of this chapter. I also would like to thank the two anonymous readers who have reviewed the manuscript for the publisher for their time and careful reading.

India, Egypt, Turkey, and Saudi Arabia. The latter enjoyed special status in this context due to the location of the 'two holy cities' of Islam (Arabic: *al-Ḥaramayn*, i.e. Mecca and Medina), where a significant diaspora of Central Asian Muslim scholars (*ʿulamāʾ*) found refuge.² Despite the remoteness from their homeland, the Turkestani emigrants who settled in Saudi Arabia in the first half of the twentieth century maintained contact with their fellow Muslims in Uzbekistan. During the Cold War period, these relations were necessarily limited and were largely confined to interactions during visits by members of the Soviet delegation to Mecca and Medina in the Hajj seasons.³ With the fall of the Soviet Union (1922–91) and the Republic of Uzbekistan's declaration of independence, the once

---

2   Manṣūr b. ʿAbd al-Bāqī al-Andījānī al-Bukhārī, *ʿUlamāʾ Mā warāʾ al-nahr al-muhājirīn lil-Ḥaramayn* (Istanbul: Dār al-Mīrāth al-Nabawī lil-Dirāsāt al-Taḥqīq wa-Khidmat al-Turāth, 1434/2013). For a brief overview of al-Bukhārī's book and perspectives on its use in the context of Central Asian Islamic studies, see Filipp Khusnutdinov, 'From Soviet to Saudi: On Central Asian Ulama and their Hijra', *SICE Blog*, 2022, https://www.oeaw.ac.at/sice/sice-blog/from-soviet-to-saudi-on-central-asian-ulama-and-their-hijra

3   Eren Tasar, *Soviet and Muslim: The Institutionalization of Islam in Central Asia, 1943–1991* (New York: Oxford University Press, 2017), pp. 269–73. One can learn about such interactions between Soviet pilgrims and their former compatriots not only through archival documents and oral testimonies of eyewitnesses, but also through Soviet fiction. In this respect, a novel by the Tajik writer Fazliddin Muhammadiev (1928–1986) deserves special attention. It describes in detail (of course, not without a fair share of irony) the story of one Hajj pilgrimage by Soviet Muslims and, in particular, their encounters with Turkestani emigrants: *Puteshestvie na tot svet ili povest' o velikom khadzhzhe*, trans. by Yuri Smirnov (Dushanbe: Irfon, 1970), pp. 121–25, 133–35, 174–75, 180–81, 191–92, 198, 201, 220, 228, 239–40, 243–49, 265–67. For more on this work and its author, see, for example, Vladimir Bobrovnikov and Artemy Kalinovsky, 'Fazliddin Muhammadiev's Journey to the "Other World": The History of a Cold War *Ḥajjnāma*', *Die Welt des Islams*, 62:1 (2021), 21–52, https://doi.org/10.1163/15700607-61020007; Vladimir Bobrovnikov, 'From Moscow to Mecca: Entangled Soviet Narratives of Pilgrimage in the Unlikely 1965 *ḥajjnāme* of Fazliddin Muhammadiev', in *Narrating the pilgrimage to Mecca: historical and contemporary accounts*, ed. by Marjo Buitelaar and Richard van Leeuwen (Boston: Brill, 2023), pp. 221–41. Originally published in 1965 in Tajik, the novel was later translated into a number of languages, including Russian. As Vladimir Bobrovnikov and Artemy Kalinovsky write, Muhammadiev's work has seen more than thirty editions, with a total print run of over one million copies. Bobrovnikov and Kalinovsky, 'Fazliddin Muhammadiev's Journey', p. 51.

sporadic ties began to grow rapidly stronger, especially in the context of the Islamic revival within Uzbekistan.[4]

One of the vectors of this interaction, which began to crystallise as early as the late 1950s, was the infiltration of Islamic literature written by Turkestani émigrés into the Uzbek SSR (1924–91).[5] According to the historian Manṣūr al-Bukhārī, Muslim scholars from Turkestan who settled in Medina worked to clandestinely distribute their books in their native region, with the aim 'to teach [their] descendants the prescriptions of their religion under socialist occupation.'[6] And some books did indeed reach Soviet Central Asia, although initially the number of copies was hardly significant. However, by 1990, such works were being imported into what was still Soviet Uzbekistan by the thousand.[7] Despite this, when, only a few years later, writings by these Turkestani emigrants were distributed gratis in a number of Tashkent mosques or published in an adaptation using the modern Uzbek script,[8] they never really became widely popular.

In this chapter, I argue that the Islamic literature written by Turkestani emigrants fell on fertile ground among Muslim intellectuals and secular scholars in Central Asia precisely during the Soviet era, when there was virtually no alternative available in the vernacular languages of the Muslim peoples of the USSR. Following the fall of the Iron Curtain and the national-religious revival that swept across

---

4 Sayfiddin Jalilov, *Buxoriylar qissasi (Muhojirat tarixidan lavhalar)* (Tashkent: Toshkent islom universiteti nashriyot-matbaa birlashmasi, 2006), pp. 4–8, 64–68, 77–149; Bayram Balci, *Islam in Central Asia and the Caucasus since the Fall of the Soviet Union*, trans. by Gregory Elliott (New York: Oxford University Press, 2018), pp. 121–23, 125–26.

5 The Uzbek Soviet Socialist Republic was one of the union republics of the former Soviet Union, situated in Central Asia. It was established in 1924 as a result of the so-called national-territorial delimitation in the USSR. For more information on the topic, see Adeeb Khalid, *Making Uzbekistan: Nation, Empire, and Revolution in the Early USSR* (Ithaca and London: Cornell University Press, 2015).

6 al-Bukhārī, ʿUlamāʾ, pp. 255–56 (reference 1).

7 Sayyid Mahmud Taroziy, *Nurul basar*, ed. by Abdul Azim Ziyouddin (Samarkand: Imom Buxoriy xalqaro markazi nashriyoti, 2017), pp. 5–6.

8 In this case, I am referring to Cyrillic script, which has been and remains the main script for Islamic literature in Uzbekistan, although the official script in the country is Latin. More details about the current situation regarding the script used in Qur'an translations in Uzbekistan will be provided in the last section of this chapter.

the country, Islamic literature in vernacular languages experienced an enormous increase in popularity, and the vacuum that had previously existed in this segment of the book market has begun to rapidly fill. Books written by local authors living in Uzbekistan began to appear rather quickly, and quite successfully superseded their old predecessors. This rapid development can be explained by the fact that the 'new' Islamic literature was more in line with the demands of a wider readership and had a corresponding socio-political capital. To illustrate this, I will highlight how the fate of the Qur'an translation and exegesis by al-Sayyid Maḥmūd al-Ṭarāzī—the leader of the Turkestani émigré community in Saudi Arabia in the 1950s and 1980s—has changed within post-Soviet Uzbekistan when compared to its reception during the Soviet period.

Al-Sayyid Maḥmūd al-Ṭarāzī was born in around 1895 in the city of Awliya Ata, nowadays called Taraz, in Kazakhstan, and died in 1991 in Medina (see Fig. 2.1).[9] Having emigrated from Soviet Central Asia in around 1930 against the backdrop of the mass persecution of 'cult servants' (Russian: *sluzhiteli kul'ta*), over the next thirty years he became a prominent Muslim scholar and head of the Religious Administration of the National Turkestanian Unity Committee (1942–76), the largest and most influential Turkestani emigrant political organisation.[10] He is also notable for being the author of arguably the first known full interlinear translation of the Qur'an with commentary (*tafsīr*) to be written in Central Asian Turki.

---

9   al-Ṭarāzī is also known by his honorary nickname (*laqab*) of Āltūn-*khān*-*tūra* (Uzbek: *Oltinxonto'ra*). For his biography, see Filipp Khusnutdinov, 'Altin-*khan*-*tura*: biobibliograficheskii ocherk', *Journal of Central Asian History*, 1:2 (2022), 329–38.

10 For more information on this organisation, see Ahat Andican, *Turkestan Struggle Abroad (From Jadidism to Independence)* (Haarlem: SOTA, 2007), pp. 471–503, 553–58, 570–75, etc.

2. 'Vernacular Qur'anic Space' within Post-Soviet Uzbekistan

Fig. 2.1. Undated photograph of al-Sayyid Maḥmūd al-Ṭarāzī. The identity of the photographer is unknown. ©Filipp Khusnutdinov, Creative Commons license CC BY.

Existing scholarship on al-Ṭarāzī's Qur'an translation in Arabic-, Persian-, Turkish-, and Uzbek-language academic spaces is mainly based on a philological analysis of some fragments of al-Ṭarāzī's text itself, or is limited to a brief mention of the place and time of publication of a particular edition of this translation.[11] Researchers have not focused

---

11 See, for example, Ḥasan ʿAbd al-Majīd al-Maʿāyirijī, 'Tarjamat ḥayāt al-muʾallif', in *Qurʾān-i karīm. Mutarjam wa-muḥashshā bi-l-lugha al-tūrkistāniyya bi-qalam al-ʿājiz al-Sayyid Maḥmūd b. al-Sayyid Nadhīr al-Ṭarāzī al-Madanī* (Qatar: n.p., 1993), pp. 709–10; *Al-Qurʾon ul-karim (oʻzbek tilida izohli tarjima)*, trans. and comm. by Sayyid Mahmud ibn Sayyid Nazir at-Taroziy al-Madiniy (Oltinxon Toʻra), ed. by Hoji Ismatullo Abdulloh (Tashkent: Gʻafur Gʻulom nomidagi Adabiyot va sanʼat nashriyoti, 1994), pp. 5–6; Ibrāhīm Khudāyār, 'Muʿarrifī-yi chand tarjuma-yi Qurʾān-i karīm ba zabān-i uzbakī', *Tarjumān-i vahī*, 7 (1379/2000–1), 92–96 (pp. 94–95), http://ensani.ir/file/download/article/20101106123337-58. pdf; Rahmatulloh qori Obidov, *Markaziy Osiyo olimlarining tafsir sohasida tadqiqotlari (Toshkent islom universiteti malaka oshirish kursi uchun maʼruza matni)* (Tashkent: n.p., 2008), pp. 9–10; Ibrohim Gʻafurov, 'Qurʼon tarjimalari: tajribalar', *Oʻzbekiston adabiyoti va sanʼati*, 16:3999 (2009), 3–4; Nevin Mazman, 'Hindistan'da basılmış bir Kurʼan tercümesi: mütercem ve muhaşşa bi'l-lugati't-türkistâniyye', *Çukurova Üniversitesi Türkoloji Araştırmaları Dergisi*, 3:1 (2018), 131–53; Yunus

on analysing its theological or legal characteristics, and even less on the specifics of the circulation of this book in the past and present in any of the regions where it may have been disseminated.

Al-Ṭarāzī's work first appeared in 1956 in Indian Bombay (now Mumbai), in the form of a lithographed six-volume publication.[12] The author positioned his translation as the first complete translation of the main sacred text of Islam 'into the Turkestani language'[13] (Arabic: *bi-l-lugha al-tūrkistāniyya*; Uzbek: *Turkiston tilida/shevasida*).[14] In the introductory part of the book, al-Ṭarāzī lamented that '[...] the [Qur'anic] translations and *tafsīr*s written in Persian and Urdu, praise be to Allah, exist in abundance. However, the Turkestani Muslim communities who do not master these two languages have been deprived of this happiness.'[15] According to this introduction, al-Ṭarāzī was not the main initiator of the translation; it was instead the fulfilment of a 'great sacred task' entrusted to him by a group of Muslim scholars,

---

Abdurahimoğlu, 'Seyyid Mahmûd et-Tarazî ve Kur'an-ı Kerim'i Türkistan Diline Tercüme ve Haşiyesi', *Türkiye İlahiyat Araştırmaları Dergisi*, 6:2 (2022), 827–44.

12 *Qur'ān-i karīm. Mutarjam wa-muḥashshā bi-l-lugha al-tūrkistāniyya*, 6 vols, trans. and comm. by al-Sayyid Maḥmūd al-Ṭarāzī al-Madanī (Bombay: al-Maṭbaʿa al-Karīmiyya al-Kāʾina fī Bambay al-Hind, 1375/1956), al-Biruni Institute of Oriental Studies, Fund of Hamid Sulaymanov, Litho. №№ 4015–4020.

13 In many of his writings, by 'Turkestani language/dialect' al-Ṭarāzī essentially meant the Uzbek language that was in use in Central Asia in the early twentieth century, also referred to by specialists as 'Central Asian Turki.' See Emir Nadzhip and Galina Blagova, 'Tiurki iazyk', in *Iazyki mira. Tiurkskie iazyki* (Moscow and Bishkek: Izdatel'skii Dom 'Kyrgyzstan', 1997), pp. 126–38 (pp. 126–29). For some comments on the language of al-Ṭarāzī's Qur'an translation, see Abdurahimoğlu, 'Seyyid Mahmûd et-Tarazî', pp. 837–38. Regarding the term 'Turkestani language', researchers have not yet been able to give a definitive answer as to when it was first coined and by whom. However, a glance at the writings of émigré Turkestani ʿulamāʾ illustrates that al-Ṭarāzī was not the only one who employed this expression. See, for example: Muḥammad-Ẓarīf al-Kāshgharī, *Tafsīr juzʾ ʿamma yatasāʾalūn* (*bi-l-lugha al-turkistāniyya*), abridged by Raḥmatallāh ʿInāyatallāh (Makka al-Mukarrama: Rābiṭat al-ʿĀlam al-Islāmī, 1403/1983); *Muqaddimat al-Jazariyya wa-tarjamatuhā bi-l-lugha al-turkistāniyya*, trans. and comm. by 'Abd al-Salām b. al-Shaykh Shīr-Muḥammad al-Khūqandī (Madīna al-Munawwara: n.p., n.d.).

14 Previously, there were translations and exegeses of individual *sūra*s or groups of *sūra*s in very limited quantities. As an example, I can mention the interpretation of the thirtieth part (*juzʾ*) of the Qur'an in Central Asian Turki by Muḥammad-Ẓarīf al-Kāshgharī (1872–1959). This work, of over 730 pages, was completed in Kashgar in 1926 and published there in 1937. See Muḥammad-Ẓarīf al-Kāshgharī, *Tafsīr ʿAmma yatasāʾalūn* (Doha: Maṭābiʿ al-ʿArūba, 1413/1992). For more on al-Kāshgharī's biography, see al-Bukhārī, *ʿUlamāʾ*, p. 32.

15 *Qur'ān-i karīm*, vol. I, trans. by al-Ṭarāzī, p. i.

after representatives of the Turkestani diaspora approached them with a request for a translation of the Qur'an into their native language. At the same time, al-Ṭarāzī warns readers that for him to 'write a proper translation and commentary (Uzbek: *tarjima va tafsir*) on the 'Pure Word' (Uzbek: *Pak Kalam*, i.e. the Qur'an) [all by himself] is beyond his ability.' For this reason, the '[Qur'anic] translations and exegesis carried out earlier by Indian Muslim scholars' serve as his guidance.[16]

In the commentary he includes in *Qur'ān-i karīm*, al-Ṭarāzī follows the Sunni exegetical tradition of past centuries. His work is in many respects an imitation of the classics. This tendency can be traced in the content of the commentary and in the methodology of its narration. The author dwells on the sacred history of Islam; explains the occasions of revelation (*asbāb al-nuzūl*) of certain verses of the Qur'an, providing excerpts from the biography of the Prophet Muḥammad (*al-sīra al-nabawiyya*); clarifies a number of ritual-legal and doctrinal issues (*al-masāʾil al-fiqhiyya, al-masāʾil al-ʿaqāʾidiyya*); and gives lexical comments elucidating the meanings of some Qur'anic words and expressions. His commentary on the *āyāt* is rather laconic, and does not reflect the deep scholarly discussions between different factions of Islamic theological thought.[17] Al-Ṭarāzī prepared his annotated Qur'an translation in accordance with the Ḥanafī school of law (*madhhab*), a fact which is especially evident in the articulation of ritual-legal prescriptions. The names of the personalities and writings that served as the foundation for his commentary are only rarely mentioned in the text, but include recognised Sunni authorities such as the founders of the four *madhhabs*, the authors of the authentic six *hadith* collections (*al-ṣiḥāḥ al-sitta*), companions of the Prophet (*aṣḥāb al-nabī*) and their followers (*al-tābiʿūn*), and medieval Muslim intellectuals like Ibn Kathīr (c. 1300–73), Abū Muḥammad al-Ḥusayn al-Baghawī (c. 1041–1122), Ibn Ḥajar al-ʿAsqalānī (1372–1449) and Jalāl al-Dīn al-Suyūṭī (1445–1505). Scholars from the Indian subcontinent are represented by Mullā Jīwan (c. 1637–1717), the author of the best-known *tafsīr* from the time of Aurangzeb ʿĀlamgīr (1618–1707, r. 1658–1707), the historian Muḥammad-Qāsim Firishta (c. 1572–1620), the prominent religious figure Shabbīr Aḥmad ʿUthmānī (1886/87–1949), and others.

---

16   Ibid., pp. i–ii.
17   In total, al-Ṭarāzī's text is a little over 700 pages long.

In less than fifty years after its first publication, this translation by al-Ṭarāzī has been issued in more than ten reprints and editions in various regions of the Muslim world—in India (Bombay, 1956); Pakistan (Karachi, 1975, (not earlier than) 1992); Saudi Arabia (Medina, 1975; Jeddah, 1980–81); Qatar (Doha, 1975, 1980, 1993); Turkey (Istanbul, 1990); and Uzbekistan (Tashkent, 1994, 2002).[18] In one way or another—for example, through Hajj pilgrimages and foreign trips taken by religious figures and secular scholars from the Uzbek SSR—some of these editions reached Soviet Central Asia, where they developed their own rich history.

Until practically the last years of the USSR's existence, translations of Islamic materials were restricted to the official state language of Russian and the authorities forbade the publication of any Qur'an translation in a vernacular language[19]—whether this be a translation prepared in accordance with all the canons of Islam by a major Muslim scholar who held the post of chairman of one of the Muslim spiritual boards, or even a translation made by a retired militia officer who wanted to show through his writing that 'the Islamic tradition contains many errors and misinterpretations aimed at deceiving ordinary people and enriching the bourgeoisie.'[20] Despite this, a few decades before the Islamic revival in the region, al-Ṭarāzī's Qur'an translation was actively circulating in Uzbekistan, the main Islamic outpost of the USSR.[21]

---

18 The wide geographical spread of the publication might perhaps be explained by the concentration of Turkestani emigrants in these locations.

19 Meanwhile, the publication of the Qur'an in Arabic was authorised. On the first official Soviet edition of the Qur'an, realised in Tashkent in 1956, and the foreign policy goals of this action, see Viacheslav Akhmadullin, 'Deiatel'nost' gosudarstvennykh organov SSSR i dukhovnykh upravlenii musul'man po izdaniiu Korana na arabskom iazyke v SSSR i ego rasprostraneniiu v 50-e gody XX v.', *Vestnik Dagestanskogo nauchnogo tsentra*, 52 (2014), 84–89, http://vestnikdnc.ru/IssSources/52/Akhmadullin.pdf

20 Alfrid Bustanov, 'The Qur'an for Soviet Citizens: The Rhetoric of Progress in the Theological Writings of 'Abd al-Bari Isaev', *Antropologicheskij forum*, 37 (2018), 93–110 (pp. 95–97, 100–01), https://anthropologie.kunstkamera.ru/files/pdf/037/bustanov.pdf

21 Among the Muslim republics of the Soviet Union, Uzbekistan enjoyed the most significant historical and cultural Islamic heritage and the largest Muslim population. The Central Asian Muftiate was headquartered in the UzSSR and played the most prominent role of all the Soviet muftiates in the state's approach to Islamic affairs in the international arena. The Mir-i ʿArab Madrasa and the Imam al-Bukhari Tashkent Islamic Institute also operated in Uzbekistan. These

My field studies have revealed that, since at least the 1970s, despite the isolation of most Soviet Muslims from the Islamic world, al-Ṭarāzī's Qur'an translation still found its way to the author's homeland. The book circulated there in the private libraries of major Central Asian Muslim intellectuals as well as local secular scholars.[22] It used to be seen illegally on sale at the Friday markets (*jumʿa-bazaar*s) held in Kokand and Tashkent. It was also found in the collection of the Central Asian Muftiate (SADUM, 1943–92),[23] and in the confessional and educational institutions under its jurisdiction, and even in state academic depositaries.[24]

Due to the changing nature of the socio-political situation in Uzbekistan in the early 1990s, the use of al-Ṭarāzī's Qur'an translation became more widespread. Simultaneously during this period, other translations of the holy scripture of Islam began to appear in Uzbekistan. These also gained an enthusiastic readership, and competed directly with their illustrious predecessor. In this chapter, I discuss some aspects

---

were the only official Islamic educational institutions in the USSR that opened in the post-war period.

22 Among them were probably the most notable Ḥanafī scholar of Soviet Central Asia, *dāmlā* (teacher) al-Hindustānī (Muhammadjon Rustamov, 1892–1989); the Kokand Sufi Shaykh Ibrāhīm-*ḥaḍrat* (Ibrahimjon Mamatqulov, 1937–2009); a number of theologians of the SADUM; and the last Mufti of the SADUM, Shaykh Muhammad Sodiq Muhammad Yusuf (1952–2015). For more on their biographies and intellectual legacies, see Bakhtiiar Babadzhanov, 'Hindustani', in *Islam na territorii byvshei Rossiiskoi imperii: Entsiklopedicheskii slovar'*, vol. I, ed. by Stanislav M. Prozorov (Moscow: Vostochnaia Literatura, 2006), pp. 426–28; Bakhtiiar Babadzhanov, 'Ibrahim-hazrat', in *Islam na territorii byvshei Rossiiskoi imperii*, pp. 155–56; Haydarxon Yo'ldoshxo'jaev and Irodaxon Qayumova, *O'zbekiston ulamolari*, ed. by Usmonxon Alimov and Baxtiyor Bobojonov (Tashkent: Movarounnahr, 2015), pp. 82–83; Bakhtiiar Babadzhanov and Muhammad-Ayyubxon Hamidov, 'Muhammad-Sodiq', in *Islam na territorii byvshei Rossiiskoi imperii: Entsiklopedicheskii slovar'*, vol. II, ed. by Stanislav M. Prozorov (Moscow: Nauka—Vostochnaia Literatura, 2018), pp. 267–70.

23 SADUM is a common acronym for the Central Asian Muftiate (from Russian: *Sredneaziatskoe dukhovnoe upravlenie musulman*). The official name of the institution is the Spiritual Board of Muslims of Central Asia and Kazakhstan. In 1992, it was renamed as the Spiritual Board of Muslims of Mawerannahr, and in 1996, its name was changed to the Muslim Board of Uzbekistan. For recent major studies on the Central Asian Muftiate, see, for example: Tasar, *Soviet and Muslim*; Talgat Zholdassuly, *Sovyetler'in İslam Siyaseti ve Orta Asya'da Dini İdare (1943–1990)* (Leiden: SOTA, 2022).

24 I have dealt with these storylines in an article: Filipp Khusnutdinov, '"Turkestani Muslim Communities … Have Been Deprived of This Happiness". The Dissemination of Tarazi's Qur'an Translation and Exegesis in Soviet Uzbekistan', *Islamology*, 11:1 (2021), 84–103.

of the circulation history of al-Ṭarāzī's Qur'an translation within Soviet—and especially post-Soviet—Uzbekistan, and offer my thoughts on why his writing has not been as widely disseminated in the country as the other full Qur'an translations produced by Shaykh Alouddin (ᶜAlāʾ al-Dīn) Mansur (1952–2020), Shaykh Muhammad Sodiq Muhammad Yusuf (Muḥammad-Ṣādiq Muḥammad-Yūsuf), and Shaykh Abdulaziz (ᶜAbd al-ᶜAzīz) Mansur (b. 1944).[25]

By using a creative reinterpretation of the Foucauldian idea of heterotopia, or 'other' spaces, in this chapter I propose to introduce the concept of 'vernacular Qur'anic space' and demonstrate how this is relevant to Uzbekistan.[26] In this case, by the term 'vernacular Qur'anic space', I mean: (1) translations of the Qur'an into Uzbek, produced within Uzbekistan and/or circulating within its borders; as well as (2) the complex of social and political processes that accompanied the publication and circulation of these translations. Moreover, this reveals (3) the production practices (publication, open or clandestine sale, free distribution, etc.) associated with translations of the Qur'anic text in Uzbekistan, and (4) the main actors and institutions that shape and regulate this space.[27] I consider the case of al-Ṭarāzī's Qur'an translation to be quite informative in this respect. This translation, by nature of being the first complete modern translation of the Qur'an into Central Asian Turki, has the longest history of dissemination in Uzbekistan of all Uzbek Qur'an translations. Furthermore, I believe that turning to the

---

25   For a brief biography of the latter, see Yo'ldoshxo'jaev and Qayumova, *O'zbekiston ulamolari*, pp. 110–12.

26   Being both a word and a thing, the Qur'an—like its translations into other languages, by interacting with the 'places' of its presence within the outside world—creates its own unique 'Qur'anic space.' I owe my broader understanding of the concept of heterotopia to a collection of articles in *Heterotopias: Worlds, Borders, Narratives*, ed. by Galina Michailova, Inga Vidugiryte, and Pavel Lavrinec (Vilnius: Vilniaus Universiteto Leidykla, 2015).

27   The concept of 'Qur'anic space' itself—not limited to the word 'vernacular'—in my view, carries a broader semantic load because, in addition to characteristics and practices 1–4 mentioned above, it can also comprise of: (5) the original texts of the Qur'an and its various translations imported from abroad or published within the country; (6) the teaching of Qur'anic disciplines within the state and the people and books involved in this practice—teachers, students, and writings used as educational material; and (7) the authors of various books as well as audio and video products related to the Qur'an and its sciences. Certainly, I do not claim to be all-encompassing here, and I am convinced that this line of logic could be continued.

circulation history of al-Ṭarāzī's book will enable us to trace the dynamics and trends of the vernacular Qur'anic space within Uzbekistan, from the late 1950s up to the present day.

This chapter will now move on to provide a brief description of the history of the circulation of al-Ṭarāzī's writing within Soviet Uzbekistan. It then discusses the features of this story in the context of the significantly altered social and political realities within post-Soviet Uzbekistan. I also provide a general overview of the situation within the vernacular Qur'anic space of the country at the turn of the 1990s. This is important in order to have an idea of the dominant trends in Uzbekistan that served as the background to the events surrounding the reception of al-Ṭarāzī's writing. Finally, the last part of the chapter will be devoted to an analysis of the factors that may have hindered the proliferation of al-Ṭarāzī's Qur'an translation and exegesis in post-Soviet Uzbekistan.

My main sources include, firstly, various editions of al-Ṭarāzī's Qur'an translation and archival materials that mention this work (in particular, the accounts of Soviet delegations on their visits to Saudi Arabia, the inventories of official academic and Islamic institutions, and the drafts that formed the basis of the Cyrillic edition of al-Ṭarāzī's Qur'an translation). This corpus of heterogeneous sources has been generated by various state institutions and private individuals for multiple purposes (for submission to the authorities, including security bodies, or for official, public, or private use). This context needs to be borne in mind in order to avoid normalising the sometimes politically biased connotations of the material presented here.[28] I found these documents in the State Archive of the Russian Federation (Moscow), the al-Biruni Institute of Oriental Studies (Tashkent), the libraries of the Mir-i ʿArab Madrasa (Bukhara), the Imam al-Bukhari Tashkent Islamic Institute (Tashkent), the Muslim Board of Uzbekistan (Tashkent), and a number of private libraries of local Uzbek scholars and bibliophiles. The second group of sources consists of oral accounts by people who were directly or indirectly involved in the dissemination of writings by al-Ṭarāzī in Soviet and post-Soviet Uzbekistan.[29] A final, third group of sources I have used comprises a number of editions of several full

---

28 See, for instance, the next section of this chapter.
29 Here, I am referring mainly to material from interviews I conducted between 2018 and 2022.

Qur'an translations into Uzbek that have been officially published in Uzbekistan since 1990.[30]

Al-Ṭarāzī's Qur'an Translation in Soviet Uzbekistan[31]

The earliest reference I have seen to al-Ṭarāzī's translation of the Qur'an in official Soviet documents dates back to 1959. That year, al-Ṭarāzī visited a group of Soviet pilgrims in Mecca. The Soviet delegation's report of this visit describes him as an 'evident enemy' of the Soviet state, who 'tried to engage in anti-Soviet discourse about the alleged oppression of the religion of Islam in the Soviet Union.'[32] At the same time, the document acknowledges that 'at present [al-Ṭarāzī is] one of the most famous *mudarris*es in Mecca and Medina.'[33] Moreover, it says that he invited several pilgrims 'from among the Uzbeks' to his home and 'showed them the quran,[34] which he himself had translated into the Uzbek language. Along the way, Mr. Ishankhanov [i.e. al-Ṭarāzī] tried to engage in anti-Soviet discourse about the alleged oppression of the

---

30 Uzbek translations of the Qur'an that have been published abroad or that translate only part of the Qur'an are not taken into consideration. This selection may be explained by the fact that these editions of the Qur'an are very unpopular in Uzbekistan. For example, there are translations by the third Mufti of SADUM Shamsuddin (Shams al-Dīn) Babakhanov (1937–2003), and by a group of translators led by the Uzbek scholar-philosopher Mutalib Usmanov (1924–94): *Qur'oni karim (30-pora)*, trans. by Shamsiddinxon Boboxonov (Moscow: COMIL, 1992); *Qur'oni karim. Tarjima va ilmiy-tarixiy izohlar. I-kitob. (1992 y.)*, trans. and comm. by Mutallib Usmon, Abdusodiq Irisov, Hoji Ismatullo Abdullo, and Ubaydulla Uvatov, ed. by Mutallib Usmon (Tashkent: Fan, 2004). For recent translations published outside Uzbekistan, see, for example: *Qur'oni karimning yengil tafsiri*, 2nd edn trans. by Abdulloh Kamol Yusuf, (Istanbul: n.p., 2019); *Qur'on ma'nolarining arab tilidan ilmiy-izohli akademik tarjimasi*, trans. and comm. by Mahmudhodja Nuritdinov (Germany: GlobeEdit, 2018/2021).
31 In this section of the chapter, I partially utilise material presented in my previous article: Khusnutdinov, 'Turkestani Muslim Communities'.
32 Gosudarstvennyi arkhiv Rossiiskoi Federatsii. F. R-6991 (Sovet po delam religii pri Sovete Ministrov SSSR). Op. 4. D. 102. L. 48. (Spravka o poezdke palomnikov v Mekku v 1959 godu).
33 Ibid.
34 Ibid. In the text, the word 'Qur'an' is written with a lower-case letter, and I have replicated this in my translation.

religion of Islam in the Soviet Union. Our pilgrims responded to him with dignity and left his house.'[35]

During the same period, in the late 1950s, in his *The Pilgrimage Book*, al-Ṭarāzī unequivocally expressed the hope that his Qur'an translation would spread to Soviet Central Asia:

> Praise and gratitude to Allah, [...] the translation of the Holy Qur'an with commentary in our mother tongue that we embarked upon was completed within two years, [and then] published. O Lord of the Worlds, accept this humble service from Your humble servant and make it suitable and useful for my compatriots both in the homeland and abroad![36]

And it seems that soon, by the mid-1970s and early 1980s, the author's aim was gradually being achieved. Arguably, by that time the wider circles of ʿulamāʾ and secular scholars in Soviet Central Asia were becoming aware of the existence of this translation. I will provide some examples to demonstrate this increasing awareness.

The exemplar of al-Ṭarāzī's Qur'an translation depicted in Fig. 2.2 was preserved, until 1983, in the book collection of Shaykh Ibrāhīm-ḥaḍrat, a famous Sufi and a representative of the Naqshbandiyya-Ḥusayniyya from Kokand. However, as a result of his arrest, the translation and dozens of other books were confiscated from the Shaykh's library and removed to the Hamid Sulaymanov Institute of Manuscripts in Tashkent (1978–98). A few months later, when Ibrāhīm-ḥaḍrat was released, it was instructed that his books be returned to their rightful owner. Before returning the confiscated books, an employee of the Institute—whose name was Boboxon Qosimxonov (d. 2018)—asked the Shaykh to leave the complete six-volume set of al-Ṭarāzī's Qur'an translation in the Institute's collection. Negotiations were successful, and the books found

---

35 Ibid. The last two sentences clearly show the biased nature of the document, which ought to be taken into consideration—the circle of readers of these reports included representatives of the Soviet secret services. For an analysis of this and other similar documents in the context of al-Ṭarāzī's relations with Soviet pilgrims, see Tasar, *Soviet and Muslim*, pp. 270–71.
36 al-Sayyid Maḥmūd b. al-Sayyid Nadhīr al-Ṭarāzī al-Madanī, *Ḥajj kitābī* (*Türkistān tīlīda imām Abū Ḥanīfa raḥimahu Allāh madhhablārīgha muṭābiq*) (Jeddah: Dār al-Funūn lil-Ṭibāʿa wa-l-Nashr, 1378/1958–9), p. 2.

a new home. In 1998, after the Institute of Manuscripts was abolished, the collection was transferred to the al-Biruni Institute of Oriental Studies.[37]

Fig. 2.2. The first edition of al-Ṭarāzī's Qur'an translation and exegesis, published in six volumes in Bombay (1956), vol. I, al-Biruni Institute of Oriental Studies, Tashkent. ©al-Biruni Institute of Oriental Studies, Creative Commons license CC BY.

However, before officially moving permanently to the al-Biruni Institute in 1998, al-Ṭarāzī's translation had already paid a visit to this Institute, albeit in a different form. Around 1978–79, one of the staff members (Hamidulla Hikmatullaev, d. 1994)[38] brought to the Institute a microfilm he had had delivered from Pakistan or Afghanistan which contained

---

37 *Qur'ān-i karīm*, trans. and comm. by al-Ṭarāzī, al-Biruni Institute of Oriental Studies, Fund of Hamid Sulaymanov, Litho. №№ 4015–4020. Personal interview with Bobokhon Qosimkhonov on 23 February 2018. On his biography, see Sharifjon Islamov, 'Ustoz Boboxon Qosimxonovni xotiralab', *Meros*, 1 (2019), 150–52.

38 Malik Abdusamatov, *O'zbekiston sharqshunoslari (bibliografik ocherk)* (Tashkent: Qomuslar Bosh tahririyati, 1996), pp. 496–97.

al-Ṭarāzī's work.³⁹ Colleagues at the Institute helped him to print the full text of the book on photographic paper and prepared its binding.

Despite the risk of possible criminal prosecution for the distribution of religious literature, al-Ṭarāzī's Qur'an translation could be found illegally for sale at Friday markets (*jumʿa-bazaars*) in Kokand and Tashkent.⁴⁰ Thus, in the early 1980s the translation—especially its thirtieth part, the *juzʾ ʿamma*—enjoyed a certain circulation (mostly in the form of photocopies) in Kokand. The full translation of the Qur'an in its original edition was less commonly available and cost up to 1,000 Soviet rubles.⁴¹

The reason for the popularity (if that word is appropriate in this context) of al-Ṭarāzī's Qur'an translation seems to lie in the fact that for several decades, this Qur'an translation into Uzbek was basically the only one of its kind. The next full translation did not appear on the scene until the second half of the 1980s.⁴² Its author, *dāmlā* al-Hindustānī—the

---

39 The process of smuggling Islamic literature from abroad into the USSR deserves a specific study. For a brief analysis of the ways Islamic publications penetrated into Soviet Central Asia, see Bakhtiyar Babajanov, Ashirbek Muminov, and Anke von Kügelgen, *Disputes on Muslim Authority in Central Asia in 20th Century: Critical Editions and Source Studies* (Almaty: Daik-Press, 2007), pp. 21–24.

40 The activities of selling Islamic literature from abroad fell under a number of administrative and criminal offences. These include, for example, 'smuggling', 'hand trade in unauthorized places', and 'petty speculation.' Moreover, considering the anti-Soviet message of most of al-Ṭarāzī's works, the distribution, production, or possession of his books could be regarded as 'dissemination of deliberately false fabrications defaming the Soviet state and social order', or 'anti-Soviet agitation and propaganda'. The latter is taken from articles of the Criminal Code of the Uzbek SSR that characterise particularly dangerous offences against the state. See *Ugolovnyi kodeks Uzbekskoi SSR* (Tashkent: Uzbekistan, 1977), pp. 54–55, 58, 113, 127; *Kodeks Uzbekskoi SSR ob administrativnykh pravonarusheniiakh* (Tashkent: Uzbekistan, 1986), pp. 91–92, 113–15.

41 At that time, the average salary of an ordinary Soviet citizen was about 120 rubles, and that of a doctor of science at the al-Biruni Institute was 400–450 rubles, and the cost of a mid-range car was about 5,000 rubles.

42 There also existed translations into Uzbek of parts of the Qur'anic text. These were produced by private individuals (mainly religious figures) for their own use (not for open publication) and were aimed at teaching the basics of the Qur'an to their children. One such example was written in 1970 by Muhammadxon (Muḥammad-*khān*) Mahjuri (1889–1973), a prominent religious scholar who at various times was a member of the Uzbek SSR Academy of Sciences and a teacher at the Mir-i ʿArab Madrasa: Muhammadxon mullo Is'hoq qori o'g'li Mahjuriy, *Fotiha, Yosin, Taborak va Amma suralarining tafsiri*, ed. by Sayfiddin Sayfulloh and Maqsudxon hoji Muhammadxon o'g'li (Tashkent: Movarounnahr, 2004). See also Yo'ldoshxo'jaev and Qayumova, *O'zbekiston ulamolari*, pp. 158–60.

most eminent Muslim scholar of the Fergana Valley and Tajikistan in the second half of the twentieth century—wrote his work in Arabic script and then published it as a *samizdat* of 500 copies which was distributed to a narrow circle of trusted people. Thereafter, the official edition of this text, as far as I know, did not come out until 2006, by which time it had been transliterated into Cyrillic.[43]

In the capital of the Uzbek SSR, Tashkent, in the mid-1970s, al-Ṭarāzī's translation had been hijacked by the state—meaning that a book authored by an anti-Soviet figure was exhibited among other translations of the Qur'an in the SADUM library so as to serve the interests of the Soviet state's policy vis-à-vis Islamic affairs. Naturally, there were impediments in place to prevent ordinary citizens holding this book in their hands. The purpose of exhibiting Qur'an translations in the SADUM library, along with other Islamic objects, was primarily to provide a symbolic demonstration of religious freedom in the USSR and to create a positive image of the state during visits by foreign delegations.[44] However, almost twenty years later, between 1990 and 1993, al-Ṭarāzī's work was openly available at the local *jumʿa-bazaar* in the Old City on the territory of the Ḥast-i Imām (*Ḥaḍrat-i Imām*) architectural complex. According to witnesses, in the years 1991 to 1992, when Uzbekistan gained state independence, there were occasions when the Qur'an translation and other writings by al-Ṭarāzī that had been published abroad were given away for free in the mosques of Tashkent.

Given the substantive history of al-Ṭarāzī's Qur'an translation and exegesis during the Soviet era, it is of clear interest to explore the reception of this text in the post-Soviet period. Before moving on to do

---

43 For more on al-Hindustānī's Qur'an translation and the history of its publication, see *Qur'oni karim. Oyatlari ma'nolarining izohli tarjimasi*, trans. and comm. by Shayx Muhammadjon mullo Rustam o'g'li (Mavlaviy hoji Hindistoniy), ed. by Sayfiddin Sayfulloh (Tashkent: Movarounnahr, 2006).

44 A similar situation could be observed when it came to the Soviet Islamic press. As Shamil Shikhaliev points out, the magazine *Muslims of the Soviet East*, which was published by SADUM from the end of the 1960s, 'was largely aimed at an external audience—Islamic and European countries. Perhaps, under the Iron Curtain it served as a kind of message to foreign Muslim countries about the Soviet government's support of religious communities and as a consequence—a certain attempt to legitimise the USSR in its domestic religious policy'. Shamil Shikhaliev, 'Islamic Press in the Early Soviet Dagestan and the Journal "Muslims of the Soviet Orient"', *Islamology*, 7:2 (2017), 74–100 (p. 94).

this, however, attention should be paid to the historical context in which events unfolded.

The Vernacular Qur'anic Space in Uzbekistan at the Turn of the 1990s

One of the markers of the changing socio-political situation in Uzbekistan in the late 1980s and early 1990s was a rapid rise in interest in religion among the local Muslim community.[45] This process was accompanied by a change in leadership within SADUM. The new Mufti, Muhammad Sodiq Muhammad Yusuf, and his supporters largely represented that generation of young Soviet theologians who, unlike their older colleagues, actively sought to liberate the religious sphere from the meticulous tutelage of the state. They were perfectly conscious of the trends of their time and strove to realise what they considered to be their paramount objectives. Alongside an increase in the number of mosques—and the extension of quotas for Islamic educational institutions, with the direct involvement of religious elites—many thousands of copies of Islamic literature were printed and distributed within the country.

It was at this time that the first Qur'an translations into modern Uzbek appeared in the official public space. In 1990, perhaps the most authoritative 'literary and artistic, social and political' magazine in Uzbekistan, *Sharq yulduzi* ('Star of the East'),[46] began to serialise publication of a Qur'an translation prepared by Alouddin Mansur.[47] The release of

---

45 Adeeb Khalid, *Islam after Communism: Religion and Politics in Central Asia* (Berkeley: University of California Press, 2007), pp. 117–18; Bayram Balci, *Islam in Central Asia and the Caucasus Since the Fall of the Soviet Union*, trans. by Gregory Elliott (New York: Oxford University Press, 2018), pp. 29–33.
46 During these years, the editor-in-chief of the magazine was Utkir Hoshimov (1941–2013), People's Writer of the Uzbek SSR.
47 'Qur'on', trans. and comm. by Alouddin Mansur, *Sharq yulduzi* (1990), 3–12; 'Qur'on', trans. and comm. by Alouddin Mansur, *Sharq yulduzi* (1991), 1–12; and 'Qur'on', trans. and comm. by Alouddin Mansur, *Sharq yulduzi* (1992), 1–2. The magazine's print run at the end of 1990 numbered about 206,000 copies; at the end of 1991, it was 98,000; and at the beginning of 1992 it was 111,000. Interestingly, the Russian-language version of the magazine, appropriately titled *Zvezda Vostoka*, published a full translation of the Qur'an by the academic Ignatii Krachkovskii (1883–1951), with commentary by Mutalib Usmanov, alongside Mansur's Uzbek translation. The Uzbek translation appeared after the publication of the Russian translation had begun: see 'Koran', trans. by Ignatii

the first fragments of this work sparked a heated public debate about the advisability of continuing the project, and the Office of the President of Uzbekistan received numerous letters from local citizens on the subject. The arguments were various. Some people believed that printing passages from the Holy Book of Islam in a magazine was disrespectful to the Qur'an, as the pages of these magazine editions could then end up anywhere: they might be sent for recycling, or even used as packaging by vendors who have traditionally used sheets of paper from newspapers and magazines for their products (e.g. for sunflower seeds, nuts, or condiments).

The public outcry reached as high as the President of the Republic. In response, Islam Karimov (1938–2016), the President of Uzbekistan between 1989 and 2016, convened a special public council of government officials, clerics, and prominent figures in science, art, and culture to address the issue. The council decided to proceed with the publication.[48] Later, in 1992, Cho'lpon publishing house undertook the publication of Alouddin Mansur's complete work, with a print run of half a million copies. This was the first ever edition of a complete translation of the Qur'an into modern Uzbek produced within Uzbekistan.[49]

Some six months before Mansur's work was first published in *Sharq yulduzi*, in August 1989, the popular science journal *Fan va turmush* ('Science and Life') included translations of brief Qur'anic passages with commentary. The author of this translation was a scholar-Arabist

---

Krachkovskii, comm. by Mutalib Usmanov, *Zvezda Vostoka* (1990), 1–12; 'Koran', trans. by Ignatii Krachkovskii, comm. by Mutalib Usmanov, *Zvezda Vostoka* (1991), 1–12. The magazine's print run in Russian at the end of 1990 numbered about 212,000 copies; at the end of 1991 it was 73,000. For a concise description of Alouddin Mansur's Uzbek translation of the Qur'an, as well as this scholar's activity in translating the holy scripture of Islam into other Turkic languages, and the influence of his work on later Qur'an translation into Crimean Tatar, see Mykhaylo Yakubovych, 'Qur'an translation of the week #08: Kur'oni Karim. Uzbekcha Izoxli Tarjima', *Qur'an Translation of the Week*, https://gloqur.de/quran-translation-of-the-week-08-kuroni-karim-uzbekcha-izoxli-tarjima/

48 This story was kindly shared with me by a former employee of the Office of the President of Uzbekistan, who wished to remain anonymous. Personal interview on 18 September 2021.

49 *Qur'oni Karim*, trans. and comm. by Alouddin Mansur (Tashkent: Cho'lpon, 1992). At the end of the same year, the translation was reprinted again, this time in a print run of 100,000 copies: see *Qur'oni karim. O'zbekcha izohli tarjima*, trans. and comm. by Alouddin Mansur (Tashkent: G'afur G'ulom nomidagi nashriyot-matbaa birlashmasi; O'zbekiston Respublikasi prezidenti mahkamasining ishlar boshqarmasi huzuridagi «Sharq» nashriyot-matbaa konserni, 1992).

from Namangan, Ismatulla Abdullayev (1927–2005).[50] The publication of this fragmentary translation, unlike Mansur's, did not receive much public recognition, did not generate any visible discussion, and was limited to only two issues of the magazine.

---

50 'Qur'oni karim', trans. and comm. by Ismatulla Abdullayev, *Fan va turmush*, 8 (1989), 20–21; 'Qur'oni karim', trans. and comm. by Ismatulla Abdullayev, *Fan va turmush*, 9 (1989), 22–23.

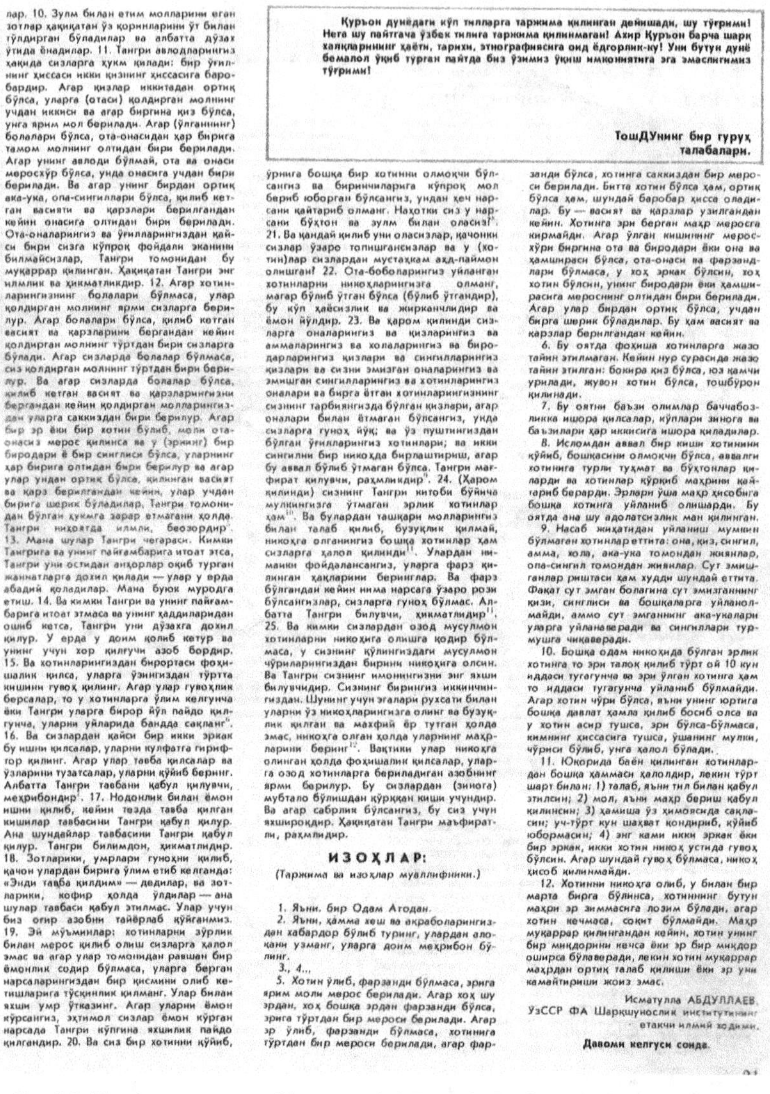

Қуръон дунёдаги кўп тилларга таржима қилинган дейишади, шу тўғрими! Нега шу пайтгача ўзбек тилига таржима қилинмаган! Ахир Қуръон барча шарқ халқларининг ҳаёти, тарихи, этнографиясига оид ёдгорлик-ку! Уни бутун дунё бемалол ўқиб турган пайтда биз ўзимиз ўқиш имкониятига эга эмаслигимиз тўғрими!

ТошДУнинг бир гуруҳ талабалари.

лар. 10. Зулм билан етим молларини еган зотлар ҳақиқатан ўз қоринларини ўт билан тўлдирган бўладилар ва албатта дўзах ўтида ёнадилар. 11. Тангри авлодларингиз ҳақида сизларга ҳукм қилади: бир ўғилнинг ҳиссаси икки қизнинг ҳиссасига баробардир. Агар қизлар иккитадан ортиқ бўлса, уларга (отаси) қолдирган молнинг учдан иккиси ва агар биргина қиз бўлса, унга ярим мол берилади. Агар (ўлганнинг) болалари бўлса, ота-онасидан ҳар бирига тамом молнинг олтидан бири берилади. Агар унинг авлоди бўлмай, ота ва онаси меросхўр бўлса, унда онасига учдан бири берилади. Ва агар унинг бирдан ортиқ ака-ука, опа-сингиллари бўлса, қилиб кетган васияти ва қарзлари берилгандан кейин онасига олтидан бири берилади. Ота-оналарингиз ва ўғилларингиздан қайси бири сизга кўпроқ фойдали эканини билмайсизлар, Тангри томонидан бу муқаррар қилинган. Ҳақиқатан Тангри энг илмлик ва ҳикматликдир. 12. Агар хотинларингизнинг болалари бўлмаса, улар қолдирган молнинг ярми сизларга берилур. Агар болалари бўлса, қилиб кетган васият ва қарзларини бергандан кейин қолдирган молнинг тўртдан бири сизларга бўлади. Агар сизларда болалар бўлмаса, сиз қолдирган молнинг тўртдан бири берилур. Ва агар сизларда болалар бўлса, қилиб кетган васият ва қарзларингизни бергандан кейин қолдирган молларингиздан уларга саккиздан бири берилур. Агар бир эр ёки бир хотин бўлиб, моли ота-онасиз мерос қилинса ва у (эрнинг) бир биродари ё бир синглиси бўлса, уларнинг ҳар бирига олтидан бири берилур ва агар улар ундан ортиқ бўлса, қилинган васият ва қарз берилгандан кейин, улар учдан бирига шерик бўладилар, Тангри томонидан бўлган ҳукмга зарар етмагани ҳолда. Тангри ниҳоятда илмли, беозордир[5]. 13. Мана шулар Тангри чегараси. Кимки Тангрига ва унинг пайғамбарига итоат этса, Тангри уни остидан анҳорлар оқиб турган жаннатларга дохил қилади — улар у ерда абадий қоладилар. Мана буюк муродга етиш. 14. Ва кимки Тангри ва унинг пайғамбарига итоат этмаса ва унинг ҳаддиларидан ошиб кетса, Тангри уни дўзахга дохил қилур. У ерда у доим қолиб кетур ва унинг учун хор қилғучи азоб бордир. 15. Ва хотинларингиздан бирортаси фоҳишалик қилса, уларга ўзингиздан тўртта кишини гувоҳ қилинг. Агар улар гувоҳлик берсалар, то у хотинларга ўлим келгунча ёки Тангри уларга бирор йўл пайдо қилгунча, уларни уйларида бандда сақланг[6]. 16. Ва сизлардан қайси бир икки эркак бу ишни қилсалар, уларни кулфатга гирифтор қилинг. Агар улар тавба қилсалар ва ўзларини тузатсалар, уларни қўйиб беринг. Албатта Тангри тавбани қабул қилувчи, меҳрибондир[7]. 17. Нодонлик билан ёмон ишни қилиб, кейин тезда тавба қилган кишилар тавбасини Тангри қабул қилур. Ана шундайлар тавбасини Тангри қабул қилур. Тангри билимдон, ҳикматлидир. 18. Зотларики, умрлари гуноҳни қилиб, қачон улардан бирига ўлим етиб келганда: «Энди тавба қилдим» — дедилар, ва зотларики, кофир ҳолда ўлдилар — ана шулар тавбаси қабул этилмас. Улар учун биз оғир азобни тайёрлаб қўйганмиз. 19. Эй мўъминлар: хотинларни зўрлик билан мерос қилиб олиш сизларга ҳалол эмас ва агар улар томонидан равшан бир ёмонлик содир бўлмаса, уларга берган нарсаларингиздан бир қисмини олиб кетишларига тўсқинлик қилманг. Улар билан яхши умр ўтказинг. Агар уларни ёмон кўрсангиз, эҳтимол сизлар ёмон кўрган нарсада Тангри кўпгина яхшилик пайдо қилгандир. 20. Ва сиз бир хотинни қўйиб, ўрнига бошқа бир хотинни олмоқчи бўлсангиз ва биринчиларига кўпроқ мол бериб юборган бўлсангиз, ундан ҳеч нарсани қайтариб олманг. Наҳотки сиз у нарсани бўҳтон ва зулм билан оласиз?[8]. 21. Ва қандай қилиб уни оласизлар, қачонки сизлар ўзаро топишгансизлар ва у (хотин)лар сизлардан мустаҳкам аҳд-паймон олишган! 22. Ота-боболарингиз уйланган хотинларни никоҳларингизга олманг, магар бўлиб ўтган бўлса (бўлиб ўтгандир), бу кўп ҳаёсизлик ва жирканчлидир ва ёмон йўлдир. 23. Ва ҳаром қилинди сизларга оналарингиз ва қизларингиз ва аммаларингиз ва холаларингиз ва биродарларингиз қизлари ва сингилларингиз қизлари ва сизни эмизган оналарингиз ва эмишган сингилларингиз ва хотинларингиз оналари ва бирга ётган хотинларингизнинг сизнинг тарбиянгизда бўлган қизлари, агар оналари билан ётмаган бўлсангиз, унда сизларга гуноҳ йўқ; ва ўз пуштингиздан бўлган ўғилларингиз хотинлари; ва икки сингилни бир никоҳда бирлаштириш, агар бу аввал бўлиб ўтмаган бўлса. Тангри мағфират қилувчи, раҳмликдир[9]. 24. (Ҳаром қилинди) сизнинг Тангри китоби бўйича мулкингизга ўтмаган эрлик хотинлар ҳам[10]. Ва булардан ташқари молларингиз билан талаб қилиб, бузуқлик қилмай, никоҳга олганингиз бошқа хотинлар ҳам сизларга ҳалол қилинди[11]. Улардан нимаики фойдалансангиз, уларга фарз қилинган ҳақларини беринглар. Ва фарз бўлгандан кейин нима нарсага ўзаро рози бўлсангизлар, сизларга гуноҳ бўлмас. Албатта Тангри билувчи, ҳикматлидир[11]. 25. Ва кимки сизлардан озод мусулмон хотинларни никоҳига олишга қодир бўлмаса, у сизнинг қўлингиздаги мусулмон чўриларингиздан бирини никоҳига олсин. Ва Тангри сизнинг имонингизни энг яхши билувчидир. Сизнинг бирингиз иккинчингиздан. Шунинг учун эгалари рухсати билан уларни ўз никоҳларингизга олинг ва бузуқлик қилган ва махфий ёр тутган ҳолда эмас, никоҳга олган ҳолда уларнинг маҳрларини беринг[12]. Вақтики улар никоҳга олинган ҳолда фоҳишалик қилсалар, уларга озод хотинларга бериладиган азобнинг ярми берилур. Бу сизлардан (зинога) мубтало бўлишдан қўрққан киши учундир. Ва агар сабрлик бўлсангиз, бу сиз учун яхшироқдир. Ҳақиқатан Тангри мағфиратли, раҳмлидир.

ИЗОҲЛАР:

(Таржима ва изоҳлар муаллифники.)

1. Яъни, бир Одам Атодан.
2. Яъни, ҳамма хеш ва ақраболарингиздан хабардор бўлиб туринг, улардан алоқани узманг, уларга доим меҳрибон бўлинг.

3., 4...

5. Хотин ўлиб, фарзанди бўлмаса, эрига ярим моли мерос берилади. Агар хоҳ шу эрдан, хоҳ бошқа эрдан фарзанди бўлса, эрига тўртдан бир мероси берилади. Агар эр ўлиб, фарзанди бўлмаса, хотинига тўртдан бир мероси берилади, агар фарзанди бўлса, хотинга саккиздан бир мероси берилади. Битта хотин бўлса ҳам, ортиқ бўлса ҳам, шундай баробар ҳисса оладилар. Бу — васият ва қарзлар узилгандан кейин. Хотинга эри берган маҳр меросга кирмайди. Агар ўлган кишининг меросхўри биргина ота ва биродари ёки она ва ҳамшираси бўлса, ота-онаси ва фарзандлари бўлмаса, у хоҳ эркак бўлсин, хоҳ хотин бўлсин, унинг биродари ёки ҳамширасига мероснинг олтидан бири берилади. Агар улар бирдан ортиқ бўлса, учдан бирга шерик бўладилар. Бу ҳам васият ва қарзлар берилгандан кейин.
6. Бу оятда фоҳиша хотинларга жазо тайин этилмаган. Кейин нур сурасида жазо тайин этилган: бокира қиз бўлса, юз қамчи урилади, жувон хотин бўлса, тошбўрон қилинади.
7. Бу оятни баъзи олимлар баччабозликка ишора қилсалар, кўплари зинога ва баъзилари ҳар иккисига ишора қиладилар.
8. Исломдан аввал бир киши хотинини қўйиб, бошқасини олмоқчи бўлса, аввалги хотинига турли туҳмат ва бўҳтонлар қиларди ва хотинлар қўрқиб маҳрини қайтариб берарди. Эрлари ўша маҳр ҳисобига бошқа хотинга уйланиб олишарди. Бу оятда ана шу адолатсизлик ман қилинган.
9. Насаб жиҳатидан уйланиш мумкин бўлмаган хотинлар еттита: она, қиз, сингил, амма, хола, ака-ука томондан жиянлар, опа-сингил томондан жиянлар. Сут эмишганлар риштаси ҳам худди шундай еттита. Фақат сут эмган болагина сут эмизганнинг қизи, синглиси ва бошқаларга уйланолмайди, аммо сут эмганнинг ака-укалари уларга уйланаверади ва сингиллари турмушга чиқаверади.
10. Бошқа одам никоҳида бўлган эрлик хотинга то эри талоқ қилиб тўрт ой 10 кун иддаси тугагунча ва эри ўлган хотинга ҳам то иддаси тугагунча уйланиб бўлмайди. Агар хотин чўри бўлса, яъни унинг юртига бошқа давлат ҳамла қилиб босиб олса ва у хотин асир тушса, эри бўлса-бўлмаса, кимнинг ҳиссасига тушса, ўшанинг мулки, чўриси бўлиб, унга ҳалол бўлади.
11. Юқорида баён қилинган хотинлардан бошқа ҳаммаси ҳалолдир, лекин тўрт шарт билан: 1) талаб, яъни тил билан қабул этилсин; 2) мол, яъни маҳр бериш қабул қилинсин; 3) ҳамиша ўз ҳимоясида сақласин; уч-тўрт кун шаҳват қондириб, қўйиб юбормасин; 4) энг ками икки эркак ёки бир эркак, икки хотин никоҳ устида гувоҳ бўлсин. Агар шундай гувоҳ бўлмаса, никоҳ ҳисоб қилинмайди.
12. Хотинни никоҳга олиб, у билан бир марта бирга бўлинса, хотиннинг бутун маҳри эр зиммасига лозим бўлади, агар хотин кечмаса, соқит бўлмайди. Маҳр муқаррар қилингандан кейин, хотин унинг бир миқдорини кечса ёки эр бир миқдор оширса бўлаверади, лекин хотин муқаррар маҳрдан ортиқ талаб қилиши ёки эр уни камайтириши жоиз эмас.

Исматулла АБДУЛЛАЕВ,
УзССР ФА Шарқшунослик институтининг етакчи илмий ходими.

Давоми келгуси сонда.

Fig. 2.3. The fragmentary publication of al-Ṭarāzī's Qur'an translation in Cyrillic by Ismatulla Abdullayev in *Fan va turmush*, 8 (1989), pp. 20–21. ©*Fan va turmush*, Creative Commons license CC BY.

It is notable that there was no mention of al-Ṭarāzī's name in either the preface to Abdullayev's translation or the commentary it contained. However, even a cursory comparative analysis shows that Abdullayev's translation was based on al-Ṭarāzī's work, with some adaptations to bring in more modern vocabulary. This is clearly evident from the text of the commentary. As for the fact that Abdullayev does not credit or mention al-Ṭarāzī, this may have been due to censorship considerations (perhaps self-censorship on the part of the translator or editors), given al-Ṭarāzī's anti-Soviet positions in the past.

A few years later, in 1994, Abdullayev published the full text of al-Ṭarāzī's Qur'an translation which had been reworked using the Uzbek Cyrillic alphabet. As far as I know, this publication did not generate much public excitement and had a fairly restricted circulation, in only a few circles. The same fate befell the second edition of this adaptation, published in 2002. I shall return later to these editions, but for now I will turn to a few anecdotes about the history of circulation of the original text of al-Ṭarāzī's translation within post-Soviet Uzbekistan.

The Circulation of al-Ṭarāzī's Qur'an Translation within Post-Soviet Uzbekistan

The circulation history of al-Ṭarāzī's Qur'an translation, as well as a number of his other writings, in the post-Soviet period will be outlined here. Their dissemination was primarily linked to former Turkestani émigrés who visited Uzbekistan, their descendants, and other foreign emissaries, alongside local confessional and educational institutions. In addition, as in Soviet times, al-Ṭarāzī's writings continued to be available through *jumʿa-bazaar*s and pilgrimage trips made by citizens of Uzbekistan to Mecca and Medina.

The Gifts of a Turkestani Emigrant from the USA

In the early years after Uzbekistan gained independence, access to the country was open and easy, even for those who might have been explicitly denied entry in the recent Soviet era. Former Turkestani emigrants and their descendants, in particular, began to visit their historical homeland. Some of them attempted to participate in the local religious agenda,[51] and they sponsored the construction of numerous

---

51 For a concise analysis of the cumulative contribution of Turkestani emigrants living in Saudi Arabia to the reconstruction of the Islamic sphere in post-Soviet Uzbekistan, see Balci, *Islam in Central Asia and the Caucasus*, pp. 121–23, 125–26.

mosques, participated in official SADUM events,⁵² and/or brought with them religious literature, which included writings by al-Ṭarāzī.

In 1992, Abdulla Chighatay (c. 1928–c. 2018), a well-known figure in Turkestani émigré circles in the United States, visited Tashkent. When he was four or five years old, in 1932–33, he had emigrated with his parents from Tashkent to Afghanistan, later moving to Turkey, and from there relocating to the United States in 1965. There, one of his most noteworthy jobs was working for the Uzbek section at the news outlet Voice of America from 1971 to 1977.⁵³

On returning to Tashkent, Chighatay visited his native neighbourhood community (*mahalla*) on Boyko'cha Street in the old part of the city, met with local residents, and told them about himself. A number of the people attending this meeting already knew of him from his radio broadcasts. To one of them (namely Marif Salimov, who told me this story),⁵⁴ Chighatay gave a pocket-sized version of al-Ṭarāzī's Qur'an translation (in paperback) that he had brought with him.⁵⁵ This testimony is pertinent because it affirms that al-Ṭarāzī's work had reached the USA, and was then transferred by an intricate route to the cultural and linguistic area it was originally intended for.

Al-Ṭarāzī's Qur'an Translation in the Collections Held at the Mir-i ʿArab Madrasa and the Tashkent Islamic Institute

Foreign emissaries also played a major role in the dissemination of al-Ṭarāzī's Qur'an translation. This observation is especially relevant in regard to the famous Bukharan Madrasa Mir-i ʿArab. Some graduates of the *madrasa* who studied there in 1995–99 told me that in around 1997, a group of visitors from the Near East donated dozens

---

52 For example, the Extraordinary Fifth Kurultai (Congress) of Muslims of Central Asia and Kazakhstan, held in Tashkent on 26–27 February 1992, was also attended by representatives of Turkey, Saudi Arabia, Libya, and other foreign countries. See P. Nishanov, 'Kurultai musul'man Srednei Azii i Kazakhstana', *Narodnoe slovo*, 41:292 (1992), 1.

53 Shodmon Hayitov, *O'zbek muhojirligi tarixi (1917–1991 yillar)* (Tashkent: Abu Matbuot Konsalt, 2008), pp. 66–67.

54 Marif Salimov (d. 2023) was a renowned Uzbek specialist in the conservation of Arabic manuscripts, and a long-time staff member of the al-Biruni Institute.

55 Personal interview with Marif Salimov on 15 April 2021.

of copies of the Qur'an translation by al-Ṭarāzī to this educational institution. Many of them were then gifted to the students, but some remain in the library and are still there today. In February 2021, I counted twenty-four copies of the translation in the *madrasa* library: one copy published in Jeddah in 1980–81, and twenty-three of the Doha edition of 1993.⁵⁶

Fig. 2.4. Al-Ṭarāzī's writings, preserved in the library of the Mir-i ʿArab Madrasa (2021). ©Filipp Khusnutdinov, Creative Commons license CC BY.

According to my informants, in the mid-1990s al-Ṭarāzī's work served as a kind of propaedeutic textbook on the subject of *tafsīr* for first-year students at the *madrasa*.⁵⁷ Its use may have served several purposes:

---

56 The 1993 Doha edition was prepared by Ḥasan ʿAbd al-Majīd al-Maʿāyirijī (1927–2008), a renowned Egyptian-Qatari scholar and a specialist in Qur'an translation into various languages. Under his supervision, translations of the Qur'an into a number of other Turkic languages were also published. See Mykhaylo Yakubovych, 'Qur'an Translations into Central Asian Languages: Exegetical Standards and Translation Processes', *Journal of Qur'anic Studies*, 24:1 (2022), 89–115 (p. 89). For more on al-Maʿāyirijī and his professional activities, see *al-Duktūr Ḥasan al-Maʿāyirjī raḥimahu Allāh taʿālā: al-rāʾid al-ʿimlāq al-majhūl*, ed. by ʿAbd al-Salām al-Basyūnī/al-Bassiyūnī (n.p., no earlier than 2018), https://islamsyria.com/storage/NewResearch/%D8%A7%D9%84%D8%AF%D9%83%D8%AA%D9%88%D8%B1-%D8%AD%D8%B3%D9%86-%D8%A7%D9%84%D9%85%D8%B9%D8%A7%D9%8A%D8%B1%D8%AC%D9%8A/f9541e4de0b59610043e8e95d0cad649.pdf

57 Also among the study books was an abridged version (*mukhtaṣar*) of al-Kāshgharī's translation of the thirtieth part of the Qur'an, *Tafsīr juzʾ ʿamma yatasāʾalūn* (*bi-l-lugha al-turkistāniyya*).

preparing students to read Arabic books in general and the Qur'an in particular; teaching some features of *tafsīr* in a language that was familiar to the students; and acquainting students with elements of *tafsīr* written mostly in the spirit of Ḥanafī law.⁵⁸ It seems that by the early 2000s, however, this book had disappeared from the *madrasa*'s curriculum. The lack of demand for al-Ṭarāzī's Qur'an translation among today's students is demonstrated by the fact that neither the administration of Mir-i ʿArab and its library, nor the students whom I talked to, were even aware of the availability of this book in the *madrasa*.⁵⁹

The library of the Tashkent Islamic Institute also possesses copies of al-Ṭarāzī Qur'an translations, but considerably fewer than are held in the library of Mir-i ʿArab—only six copies.⁶⁰ And unlike in Mir-i ʿArab, according to staff and students this translation was never used as a textbook at the Islamic Institute in the 1990s.⁶¹

Pilgrimage Trips and *jumʿa-bazaars*

At the beginning of the 1990s, as in Soviet times, al-Ṭarāzī's Qur'an translation was brought back home by pilgrims. For instance, during an expedition to Namangan in June 2021, my colleagues from the al-Biruni Institute and I had a chance to take a close look at the library of Ahmad Ubaydulloh (b. 1945), a renowned bibliophile who lived in the city. This collection consists of about 2,500 manuscripts and lithographs. Ubaydulloh inherited it from his grandfather,

---

58   Personal interviews with Komiljon Rakhimov and Ahtam Akhmedov in August 2019 and on 16 February 2021, respectively. The repertoire of al-Ṭarāzī's writings was not limited to one title. For instance, first-year students also studied *Nūr al-baṣar*, his biography of the Prophet Muhammad, and his annotated translations into 'Turkestani' of *al-Fiqh al-akbar* by Abū Ḥanīfa (c. 699–767) and *Riyāḍ al-ṣāliḥīn* by Muḥyī l-Dīn al-Nawawī (1233–77).
59   At the same time, the *Nūr al-baṣar* and the translations of *al-Fiqh al-akbar* and *Riyāḍ al-ṣāliḥīn* were widely known. It transpired that these books continue to be used as preparation or supplementary manuals for students.
60   One book is an edition from Jeddah (1980–1), the others are 1993 editions from Doha. One of the Doha copies has an oval-shaped seal with an inscription in Uzbek: '*Shaxsiy kutubxonasi. №. 428. Saydaliev Moʻminjon Andijoniy*' [Private Library. №. 428. Saydaliev Muminjon Andijoniy].
61   However, the Institute holds about 200 copies of *al-Fiqh al-akbar* translated by al-Ṭarāzī, and several dozen copies of *Nūr al-baṣar*.

Khwādja ʿUbaydallāh-*makhdūm*, who was chief *mudarris* in one of the *madrasas* in the city of Namangan during the rule of the Kokandian *khān* Muḥammad Khudāyār (c. 1831–81, r. 1844–75).[62] This private library also includes a number of modern works, among which was one copy of al-Ṭarāzī's translation of the Qur'an, published in Medina in 1975. Ubaydulloh personally brought the book back with him in 1994, when he went on the Hajj. It was given to him as a gift by relatives of Namanganians who had ended up in Saudi Arabia as a result of leaving the USSR.

With regard to the *jumʿa-bazaar*s, translations of the Qur'an and a number of other writings by al-Ṭarāzī published abroad continued to be available in Uzbekistan until the mid-1990s, where they have been seen on sale at the Tashkent Friday bazaar at the Ḥast-i Imām complex and in Kokand. In addition, according to eyewitness accounts, al-Ṭarāzī's Qur'an translation could be found on book stalls in Bukhara in the second half of the 1990s, for instance at the Tāk-i Sarrafān (Persian for 'Dome of the (Money) Changers'): a famous traditional covered bazaar in the historic heart of Bukhara.

The Tashkent Editions of al-Ṭarāzī's Qur'an Translation, and Their Competition

The survey presented in the previous section is sporadic, and in no way systematic or exhaustive. However, the considerable number and geographical distribution of copies of al-Ṭarāzī's Qur'an translation across Uzbekistan suggest that it was not perceived as marginal in

---

62 In approximately 1920, their family was forced to move from Namangan to Samarkand. Before leaving, ʿUbaydallāh-*makhdūm* hid his library in a wall—in a niche which he walled up, adding broken glass to the lime to protect the books in case anyone decided to dismantle the wall. After Stalin's death (1953), the family returned to Namangan to find that the library was still in place—it was opened up and began serving the family again (personal interview with Ahmad Ubaydulloh on 10 June 2021). On the current situation regarding private manuscript collections in the Fergana Valley and the practices of concealment of manuscripts in Arabic script during the Soviet period, see Ashirbek Muminov and Nodirjon Abdulahatov, 'Chastnye sobraniia vostochnykh rukopisei i redkikh knig v Ferganskoi doline: perspektivy ikh izucheniia' (unpublished report presented at the 'Ethnography of Book Collections in the Islamicate World' workshop, Istanbul, 27–28 April 2023).

the local environment, and it is clear that its copies reached their readers in a variety of ways. The final outcome of this process was the eventual publication of al-Ṭarāzī's Qur'an translation in Cyrillic. This adaptation represented an effort to promote his translation to a wider audience who could not access the original text in the Arabic script.

Fig. 2.5. The front cover of the first Tashkent edition of al-Ṭarāzī's Qur'an translation (1994). ©*Al-Qur'on ul-karim (o'zbek tilida izohli tarjima)*, Creative Commons license CC BY.

The first edition of al-Ṭarāzī's Qur'an translation in Cyrillic was published in 1994. Due to lack of funding, its author, Ismatulla Abdullayev, was forced to publish the book at his own expense.[63] For this reason, the print run was only a hundred copies. The lack of finances had an impact not only on the number of copies distributed,

---

63 *Al-Qur'on ul-karim (o'zbek tilida izohli tarjima)*, trans. and comm. by at-Taroziy, p. 438.

but also on the quality of the publication—it was printed on newsprint paper and in small font (there were an average of 60–62 lines per page, which was close to A4 size).

Abdullayev provided this extensive adaptation with a brief introductory historical overview, and a short glossary of some terms used in the translation and a thematic index of the *āyāt* on Qur'anic prescriptions and guidelines (Uzbek: *'Qur'on hukmlari va yo'l-yo'riqlari haqidagi oyatlar ko'rsatkichi'*). The introductory part provided general information about the Qur'an, its history, structure, and popular interpretations and translations into the Turkic languages, including the new translations into Uzbek appearing at the time. The book also contains a succinct discussion of al-Ṭarāzī's life, his translation of the Qur'an, and the principles of the Cyrillic adaptation. Abdullayev stipulates that he tried to retain al-Ṭarāzī's style and language, but in some cases had to change the structure of sentences to make them understandable to the modern reader.[64]

A second expanded edition of the book was published in 2002.[65] It was printed at the Fan publishing house of the Uzbekistan Academy of Sciences and was of noticeably higher quality than the first. The preface provides new information about al-Ṭarāzī's translation and corrects the previous edition's misprints and omissions. Furthermore, the glossary that accompanies the adaptation has undergone a significant expansion, and has been extended by more than tenfold (from 83 words to approximately 1,030).

---

64   Ibid., p. 6. As a preliminary comparison of the text of Abdullayev's edition with al-Ṭarāzī's original text has shown, the changes made by Abdullayev cover mainly morphological and lexical features of the text. Such changes are quite numerous. They are characterised by the replacement of archaic/classical word forms with modern ones, fairly frequent omission of words or individual phrases, and the rare addition of explanatory words. Unfortunately, all these editorial changes are not labelled in any way in the text of the edition.

65   *Al-Qur'on al-karim ma'nolarining tarjimasi va sharhlar*, 2nd edn, trans. and comm. by Sayyid Mahmud ibn Sayyid Nazir at-Taroziy al-Madaniy (Oltinxon To'ra), ed. by Hoji Ismatullo Abdulloh (Tashkent: Fan, 2002).

Fig. 2.6. The front cover of the second Tashkent edition of al-Ṭarāzī's Qur'an translation (2002). ©*Al-Qur'on al-karim ma'nolarining tarjimasi va sharhlar*, Creative Commons license CC BY.

It should be recognised that neither the first nor second editions are free from occasional errors, including factual ones. For example, in several cases Abdullayev's adaptation gives a different location for the revelation of certain chapters of the Qur'an in comparison to al-Ṭarāzī's text.[66] There are also some misreadings of names: instead of the famous scholar from Deoband, 'Shabbīr Aḥmad ᶜUthmānī', there appears a certain 'Sherahmad Usmani'.[67] In addition, incorrect reading of individual words, as well as their omission, is not uncommon. In this regard, these adaptations should be handled with a fair degree of caution and, if necessary, reference should be made directly to the original text in the Arabic script.

---

66   See, for example, *sūras* 67, 98, and 108.
67   *Al-Qur'on ul-karim (o'zbek tilida izohli tarjima)*, trans. and comm. by at-Taroziy, p. 333; *Al-Qur'on al-karim ma'nolarining tarjimasi va sharhlar*, trans. and comm. by at-Taroziy, p. 567.

As it turned out, in terms of the number of copies printed, the second edition met the same fate as the first one—again only a hundred copies were produced, for reasons that are as yet unclear. However, I am more interested in another question: why has al-Ṭarāzī's Qur'an translation not been widely disseminated within post-Soviet Uzbekistan? As I see it, there are several reasons for this.

Firstly, as was already noted, a whole group of translations of the Qur'an into modern Uzbek appeared during the 1990s and 2000s. In terms of language, they were better suited to the demands of the times and were aimed at a wider readership. Even *dāmlā* al-Hindustānī, explaining his motivation for writing his own Qur'an translation, noted in the early 1980s that al-Ṭarāzī's language was already difficult for ordinary people and young students to understand.[68] Indeed, this observation by al-Hindustānī seems quite astute: the language of al-Ṭarāzī's Qur'an translation, both morphologically and lexically speaking, was different from that which prevailed in Uzbekistan at the end of the twentieth century (this was a problem for virtually all émigré Central Asian writers, not just al-Ṭarāzī).

There is no reliable data on what percentage of the population of Soviet Central Asia in the 1970s and afterwards was able to read texts in Central Asian Turki, but it is clear that the number of such people did not constitute a majority. To the average man of the time (let alone the present day), al-Ṭarāzī's vocabulary would have seemed archaic,[69] especially his use of a large number of Arabisms and Persianisms that have fallen out of active use in modern Uzbek.[70] In addition, both al-Ṭarāzī and al-Hindustānī, educated in the pre-Soviet period or abroad, remained committed to their adopted linguistic practice throughout their lives and continued to write in the Arabic script. It is therefore not entirely clear why they would expect their books to be widely disseminated without being adapted to the dominant script in use in Soviet Central Asia.

---

68 *Qur'oni karim. Oyatlari ma'nolarining izohli tarjimasi*, trans. and comm. by Hindistoniy, p. 14.
69 Abdurahimoğlu, 'Seyyid Mahmûd et-Tarazî', pp. 838–41.
70 For this reason, Abdullayev compiled such an extensive explanatory dictionary for the second edition of al-Ṭarāzī's translation.

Qur'an translations into Uzbek produced after 1990 were characterised by a more comprehensible vocabulary and were written in Cyrillic. This gives them an advantage over editions written in both the Arabic script and the official Uzbek Latin alphabet today.[71] In general, the publication of Qur'an translations in Uzbekistan has followed in line with the established tradition of publishing Islamic literature in Cyrillic over the last few decades. Religious books written in this script vastly outnumber those issued in the Latin alphabet.[72] Thus, the foremost factor that may have limited the spread of al-Ṭarāzī's Qur'an translation is its linguistic inaccessibility to a wide range of readers.[73]

The second reason behind the failure of al-Ṭarāzī's work to thrive in the post-Soviet era relates to the popularity and authority in the religious sphere of the personality behind this translation of the Qur'an. While Alouddin Mansur, Muhammad Sodiq Muhammad Yusuf, and Abdulaziz Mansur were popular with the believing masses, al-Ṭarāzī remained far less known. Perhaps if al-Ṭarāzī's Qur'an translation had been actively promoted by any of the aforementioned translators or by the Muslim Board of Uzbekistan, its fate would have been different. However, given that the process of domesticising a translation by transcribing it into Cyrillic with the aim of popularising it was handled by an enthusiastic scholar rather than a renowned religious figure—and at his own, frankly modest, expense—the potential for success was naturally rather limited.

The impressive numbers involved in the print runs of newer, modern Uzbek translations of the Qur'an suggest that their authors and/or publishers had both authority within the community of believers and certain financial resources. For instance, the first print run of Alouddin Mansur's translation in 1992 numbered half a million copies. Shaykh Muhammad Sodiq Muhammad Yusuf's translation of the twenty-seventh through to the thirtieth parts of the Qur'an was published in

---

71 As a side note, most translations of the Qur'an produced since 1991 have their prototypes in the Latin alphabet as well.
72 This trend seems to be primarily due to the preferences of the older generation (both book authors and their audiences) brought up on the Cyrillic script in the Soviet and early post-Soviet period.
73 On the other hand, as far as I know, certain philologists (among them some Arabists and Turkologists) sympathise with al-Ṭarāzī's translation, noting its lexical purity and elegance of the language.

separate volumes in Tashkent between 1991 and 1993. Each of these had a circulation of between 100,000 to 150,000 copies. From this, we can conclude at least that Abdullayev did not have as much social and financial capital as his competitors to help him successfully roll out his product.

The final important factor in determining the proliferation of a given Qur'an translation in post-Soviet Uzbekistan (apart from its conformity to the prevailing Ḥanafī Islamic tradition in the region,[74] the accessibility of its language to a wide audience, and the financial capacity of the author and/or publisher) is the backing and approval of the official authorities. In the late 1990s, there was debate in political high circles over whether or not to publish an 'official' translation of the Qur'an authored by Abdulaziz Mansur, who had worked for a long time for the Muslim Board of Uzbekistan and was, by then, the State Adviser to the President on Religious Affairs. There are testimonies that President Karimov initially suggested that such a publication should be delayed, on the basis that there was already one translation available in the country (i.e. that by Alouddin Mansur) and that publishing a new one might lead to unnecessary social divisions.[75]

Over the next two years, in a bid to instill 'good' Islam within the country,[76] this opinion changed. Perhaps the terrorist attacks that took place in Tashkent in February 1999, and the opening of Tashkent Islamic University in April that year, made it necessary to publish a new translation of the Qur'an: a translation that would be positioned as corresponding to the Hanafi school of law. The reference to the Hanafi doctrine—adherence to which has often been encouraged at the state level—was a major factor leading to the authorities' favourable

---

74 A brief yet insightful overview of the Ḥanafī legal doctrine's hegemony in Central Asia over the centuries has been provided, for example, by Paolo Sartori: *Visions of Justice: Sharīʿa and Cultural Change in Russian Central Asia* (Leiden and Boston: Brill, 2016), p. 250. Basic bibliography is also provided there. On the history of the formation and development of the Ḥanafī school of law in Central Asia up to the fifteenth century, see the outstanding study by Ashirbek Muminov: *Khanafitskii mazkhab v istorii Tsentralnoi Azii*, ed. by Stanislav M. Prozorov (Almaty: Qazaq entsiklopediiasy, 2015).

75 Personal interview with one of the former employees of the Office of the President of Uzbekistan on 18 September 2021.

76 Bakhtiiar Babadzhanov, '"Good" and "Bad" Islam: From Personal Experience of Participation in Religious Expertise', *Alatoo Academic Studies*, 4 (2015), 34–46.

decision regarding the publication of Abdulaziz Mansur's commentary translation of the Qur'an in 2001. Over the following twenty years, the book has seen ten editions and has become perhaps the main official Qur'an translation in the country.[77]

Another prime example of the power of official sanction can be seen in the case of Muhammad Sodiq Muhammad Yusuf's translation. According to oral evidence, after the Shaykh decided to emigrate in 1993, a ban was imposed on the publication and distribution of his writings. Almost ten years later, when he returned to the country, his books were again granted legal status, a change that was not possible without the permission of the relevant authorities (in particular, the Committee for Religious Affairs).[78]

As for the *Tafsiri Irfon*—authored by the former chairman of the Muslim Board of Uzbekistan Shaykh Usmonxon ('Uthmān-*khān*) Alimov (1950–2021, chairman 2006–21)[79]—a complete version of this text has appeared only recently (in 2019) and is not yet as popular as the Qur'an translations mentioned earlier.[80] This work is noteworthy for being the only one among those discussed here in which al-Ṭarāzī's *tafsīr* is included as an accredited source.[81]

---

77 *Qur'oni karim ma'nolarining tarjima va tafsiri*, 10th edn, trans. and comm. by Shayx Abdulaziz Mansur (Tashkent: «Munir» nashriyoti, 2021) (the print run is 20,000 copies). The status of the 'main official translation' is confirmed, for example, by the fact that some publishers (for instance, 'Maverannahr': the publishing house of the Muslim Board of Uzbekistan) have for many years advised authors of works published in Uzbek to use this particular translation. The same is true of the textbooks published for the Tashkent Islamic University and then for its successor, the International Islamic Academy of Uzbekistan (founded on 16 April 2018 on the basis of the Tashkent Islamic University (1999–2018) and the Islamic Academy of Uzbekistan (2017–18)).

78 The Committee for Religious Affairs under the Cabinet of Ministers of the Republic of Uzbekistan is the state body responsible for coordinating relations between the state and religious organisations located in the territory of the Republic. The Committee was established in March 1992 and de facto succeeded the Office of the Plenipotentiary of the Council for Religious Affairs under the USSR Council of Ministers across the Uzbek SSR.

79 For more about him, see Yo'ldoshxo'jaev and Qayumova, *O'zbekiston ulamolari*, pp. 90–91.

80 *Tafsiri Irfon. Qur'oni karim ma'nolarining o'zbekcha tarjimasi va tafsiri*, 6 vols, trans. and comm. by Shayx Usmonxon Temurxon Samarqandiy (Tashkent: Sharq, 2019) (the print run is 5,000 copies).

81 *Tafsiri Irfon*, vol. VI, trans. and comm. by Samarqandiy, p. 747. It is noteworthy that not one of the Arabic-script editions is cited, but rather Abdullayev's adaptation from 2002.

It seems that, for a number of reasons, al-Ṭarāzī's translation was not equipped to take on the competition presented by more modern, vernacular renditions of the Qur'an and so remained in the shadows, even though it possessed the honourable rank of being the first full interlinear modern translation of the Qur'an into Central Asian Turki. It may well be that, in addition, al-Ṭarāzī's writing—two adaptations of which were published in Uzbekistan—was simply unlucky in terms of both its time and place of publication. The first edition came out in 1994, following the stellar appearance of Alouddin Mansur's translation, while the second one was brought out in 2002, following the publication of Abdulaziz Mansur's translation—which was officially positioned to take the mantle of the primary translation of the Qur'an in the country. Moreover, the first fragments of al-Ṭarāzī's Qur'an translation were published (without attribution) in *Fan va turmush* rather than in the much more popular and authoritative *Sharq yulduzi*, which released Alouddin Mansur's translation. Had the text by al-Ṭarāzī been published in the latter, perhaps it would have been disseminated more broadly and would have received the greater recognition it is due.[82]

Concluding Remarks

The material presented in this chapter enables one to reflect on the complexity of recent Islamic intellectual history within Soviet and post-Soviet Uzbekistan. This chapter also shows that the local vernacular Qur'anic space was shaped not only by Muslim scholars of the region, but also by those religious figures who once emigrated from Soviet Central Asia. Islamic literature authored by Turkestani emigrants was circulating in the area and finding its readership decades before the fall of the Iron Curtain. In the post-Soviet period, these books moved from the underground to the official public sphere and at first were

---

82 As it turned out, the influence of al-Ṭarāzī's translation spread beyond the Uzbek-speaking community as well. For instance, al-Ṭarāzī's book is mentioned among the sources used by Xalifa Altay (1917–2003) in his Qur'an translation into Kazakh. See *Quran Kärim: qazaqşa mağına jäne tüsinigi*, trans. by Xalïfa Altay (Medina: Şarapattı eki xaramnıñ qızmetkeri Fahd patşanıñ Quran Şärïf basım kombïnatı, 1411/1991), pp. iii, vi. I owe this valuable reference to Mykhaylo Yakubovych.

actively used, but they eventually gave way to the proliferation of more numerous and up-to-date local content.

Al-Ṭarāzī's Qur'an translation provides an illustrative example of this process. Despite its early circulation history, it has not seriously competed with those translations of the Qur'an that have emerged in Uzbekistan since 1990. The situation can be primarily explained by such factors as the comprehensibility of its language to the average reader, the level of public prestige of the translator and the financial power behind them, as well as the approval of the official Uzbekistan authorities.

Al-Ṭarāzī's writing did, however, possess a combination of these factors abroad, in the places where Turkestani émigré communities were concentrated. Because of this, it seems that this translation was more relevant not for historical Turkestan, but for its 'islets' in emigration. The 'Turkestani' language chosen, with its Arabic script, made this text understandable mainly to the various Turkic-speaking diasporas scattered across the expanses of the Muslim world.

In fact, al-Ṭarāzī's Qur'an translation might be seen as part of a global process of 'nationalisation' of Muslim written heritage that began during the rise of Islamic modernism with the production of translations and wide dissemination of the Qur'anic text, *hadīths*, and a range of writings on Muslim law in 'the languages of non-Arabs' (ʿajamī). Under the restrictive official framework for publishing Islamic literature in the Soviet Union, al-Ṭarāzī's writing—while being a product of its time and linguistic range—has nevertheless played a notable role in shaping the vernacular Qur'anic space within Soviet Uzbekistan. However, in the post-Soviet period, with the advent of new Qur'an translations into Uzbek, the window of opportunity for the dissemination of al-Ṭarāzī's text has substantially narrowed, and his translation has lost its former significance.

Bibliography

Abdullayev, Ismatulla (trans. and comm.), 'Qur'oni karim', *Fan va turmush*, 8 (1989), 20–21.

——, (trans. and comm.), 'Qur'oni karim', *Fan va turmush*, 9 (1989), 22–23.

Abdurahimoğlu, Yunus, 'Seyyid Mahmûd et-Tarazî ve Kur'an-ı Kerim'i Türkistan Diline Tercüme ve Haşiyesi', *Türkiye İlahiyat Araştırmaları Dergisi*, 6:2 (2022), https://doi.org/10.32711/tiad.1169273

Abdusamatov, Malik, *O'zbekiston sharqshunoslari (bibliografik ocherk)* (Tashkent: Qomuslar Bosh tahririyati, 1996).

Akhmadullin, Viacheslav, 'Deiatel'nost' gosudarstvennykh organov SSSR i dukhovnykh upravlenii musul'man po izdaniiu Korana na arabskom iazyke v SSSR i ego rasprostraneniiu v 50-e gody XX v.', *Vestnik Dagestanskogo nauchnogo tsentra*, 52 (2014), http://vestnikdnc.ru/IssSources/52/Akhmadullin.pdf

Altay, Xalïfa (trans.), *Quran Kärim: qazaqşa mağına jäne tüsinigi* (Medina: Şarapattı eki xaramnıñ qızmetkeri Fahd patşanıñ Quran Şärïf basım kombïnatı, 1411/1991).

Andican, Ahat, *Turkestan Struggle Abroad (From Jadidism to Independence)* (Haarlem: SOTA, 2007).

Babadzhanov, Bakhtiiar, '"Good" and "Bad" Islam: From Personal Experience of Participation in Religious Expertise', *Alatoo Academic Studies*, 4 (2015).

——, 'Hindustani', in *Islam na territorii byvshei Rossiiskoi imperii: Entsiklopedicheskii slovar'*, vol. I, ed. by Stanislav M. Prozorov (Moscow: Vostochnaia Literatura, 2006), pp. 426–28.

——, 'Ibrahim-hazrat', in *Islam na territorii byvshei Rossiiskoi imperii: Entsiklopedicheskii slovar'*, vol. I, ed. by Stanislav M. Prozorov (Moscow: Vostochnaia Literatura, 2006), pp. 155–56.

——, and Muhammad-Ayyubxon Hamidov, 'Muhammad-Sodiq', in *Islam na territorii byvshei Rossiiskoi imperii: Entsiklopedicheskii slovar'*, vol. II, ed. by Stanislav M. Prozorov (Moscow: Nauka–Vostochnaia Literatura, 2018), pp. 267–70.

——, Ashirbek Muminov, and Anke von Kügelgen, *Disputes on Muslim Authority in Central Asia in 20th Century: Critical Editions and Source Studies* (Almaty: Daik-Press, 2007).

Balci, Bayram, *Islam in Central Asia and the Caucasus Since the Fall of the Soviet Union*, trans. by Gregory Elliott (New York: Oxford University Press, 2018).

al-Basyūnī/al-Bassiyūnī, ʿAbd al-Salām (ed.), *al-Duktūr Ḥasan al-Maʿāyirjī raḥimahu Allāh taʿālā: al-rāʾid al-ʿimlāq al-majhūl* (n.p., no earlier than 2018), https://islamsyria.com/storage/NewResearch/%D8%A7%D9%84%D8%AF%D9%83%D8%AA%D9%88%D8%B1-%D8%AD%D8%B3%D9%86-%D8%A7%D9%84%D9%85%D8%B9%D8%A7%D9%8A%D8%B1%D8%AC%D9%8A/f9541e4de0b59610043e8e95d0cad649.pdf

Boboxonov, Shamsiddinxon (trans.), *Qur'oni karim (30-pora)* (Moscow: COMIL, 1992).

Bobrovnikov, Vladimir, 'From Moscow to Mecca: Entangled Soviet Narratives of Pilgrimage in the Unlikely 1965 ḥajjnāme of Fazliddin Muhammadiev', in *Narrating the pilgrimage to Mecca: historical and contemporary accounts*, ed. by Marjo Buitelaar and Richard van Leeuwen (Boston: Brill, 2023), pp. 221–41.

——, and Artemy Kalinovsky, 'Fazliddin Muhammadiev's Journey to the "Other World": The History of a Cold War Ḥajjnāma', *Die Welt des Islams*, 62:1 (2021), https://doi.org/10.1163/15700607-61020007

al-Bukhārī, Manṣūr b. ʿAbd al-Bāqī al-Andījānī, *ʿUlamāʾ Mā warāʾ al-nahr al-muhājirīn lil-Ḥaramayn* (Istanbul: Dār al-Mīrāth al-Nabawī lil-Dirāsāt al-Taḥqīq wa-Khidmat al-Turāth, 1434/2013)

Bustanov, Alfrid, 'The Qur'an for Soviet Citizens: The Rhetoric of Progress in the Theological Writings of 'Abd al-Bari Isaev', *Antropologicheskij forum*, 37 (2018), https://anthropologie.kunstkamera.ru/files/pdf/037/bustanov.pdf, https://doi.org/10.31250/1815-8870-2018-14-37-93-110.

G'afurov, Ibrohim, 'Qur'on tarjimalari: tajribalar', *O'zbekiston adabiyoti va san'ati*, 16:3999 (2009), 3–4.

Gosudarstvennyi arkhiv Rossiiskoi Federatsii. F. R-6991 (Sovet po delam religii pri Sovete Ministrov SSSR). Op. 4. D. 102. L. 48. (Spravka o poezdke palomnikov v Mekku v 1959 godu).

Hayitov, Shodmon, *O'zbek muhojirligi tarixi (1917–1991 yillar)* (Tashkent: Abu Matbuot Konsalt, 2008).

Hindistoniy, Shayx Muhammadjon mullo Rustam o'g'li Mavlaviy hoji (trans.), *Qur'oni karim. Oyatlari ma'nolarining izohli tarjimasi*, ed. by Sayfiddin Sayfulloh (Tashkent: Movarounnahr, 2006).

Islamov, Sharifjon, 'Ustoz Boboxon Qosimxonovni xotiralab', *Meros*, 1 (2019).

Jalilov, Sayfiddin, *Buxoriylar qissasi (Muhojirat tarixidan lavhalar)* (Tashkent: Toshkent islom universiteti nashriyot-matbaa birlashmasi, 2006).

al-Kāshgharī, Muḥammad-Ẓarīf, *Tafsīr juzʾ ʿamma yatasāʾalūn (bi-l-lugha al-turkistāniyya)*, abridged by Raḥmatallāh ʿInāyatallāh (Makka al-Mukarrama: Rābiṭat al-ʿĀlam al-Islāmī, 1403/1983).

——, *Tafsīr ʿAmma yatasāʾalūn* (Doha: Maṭābiʿ al-ʿArūba, 1413/1992).

Khalid, Adeeb, *Islam after Communism: Religion and Politics in Central Asia* (Berkeley: University of California Press, 2007).

——, *Making Uzbekistan: Nation, Empire, and Revolution in the Early USSR* (Ithaca and London: Cornell University Press, 2015).

al-Khūqandī, ʿAbd al-Salām b. al-Shaykh Shīr-Muḥammad (trans. and comm.), *Muqaddimat al-Jazariyya wa-tarjamatuhā bi-l-lugha al-turkistāniyya* (Madīna al-Munawwara: n.p., n.d.).

Khudāyār, Ibrāhīm, 'Muᶜarrifī-yi chand tarjuma-yi Qur'ān-i karīm ba zabān-i uzbakī', *Tarjumān-i vahī*, 7 (1379/2000–1), http://ensani.ir/file/download/article/20101106123337-58.pdf

Khusnutdinov, Filipp, 'Altin-*khan-tura*: biobibliograficheskii ocherk', *Journal of Central Asian History*, 1:2 (2022), https://doi.org/10.1163/27728668-12340010

——, 'From Soviet to Saudi: On Central Asian Ulama and their Hijra', *SICE Blog*, 2022, https://www.oeaw.ac.at/sice/sice-blog/from-soviet-to-saudi-on-central-asian-ulama-and-their-hijra.

——, '"Turkestani Muslim Communities ... Have Been Deprived of This Happiness". The Dissemination of Tarazi's Qur'an Translation and Exegesis in Soviet Uzbekistan', *Islamology*, 11:1 (2021), http://dx.doi.org/10.24848/islmlg.11.1.07

Kodeks Uzbekskoi SSR ob administrativnykh pravonarusheniiakh (Tashkent: Uzbekistan, 1986).

Krachkovskii, Ignatii (trans.), 'Koran', comm. by Mutalib Usmanov, *Zvezda Vostoka* (1990), 1–12.

——, comm. by Mutalib Usmanov, 'Koran', *Zvezda Vostoka* (1991), 1–12.

al-Maᶜāyirjī, Ḥasan ᶜAbd al-Majīd, 'Tarjamat ḥayāt al-muʾallif', in *Qur'ān-i karīm. Mutarjam wa-muḥashshā bi-l-lugha al-tūrkistāniyya bi-qalam al-ᶜājiz al-Sayyid Maḥmūd b. al-Sayyid Nadhīr al-Ṭarāzī al-Madanī* (Qatar: n.p., 1993), pp. 709–10.

Mahjuriy, Muhammadxon mullo Is'hoq qori o'g'li, *Fotiha, Yosin, Taborak va Amma suralarining tafsiri*, ed. by Sayfiddin Sayfulloh and Maqsudxon hoji Muhammadxon o'g'li (Tashkent: Movarounnahr, 2004).

Mansur, Alouddin (trans. and comm.), 'Qur'on', *Sharq yulduzi* (1990), 3–12.

——, 'Qur'on', *Sharq yulduzi* (1991), 1–12.

——, 'Qur'on', *Sharq yulduzi* (1992), 1–2.

—— (trans. and comm.), *Qur'oni Karim* (Tashkent: Cho'lpon, 1992).

—— (trans. and comm.), *Qur'oni karim. O'zbekcha izohli tarjima* (Tashkent: G'afur G'ulom nomidagi nashriyot-matbaa birlashmasi; O'zbekiston Respublikasi prezidenti mahkamasining ishlar boshqarmasi huzuridagi «Sharq» nashriyot-matbaa konserni, 1992).

Mansur, Shayx Abdulaziz (trans. and comm.), *Qur'oni karim ma'nolarining tarjima va tafsiri*, 10th edn (Tashkent: «Munir» nashriyoti, 2021).

Mazman, Nevin, 'Hindistan'da basilmiş bir Kur'an tercümesi: mütercem ve muhaşşa bi'l-lugati't-türkistâniyye', *Çukurova Üniversitesi Türkoloji Araştırmaları Dergisi*, 3:1 (2018).

Michailova, Galina, Inga Vidugiryte, and Pavel Lavrinec (eds), *Heterotopias: Worlds, Borders, Narratives* (Vilnius: Vilniaus Universiteto Leidykla, 2015).

Muhammadiev, Fazliddin, *Puteshestvie na tot svet ili povest' o velikom khadzhzhe*, trans. by Yuri Smirnov (Dushanbe: Irfon, 1970).

Muminov, Ashirbek, *Khanafitskii mazkhab v istorii Tsentralnoi Azii*, ed. by Stanislav M. Prozorov (Almaty: Qazaq entsiklopediiasy, 2015).

Muminov, Ashirbek, and Nodirjon Abdulahatov, 'Chastnye sobraniia vostochnykh rukopisei i redkikh knig v Ferganskoi doline: perspectivy ikh izucheniia' (unpublished report presented at the 'Ethnography of Book Collections in the Islamicate World' workshop, Istanbul, 27–28 April 2023).

Nadzhip, Emir, and Galina Blagova, 'Tiurki iazyk', in *Iazyki mira. Tiurkskie iazyki* (Moscow and Bishkek: Izdatel'skii Dom 'Kyrgyzstan', 1997), pp. 126–38.

Nishanov, P., 'Kurultai musul'man Srednei Azii i Kazakhstana', *Narodnoe slovo*, 41:292 (1992).

Nuritdinov, Mahmudhodja (trans. and comm.), *Qur'on ma'nolarining arab tilidan ilmiy-izohli akademik tarjimasi* (Germany: GlobeEdit, 2018/2021).

Obidov, Rahmatulloh qori, *Markaziy Osiyo olimlarining tafsir sohasida tadqiqotlari (Toshkent islom universiteti malaka oshirish kursi uchun ma'ruza matni)* (Tashkent: n.p., 2008).

Samarqandiy, Shayx Usmonxon Temurxon (trans. and comm.), *Tafsiri Irfon. Qur'oni karim ma'nolarining o'zbekcha tarjimasi va tafsiri*, 6 vols (Tashkent: Sharq, 2019).

Sartori, Paolo, *Visions of Justice: Sharīʿa and Cultural Change in Russian Central Asia* (Leiden and Boston: Brill, 2016).

Shikhaliev, Shamil, 'Islamic Press in the Early Soviet Dagestan and the Journal "Muslims of the Soviet Orient"', *Islamology*, 7:2 (2017), http://dx.doi.org/10.24848/islmlg.07.2.04

al-Ṭarāzī al-Madanī, al-Sayyid Maḥmūd (trans. and comm.), *Qur'ān-i karīm. Mutarjam wa-muḥashshā bi-l-lugha al-tūrkistāniyya*, 6 vols (Bombay: al-Maṭbaʿa al-Karīmiyya al-Kāʾina fī Bambay al-Hind, 1375/1956), al-Biruni Institute of Oriental Studies, Fund of Hamid Sulaymanov, Litho. №№ 4015–4020.

——, *Ḥajj kitābī* (*Tūrkistān tīlīda imām Abū Ḥanīfa raḥimahu Allāh madhhablārīgha muṭābiq*) (Jeddah: Dār al-Funūn lil-Ṭibāʿa wa-l-nashr, 1378/1958–9).

—— [at-Taroziy al-Madiniy, Sayyid Mahmud ibn Sayyid Nazir (Oltinxon To'ra)] (trans. and comm.), *Al-Qur'on ul-karim (o'zbek tilida izohli tarjima)*, ed. by Hoji Ismatullo Abdulloh (Tashkent: G'afur G'ulom nomidagi Adabiyot va san'at nashriyoti, 1994).

—— [at-Taroziy al-Madaniy, Sayyid Mahmud ibn Sayyid Nazir (Oltinxon To'ra)] (trans. and comm.), *Al-Qur'on al-karim ma'nolarining tarjimasi va sharhlar*, 2nd edn, ed. by Hoji Ismatulla Abdullayev (Tashkent: Fan, 2002).

—— [Taroziy, Sayyid Mahmud], *Nurul basar*, ed. by Abdul Azim Ziyouddin (Samarkand: Imom Buxoriy xalqaro markazi nashriyoti, 2017).

Tasar, Eren, *Soviet and Muslim: The Institutionalization of Islam in Central Asia, 1943–1991* (New York: Oxford University Press, 2017).

Ugolovnyi kodeks Uzbekskoi SSR (Tashkent: Uzbekistan, 1977).

Usmon, Mutallib, Abdusodiq Irisov, Hoji Ismatullo Abdullo, and Ubaydulla Uvatov (trans. and comm.), *Qur'oni karim. Tarjima va ilmiy-tarixiy izohlar. I-kitob. (1992 y.)*, ed. by Mutallib Usmon (Tashkent: Fan, 2004).

Yakubovych, Mykhaylo, 'Qur'an translation of the week #08: Kur'oni Karim. Uzbekcha Izoxli Tarjima', *Qur'an Translation of the Week*, https://gloqur.de/quran-translation-of-the-week-08-kuroni-karim-uzbekcha-izoxli-tarjima/

——, 'Qur'an Translations into Central Asian Languages: Exegetical Standards and Translation Processes', *Journal of Qur'anic Studies*, 24:1 (2022), http://dx.doi.org/10.3366/jqs.2022.0491

Yo'ldoshxo'jaev, Haydarxon, and Irodaxon Qayumova, *O'zbekiston ulamolari*, ed. by Usmonxon Alimov and Baxtiyor Bobojonov (Tashkent: Movarounnahr, 2015).

Yusuf, Abdulloh Kamol (trans.), *Qur'oni karimning yengil tafsiri*, 2nd edn (Istanbul: n.p., 2019).

Zholdassuly, Talgat, *Sovyetler'in İslam Siyaseti ve Orta Asya'da Dini İdare (1943–1990)* (Leiden: SOTA, 2022).

3. 'I Quenched the Thirst of Seventy Million':[1] Sumayya ʿAfīfī, an Egyptian Qurʾan Translator for a Post-Soviet Readership[2]

Elvira Kulieva

Introduction

In 2000, at the end of the first decade following the collapse of the USSR, a joint project undertaken by a number of Egyptian institutions produced a Russian translation of an Arabic *tafsīr* work entitled *al-Muntakhab*, the primary translator of which was an Egyptian woman named Sumayya ʿAfīfī (1935–2005).[3] The translation, known primarily by its Russian-speaking readers as *Azkharovskii perevod* ('the al-Azhar translation') transcended national borders and was republished and

---

1　Najwā Ṭanāwī, 'Rāʾida al-lugha al-Rūsiyya wa-mutarjima ʿAbd al-Nāṣir, Dr. Sumayya ʿAfīfī: rawītu ẓamaʾan sabʿīna milyūnan', *al-Ittiḥād Dunyā*, 21 August 2003.
2　This publication is the result of the project 'GloQur—The Global Qurʾan', which has received funding from the European Research Council (ERC) under the European Union's Horizon 2020 research and innovation programme (grant agreement no. 863650).
3　*al-Muntakhab fī tafsīr al-Qurʾān al-karīm*, trans. by Sumayya ʿAfīfī and ʿAbd al-Salām al-Mansī (Cairo: al-Ahrām al-Tijāriyya, 2000).

disseminated in a number of post-Soviet countries where Russian continued to be used alongside local languages. It primarily reached its readership through a number of local institutions but also gained a grassroots circulation, and it continues to be used and reprinted up to this day.[4] The original, Arabic source text was a short *tafsīr* composed by a committee of thirty-two al-Azhar scholars with diverse specialisations, and designed to be translated into multiple languages in a project that was directly supported by the Egyptian Ministry of Religious Affairs and Supreme Council for Islamic Affairs. The publication of *al-Muntakhab* in Russian was part of a larger, ambitious, Egyptian state project intended to win global influence in a region recently liberated from communism that represented a new horizon for Egyptian *daʿwa* (Islamic missionary activity). In contemporary contexts, *daʿwa* primarily refers to efforts aimed at educating or revitalising fellow Muslims and encouraging conversions among non-Muslims. Since the early twentieth century, *daʿwa* has experienced significant global growth, supported by advancements in technologies such as printing and the internet. It now includes diverse methods of Islamic propagation and features various grassroots initiatives led by Muslim laypeople, including women and children, highlighting the modern democratisation of religious and political authority alongside state-led efforts.[5] Egypt has been one of the key centres of *daʿwa* in the modern Middle East and it has received significant scholarly attention. Studies have focused on the pioneering approaches of Egyptian modernists such as Rashīd Riḍā (1865–1935), the religio-political *daʿwa* of the Muslim Brotherhood, the global *daʿwa* efforts of Shaykh Yūsuf al-Qaraḍāwī (1926–2022), and anthropological explorations of domestic *daʿwa* within Egypt.[6] However, the use of Qur'an

---

4 For instance, one of the recent reprints was produced in 2017 by the Russian state-related religious institution Spiritual Administration of Muslims of Kabardino-Balkaria, which distributed 30,000 copies of the Russian translation of *al-Muntakhab*. See Khyzir Otarov, *Raz"iasnenie po povodu izdaniia knigi Al' Muntakhab Tolkovanie Sviashchennogo Korana (perevod s arabskogo na russkiĭ)*, online video recording, *kbrdum*, 4 August 2017, https://www.kbrdum.ru/video/2186-raz-yasnenie-po-povodu-izdaniya-knigi-al-muntakhab-tolkovanie-svyashchennogo-korana-perevod-s-arabskogo-na-russkij-imam-khatyb-otarov-khyzir

5 For more on Islamic *daʿwa*, see Matthew J. Kuiper, *Da'wa: A Global History of Islamic Missionary Thought and Practice* (Edinburgh: Edinburgh University Press, 2021), pp. 4–5.

6 For the list of bibliographical references, see Matthew J. Kuiper, 'Daʿwa', 27 June 2018, https://doi.org/10.1093/obo/9780195390155-0252

translations as a tool of *daʿwa*, particularly through state-sponsored initiatives and the role of al-Azhar, remains a largely unexplored aspect of modern *daʿwa*.

The story of the Russian translation of *al-Muntakhab* and its Egyptian female translator is intriguing on several levels. Sumayya ʿAfīfī was an Egyptian Muslim who had studied in the USSR in the 1960s, a very unusual situation that came about because of the political and ideological circumstances during the Cold War. In a paradoxical twist, given the Nasserist and communist policies that had led her to learn Russian in the first place as part of her secular education, ʿAfīfī subsequently turned to *daʿwa*, and her inclusion in an Egyptian state-sponsored soft-power Islamic initiative is notable given the historical scarcity of women in Qur'anic fields. Those women who have produced translations of the Qur'an and other Islamic works are of particular interest, as they enjoy a rare degree of agency in a male-dominated field.[7] What was the nature of this agency during that specific historical period, and how can it be understood? What were the constraints and possibilities it presented? As a transnational project, the Russian *al-Muntakhab* not only highlights the existence of Egyptian *daʿwa* efforts in the region, but also demonstrates how, during the 1990s, the Arabic media celebrated ʿAfīfī as a national heroine, while her personality remained rarely discussed in the target language context, where the focus shifted to al-Azhar's institutional authority. This chapter suggests that the narrative built up around ʿAfīfī in Egypt can only really be understood in the context of al-Ṣaḥwa al-Islāmiyya (the 'Islamic revival'), which facilitated women's 'pious' involvement with the Qur'an, as opposed to feminist hermeneutical 'resistance' to traditional exegesis and interpretations.

The exploration of ʿAfīfī's biography as an Egyptian national heroine who 'quenched the thirst of seventy million'[8] undertaken in this chapter entails an examination of the relevant Arabic print sources as well as the personal testimonies of people who knew her, or who were also involved in the Russian translation of *al-Muntakhab*. This chapter uncovers some

---

7   To my knowledge, only two women have acted as the main translators in published translations of the Qur'an and *tafsīrs* into Russian. See Iman Valeriia Porokhova (trans.), *Koran: perevod smyslov i kommentarii* (Moscow: Ripol Klassik, 2022), and Ibn Kathīr al-Dimashqī, *Tolkovanie Korana*, trans. by Anastasiia Shipilina (Moscow: Al' Kitab, 2022).

8   Ṭanāwī, 'Rāʾida al-lugha al-Rūsiyya'.

significant differences in the Egyptian and Russian reception of ʿAfīfī's persona which cast light on notions of female religious agency held by conservative religious authorities. It begins with a biographical sketch of Sumayya ʿAfīfī before she turned to Islamic translation, situated in the political context of the USSR and Nasserist Egypt which facilitated the emergence of the professionals later involved in daʿwa projects such as *al-Muntakhab*. The subsequent section analyses how the Islamic revival that took place in Egypt facilitated female involvement in Egyptian religious institutions, and how this in turn affected Sumayya ʿAfīfī's 'Islamic' persona as a female translator of the Qur'an. The following two sections look at her early translations of a number of Islamic works, notably *al-Muntakhab*, after which I discuss the spiritual significance of Qur'an translation within the framework of the overall state project. Finally, I highlight the challenges and limitations of the reception of *al-Muntakhab* in the Russian-speaking context.

Between Nasserism and Communism: Sumayya ʿAfīfī's Life Trajectory

Sumayya ʿAfīfī was born in 1935 into an upper-class Egyptian family with a respectable social standing during the rule of King Farouk, prior to the Egyptian revolution of 1952. Her mother was one of the first Egyptian women to study in Europe, which indicates that the family had very progressive views on the spectrum of societal roles for Egyptian women. She attended an elite school for girls in the Cairo district of Zamalek, where she was taught in English and French by foreigners. As in other affluent Cairo neighbourhoods, her social and cultural life reflected the strong European influences favoured by the upper class and bourgeoisie. ʿAfīfī was the youngest of three girls, all of whom also received higher education, and she was firm in her intention to pursue a similar intellectual trajectory to her elder sisters. Her family can be placed within the urban upper and middle class of the so-called *effendiyya*, who were the beneficiaries of the monarchy's pre-revolutionary promotion of education, as well as the post-revolutionary expansion of a modernised civil service. While her family was eager to assert that ʿAfīfī was always a religious person, it is significant that her student and early professional life were lived under Nasser's Arab

Socialism, in which religion was not seen as a driving force for societal change. This may explain why outward expressions of Islam such as involvement in daʿwa activity, as well as her choices in public attire, only became visible during the time of Anwar Sadat (d. 1981) and Husni Mubarak (d. 2020), reflecting larger societal trends, as will be discussed in the next section.

ʿAfīfī's quest for education has been emphasised in the press, which has highlighted her ambitions in this arena. In the Egyptian public discourse of the early 1990s, media portrayal of successful women often aimed to engender admiration for confident women who successfully balanced a career forged through secular education while also prioritising family responsibilities, rather than the 'traditional' housewife, who remained unseen.[9] This is reflected in the recurring narrative about our heroine, which reads as follows: in 1956, she successfully graduated from Ain Shams University in Cairo with a BA in English Language and Literature, following which she intended to pursue a Master's degree in an English-speaking country; despite her marriage, her plans remained intact. However, fate intervened and ʿAfīfī's graduation coincided with the 1956 Tripartite Invasion of Egypt (otherwise known as the Suez Crisis),[10] and Gamal Abdel Nasser Nasser's (1918–1970) radical reconsideration of foreign policy in its aftermath impacted scholarship grants. Funding was withdrawn for scholarships in Western countries during that particular period and, instead of her planned destination, ʿAfīfī found herself presented with the opportunity to pursue further studies in the USSR. In a coincidence that eased the risky venture of travelling to the USSR, her husband, who was a scholar of chemistry, was suddenly appointed as cultural attaché to Moscow.[11]

The political context that made such educational initiatives possible rested on two factors: the Soviet Union's shift in foreign policy focus in the late 1950s towards the Global South, and President Nasser's drastic reconsideration of his foreign policy after the Tripartite Invasion. His

---

9 Aaron Rock-Singer, *Practicing Islam in Egypt: Print Media and Islamic Revival* (Cambridge: Cambridge University Press, 2019), pp. 159–60.

10 Israel, France, and the UK invaded Egypt, seeking to depose the Egyptian president Gamal Abdel Nasser and regain control of the Suez Canal, which Nasser had recently nationalised.

11 His appointment illustrates the general lack of Russian-speaking specialists in Egypt at the time, as he did not speak Russian.

opening of Egypt to a new strategic alliance with the USSR went far beyond simply obtaining Soviet military aid, and the period of collaboration has been called 'the Soviet-Egyptian marriage' by some scholars because it included a wide range of scientific and cultural endeavours.[12] However, the implementation of Soviet-inspired, non-capitalist developments and modernisation—which was an integral element of Soviet aid to the Global South—would have been impossible without specialists on the ground who had been educated by the Soviets.[13] Recognising this critical need led to a remarkable influx of foreign students over several decades, drawn to the Soviet Union in pursuit of higher education at its various universities. That some of these individuals turned in subsequent decades to *daʿwa* activism and became involved in religious projects such as the Russian *al-Muntakhab* translation was an unexpected outcome of these Soviet and Nasserist policies.[14]

Sumayya ʿAfīfī, who was renowned as *umm al-lugha al-Rūsiyya* ('the mother of Russian') in Egypt, earned recognition as a successful translator and academic,[15] and embodied the 'state feminism' approach

---

12 Paul B. Henze, 'Flexible Opportunism', in *Soviet Strategy and Islam*, ed. by Alexandre Bennigsen, Paul B. Henze, George K. Tanham, and S. Enders Wimbush (New York: Palgrave Macmillan, 1989), pp. 79–100 (p. 84). Playing the game of anti-imperialism, Soviets began to see the countries of the post-colonial South—which had just achieved formal independence but not yet full 'sovereignty'—as targets for its exertion of soft power. Soviet aid included a wide range of assistance, such as financial, military, technological, technical, cultural, and most importantly, scientific aid. Soviet specialists were sent abroad to undertake research and teaching at the educational institutions of host countries as well as to assist with various costly construction projects that were crucial for national development, such as the Aswan and Euphrates dams. See Constantin Katsakioris, 'Soviet Lessons for Arab Modernization: Soviet Educational Aid to Arab Countries after 1956', *Journal of Modern European History*, 8:1 (2010), 85–106 (p. 89).

13 Katsakioris, 'Soviet Lessons', p. 92.

14 The history of Arab students benefiting from Soviet education policies and influencing Islamic *daʿwa* in post-Soviet countries represents an area of study that remains relatively unexplored. Specifically, within the domain of Qur'an translations, noteworthy Arab figures (beyond ʿAfīfī) have directly or indirectly engaged in translating the Qur'an. For instance, another popular Qur'an translation by a woman, Iman Valeriia Porokhova's poetic Qur'an translation, highlights this trend. Her Syrian husband, Muḥammad Saʿīd al-Rushd (b. 1946), arrived in the USSR to study engineering and influenced her conversion to Islam. Subsequently, he assumed the role of editor for her widely read Qur'an translation. See footnote 7.

15 ʿAbd al-Fattāḥ al-Maghāwrī, 'Sumayya ʿAfīfī ... riḥla ʿaṭāʾ', *Afāq ʿArabiyya*, 8 September 2005.

espoused by the authoritarian, socialist Nasserist state.[16] Her career trajectory resonated with state-driven public debates about women's active participation in government-led development, whereby Egyptian-educated urban women were made 'agents of modernization'.[17] Successful, educated, and not restrained by 'obscurantist' views on women's roles, ʿAfīfī could be said to represent a symbolic nationalist Egyptian ideal of that time: a married woman who fulfilled her supportive domestic role at home, but also worked outside of her household in 'the service of the nation', and played a part in shaping a prosperous future for the state.[18] Her personal life and career took shape within the framework of the prevailing discourse of secular nationalism, which regarded certain public religious manifestations—such as wearing the veil—as culturally outdated symbols. Instead of relying on such traditional symbols, as Laura Bier explains, the public discourse of the pre-Ṣaḥwa period emphasised 'veiling of conduct'. This involved shaping new societal roles for Egyptian middle-class women, who were integrated into male-dominated workspaces, with an emphasis on modest behaviour, coupled with education and professionalism.[19] This period of ʿAfīfī's life is not reflected in the images of her that are available in public sources, which instead often feature later photos of her, in which she is wearing a Muslim veil, a practice she adopted in the 1980s while working at Ain Shams University.

---

16 'State feminism entailed the recognition of women as enfranchised citizens and the explicit commitment by the Nasser regime to liberate women in order to guarantee their inclusion and participation in the postrevolutionary nation on the equal footing with men. Through laws, social programmes, and the creation of new institutions that redrew the parameters of the public, state feminism aimed to make women into modern political subjects by dismantling traditional patriarchal structures in the family, creating new gender subjectivities, and mobilising them in the service of national development'. Laura Bier, *Revolutionary Womanhood: Feminisms, Modernity, and the State in Nasser's Egypt* (Stanford: Stanford University Press, 2011), p. 3.

17 Nasser's nation-state project placed a significant emphasis on women's empowerment and mobilised Egyptian women for labour, considering this an integral aspect of national development. In her *Revolutionary Womanhood*, Bier critically explores this state feminism project and demonstrates how Nasserist emancipation also led to new patterns of state involvement in women's lives. She highlights the interconnectedness between these novel forms of emancipation and the emerging mechanisms of social control and coercion. See Bier, *Revolutionary Womanhood*, pp. 6–7, 10.

18 Bier, *Revolutionary Womanhood*, p. 34.

19 Ibid., p. 91.

In 1959, ʿAfīfī travelled to the USSR as one of the first cohort of Egyptian students who were part of Egypt's sponsored programme. Most of the sources emphasise that while she was abroad studying in the USSR, she was accompanied by her husband—an important aspect of the Egyptian moral exemplar of a woman. While the Nasser era promoted socialist progressive ideas concerning women's rights, it retained its fundamentally conservative social values. Thus, her narrative during that period intertwines two elements: there is a 'transgression' of the norm, i.e. her travels to unknown lands governed by communist dogma, but she is accompanied there by a *maḥram* ('guardian'), her husband. She is thus represented in a way that is intended to depict her as successful, but uncontroversial, particularly in terms of religious concerns and ideas.

The influx of students to the USSR raises the question of to what extent they were subject to indoctrination and the promotion of communist ideas.[20] While this was certainly one of the long-term objectives of Soviet policy, the Soviet approach towards Arab students reflected a wider policy towards Arab countries, which represents what Henze has named 'flexible opportunism'—a pragmatic and adaptable approach to foreign politics.[21] Egyptian-Soviet collaboration existed alongside Nasser's persecution of communists in Egypt, which the Soviets knew about but decided to disregard in favour of their short-term objectives and the longer-term effects of social engineering through education. Egyptian students were thus released from any obligation to enrol for courses related to the study of Marxism or Leninism, because these were viewed as a clear threat to the political status quo of Middle

---

20 For statistics and dates on foreign students from the Global South, see Constantin Katsakioris, 'Statistics on Arab Students in the USSR (1959–1991)', in *Russian-Arab Worlds: A Documentary History*, ed. by Eileen Kane, Masha Kirasirova, and Margaret Litvin (Abingdon: Oxford University Press, 2023), pp. 236–44.

21 Karan Dawisha's analysis of the Soviet policy in Egypt suggests that we view the USSR as having two types of approach, namely 'short-term objectives' and 'long-term goals.' The short-term objectives aimed to diminish Western influence and strengthen the target countries' independence, while the long-term goals were intended to promote communist ideals, which included the promotion of a political, economic, and social system similar to that of the Soviet Union. See Karen Dawisha, 'Soviet Cultural Relations with Iraq, Syria and Egypt 1955–70', *Soviet Studies*, 27:3 (1975), 418–42; Henze, 'Flexible Opportunism', p. 73.

Eastern regimes and were seen as having clear communist propaganda and revolutionary potential.

The Egyptian approach was also to support its established specialist professionals, particularly by requalifying, retraining, and strengthening the skills of those who were already qualified. Postgraduate degrees were prioritised for study in the USSR because the Egyptian government relied on the assumption that these students had mature personalities, which would reduce their vulnerability to communist indoctrination. As a result, compared to other African countries, a much greater proportion of Egyptian students pursued postgraduate degrees in the USSR rather than their first higher education degree.[22] Despite lacking any formal training in Russian language, culture, or history, ʿAfīfī was enrolled at Moscow State University to pursue a PhD (*'kandidat nauk'*) in the philology of the Russian language.[23] The acceptance of a foreign student without any relevant prior training at the undergraduate level for such a course of study can only be read as signifying a vested interest on the part of the Soviets. In order to compensate for her lack of linguistic background knowledge, ʿAfīfī received language immersion training with a private tutor on a daily basis, facilitated by the Russian authorities.

Despite their agreement with the Egyptian government that communism-related courses would be optional for all students, the Soviet authorities found other ways to implement their long-term objective of immersing students in Soviet ideology, for example through the mandatory but vaguely defined 'USSR Today' course, as well as various other extracurricular activities. The Soviets also imposed these courses as a punitive measure for student misconduct, as indicated by a number of private testimonies.[24] However, in 1968, in a change in policy, the USSR made enrollment in Marxism-Leninism courses compulsory

---

22 Constantin Katsakioris, 'Soviet Lessons for Arab Modernization: Soviet Educational Aid to Arab Countries after 1956', *Journal of Modern European History*, 8:1 (2010), 85–106 (p. 96).

23 Somaiia M. Afifi, 'Leksikologicheskii analiz glagolov idti-khodit' i ikh proizvodnykh v sovremennom russkom iazyke.' (unpublished dissertation, M. V. Lomonosov Moscow State University, 1964).

24 Katsakioris, 'Soviet Lessons', p. 98; Margaret Litvin, 'Should Dormitory Bathrooms Have Doors? Zakaria Turki's *An Upper Egyptian among the Russians* (1967–1972)', in *Russian-Arab Worlds: A Documentary History*, ed. by Eileen Kane, Masha Kirasirova, and Margaret Litvin (Oxford: Oxford University Press, 2023), pp. 245–54 (p. 251).

for all foreign students.²⁵ This shift reflects the weakened Arab position post 1967, which made Nasser more dependent on the Soviet Union and provided the Soviets with an opportunity to assert their worldview more vigorously.

Sumayya ʿAfīfī was among the first cohort of Egyptian students to study in the USSR, and her time there thus corresponds to the earlier period when it was possible to avoid the more overt attempts at political indoctrination; but ʿAbd al-Salām al-Mansī, who worked under ʿAfīfī and also contributed to the translation of *al-Muntakhab* as a second translator, was not able to avoid these courses.²⁶ However, according to his recollection, despite the fact that foreign students attended the same classes as the Soviets, they were usually graded more leniently and it was often enough to simply positively mention Friedrich Engels and Vladimir Lenin in relation to various subjects to be deemed to have shown some kind of familiarity with communist ideas.²⁷ Importantly, neither the philosophy of dialectical materialism nor an anti-Western orientation seem to have been instilled in the Arab students who went on to form the new educated class in their home countries. For instance, many of those who studied technical specialisations later used their Soviet degrees to work for American companies in the Gulf.²⁸

Now fluent in Russian, upon her return to Egypt Sumayya ʿAfīfī undertook various literary translations from Russian into Arabic, thereby popularising Russian and Soviet classics, such as the plays of Ivan Turgenev and Aleksandr Vampilov.²⁹ However, despite her education in a 'Soviet' school of thought, ʿAfīfī's educational background did not bind her to any fixed ideological stance. This is evident in her decision to pursue an additional MA degree from the American University in Cairo

---

25 Katsakioris, 'Soviet Lessons', p. 98.
26 ʿAfīfī also visited the USSR after completing her degree, but subsequent trips were for research rather than study purposes.
27 Based on an interview conducted by the author with ʿAbd al-Salām al-Mansī in Cairo (Egypt) in February 2023.
28 Katsakioris, 'Soviet Lessons', p. 88.
29 A series of theatre plays was published in Kuwait under the title *The World Theater* (*Min al-masraḥ al-ʿālamī*) and included ʿAfīfī's translations, for example: Ivan Turgenev, *al-Aʿzab*, trans. by Sumayya ʿAfīfī (Kuwait: Ministry of Information, 1983); Alexander Vampilov, *Wadāʿ fi Yūniyū*, trans. by Sumayya ʿAfīfī (Kuwait: Ministry of Information, 1993).

(AUC) in 1985.³⁰ Moreover, as time went on, she shifted her focus to the translation of religious works, indicating the personal transformations she underwent, which also reflected changes in her broader social milieu.

It is important to note, however, that ʿAfīfī's life in the USSR was truly exceptional compared to other foreign students who went to the USSR. As the wife of an Egyptian diplomat who represented not only Egypt but also the United Arab Republic (which included both Egypt and Syria) during the partial period of Nasser's rule, her family's life in the USSR was luxurious. They were very affluent, largely thanks to her husband's high income as a diplomat—which was paid in foreign currency and which, when exchanged into rubles, amounted to an extravagant sum by local standards. A demonstrative example of this is the fact that, for the entire five-year period of her PhD, they were able to live in a spacious suite in the iconic Hotel Moskva: a symbol of Stalinist grandeur located in the city centre near the Red Square. During this time she also gave birth to her two sons and her husband's salary was enough for private babysitters for each child, allowing her to focus on her studies and travel throughout the USSR and Eastern Bloc. As the wife of a diplomat, she enjoyed a range of opportunities, including meeting politicians and celebrities at events such as film festivals. The lavish income of the family, in contrast to the average Soviet living wage, allowed her to enjoy the social life of the Soviet capital to the full; for example, she attended numerous performances of the iconic Swan Lake ballet at the Bolshoi Theater in the company of various delegations.³¹ The descriptions of her academic and life experiences in the USSR provided in public sources, as well as in family narratives, are overwhelmingly positive. However, press reports and interviews that discuss her life in the USSR tend to be limited to a few lines outlining her studies and the fact that she was accompanied by family. This is not surprising, given that her cultural immersion in the USSR was purely secular in nature. To the general public, she was portrayed by the media as a woman whose life was dedicated to scholarship and knowledge, and who would later

---

30   Her degree from American University of Cairo was in Teaching English as a Foreign Language.
31   Information about the family's income and their pastimes while in the USSR is taken from an interview conducted by the author with ʿAfīfī's family members Dr Khaled Abdelazim Abbas and Dr Yasser Abdelazim Abbas in Cairo (Egypt), February 2023, as well through online communications.

translate the Qur'an, as if the details of the more secular aspects of her everyday life could diminish the seriousness of the religious narrative that was built around her, or bring it into question.

Upon ʿAfīfī's return to Egypt, she first taught Russian and then became a professor at Ain Shams University,[32] eventually being appointed as the head of the Department of Slavic Languages.[33] Her appointment reflects the Egyptian policy of 'state feminism', which allowed professional women to access the higher ranks of a number of professions, especially in the area of education.[34] In this regard, ʿAfīfī can be regarded as a successful career woman and an exemplar of an educated Egyptian wife-mother-scholar-civil servant—in other words, as a demonstrative case of the regime's symbolic achievements, on which the state modernising project discursively depended.[35] Another facet of her public image, that of the female *dāʿiya* ('preacher') and Qur'an translator, can be connected to the social reconfigurations of post-Nasserism which we will now turn to.

The Ṣaḥwa and Sumayya ʿAfīfī's 'Islamic' Persona

The social movement known as the Ṣaḥwa ('the Egyptian Islamic revival') emerged after the end of a period pursuing an Arab Socialist dream under the charismatic leadership of Nasser, who died in 1970. The Six-Day War of 1967—in which Egypt was part of the Arab coalition that was defeated by Israel—played a part in changing Egypt's socio-political outlook. For many Egyptians, from ordinary Muslim citizens to religious and political leaders, this defeat had a significant impact. It served as a catalyst for self-reflection, sparking a new public discourse grounded in the Islamic faith which led to a renewed focus on religion as a potential source for positive transformation. The Egyptian Islamic

---

32 Thanāʾ al-Baṭil, 'D. Sumayya ʿAfīfī: tarjamat tafsīr al-Qurʾān al-karīm lil-Rūsiyya', *al-Jumhūriyya*, 20 May 2004.
33 It was not her only experience of visiting the USSR. Subsequently, the family returned to Moscow for shorter research trips.
34 Bier points out that this trend was in many respects a continuation of the prerevolutionary trends when these professions had experienced significant feminisation: see Bier, *Revolutionary Womanhood*, p. 66.
35 Bier, *Revolutionary Womanhood*, p. 69.

revival became an important subject of scholarly investigation, offering diverse perspectives to understand this transformative period.[36]

For the purpose of this chapter, which situates the intellectual path of a female Qur'an translator, a recent study by Aaron Rock-Singer is particularly relevant for understanding the context that shaped Sumayya ʿAfīfī's public image. He argues that the newly emerged Islamic discourses of the time about pious Muslim public practices came out of the interplay between various non-state Islamic groups, such as the Salafis and the Muslim Brotherhood, and state-related actors such as al-Azhar and its associated institutions, which influenced changing perceptions of the role of religion in the public sphere. The outward architecture of Egyptian society was rapidly changing, and the features of modernisation became very much connected with public expressions of religion that were incorporated into the state project. These included the rise of debates over, and the practice of, veil-normativity, segregation on public transport, and the right to pray within work and educational settings. Notably, Rock-Singer demonstrates how the inclusion of middle-class women within the Egyptian public sphere by various Islamic actors was a side effect of the 'state feminism' policies of the Nasserist era, and this became an inevitable part of evolving modern social reality. As a result, new, pious public figures who demonstrated the proper models of public comportment had to be established. By utilising print media and delivering sermons, Muslim intellectuals and preachers—who (with rare exceptions) were all male—actively shaped the public discourse on *adab* ('etiquette' or 'deportment'), encompassing a range of topics related to the proper conduct and behaviour expected of pious women in academic and professional working environments,

---

36   As noted throughout the literature, the religious revival during this period was not an exclusively Egyptian phenomenon but rather part of a global trend that challenged prevailing assumptions about modernisation in various parts of the world, with manifestations differing according to specific political, religious, and cultural contexts. Regarding the Egyptian Ṣaḥwa, Aaron Rock-Singer's recent study, *Practicing Islam in Egypt: Print Media and Islamic Revival* (Cambridge: Cambridge University Press, 2019) offers a useful overview of the literature on this topic in both the Egyptian context and beyond (pp. 1–2). For discussions of female agency in the context of the Islamic revival, as well as a general overview of the period, see Saba Mahmood, *The Politics of Piety: The Islamic Revival and the Feminist Subject* (Princeton: Princeton University Press, 2005), pp. 3–4; and Ellen Anne McLarney, *Soft Force: Women in Egypt's Islamic Awakening* (Princeton: Princeton University Press, 2015).

as well as in public spaces more broadly. This discourse covered such aspects of daily life as adhering to prescribed Islamic dress codes (which varied across different Islamic groups in terms of strictness), and the observance of gender-specific behaviours and manners in mixed-gender settings such as work environments.

In the beginning stages of al-Ṣaḥwa, most Egyptian preachers approached the inclusion of women in public life through the lens of the legal concept of 'necessity' (*ḍarūra*). The implication was that it was only due to the 'necessities or demands of social and economic life'[37] that women's default mode of home seclusion had shifted to one of public participation, and thereby their public morality now had to be regulated. However, in subsequent decades (from the late 1980s onwards, and throughout the Mubarak era), the discourse changed to approaching the behaviour and deportment of women as 'a barometer of public morality'—women's public presence became a norm, and in fact the whole of society was now evaluated on the basis of women's public behaviour and garments.[38] This shift within the later stage of al-Ṣaḥwa was evident in public discourse, particularly in contrast to that of the early Sadat era. In the late Mubarak period, women's employment and visibility gained such importance that women became 'necessarily public objects and agents of change'.[39] Consequently, many preachers and spokesmen for Islamic institutions and organisations demonstrated an acceptance of the widening of the range of professions available to women in the labour market. These Islamic spokesmen and preachers covered a spectrum of ideological orientations, but despite their differing perspectives and often contentious relationships, they all agreed—either directly or indirectly—on the acceptability of women's inclusion in public life; yet it was primarily men who retained the power and authority to regulate and navigate the boundaries of women's inclusion in this modern reality.

The formation of a new public morality within the context of al-Ṣaḥwa, which included the perception of women as active participants of social change, highlights the idea that 'Religious principle[s] can be lived not

---

37   Y. Linant de Bellefonds, 'Ḍarūra', in *Encyclopaedia of Islam New Edition Online*.
38   Aaron Rock-Singer, *Practicing Islam in Egypt: Print Media and Islamic Revival* (Cambridge: Cambridge University Press, 2019), p. 155.
39   Ibid., p. 155.

merely through resistance to an unjust regime, but also through attempts to morally shape society under the leadership of state-aligned scholars and intellectuals.'⁴⁰ In such circumstances, the emergence in Egypt of various local piety projects, the idealisation of a number of exemplary figures, and the pursuit of influential global Islamic initiatives may be understood as the results of al-Ṣaḥwa, as the interests of the state, religiously motivated women, and various ideological Muslim factions intersect and overlap.

The life trajectory of ʿAfīfī is very demonstrative of these overlaps and changes. Looking at the various Egyptian journals that mention ʿAfīfī and her work, a reader is left with the impression that she was no ordinary person. For example, there is a repetitive emphasis on her 'being the first'. 'Firstness' in this context was not only a description, but also a rhetorical tool that was employed effectively by newspapers to persuade the reader of her success as a woman, as well as to emphasise the uniqueness and extraordinariness of her actions.⁴¹ While any activity or action can be repeated and improved upon, the idea of placing someone on the pedestal of 'firstness' necessarily entails the breaking of boundaries. Being a pioneer in a given field implies that all later contributions or efforts follow a path that has already been paved, that the person in question is someone who has already made the work easier for those who would want to repeat or improve upon it.

However, ʿAfīfī was not, in actual fact, the first to translate the Qur'an into Russian, as there was already a history of Qur'an translations into Russian. Following the dissolution of the USSR a few Russian Qur'an translations had already been published by Muslims, and these even include one by a Muslim woman. This information was well-known in the Russian-speaking context, and was also recognised by ʿAfīfī in a number of interviews.⁴² She is on record as mentioning both that there were other Russian translations of the Qur'an, and that her work was

---

40   Ibid., p, 181.
41   The trope of firstness in titles related to ʿAfīfī can be rightfully interpreted as a modern manifestation of the literary practice found in Arabic literature, known as the genre of awāʾil. See Shosh Ben-Ari, 'The "Awāʾil" Stories: Legitimization of Norms and Customs', *Quaderni Di Studi Arabi*, 2 (2007), 103–18.
42   For example, in this video, she mentions some of the earlier works: 'Barnāmaj Muwājihāt maʿa d. Sumayya Muḥammad Mūsa ʿAfīfī', online video recording, *YouTube*, https://www.youtube.com/watch?v=2m3784QUzyc&t=1704s

in fact a translation of *al-Muntakhab* and not a translation of the Qur'an itself. However, the media emphasis on her 'firstness' can be understood as a necessary step in the creation of an heroic figure, as it 'refers to [the] phenomena of singularity' which builds up a picture of the uniqueness of certain individuals.⁴³ Accordingly, the titles of some articles written about ʿAfīfī pointed to the fact that she had translated the first *tafsīr* in Russian, others to the claim that she had published the first Russian Qur'an translation, giving rise to titles such as 'The First Russian Translation of the *tafsīr* of the Noble Qur'an', and 'Finally, the Qur'an in Russian!'⁴⁴ All aimed to underscore the exceptional nature of her intellectual endeavour using the rhetorical strategy of emphasising her 'firstness'.

The titles of many of these articles also specifically emphasised the female gender of the translator as an important aspect of her achievement: 'The First Female Translator of the Meanings of the Noble Qur'an into Russian', 'The First Arab Woman to Translate the Meanings of the Noble Qur'an into Russian', and 'The First Egyptian Woman Translator of the Exegesis of the Noble Qur'an into Russian'.⁴⁵ Her story appeared in the 'Successful Woman' column of the governmental journal *al-Liwāʾ al-Islāmī*,⁴⁶ which directed readers' attention not only to her works, but also to the exemplary nature of female participation in an endeavour that was considered to be tough and challenging. Not only was the task considered difficult in itself, it was also believed to be dangerous, given the grave consequences Islamic tradition associates with misinterpreting the Qur'an. Highlighting the fact that a woman was contributing to a historically male enterprise—and a precarious one at that—was a strategic means by which journalists demonstrated her transgression of established religio-societal boundaries whilst simultaneously conveying

---

43   Olmo Gölz, 'Collectives', in *Compendium heroicum*, ed. by Ronald G. Asch, Achim Aurnhammer, Georg Feitscher, Anna Schreurs-Morét, and Ralf von den Hoff (Freiburg: University of Freiburg).

44   For example: Narmīn Khashaba, "Sumayya ʿAfīfī: awwal tarjama Rūsiyya li-tafsīr al-Qurʾān al-karīm', *Kolenas/ Kull al-nās*, 20–26 February 2002, pp. 38–40; Hiba al-Sayyid ʿAlī, 'Akhīran al-Qurʾān bi-l-Rūsiyya', *Ḥawāʾ*, 10 June 1995, pp. 26–27.

45   Īmān Muḥammad Imbābī, 'Awwal mutarjima li-maʿānī al-Qurʾān al-karīm lil-lugha al-Rūsiyya', *al-Ahrām*, 1 December 2001; 'Awwal ʿArabiyya tutarjimu maʿānī al-Qurʾān al-karīm ilā al-Rūsiyya ... al-duktura Sumayya ʿAfīfī: al-lugha hiya silāḥunā li-nashr dīninā wa-thaqāfatinā', *Kull al-Usra*, 23 August 1995, pp. 70–71; Īmān Muḥammad Imbābī, 'Miṣriyya tutarjimu maʿānī al-Qurʾān ilā al-Rūsiyya', *al-Ahrām al-Masāʾiyy*, 27 May 1995.

46   'Imraʾa nājiḥa', *al-Liwāʾ al-Islāmī*, 31 July 2003.

the acknowledgement of her translation by established male scholarly authorities, adding extra significance to ʿAfīfī's achievement.⁴⁷

Fig. 3.1. Sumayya ʿAfīfī (1935–2005). ©Elvira Kulieva, Creative Commons license CC BY.

Some other titles have pointed to her Egyptian nationality, using such wording as 'Egyptian Woman Translates the Meanings of the Qurʾan into Russian!', for example. However, when articles on her were published in other Arab countries such as the UAE, her Arab origin was noticeably emphasised instead.⁴⁸ This is clearly intended to trigger nationalistic sentiments and feelings of pride in readers, who can share in being a part of an 'imaginary community' in which women play an important role.⁴⁹ Another way that nationalistic elements are brought into stories about ʿAfīfī is through connection of this female heroine to other, 'bigger' and more famous national heroes. For instance, the titles of some newspaper

---

47 Tobias Schlechtriemen, 'Transgressiveness', in *Compendium heroicum*, ed. by Ronald G. Asch, Achim Aurnhammer, Georg Feitscher, Anna Schreurs-Morét, and Ralf von den Hoff (Freiburg: University of Freiburg), 19 August 2002, https://www.compendium-heroicum.de/lemma/transgressiveness/
48 Imbābī, 'Miṣriyya'.
49 Benedict Anderson, *Imagined Communities: Reflections on the Origin and Spread of Nationalism* (London: Verso, 2006). For more on the conceptualisation of the national hero, see Johanna Pink, 'National Hero', in *Compendium heroicum*, ed. by Ronald G. Asch, Achim Aurnhammer, Georg Feitscher, Anna Schreurs-Morét, and Ralf von den Hoff (Freiburg: University of Freiburg), 19 September 2022, https://www.compendium-heroicum.de/lemma/national-hero/

articles specifically pointed to her close work in the early years with Gamal Abdel Nasser, explicitly incorporating his name in their titles—as in *al-Shabāb*'s use of the title 'Mutarjima ᶜAbd al-Nāṣir' ('Nasser's Translator'). [50] By linking ᶜAfīfī with the former Egyptian president, a symbolic figure of Arab nationalism, such titles used his name as a hook to inform readers about the importance of this woman, who had worked for him, unknown, in the shadows. The press adopted this idea with great enthusiasm, dubbing ᶜAfīfī the 'unknown soldier behind the army forces', and highlighting her role in facilitating the smooth running of national military operations, as well as preparing specialist professionals to work with the Soviets in the industrial sector.[51] At one point in her career, ᶜAfīfī also worked as a simultaneous interpreter for Nasser's meetings with Soviet top officials such as Nikita Khrushchev (1894–1971) and Alexei Kosygin (1904–1980), and had been involved in translating Soviet press reports for the Egyptian president. She had also accompanied him and his family on unofficial trips in 1969 to Tsqaltubo in Soviet Georgia, when Nasser travelled there for medical treatment.[52] Thus, ᶜAfīfī was characterised as an important personality who had served the state during a crucial historical period—but her feminine character is subordinated, which only served to emphasise the heroic nature of her endeavours for the state. Her association with Nasser was a detail that was frequently mentioned, and appears repeatedly in numerous sources, adding prestige to her image as a translator. This also served as a pretext for her later role as translator of the Qur'an, giving her persona a definite sense of gravitas.

ᶜAfīfī's belief in the importance of women in the public sphere is clear from press interviews, and she especially highlights the part women have to play in *daᶜwa*. She stresses that by learning foreign languages, women— as the 'keys to society' [53]—can pave the way to open people's hearts to

---

50 'Mutarjima ᶜAbd al-Nāṣir', *al-Shabāb*, June 2004, p. 46.
51 During Nasser's rule, the Department had a strong cooperative relationship with the Egyptian military, as this was the only institution in which the Russian language was taught. ᶜAfīfī focused on teaching Russian to meet the needs of the army, training around 200 translators every six months. See Ṭanāwī, 'Rāʾida al-lugha al-Rūsiyya; Ṣafiyya al-Khūlī, 'D. Sumayya ᶜAfīfī: dīnunā al-samḥ ... bi-l-lugha al-Rūsiyya', *al-Jumhūriyya*, 21 November 2002.
52 Interview conducted by the author with ᶜAfīfī's family members in February 2023, Cairo.
53 'Awwal ᶜarabiyya', p. 71.

Islam, and she believes that 'with a little time-management, any woman can become a great scholar, as well as a dedicated home keeper with no shortcomings.'[54] These ideas correspond to the socio-historical background of the Egyptian Ṣaḥwa through which she lived and worked (and in this light, it is interesting that the interview with ʿAfīfī cited here—which focused on women's career paths—was accompanied by a table showing statistical data relating to women's employment, which illustrates the social demand for female participation in the nation-state project).[55]

The Beginning of ʿAfīfī's Involvement with *daʿwa* and the Russian *al-Muntakhab*

The social processes related to state feminism that had their origins in the Nasser era continued to evolve during the periods of Anwar Sadat and, particularly, his successor Husni Mubarak; and women's involvement in the Islamic revival, especially in terms of writing and teaching, became increasingly evident. The inclusion of women in state-related religious institutions (such as the Ministry of Endowments, the Supreme Council for Islamic Affairs, and even al-Azhar itself) is also an element of the late period of al-Ṣaḥwa, and is particularly observable in the 1990s. In 1989 or 1990, Dr Muḥammad Alī al-Mahjūb—who was then the Minister of Endowments—approached ʿAfīfī—who worked at Ayn Shams University at the time—with the proposal that she translate into Russian a number of short books related to the pillars of Islam. Aside from her qualifications, it might be that she was also approached in part due to the practical aspect that Russian was not studied or taught at al-Azhar University (which only had the relevant expertise in English, German, and French), and thus an appropriate candidate to publish Russian language *daʿwa* books had to be found from outside al-Azhar. It seems that ʿAfīfī was approached on the basis of her professional reputation, but also her reputation for piety: her visibility as a devout, practising Muslim woman was as important as the prestige of being Nasser's translator. (This contrasts somewhat with the Saudi approach to selecting translators, which primarily focuses on creedal aspects, which often served as a decisive factor in recommendations for

---

54 al-Sayyid ʿAlī, 'Akhīran al-Qurʾān', p. 27.
55 Ibid., p. 27.

translators, made via the extensive Salafi global network.⁵⁶ This creedal aspect appears to carry less weight when it comes to Egyptian *daʿwa*, which exhibits a less sectarian and more easy-going approach to such matters.)⁵⁷

ʿAfīfī has confirmed in many interviews, both in print and on television, that it was her translations of the religious booklets about the pillars of Islam that she undertook in the early 1990s at the request of al-Maḥjūb that made her confident enough to take on translating *al-Muntakhab*.⁵⁸ It is still possible to find some of these books, in various editions, in libraries in the region. These Russian translations were part of the 'Essentials of Islam' series that had been published in other languages, including English, French, and German, and deal with subjects such as praying (*ṣalāt*), compulsory almsgiving (*zakāt*), fasting (*ṣiyām*), and pilgrimage (*ḥajj* and *ʿumra*).⁵⁹ The books are short (all are

---

56 By creedal aspects, I refer here to *ʿaqīda*-related criteria: that is, matters of Islamic creed. While these may vary slightly depending on the context, they can carry serious social consequences. For example, a translator who adheres to Ashʿarī theology (as is common among many traditional Egyptian scholars) may be excluded from Salafi translation circles, even if their Arabic and English are excellent, because their theological framework is not considered 'pure' according to the Salafi standards widely accepted among Saudi scholars. The Salafi global network refers to the transnational infrastructure of interconnected Muslims who subscribe to the Salafi creed. While they are often represented by graduates of the Islamic University of Madinah, the network is not limited to them.

57 Based on an official letter from the Wizārāt al-Awqāf to ʿAfīfī, al-Maḥjūb's proposal for these short booklets was made on a purely voluntary basis and did not involve any financial compensation for the translator. However, working on *al-Muntakhab* was not a purely voluntary project, as Zaqzūq stated in his interview that the translators were reimbursed on the basis of a salary of 40 Egyptian pounds for every 200 words. See Ṣalāḥ al-Bīlī, 'al-Qurʾān al-karīm: awwal tarjama kāmila li-tafsīrihi bi-l-Injlīzī wa-l-Faransī wa-l-Almānī wa-l-Rūsī', *al-Muwassar / al-Muṣawwar*, 18 May 1999, 28–30 (p. 30).

58 For example, https://www.youtube.com/watch?v=2m3784QUzyc&t=1710s; https://www.youtube.com/watch?v=NM_QLJBErRU

59 For example, Al-Bakhi Al-Kholi [al-Bahī al-Khūlī], *As-Siiam*, trans. by Somayia Afifi [Sumayya ʿAfīfī] (Cairo: Supreme Council for Islamic Affairs Ministry of Awqaf of the Arab Republic of Egypt, 1991); *Hadzh i Umra/palomnichestvo i maloe palomnihestvo*, trans. by A. Voronin, ed. by Somayia Afifi [Sumayya ʿAfīfī] (Cairo: Supreme Council for Islamic Affairs Ministry of Awqaf of the Arab Republic of Egypt, 1991); Abdel' Razzak Nofal' [ʿAbd al-Razzāq Nawfal], *As-Salat Molitva*, trans. by Sumayya ʿAfīfī (Cairo: The Supreme Council for Islamic Affairs Ministry of Awqaf of the Arab Republic of Egypt, 1991); Abdel' Razzak Nofal' [ʿAbd al-Razzāq Nawfal], *Zakiat*, 3rd edn, trans. by Somayia Afifi [Sumayya ʿAfīfī] (Cairo: The Supreme Council for Islamic Affairs Ministry of Awqaf of the Arab Republic of Egypt, 1991). The Russian translations were completed by ʿAfīfī, except for the *ḥajj-ʿumra* booklet, which was translated by someone named A.

3. 'I Quenched the Thirst of Seventy Million' 129

around fifty pages in Russian), and were first published in 1991, in a small format, under the auspices of the Supreme Council for Islamic Affairs in Cairo. The front matter states that: 'This book was prepared by The Supreme Council for Islamic Affairs of the Arab Republic of Egypt, which is trying to do its duty to our brothers in the Soviet Union, especially at this critical period, when our brothers there need support, guidance, and help.'[60] In comparison to later English editions, which have different content, the Russian versions have lower clarity and quality.[61] They also highlight the challenges of transliterating Islamic terms and Arabic names into Russian, a lexicon that had not yet been firmly established in the Russian Islamic context, and the sometimes peculiar transcriptions ʿAfīfī provided in these books have not been perpetuated.[62] The challenge of identifying suitable terminology for Islamic terms was an issue that ʿAfīfī openly acknowledged in several interviews,[63] and the difficulty it presents is evident in, for example, the definition of *ḥajj* ('pilgrimage') in one of the books that she edited in this series, where it is described as the 'yearly congress', or *kongress* (конгресс) of Muslims.[64] There are inaccuracies connected to Russian syntax, prepositions, and word endings, as well as typos, and the books would clearly benefit from the editorial expertise of a native Russian speaker. This, however, was a common aspect of foreign-produced Islamic publications in Russian of this period.[65] While the books do not follow

---

Voronin (whose identity I have not been able to determine) under the editorship of ʿAfīfī.

60 For example, in Nofal', *As-Salat Molitva*.
61 For example, Muhammad M. Ghaly, *al-Salat 'Prayer'*, rev. by Shawki Sokkary (Cairo: The Supreme Council for Islamic Affairs, 1998).
62 For example, she transcribed ʿishāʾ as *a'shaa* (А'шаа) whereas today it is commonly transliterated as *isha* (Иша).
63 For example, see Islām Rifʿat, 'Tarjamat al-Qur'an al-karīm ilā al-Rūsiyya ... afḍal aʿmālī', *al-ʿAmmāl* (*Usbuʿiyya tuṣdaru ʿanal-Ittiḥād al-ʿĀmm li-Naqābāt ʿUmmāl Miṣr*), 11 November 2002.
64 *Hadzh i Umra/palomnichestvo i maloe palomnihestvo*, trans. by A. Voronin, ed. by Somayia Afifi [Sumayya ʿAfīfī] (Cairo: Supreme Council for Islamic Affairs Ministry of Awqaf of the Arab Republic of Egypt, 1991).
65 The initial years after the collapse of the USSR saw the production of subpar Islamic booklets covering fundamental tenets and practices, which were riddled with typos and incorrect conceptual issues. These booklets generally reflected an absence of cooperation with and feedback from the Islamic communities they were aimed at. It is important to note that these problems were not exclusive to Egypt; similar issues could be observed with works produced by Turkish publishers, for instance Hakikat Kitabevi.

Islamic conventions in regard to referencing *hadīth*s and other Islamic sources—a feature often observable in modern style *daʿwa* literature—it is possible to find references to *Tafsīr al-Manār* and certain positions that can be attributed to Muḥammad ʿAbduh. The default target audience is assumed to be male, as can be seen, for example, in the fact that one translation is dedicated to 'brothers in the Soviet Union', as well as the way practical aspects of Islamic rituals are handled when a specific gender is not indicated. While this lack of gender inclusivity was not generally seen as a problem in Russian-speaking Muslim communities, it is important to note that the female identity of the translator did not influence the treatment of, or attitude to, gender in the translations of these short books. Although this is partly because she is replicating the attitudes and ideas of the male authors of the texts she is translating, ʿAfīfī does occasionally add some small notes and clarifications, but it is notable that none of these relate to gender issues. Although she does not entirely adopt the mantle of the 'invisible translator', she is invisible when it comes to gender.

The source texts which the translations were based on were written by different authors with diverse ideological orientations, such as ʿAbd al-Razzāq Nawfal (d. 1984), an Egyptian writer who is mainly popular for his books about the 'scientific' and numeric miracles of the Qur'an.[66] ʿAfīfī's translation of his book on *ṣalāt* accordingly reflects his adoption of the 'scientific' (*ʿilmī*) paradigm that was popular at the time. Consider, for instance, the explanation of the pre-prayer ablution, a Qur'anic requirement, which is presented as the 'best method for prevention of any kind of infection.'[67] The *ʿilmī* approach was a popular way of seeing and explaining Islamic rituals because it gave additional 'scientific' support to their religious meanings, and was an important feature of many Qur'anic commentaries that were produced during the twentieth century, including *al-Muntakhab*.

ʿAfīfī's translations of these short books on the pillars of Islam established her credibility with Egyptian religious bureaucrats and

---

66 Another author was al-Bahī al-Khūlī (d. 1977), who played a significant role in both the Muslim Brotherhood and state-sponsored religious institutions. He held teaching positions at al-Azhar, served as a member of the Supreme Council for Islamic Affairs, and was involved in publishing the journal *Minbar al-Islam* ('The Pulpit of Islam').

67 Nawfal, *As-Salat*, p. 26.

scholars as a reliable translator with the requisite skills to undertake translations of religious texts, particularly when it came to an ambitious state-project such as *al-Muntakhab*. However, before turning to explore the Russian *al-Muntakhab*, a few important remarks must be made regarding Qur'an translation in Egypt and the role of al-Azhar during the Mubarak era.

While *al-Muntakhab* did not end up becoming a primary, internationally-acclaimed source for understanding the meaning of the Qur'an, there were certainly hopes that it would do so among the early proponents of Qur'an translation in Egypt. This vision was nurtured following the success of the Cairo edition of the Qur'an, also known as the King Fuʾād edition, which was first printed in 1924 under the authority of al-Azhar, and which gained significant global authority to the extent that, as a printed and disseminated project, it practically held greater influence than any other Qur'an manuscript or printed edition, and has since become canonical (although it now faces competition from the *muṣḥaf* produced by the Saudi King Fahd Glorious Qur'an Printing Complex). In a similar vein, having realised the practical utility of Qur'an translations and the authoritative potential of such a project, scholars and statesmen tried unsuccessfully to win King Fuʾād's approval for the creation of a similarly Egyptian Qur'an translation.[68] In this regard, the Grand Imam of al-Azhar and *ijtihād*-advocate Muṣṭafā al-Marāghī (d. 1945) is an important figure in the history of this debate,[69] not least because he published a study in favour of the permissibility of Qur'an translation, in 1936, although he did emphasise his position that it should only be undertaken with the guidance and oversight of Islamic scholars. Al-Marāghī's study was followed by a memorandum that offered a detailed conceptual explanation of how Qur'an translation should be approached.[70] He thus serves as a genealogical starting point for the acceptance of Qur'an translation in the Azhari context. However,

---

68   El-Hussein A. Y. Aly, *Qurʾān Translation as a Modern Phenomenon* (Leiden: Brill, 2023), pp. 158–71.

69   See his study on the topic: Muḥammad Muṣṭafā al-Marāghī, *Baḥth fī tarjamat al-Qurʾān al-karīm wa-aḥkāmihā* (Cairo: Maṭbaʿat al-Raghāʾib, 1932); for more on al-Marāghī, see Rainer Brunner, 'Muḥammad Muṣṭafā l-Marāghī', in *Qurʾānic Hermeneutics in the 19th and 20th Century, Vol. 4*, ed. by Georges Tamer (Berlin: De Gruyter, 2024), pp. 173–90.

70   Aly, *Qurʾān Translation*, pp. 169–70.

this project was not realised in his lifetime, and subsequent changes in the Egyptian political regimes—with their new ideological framings of Arab socialism and pan-Arabism under Nasser and Sadat—might explain why al-Marāghī's project did not quickly come into fruition.

Things changed with al-Azhar's increasing influence under Mubarak's regime. This rise in influence could be a result of the ideological gap left by Nasserism and Sadat's economic reforms. In these circumstances, al-Azhar became a pillar of the government, serving as a trustworthy force capable of guiding a society to which Islamic values were becoming an increasingly important factor. This was especially pertinent given the existence of a number of violent militant groups that had already proved themselves to be a threat to the state regime. Thus, Mubarak's government was willing to give more power to al-Azhar, both to confront militant religious groups and to gain the acclaim of citizens by empowering the Azhari centrist and moderate position. Consequently, during the Mubarak era, Azhari theologians gained influence. They had a particularly strong presence in the media, and were provided with ample resources through which they were able to shape public discourse within the local Egyptian milieu, as well as aspire to project their influence beyond national borders.[71] It was precisely at this time, in the 1990s, when the *al-Muntakhab* translational project, with its global objectives, began to be realised.[72]

While the emergence of *al-Muntakhab*—both in translation and as an Arabic *tafsīr*— represents a later outcome of al-Marāghī's project, it differed in some aspects from the initial framing al-Marāghī conceived, for example in terms of the addition of 'scientific' explanations to the scripture. We will turn to the actual content of the translation and the discrepancies connected to *tafsīr ʿilmī* in the Russian translation of *al-Muntakhab*, after a few comments on ʿAfīfī's selection as the main translator and the factors contributing to her selection.

As mentioned earlier, al-Marāghī's initial guidelines for Qur'an translation required that the translator be of sound religious credentials

---

71 Steven Barraclough, 'Al-Azhar: Between the Government and the Islamists', *Middle East Journal*, 52:2 (1998), 236–49.

72 The original Arabic *al-Muntakhab* appeared as early as in 1961, followed by a series of editions. *Al-Muntakhab fī tafsīr al-Qurʾān al-karīm* (Cairo: al-Majlis al-Aʿlā li-l-Shuʾūn al-Islāmiyya, 1961).

and have the required scholarly expertise. In addition to having language proficiency in the target language, it was important that the translator(s) be known as pious Muslim individual(s).⁷³ When Sumayya ʿAfīfī was offered the job and accepted, her commitment to it was deeply rooted in her recognition of the project's importance—a recognition fostered by her interactions with individuals from the post-Soviet region. ʿAfīfī shared stories of her interactions with Russian-speaking students who approached her seeking advice and consulted her on a variety of issues, including those related to the Arabic language used in religious texts. Despite her high profile as a university professor, she was always accessible to anyone who wished to consult with her, and is remembered for her pietistic qualities and active efforts to educate students from the ex-USSR on Islamic practices. These qualities won her recognition among Russian-speaking Muslims who came to Egypt to study Arabic, with whom she fostered close bonds that went beyond merely academic association. Many of these students viewed her as an exemplar of Muslim piety, and ʿAfīfī herself has described how they sought her counsel on matters related to their studies, personal issues related to Islam, and even marriage. ʿAfīfī shared that it was common for her to receive religious questions and give advice about fasting, make-up, and clothes, such as 'to avoid jeans in prayers and avoid makeup during fasting.'⁷⁴ She also taught some students how to pray and read the Qur'an in Arabic.⁷⁵ Thus, ʿAfīfī's public image was also an important factor in her selection as the translator of *al-Muntakhab*. In addition to her academic qualifications, the fact that she was seen as a high-profile, pious Muslim woman and Egyptian national played a crucial role in her selection for this task.

At the time, Egyptian scholars adhered to the notion that, particularly when working with Islamic texts, especially the Qur'an, native Arabic-speakers possess a distinctive edge in delivering the 'correct' interpretation, having a native capacity for precise translation. ʿAfīfī's background harmonised with this predominant viewpoint: her status as a native speaker of Arabic with extensive skills in Russian reinforced conceptions about her suitability for the role of translating

---

73   Aly, *Qur'ān Translation*, p. 169.
74   Imbābī, 'Miṣriyya'.
75   al-Sayyid ʿAlī, 'Akhīran al-Qur'ān', p. 27.

of *al-Muntakhab*. Having said that, during the 1990s, Russian-language specialists were becoming more common in Egypt, thanks to the era of political cooperation with the USSR and the work of the Slavic department of Ayn Shams University, which had been training Russian-language specialists for several decades. It is interesting that, despite the availability of potential male translators, ʿAfīfī, a devout Muslim woman, was assigned the responsibility to lead the translation. Her appointment can be seen as part of a trend of appointing female translators[76]—in contrast to another trend in Muslim Qur'an translations whereby the main translator was often a man, while a woman (or women) edited the translated text, or assisted in the actual translation process in a supportive, secondary capacity.[77] It is my contention that the selection of ʿAfīfī can be seen as a result of the Ṣaḥwa, which led to the inclusion of 'pious' women in professional roles in established, state-run, or affiliated religious projects.

To ensure the translation's quality, ʿAfīfī personally selected several people to assist her in the process. One such person was ʿAbd al-Salām al-Mansī, an Egyptian colleague at Ain Shams University with expertise in Russian literature. He translated the commentary from *Sūrat Yūnus* up to *Sūrat al-Ḥijr*, and from *Sūrat al-Shūrā* up to *Sūrat al-Nās*, which constitutes approximately one-third of the whole *tafsīr*. His involvement was primarily a result of ʿAfīfī's concern that she might not have enough time to complete the work on her own, due to her advanced age. Another person who worked on the Russian *al-Muntakhab* was the Uzbek Arabist (and another woman) Rano Umarovna Khodzhaeva (b. 1941), with whom ʿAfīfī became acquainted in 1994 when Khodzhaeva was accompanying a group of Uzbek students to Cairo. Khodzhaeva was invited to work on the project in an editorial capacity, and her knowledge of Arabic and near-native Russian language proficiency meant that she was able to handle both the source and target texts with expertise. The 'Introduction' of the translation also mentions a less well-known figure, Polina Ivanovna Belova: a Russian convert and

---

[76] The fact that it was part of a trend and not simply an exception is illustrated by the fact that the two translators of the French *al-Muntakhab* (1998) were also Egyptian women: Ruqayya Jābir and ʿAshīra Kāmil (Rokaya Gabr et Achira Kamel).

[77] For example, in English: *The Qur'an: English Translation, Commentary and Parallel Arabic Text*, trans. by Maulana Wahiduddin Khan and Prof. Farida Khanam (Bandar Lampung: Goodword Books, 2011).

native speaker who was the wife of an Egyptian national. According to information provided in the Introduction, she made contributions to the final typesetting, and also provided additional editing. Significantly, none of the people who worked on the translation had a theological background, but the sources available stress the fact that they were Muslim. Mahmood has noted that, in the context of the Ṣaḥwa, women's involvement in *daʿwa* rested 'not so much on the doctrinal expertise as on one's moral uprightness and practical knowledge of the tradition'[78]— and in this light the representation of ʿAfīfī in the press as a pious Muslim woman with life-long scholarly ambitions and a successful career, but also Muslim piety, contributes to the image of her translation of *al-Muntakhab* as a 'piety project' that intersects with the state, its institutions, and the mobilisation of Muslim women. Mahmood's ideas are also relevant to ʿAfīfī's fluidity in terms of doctrine—namely, her lack of strict allegiance to any single theological school—and her assertions in interviews that it is the practical understanding of 'the correct Islamic culture' and religiosity (*mutadayyin(a)*) that should be the main criteria for translators of the Qur'an and religious texts.[79]

In order to demonstrate the institutional authority of the project, ʿAfīfī's Russian translation of *al-Muntakhab* (as with the other languages it was translated into) was prefaced with two introductions, reflecting the fact that the book was a joint project undertaken by al-Azhar and the Ministry of Awqāf. The first was written by the late Shaykh of al-Azhar, Muḥammad Sayyid Ṭanṭāwī (d. 2010), who held the post between 1996 and 2010, and the second by the Minister of Pious Endowments in the period from 1995 to 2011, Maḥmūd Ḥamdī Zaqzūq (d. 2020)—both of whom were well-known scholars with religious and academic weight in Egypt and beyond.

In regards to the content of the Russian *al-Muntakhab*, perhaps the most striking initial observation pertains to its form: *al-Muntakhab* falls somewhere between Qur'an translation and *tafsīr*, even though it is very limited in its addition of explanatory words and phrasing to

---

78 Saba Mahmood, *The Politics of Piety: The Islamic Revival and the Feminist Subject* (Princeton: Princeton University Press, 2005), p. 65.
79 Maḥmūd ʿUshb, "al-Duktūra Sumayya ʿAfīfī ashʿuru bi-saʿāda wa-anā utarjimu maʿānā al-Qurʾān ilā al-lugha al-Rūsiyya', *ʿAqīdatī*, 29 August 1995, p. 10; Islām Rifʿat, 'Tarjamat al-Qur'an al-karīm ilā al-Rūsiyya ... afḍal aʿmālī', *al-ʿAmmāl/al Omal*, 11 November 2002.

the translation/interpretation of the Qur'an. Additionally, it features footnotes that provide a more expansive space for commentary, reflecting a common approach of the time when *al-Muntakhab* was published. During this period, many Muslim scholars framed religious meanings within the 'scientific' paradigm, as mentioned above. Accordingly, the Arabic source text of *al-Muntakhab* includes various footnotes that imbue Qur'anic verses with a supplementary 'scientific' meaning.[80] However, there are clear discrepancies in the way this 'scientific' commentary is treated in the Arabic original and its Russian translation, both of which are included in the published work.

In the initial Egyptian edition of the Russian *al-Muntakhab*, the Arabic *tafsīr*, footnotes, and Qur'anic verses are printed on the right-hand pages, while the translation is on the left-hand pages. The Arabic footnotes take up a large amount of space, and often go into extensive scientific detail, using complex technical language. For example, in the footnote to Q 36:68, the Arabic commentary explains the complexities of the metabolic process, as well as the biological processes related to human ageing. To give another example, the word *akhḍar* ('green') in Q 36:80 is described as being a reference to chlorophyll, which plays a part in the process of photosynthesis. However, most of these scientific footnotes are not carried over into the Russian translation, and the Russian footnotes largely omit such explanations, predominantly comprising only short footnotes about linguistics, classic *tafsīr* stories from the *asbāb al-nuzūl*, and discussions of the ethical importance and meaning of Islamic principles, or rituals and rules, as well as historical information. The decision to omit the 'scientific' explanations present (and preserved) in the Arabic source text is also found in the translations of *al-Muntakhab* into other languages such as German (in the first edition), and this indicates that it was probably a decision made by the official board that oversaw the project, or a practical issue related to layout, rather than a personal choice by the individual translators. This seems even more likely given the book's massive length, which extends to nearly 1,300

---

80 This stands as a significant departure from the original vision of al-Marāghī, whose time already saw the influence of *tafsīr ᶜilmī*, though he did not promote it. His memorandum explicitly stated that the translation 'should not include any scientific explanation of the Qurʾān or refer to scientific terms or theories' (Aly, *Qur'ān Translation*, p. 170).

pages. What does seem significant here is that despite the fact that the project was technically overseen by an institutional authority, there was realistically no practical way for Azhari scholars to verify the final Russian version: the contents of the final product rested on trust rather than formal approval.

The idea behind limiting the translation to a more concise, *tafsīr*-like explanation in the target language implies that the translators were deliberately constrained in how much theological interpretation they could include. The Russian *al-Muntakhab* was intended to be representative of the Azhari Islamic vision, which in later decades would more persistently self-identify as the theological brand *wasaṭiyya*. The Azhari scholars' vision for the project should thus be conceived as an attempt to produce a non-controversial work that would reflect its institutional outlook, and express a centrist, moderate, and non-radical interpretation of Islam.

In the 1990s, as today, Al-Azhar promoted 'peaceful *daʿwa*'[81]—a framing that was shaped through its distance from and opposition to militant groups, Saudi Salafi interpretations,[82] and the politically-oriented Muslim Brotherhood. Its main official creedal orientation was often considered to be Ashʿarism.[83] However, this does not mean that there was a complete absence of voices from ideological opponents within the polyphony of Muslim perspectives in the extensive structures of al-Azhar and its affiliated institutions, both historically and up to the present day. When it comes to assigning a particular theological framework to the Arabic *al-Muntakhab*, it seems fair to say that this was not considered essential and, in fact, was intentionally avoided. However, it is difficult to represent a wide, non-sectarian orientation in a Qur'an translation/short *tafsīr*, especially given the fact that certain interpretations (and consequently even more so the translations of

---

[81] Matthew J. Kuiper, *Da'wa: A Global History of Islamic Missionary Thought and Practice* (Edinburgh: Edinburgh University Press, 2021), p. 231.

[82] For more about al-Azhar's opposition to Salafism, see Raihan Ismail, 'Al-Azhar and the Salafis in Egypt: Contestation of Two Traditions', *The Muslim World*, 113 (2023), 260–80.

[83] While al-Azhar's historical orientation has been Ashʿarī and it maintains a critical stance toward Salafism, it is important to note that al-Azhar's critique of Salafism has grown stronger in recent decades, particularly with the rise of ISIS. In the 1990s, the boundaries were much more blurred. See Ismail, 'Al-Azhar and the Salafis', p. 273.

these interpretations) necessarily involve translatorial choices that are inescapably and inherently charged with a particular theology.

This contradiction was avoided in the case of the Arabic *al-Muntakhab* (and its Russian translation) by a certain inconsistency in explaining and then rendering theologically charged verses—an approach that can be seen simultaneously advantageous and disadvantageous. Since some wording assumes a specific theological understanding, the word choice of the translator may end up reflecting a particular stance in sectarian disputes over the 'correct' interpretation, even if this is not their specific intention. Theological disputes between traditional Ashʿarī and Māturīdī scholars and Salafis over the anthropomorphic depictions of God in the Qur'an and their accurate interpretation, for example, present longstanding hermeneutical problems, and there are different and competing understandings which also find their reflection in Qur'an translations. In addressing verses depicting God's anthropomorphic attributes, the Arabic text of *al-Muntakhab* lacks consistency, and does not conform to one particular theological camp. A demonstrative example of this can be found in the explanation and rendering of the phrase *al-raḥmān ʿalā al-ʿarsh istawā* in Q 20:5, where Ashʿarī and Māturīdī interpretations usually opt for understanding the word *ʿarsh* (literally '[God's] Throne') as metaphorically implying God's power and authority, or other related notions, whereas Salafis prefer a literal interpretation and rendering. The Arabic *al-Muntakhab* does not show consistency in the way it deals with such anthropomorphic phrases, and nor do ʿAfīfī and her team in their translation. The Arabic *al-Muntakhab* explains the verse as having the meaning *ʿaẓīm al-raḥmā ʿalā mulkihi istawā* ('The One of great mercy, who established Himself over His dominion'), which ʿAfīfī translates as 'Milostivyi—On utverdilsia na Nebesnom Trone' ('The Merciful—He established himself on the Heavenly Throne'), where 'utverdilsia' is a word which was apparently borrowed from Krachkovskii's literal translation of the Qur'an.[84] Q 7:54, *istawā ʿalā al-ʿarsh*, is explained in the Arabic *tafsīr* as *istawlā ʿalā al-sulṭān al-kāmil fīhā* ('He seized complete authority over it') and its

---

[84] For more on Ignatii Krachkovskii's Qur'an translation, see Elvira Kulieva, 'In the Shadow of Orientalism: Tracing the Legacy of Ignatiĭ Krachkovskiĭ in Russian Salafi Qur'an Translations', in *Retranslating the Bible and the Qur'an*, ed. by Pieter Boulogne and Marijke de Lang (Leuven: Leuven University Press, 2024).

Russian translation, while different in wording, conforms to the Ashʿarī reading, so ʿAfīfī renders it as 'ustanovil na nikh Svoiu sovershennuiu vlast'' ('[He] established His perfect authority upon them [upon the sky and the earth]').[85] In some other places such as Q 32:4, *istawā ʿalā al-ʿarsh*, the Arabic *al-Muntakhab* takes the Qur'anic words literally and does not replace them with another, theological meaning, but just adds the phrase *istiwāʾ yalīqu bihi* ('in a manner befitting Him'), and the Russian version follows this, providing a literal translation of its specific wording—'utverdilsia na Trone, kak podobaet emu' ('established on the Throne in a in a manner befitting Him'). It seems reasonable to assume that the authors of the Arabic *al-Muntakhab* aimed to leave a certain ambiguity in its reading of this sensitive theological issue, which was intended to capture theological plurality and avoid sharp sectarianism.

Qur'an translations are frequently crafted by Muslim preachers or scholars to reflect their identities and ideological orientations, thereby influencing how their work is perceived within the Muslim community. But the Russian *al-Muntakhab* did not attempt to harmonise the inconsistencies or hermeneutical plurality of the Arabic original, instead incorporating them—and one might question whether this was a deliberate approach. ʿAfīfī's individual agenda was to adhere to established theological norms within a 'secure' environment of Arabic *tafsīr* where the translator's agency was minimised. Expanding the scope of analysis beyond her Qur'an translation to encompass the broader context of her other translated works can provide a more comprehensive account of her translatorial persona.

ʿAfīfī's selection of texts to translate offers an insight into her own conception of her Muslim identity. Examining the works she chose to publish under her own name might clarify her ideological orientation, as it seems only logical that her choice of texts reflects her personal beliefs and commitments as a Muslim. During the same decade that she worked on *al-Muntakhab*, she participated in co-translating another *tafsīr*, published by the German Islamic publisher SKD Bavaria, which was associated with the European network of the Muslim Brotherhood. This

---

85 For example, a similar approach against literalism can be also seen in Q 10:3 and Q 13:2.

drew extensively on Sayyid Quṭb as one of its primary sources.[86] While Quṭb is often attributed with laying the ideological groundwork for contemporary jihadism, it would be simplistic to confine his ideas solely to this domain. His ideas on Islamic social justice, for instance, enjoyed widespread popularity, and his influence can be traced across a wide spectrum of later thinkers. However, the fact that ʿAfīfī simultaneously worked on *tafsīr* projects for al-Azhar and SKD Bavaria complicates our picture of her ideological orientation. Moreover, during her work on *al-Muntakhab*, ʿAfīfī also translated a short book about the *aqīda ṣaḥīḥa* ('correct creed'), which she also often mentioned in interviews. This was not solicited by the Egyptian Supreme Council for Islamic Affairs, but was a translation of a work by the famous Salafi Saudi preacher Ibn Bāz for a Saudi publisher, Dār al-Iʿtiṣām, which was published in 1997. Considering the fact that she had already begun the translation of *al-Muntakhab* at this time, her involvement in the translation of this clearly ultra-Salafi work shows a degree of ideological latitude on ʿAfīfī's part. While Ibn Bāz's book is about basic tenets of the Muslim faith which are largely shared by all Muslims, this short brochure gives very vocal expression to a number of specific Salafi tropes. Its main agenda is clearly to explain the Salafi hermeneutic approach to the Qur'an and to promote the literal acceptance of Qur'anic statements related to anthropomorphism, which contradicts the approach used on many occasions in *al-Muntakhab*.[87] This work, in which Ashʿarīs and their hermeneutical tenets are explicitly criticised, stands in clear contradiction to the Azharī vision that at least partially informs *al-Muntakhab*. These factors complicate the assumption that ʿAfīfī had a specific ideological affiliation with al-Azhar, and instead showcase her religious identity as an eclectic when it comes to her doctrinal orientation.[88] Her lack of a formal theological education might have contributed to her openness towards projects with competing ideologies, but her openness may also reflect the Egyptian milieu of the 1990s when she was translating,

---

86 Ignatii Krachkovskii's Qur'an translation is used by ʿAfīfī in SKD Bavaria *tafsīr* as a direct translation of the Qur'an.

87 ʿAbd al-ʿAzīz b. ʿAbdallāh Ibn Bāz, *Istinnoe Verouchenie: Istinnaia 'Akida v Islame*, trans. by Sumayya ʿAfīfī (Riyadh: Al-Iʿtisam, 1997), pp. 19–24.

88 Financial motivation may typically explain the translation of diverse and conflicting materials, yet given the family's wealth this rationale fails to account for ʿAfīfī's ideologically 'omnivorous' approach to Islamic translation.

when these issues were not as politicised as they became after 9/11 in a process which subsequently intensified with the rise of ISIS in more recent times.

Another issue that comes to mind, specifically in terms of female involvement in translation projects relating to the Qur'an, is the idea of possible feminist hermeneutical 'resistance', as ʿAfīfī's academic background suggests that she was familiar with Soviet, Egyptian, and global feminist perspectives. This raises the question of whether she felt the need to address related issues in her translation of *al-Muntakhab*, especially since, as there was effectively no editorial control over the final Russian text, she had a free hand and thus could have potentially intervened in the text's 'traditional' approach to material related to women—either through specific word choices, additions, and omissions in the translation itself, or by her use of footnotes. Her approach to gender-related material can be understood by looking at some verses that are often evoked in gender-related discourse. For example, Q 4:34 contains two of the most controversial words related to feminist interpretations in modern times, *qawwāmūna* and *iḍribūhunna*.[89] In the Arabic *al-Muntakhab*, they are interpreted in light of the most historically widespread Sunni approach. This means that *qawwāma* is explained as referring to men's guardianship over and care for women. Following this, the word *ḍaraba* is interpreted literally as 'beating' but restricted with the addition of the word *khafīf* ('lightly'). This interpretation also appeared in ʿAfīfī's Russian translation, without any significant changes. Other verses often invoked in feminist critique of the classical *tafsīr* tradition—such as that about women's inheritance in Q 4:11, or women's testimony in Q 2:282 (which equates the testimony of one man to two women) —are also translated in a way that accords with the Arabic *al-Muntakhab*'s standard Sunni approach, and ʿAfīfī does not provide any additional clarification or explanation. This is also the case for Q 4:3, in which the Qur'an sets the

---

[89] 'Husbands should take good care of their wives, with [the bounties] God has given to some *qawwāmūna* (more) than others and with what they spend out of their own money. Righteous wives are devout and guard what God would have them guard in their husbands' absence. If you fear high-handedness from your wives, remind them [of the teachings of God], then ignore them when you go to bed, then *iḍribūhunna* (hit them). If they obey you, you have no right to act against them: God is most high and great'. M. A. S. Abdel Haleem (trans.), *The Qur'an* (Abingdon: Oxford University Press, 2008).

rules for polygyny. The Arabic *al-Muntakhab* offers a lengthy apologetic commentary on this verse, which is fully reproduced in the Russian translation. Its perspective on polygyny is modern in that it does not promote it, but rather defends it as a common historical practice that is relevant today only in special circumstances, such as war-induced scarcity of marriageable men, or the dignity of being a legal wife (or even a second, third, or fourth) compared to the status of a mistress. The defence presented revolves around the benefits of marriage for women, and does not address the issue of concubinage, which is also mentioned in the Qur'anic verse. In short, it can be said that *al-Muntakhab* manifests a modern 'refined' Sunni mainstream take on such issues, meaning that, for ʿAfīfī, its interpretations of these verses were not seen to be problematic in a way that compelled her to challenge them.

ʿAfīfī, therefore, was not inclined to resist the selected meanings offered to her by the institutional authority of al-Azhar, and hence she embodied the proper image of the female *dāʿiya* whose hermeneutic approach was celebrated within the Ṣaḥwa. It is apparent that, for her, translating gender issues 'in line' with the established norm was a conscious stance, shaped by her endorsement by the patriarchal social structure as a translator and transmitter. This stance, in turn, provided room for 'pious' female hermeneutical involvement in this previously male-dominated field. This paradigm of inclusion opened up in the 1990s, when women like ʿAfīfī secured their own spaces within the various structures of Islamic revival. It is important to understand that for women operating within the Ṣaḥwa like ʿAfīfī, their participation was not merely strategic subservience to Muslim patriarchal structures—rather, they viewed their activity as submission to God, which they considered liberating.[90]

An analogous example of this paradigm can be found in the career of Karīmān Ḥamza (1942–2023), who was a pioneer of female public *daʿwa* in the media, best known for her TV show *Qurʾān rabbī* ('the Qur'an of My Lord'). Her media representation bears similarities with that of ʿAfīfī in that she was also presented in terms of her 'firstness' as the first veiled TV presenter. The path trodden by her was not easy: as a veiled female preacher working in the media, she was seen in the initial

---

90 Ellen Anne McLarney, *Soft Force: Women in Egypt's Islamic Awakening* (Princeton: Princeton University Press, 2015), p. 12.

decades of the Sahwa as resisting both secular and religious forces in Egypt.[91] She did not confine herself to media alone, but also wrote her own exegetical work, *al-Luʾluʾ wa-l-marjān fī tafsīr al-Qurʾān* ('Pearls and Corals in Qur'anic Exegesis'), which subsequently received the approval of al-Azhar because it conformed to the Azhari Sunni approach to the interpretation of the Qur'an.[92] Her contributions in areas such as her TV show about the interpretation of the Qur'an, as well as her *tafsīr* authorship, signified her inclusion in various different aspects of *daʿwa* and, consequently, led to a redefinition of the structural boundaries of the field itself. However, her *tafsīr* was described specifically as 'a work for children and the youth': a common framing that demarcates the boundaries of women's *daʿwa* influence.[93] Similarly, the neutrality of ʿAfīfī's own celebrated work—her translation of the *tafsīr al-Muntakhab*—implied limited agency as well as compliance with the 'orthodox' norms delineated by Azhari scholars, upon which she relied.

The Spiritual Significance of Qur'an Translation

Muslim translators of the Qur'an often say that the translation process serves as a pietistic practice that has a transformative personal impact and spiritual significance for those involved. In ʿAfīfī's case, there are two dimensions to this pious practice: an outer dimension and an inner one. Outwardly, the project aimed to provide service to transnational Muslim communities under the banner of national Egyptian *daʿwa*. It contributed to the extension of Egyptian religious and national influence beyond its own state borders. ʿAfīfī's Russian translation of *al-Muntakhab* was closely intertwined not only with 'ummatic' aspirations to help non-Arabic speaking Muslims, but also with national sentiments, which ʿAfīfī often expressed through patriotic utterances and expressions of appreciation for the state's support for and involvement in the project.

---

91 For more about Karīmān Ḥamza, as well as other women who have been active in the Egyptian Islamic revival, see McLarney, *Soft Force*, p. 154.

92 For more about the *tafsīr* by Karīmān Ḥamza, and specifically her exegesis on polygamy, see Johanna Pink, *Muslim Qur'anic Interpretations Today: Media, Genealogies and Interpretative Communities* (Bristol: Equinox Publishing, 2018), pp. 172–81.

93 Pink, *Muslim Qur'anic Interpretations Today*, p. 173.

In turn, through President Mubarak's public support of her, the state honoured her alongside members of the male religious and intellectual elite, granting her various awards and honours.[94] This reflects the level of state support for the overall project of translating *al-Muntakhab* into a number of languages, not just Russian. Thus, Ḥamdī Zaqzūq, the Minister of Awqāf, provided an introduction that was inserted into the *al-Muntakhab* translations in various languages, not just the Russian one produced by ᶜAfīfī. Likewise, the Shaykh al-Azhar, Muḥammad Sayyid Ṭanṭāwī, highlighted in an interview the fact that '[*al-Muntakhab*] came as a direct directive from the President Mubarak for the service of Islamic call [...] and was distributed to all embassies and cultural centers in Egypt and abroad.'[95] This is a clear example of the way that religious institutions (primarily al-Azhar) reinforced the authority of the Egyptian nation-state through participating in, and endorsing, global *daᶜwa* projects; and, in turn, the state—which had sponsored the project—used these projects to reinforce both its own authority and that of the participating institutions at both the local and global level. This intertwining of religious and nationalistic dimensions is evident in ᶜAfīfī's description of her work. Supported by the authority of al-Azhar, she reciprocated by dedicating her translation to the nation, as personified by its leadership. For instance, she says in one interview: 'So far I have finished translating the meanings of *Sūrat al-Fātiḥa* and *Sūrat al-Baqara*, and I presented these as a gift to President Mubarak on Laylat al-Qadr last Ramadan.'[96] Women such as ᶜAfīfī who were involved in these kinds of state-sponsored religious projects were important agents who reinforced this dynamic, which in turn solidified and reinforced their personal reputation and standing.

---

94 ᶜAfīfī received various awards, including the Medal of the Arab Republic of Egypt for Science and Art, First Class, and has been honoured by various Islamic scholars. See, for example, Hishām al-ᶜAjamī, 'Mishwār al-ᶜaṭāʾ lil-ᶜulamāʾ wa-l-mufakkirīn alladhīna karramahum al-rāʾis: al-ᶜulamāʾ ishamū fī al-fikr al-insānī wa-l-taqrib bayna al-diyānāt', *al-Akhbār*, 10 August 1995, p. 5; Ṣafiyya al-Khūlī, 'al-Muntakhab ...ʾtᶜabnī', *al-Jumhūriyya*, 15 June 1999.

95 al-Bīlī, 'al-Qurʾān al-Karīm', p. 30; Saᶜīd Ḥalwī and Suhayla Naẓmī, 'Fī iḥtifāl Miṣr bi-dhikrā al-mawlid al-nabawī al-sharīf, mubārak yuqallidu 12 ᶜāliman wa-mufakkiran al-awsima wa-yakrumu al-fāʾizīn fī-l-musābaqāt al-Islāmiyya lil-awqāf', *al-Ahrām*, 10 August 1995, p. 13.

96 al-Sayyid ᶜAlī, 'Akhīran al-Qurʾān', p. 27; 'Akhbārahā', *al-Ahrām*, 12 May 1995.

3. 'I Quenched the Thirst of Seventy Million'   145

Beyond this, however, *al-Muntakhab* also had an 'inward', personal significance for the women involved in its translation, who perceived the task as a 'charitable act'. ʿAfīfī described her religious motivations for embarking on the project, implying that it was not only a religious duty but a personal 'investment' in the next life:

> I know well that a person who possesses knowledge is favored in the eyes of Allah, the Almighty. There is a noble *hadīth* that says 'when a son of Adam dies, all his [good] deeds come to an end, with the exception of three: a righteous child who prays for him, ongoing charity, and beneficial knowledge.' Despite having translated numerous literary books by prominent Soviet authors into Arabic, in recent years I had been contemplating doing something that would leave a lasting impact on people in general, and Muslims in particular. It was then that the idea of translating the meanings of the Qur'an into Russian came to my mind.[97]

This statement illustrates how the translation of the Qur'an held a distinctive significance for ʿAfīfī compared to other works, and carried a unique and personal devotional importance. For all the women involved in the project, the translation of *al-Muntakhab* had a profound personal impact on their lives. It can be seen to parallel the practice of working on a *tafsīr* in the classical Islamic tradition, which was seen as a crowning achievement for (male) scholars and was often undertaken in the last period of the scholar's life, and as a final purifying *khatm* (full recitation of the Qur'an). It is with this context that one should understand ʿAfīfī's reference in an interview to the passing of the typesetter and second editor—Polina Belova, who was advanced in age—soon after the completion of her work on *al-Muntakhab*, thereby implying that her work on the translation was a 'purifying' activity that prepared her, as a pious Muslim, for the last journey.[98] ʿAfīfī's family members recall that she prioritised her work on the translation of *al-Muntakhab*, setting aside her other academic responsibilities and leisure activities to fully concentrate

---

[97] al-Sayyid ʿAlī, 'Akhīran al-Qur'ān', p. 26. The fact that the translation was commissioned to ʿAfīfī might seem to contradict her claim to have an independent idea of translating. However, this can be reconciled by noting that she agreed to become the translator of *al-Muntakhab* because she already recognised the need for such a translation and understood its importance through her interactions with Russian-speaking students in Egypt.

[98] Ṭanāwī, 'Rāʾida al-lugha al-Rūsiyya wa-mutarjima ʿAbd al-Nāṣir, Dr. Sumayya ʿAfīfī: rawītu ẓamaʾan sabʿīna milyūnan', *al-Ittiḥād Dunyā*, 21 August 2003.

on the translation.⁹⁹ ʿAfīfī herself also shared that she prayed day and night that she would be able to complete the task, and that her work on the translation was undertaken in solitude, mirroring the religious practice of *khalwa* (sole spiritual retreat). These factors show that far from being a 'mechanical' process, the translation of the Qur'anic meanings had profound personal spiritual significance for ʿAfīfī. She even shared, with slight embarrassment, that while translating *al-Muntakhab* she had the ineffable feeling of 'immense satisfaction' and a miraculous sense of being surrounded by a 'radiant aura', which she was hesitant to elaborate on for fear that people might think that she was exaggerating.¹⁰⁰

The editor Rano Khodzhaeva is likewise on record as having said that her work on *al-Muntakhab* marked the fulfilment of her longstanding dream to work with the Qur'anic text, which dated back to the Soviet era—to the time that she received a *muṣḥaf* as a gift from an Arab scholar visiting the USSR.¹⁰¹ Fearing repercussions under the Soviet regime, she donated it to the state manuscript foundation, but later, eventually, retrieved it, and placed the *muṣḥaf* in her home library. Ever since that time, she had longed to have a chance to work closely with the Qur'an, an impossible ambition during the Soviet period. When asked to become an editor of *al-Muntakhab*, she gladly accepted, as it would finally give her the opportunity to fulfil her dream. Khodzhaeva recounts a mystical experience she had when, on the first night she began work on *al-Muntakhab*, she felt herself lifted up and experienced a sense of spiritual tranquility and ease.¹⁰² She interpreted this as a beautiful sign marking the start of her participation in this religious work.

These anecdotes clearly show that for the women involved in this project, the translation was much more than simply a commissioned work. For ʿAfīfī, it was more than the performance of a religious duty under the authoritative umbrella of the Azhari global *daʿwa*: it was an opportunity for the self-cultivation of piety. For Khodzhaeva, it was also an exploration of her own heritage, the embarkation on a long-awaited journey to learn more about the Qur'an after the end of the USSR.

---

99 She also confirmed this in the interview 'Mutarjima ʿAbd al-Nāṣir'.
100 al-Sayyid ʿAlī, 'Akhīran al-Qur'ān', p. 27.
101 Personal interview with Rano Khodzhaeva conducted by the author in January 2023.
102 Ibid.

Neither they nor, presumably, Belova, felt inspired to use the project as a space to promote a feminist reading of the Qur'an, or to challenge the Azhari interpretation which sustains the patriarchal norms dominant in traditional Muslim societies. Rather, for these women it was a space in which they were able to find a combination of outer and inner significance, and which gave them the opportunity to be remembered as both professional women and pious Muslims.

It might perhaps be surprising to a modern reader that a group of women from a wealthy social stratum—who were open to and acquainted with a variety of intellectual trends, owing to their wide geographical and ideological backgrounds—willingly adhered to the existing hermeneutical conservatism of *al-Muntakhab*. However, this relies on the assumption that if such a woman decides to participate in a religious project that sustains patriarchal norms, there would be necessarily an agenda on her part to subvert the prevalent narrative. For ᶜAfīfī and the other women involved in the *al-Muntakhab* project, their participation corresponded to other, larger global *daᶜwa* projects which have been described by Mahmood as 'piety movements' that sought to educate ordinary Muslims, in which women played an integral role. Participation in a *daᶜwa* mission was not only motivated by the primary goal of providing others with access to religious texts: the process itself also provided these women with the opportunity for spiritual growth on their own personal transformative journeys. The involvement of women within larger piety movements—such as the mosque movements described by Mahmood, in which the public representation of religiosity played a significant role—meant that issues relating to women's outward appearance, and involvement in religious rituals and other aspects of an 'Islamic lifestyle', took on a deep personal relevance, which was directed towards the cultivation of virtues and formation of 'pious dispositions' within the conceptual frame of the Islamic tradition.[103] The

---

[103] Saba Mahmood described the Egyptian urban mosque movement of that period as a grassroots initiative among Muslim women (particularly in Cairo), where women increasingly began attending and organising mosque-based religious study groups led by other women. These gatherings aimed to cultivate Islamic virtues, ethical dispositions, and religious subjectivities. According to Mahmood's study, the women involved were not merely seeking religious knowledge, but rather, they were engaged in a programme of ethical self-transformation, moral cultivation, and spiritual discipline grounded in Islamic texts and practices. See Mahmood, *The Politics of Piety*, p. 133.

way that the women involved in *al-Muntakhab* describe their work also shows how, for them, working within the field of traditional Qur'anic exegesis—in this case in the guise of its modern continuum of the genre, translation—allowed them to participate in a transformative project that also benefitted their personal piety. Moreover, they clearly perceived *al-Muntakhab* as a trustworthy repository of Qur'anic meanings, which facilitated profound experiences that transcended issues of outward appearance and behavioural norms.

Some Remarks on Reception

The translation of *al-Muntakhab* into Russian signalled the recognition among Egyptian scholars and politicians of emerging opportunities in the post-Soviet region, and the potential for Egyptian soft power through the assertion of religious authority. It reflected Egypt's desire to position itself as a key player in contemporary global Islam, as a counter to other Islamic projects like Saudi Salafi *daʿwa*, which had had an active presence in Russian-language publishing since the 1990s. As early as 1991, ʿAfīfī's booklets about the pillars of Islam were actively being distributed in post-Soviet nations, as evidenced by the number of reprints of these books. This is significant, as it indicates both the ability of Egyptian actors to find distribution networks for religious materials (presumably in part due to the lack of religious books in Russian at the time) as well as the willingness of various local Islamic institutions to accept al-Azhar as a valid Islamic authority. However, the fact that these booklets were not written specifically for the post-Soviet region meant that they were unable to address regionally-specific issues. For example, they were mostly distributed among the Turkic nations, which were historically predominantly Ḥanafī in their religious practices. The books, however, lacked a clear *madhhab* focus and mostly reflected ideas held by the Shāfiʿī legal school that was predominant in Egypt, but not in the ex-Soviet countries in which they were disseminated. The securitisation of Islam in the region also resulted in a gradually increasing trend of *madhhab*isation of the state-related Islamic institutions. This is in contrast to the Egyptian paradigm, which instead aligned with the prevalent 'post-madhhab character of modern religiosity' of the Arab world.[104] This, in addition to the quality of these works, was perhaps one of the reasons why local religious organisations did not subsequently support their distribution. However, while these booklets are now largely out of use, it is still possible to find them in libraries across Russia and Kazakhstan, as well as in private collections.

The dissemination of *al-Muntakhab* in Russian was primarily driven by al-Azhar's institutional prestige. The discourse surrounding this work in the Egyptian press could not be related to the target language environment, which shows how ʿAfīfī's public representation was mainly restricted to Egypt. Al-Azhar played the main role in the institutional acceptance for and marketing of the Russian *al-Muntakhab*—and in this context, no emphasis was given to the female gender of the translator. Since its first publication in 2000, the book has been actively disseminated through al-Azhar's institutional networks, reaching audiences in Russia and neighbouring countries such as Kazakhstan, Kyrgyzstan, and Ukraine. This is one element of a wider endeavour on the part of the Egyptian state. In Kazakhstan in 1993, for example, Presidents Nursultan Nazarbayev and Husni Mubarak agreed to collaboratively establish Nur-Mubarak University. This university, whose main focus is on training imams and offering education for local *madrasa*s, promotes the Egyptian interpretation of Islam while incorporating specific aspects of Kazakhstan's religious and cultural traditions. It is managed by local Muftiate (state-promoted Islamic administrative structure) and overseen by appointed Egyptian-Azhari scholars, who serve as rectors. Up to the current date, ʿAfīfī and al-Mansī's Russian translations can be accessed through Nur-Mubarak University. On the wider stage, after the initial publication of *al-Muntakhab* there has been a continuous flow of reprints, with some changes and local adaptations. For example, the Arabic *tafsīr* has been removed in later editions due to the fact that it is incomprehensible to the

---

104 The differences between the legal schools were mentioned only in ʿAfīfī's translation of Nofal's book on *zakāt*, but Ḥanafī opinions specifically were not explained even though this was the main school of the target audience. The prevalence of the trend of *talfīq* in Egypt was clearly at odds with the growing indoctrination of state-Islam narratives in Russia and the majority of Central Asian states. The lack of understanding of these particularities on the part of the Egyptian publisher could be one of the reasons why these books were not in use for long. On *talfīq* in popular legal manuals in Egypt, see Mahmood, *The Politics of Piety*, p. 81.

majority of people and also makes the volume heavy and unwieldy, and the Qur'anic text has been localised by replacing the original Egyptian *naskh* with the locally developed Kazan *basmasi*.

The Russian *al-Muntakhab* was predominantly promoted by local statist religious organisations in the countries of the region during the years they lacked their own Qur'an translations, or before they produced these. A number of reprints have been undertaken in Russia, for example by Tatar publishers in 2009 and 2012,[105] while the most recent edition was published by the Muftiate of the Kabardino-Balkarian Republic in Russia in 2017.[106] Confirming the continued prioritisation of the institution that produced the translation over the translators themselves, the official representative of the Muftiate publicly reassured readers about the translators' affiliation with Ain Shams University, incorrectly stating that it is a branch of al-Azhar.[107] The translation is also usually present in online and offline libraries of state-related Muftiate in Kazakhstan and Kyrgyzstan, where it has also been reprinted.

In Uzbekistan, print editions have not been made available to the wider public despite the Uzbeki nationality and institutional affiliation of the main editor, Rano Khodzhaeva. However, *al-Muntakhab* can currently be accessed for free online on various websites, which perhaps explain why it features on some Uzbeki governmental websites that use Russian. The use of the Russian *al-Muntakhab* as a source for Qur'anic citations on these websites shows that many post-Soviet, state-related Islamic institutions continue to recognise al-Azhar as a reliable authority.[108] Al-Azhar's history, as well as its modern positionality, continues to generate local trust and respect.[109] In contrast, the Ashʿarī leanings of this work have made it a focal point for critique and disapproval among

---

105 See, for example, Sumayya ʿAfīfī and ʿAbd al-Salām al-Mansī (trans.), *Koran al-Muntakhab fi Tafsir al'-Kuran al'-Karim* (Kazan: Akademiia poznaniia, 2009).
106 See footnote 4.
107 Otarov, 'Raz"iasnenie po povodu'.
108 For example, see these Uzbekistan state-related Islamic websites: http://dkm.gov.uz/ru/goroda-upomanutye-v-korane-medina and http://old.muslim.uz/index.php/rus/mir/item/6094
109 This can be also supported through the statistical data of student numbers from the region. See Masuda Bano, 'Protector of the "al-Wasatiyya" Islam: Cairo's al-Azhar University', in *Shaping Global Islamic Muslim Societies Discourses: The Role of al-Azhar, al-Medina and al-Mustafa*, ed. by Masooda Bano, Keiko Sakurai, and Helena de Felipe (Edinburgh: Edinburgh University Press, 2015), pp. 73–92 (p. 75).

Salafi-oriented Muslims. Their criticism of it, and warnings against it, are apparent in numerous online debates, illustrating the ongoing contest between the state's anti-Salafi tendencies and independent Salafi circles, and reflecting the sectarian atmosphere of the Russian-speaking Islamic milieu.

It is important to note that Egyptian *daʿwa* towards the post-Soviet space has exhibited a notable lack of awareness of the national revivalist trends that emerged following the collapse of the USSR. These trends often saw local Islamic revivals intertwining with the use of national languages. Consequently, Egypt's reliance on the imperial *lingua franca* of Russian failed to demonstrate a forward-looking strategy. Additionally, the securitisation of Islam—which became a shared concern among the newly established nation-states in the region—has contributed to shaping the discourse of 'traditional Islam'. In Russia, for instance, this discourse aimed to foster loyal and local authorities, favouring them over foreign actors. In recent decades, there has also been an increase in Qur'an translation activity by local institutions, leading to competitive dynamics among these local authorities. As a result, *al-Muntakhab*, without the continuous support of robust institutional backing, lacks a distinct advantage in the market. The main reason why the large Muftiates in Russia have not promoted *al-Muntakhab* is that printing their own Qur'an translations became a means to enhance their own prestige, and to produce a marketable good. For example, Shamil Aliautdinov (b. 1974)—a popular imam who is associated with the Moscow-based Muftiate DUMRF (Spiritual Administration of Muslims of the Russian Federation), and who is himself a graduate of al-Azhar—decided to produce his own Qur'an translation in 2011.[110] In another example, Akhmad Abu Yakhya aka Kirill Ivanovich Ivaniugo (b. 1983)—an Islamic preacher associated with Tatarstan Muftiate DUMRT (Spiritual Administration of Muslims of the Republic of Tatarstan)—used to recommend *al-Muntakhab* on the basis that it was prepared by a group of Azhari scholars. However, he criticised *al-Muntakhab* for mixing the wording of the Qur'anic translation and the commentary together, and pointed out a 'number of semantic errors

---

110 *Sviashchennyi Koran. Smysly*, 4 vols, trans. by Shamil Aliautdinov (St. Petersburg: Dilia, 2009/2020).

and stylistic errors',[111] advocating that editorial volunteers rectify these errors. Ultimately, however, he opted to develop a new Qur'an *tafsīr* in Russian using his own team, and subsequently a new Russian Qur'an translation, which was more aligned with the institutional branding of Tatarstan's Muftiate. This sequence of events demonstrates the considerable impact of marketing, claims to authority, and rivalry for institutional prestige in the contemporary genre of Qur'an translation. The potential recognition of a Qur'an translation, whether produced individually or institutionally linked to a specific local authority, tends to take precedence over the inclination to share in the transnational acclaim of existing works. Despite these factors, while the narrative of ʿAfīfī remains relatively unknown among the Russian-speaking public, the impact of her *daʿwa* has undeniably left a mark on the shaping of Islam in the post-Soviet space.

Bibliography

Abdel Haleem, M. A. S. (trans.), *The Qur'an* (Abingdon: Oxford University Press, 2008).

ʿAfīfī, Sumayya, and ʿAbd as-Salām al-Mansī (trans.), *Znachenie i Smysl Korana* (Munchen: SKD Bavaria, 1999).

——, and ʿAbd al-Salām al-Mansī (trans.), *al-Muntakhab fī tafsīr al-Qurʾān al-karīm* (Cairo: al-Ahrām al-Tijāriyya, 2000).

——, and ʿAbd al-Salām al-Mansī (trans.), *Koran al-Muntakhab fi Tafsir al'-Kuran al'-Karim* (Kazan: Akademiia poznaniia, 2009).

—— [Afifi, Somaiia M.], 'Leksikologicheskii analiz glagolov idti-khodit' i ikh proizvodnykh v sovremennom russkom iazyke' (unpublished dissertation, M. V. Lomonosov Moscow State University, 1964).

al-ʿAjamī, Hishām, 'Mishwār al-ʿaṭāʾ lil-ʿulamāʾ wa-l-mufakkirīn alladhīna karramahum al-rāʾis: al-ʿulamāʾ ishamū fī al-fikr al-insānī wa-l-taqrib bayna al-diyānāt', *al-Akhbār*, 10 August 1995.

'Akhbārahā', *al-Ahrām*, 12 May 1995.

Aly, El-Hussein A. Y., *Qurʾān Translation as a Modern Phenomenon* (Leiden: Brill, 2023).

---

111 Preface to 'Tafsir Korana', https://azan.ru/tafsir

Anderson, Benedict, *Imagined Communities: Reflections on the Origin and Spread of Nationalism* (London: Verso, 2006).

ᶜUshb, Maḥmūd, 'al-Duktūra Sumayya ᶜAfīfī ashᶜuru bi-saᶜāda wa-anā utarjimu maᶜānā al-Qurʾān ilā al-lugha al-Rūsiyya', *ᶜAqīdatī*, 29 August 1995.

'Awwal ᶜArabiyya tutarjimu maᶜānī al-Qurʾān al-karīm ilā al-Rūsiyya ... al-duktura Sumayya ᶜAfīfī: al-lugha hiya silāḥunā li-nashr dīninā wa-thaqāfatinā', *Kull al-Usra*, 23 August 1995.

'Awwal Miṣriyya tutarjimu tafāsīr al-Qurʾān al-karīm lil-Rūsiyya', *Sayyidatī*, 22:1101 (2002).

al-Bakhi Al-Kholi [al-Bahī al-Khūlī], *As-Siiam*, trans. by Somayia Afifi [Sumayya ᶜAfīfī] (Cairo: Supreme Council for Islamic Affairs Ministry of Awqaf of the Arab Republic of Egypt, 1991).

Bano, Masuda, 'Protector of the "al-Wasatiyya" Islam: Cairo's al-Azhar University' in *Shaping Global Islamic Muslim Societies Discourses: The Role of al-Azhar, al-Medina and al-Mustafa*, ed. by Masooda Bano, Keiko Sakurai, and Helena de Felipe (Edinburgh: Edinburgh University Press, 2015), pp. 73–92.

'Barnāmaj Muwājihāt maᶜa d. Sumayya Muḥammad Mūsa ᶜAfīfī', online video recording, *YouTube*, n.d., https://www.youtube.com/watch?v=2m3784QUzyc&t=1704s

Barraclough, Steven, 'Al-Azhar: Between the Government and the Islamists', *Middle East Journal*, 52:2 (1998).

al-Baṭil, Thanāʾ, 'D. Sumayya ᶜAfīfī: tarjamat tafsīr al-Qurʾān al-karīm lil-Rūsiyya', *al-Jumhūriyya*, 20 May 2004.

Bier, Laura, *Revolutionary Womanhood: Feminisms, Modernity, and the State in Nasser's Egypt* (Stanford: Stanford University Press, 2011).

al-Bīlī, Ṣalāḥ, 'al-Qurʾān al-karīm: awwal tarjama kāmila li-tafsīrihi bi-l-Injlīzī wa-l-Faransī wa-l-Almānī wa-l-Rūsī', *al-Muṣawwar*, 18 May 1999.

Brunner, Rainer, 'Muḥammad Muṣṭafā l-Marāghī', in *Qur'ānic Hermeneutics in the 19th and 20th Century, Vol. 4*, ed. by Georges Tamer (Berlin: De Gruyter, 2024), pp. 173–90.

Dawisha, Karen, 'Soviet Cultural Relations with Iraq, Syria and Egypt 1955–70', *Soviet Studies* 27:3 (1975).

el-Kholy, El-Bahay, *Al Siyam 'Fasting'*, trans. by M. Hawary Ahmad (Cairo: The Supreme Council for Islamic Affairs, 1998), https://ia804701.us.archive.org/18/items/waqena/0560.pdf

Ghaly, Muhammad M., *al-Salat 'Prayer'*, rev. by Shawki Sokkary (Cairo: The Supreme Council for Islamic Affairs, 1998).

Gölz, Olmo, 'Collectives', in *Compendium heroicum*, ed. by Ronald G. Asch, Achim Aurnhammer, Georg Feitscher, Anna Schreurs-Morét, and Ralf von den Hoff (Freiburg: University of Freiburg), https://doi.org/10.6094/heroicum/kolle1.0.20220905, 5 September 2022, https://www.compendium-heroicum.de/lemma/collectives/

Hadzh i Umra/palomnichestvo i maloe palomnihestvo, trans. by A. Voronin and ed. by Somayia Afifi [Sumayya ʿAfīfī] (Cairo: Supreme Council for Islamic Affairs Ministry of Awqaf of the Arab Republic of Egypt, 1991).

Ḥalwī, Saʿīd, and Suhayla Naẓmī, 'Fī iḥtifāl Miṣr bi-dhikrā al-mawlid al-nabawī al-sharīf, mubārak yuqallidu 12 ʿāliman wa-mufakkiran al-awsima wa-yakrumu al-fāʾizīn fī-l-musābaqāt al-Islāmiyya lil-awqāf', *al-Ahrām*, 10 August 1995.

Henze, Paul B., 'Flexible Opportunism', in *Soviet Strategy and Islam*, ed. by Alexandre Bennigsen, Paul B. Henze, George K. Tanham, and S. Enders Wimbush (New York: Palgrave Macmillan, 1989), pp. 79–100.

http://dkm.gov.uz/ru/goroda-upomanutye-v-korane-medina

http://old.muslim.uz/index.php/rus/mir/item/6094.

Ibn Bāz, ʿAbd al-ʿAzīz b. ʿAbdallāh, *Istinnoe Verouchenie: Istinnaia 'Akida v Islame*, trans. by Sumayya ʿAfīfī (Riyadh: Al-Iʿtisam, 1997).

Ibn Kasir (Ibn Kathīr al-Dimashqī), *Tolkovanie Korana*, trans. by Anastasiia Shipilina (Moscow: Al' Kitab, 2022).

Imbābī, Īmān Muḥammad, 'Miṣriyya tutarjimu maʿānī al-Qurʾān ilā al-Rūsiyya', *al-Ahrām al-Masāʾiyy*, 27 May 1995.

——, 'Awwal mutarjima li-maʿānī al-Qurʾān al-karīm lil-lugha al-Rūsiyya', *al-Ahrām*, 1 December 2001.

'Imraʾa nājiḥa', *al-Liwāʾ al-Islāmī*, 31 July 2003.

Ismail, Raihan, 'Al-Azhar and the Salafis in Egypt: Contestation of Two Traditions', *The Muslim World*, 113 (2023), 260–80, https://doi.org/10.1111/muwo.12455

Katsakioris, Constantin, 'Soviet Lessons for Arab Modernization: Soviet Educational Aid to Arab Countries after 1956', *Journal of Modern European History*, 8:1 (2010), https://doi.org/10.17104/1611-8944_2010_1_85

——, 'Statistics on Arab Students in the USSR (1959–1991)', in *Russian-Arab Worlds: A Documentary History*, ed. by Eileen Kane, Masha Kirasirova, and Margaret Litvin (Abingdon: Oxford University Press, 2023), pp. 236–44.

Khan, Maulana Wahiduddin, and Farida Khanam (trans.), *The Qur'an: English Translation, Commentary and Parallel Arabic Text* (Bandar Lampung: Goodword Books, 2011).

Khashaba, Narmīn, 'Sumayya ʿAfīfī: awwal tarjama Rūsiyya li-tafsīr al-Qurʾān al-karīm', *Kolenas/ Kull al-nās*, 20–26 February 2002.

al-Khūlī, Ṣafiyya, 'al-Muntakhab ... atᶜabanī', *al-Jumhūriyya*, 15 June 1999.

——, 'D. Sumayya ᶜAfīfī: dīnunā al-samḥ ... bi-l-lugha al-Rūsiyya', *al-Jumhūriyya*, 21 November 2002.

Kuiper, Matthew J., *Da'wa: A Global History of Islamic Missionary Thought and Practice* (Edinburgh: Edinburgh University Press, 2021).

Kulieva, Elvira, 'In the Shadow of Orientalism: Tracing the Legacy of Ignatiĭ Krachkovskiĭ in Russian Salafi Qur'an Translations', in *Retranslating the Bible and the Qur'an*, ed. by Pieter Boulogne and Marijke de Lang (Leuven: Leuven University Press, 2024).

Linant de Bellefonds, Y., 'Ḍarūra', in *Encyclopaedia of Islam New Edition Online (EI-2 English)*, https://doi.org/10.1163/1573-3912_islam_SIM_1730

Litvin, Margaret, 'Should Dormitory Bathrooms Have Doors? Zakaria Turki's *An Upper Egyptian among the Russians* (1967–1972)', in *Russian-Arab Worlds: A Documentary History*, ed. by Eileen Kane, Masha Kirasirova, and Margaret Litvin (Oxford: Oxford University Press, 2023), pp. 245–54, https://doi.org/10.1093/oso/9780197605769.003.0025

al-Maghāwrī, ᶜAbd al-Fattāḥ, 'Sumayya ᶜAfīfī ... riḥla ᶜaṭāʾ', *Afāq ᶜArabiyya*, 8 September 2005.

Mahmood, Saba, *The Politics of Piety: The Islamic Revival and the Feminist Subject* (Princeton: Princeton University Press, 2005).

al-Marāghī, Muḥammad Muṣṭafā, *Baḥth fī tarjamat al-Qurʾān al-karīm wa-aḥkāmihā* (Cairo: Maṭbaᶜat al-Raghāʾib, 1932).

McLarney, Ellen Anne, *Soft Force: Women in Egypt's Islamic Awakening* (Princeton: Princeton University Press, 2015).

'Mutarjima ᶜAbd al-Nāṣir', *al-Shabāb*, June 2004.

Nofal', Abdel' Razzak [ᶜAbd al-Razzāq Nawfal], *Zakiat*, 3rd edn, trans. by Somayia Afifi [Sumayya ᶜAfīfī], (Cairo: The Supreme Council for Islamic Affairs Ministry of Awqaf of the Arab Republic of Egypt, 1991).

——, *As-Salat Molitva*, trans. by Somayia Afifi [Sumayya ᶜAfīfī] (Cairo: The Supreme Council for Islamic Affairs Ministry of Awqaf of the Arab Republic of Egypt, 1994).

Otarov, Khyzir, 'Raz"iasnenie po povodu izdaniia knigi Al' Muntakhab Tolkovanie Sviashchennogo Korana (perevod s arabskogo na russkiĭ)', online video recording, *kbrdum*, 4 August 2017, https://www.kbrdum.ru/video/2186-raz-yasnenie-po-povodu-izdaniya-knigi-al-muntakhab-tolkovanie-svyashchennogo-korana-perevod-s-arabskogo-na-russkij-imam-khatyb-otarov-khyzir

Pink, Johanna, *Muslim Qur'anic Interpretations Today: Media, Genealogies and Interpretative Communities* (Bristol: Equinox Publishing, 2018).

———, 'National Hero', in *Compendium heroicum*, ed. by Ronald G. Asch, Achim Aurnhammer, Georg Feitscher, Anna Schreurs-Morét, and Ralf von den Hoff (Freiburg: University of Freiburg), https://doi.org/10.6094/heroicum/ne1.0.20220919, 19 September 2022, https://www.compendium-heroicum.de/lemma/national-hero/

Porokhova, Iman Valeriia (trans.), *Koran: perevod smyslov i kommentarii* (Moscow: Ripol Klassik, 2022).

Rifʿat, Islām, 'Tarjamat al-Qurʾan al-karīm ilā al-Rūsiyya … afḍal aʿmālī', *al-ʿAmmāl* (*Usbuʿiyya tuṣdaru ʿan al-Ittiḥād al-ʿĀmm li-Naqābāt ʿUmmāl Miṣr*), 11 November 2002.

Rock-Singer, Aaron, *Practicing Islam in Egypt: Print Media and Islamic Revival* (Cambridge: Cambridge University Press, 2019).

al-Sayyid, Hiba ʿAlī, 'Akhīran al-Qurʾān bi-l-Rūsiyya', *Ḥawāʾ*, 10 June 1995.

Schlechtriemen, Tobias, 'Transgressiveness', in *Compendium heroicum*, ed. by Ronald G. Asch, Achim Aurnhammer, Georg Feitscher, Anna Schreurs-Morét, and Ralf von den Hoff (Freiburg: University of Freiburg), https://doi.org/10.6094/heroicum/ge1.0.20220819, 19 August 2002, https://www.compendium-heroicum.de/lemma/transgressiveness/

Sviashchennyi Koran. Smysly, 4 vols, trans. by Shamil Aliautdinov (St. Petersburg: Dilia, 2009/2020).

Tafsir Korana [online], https://azan.ru/tafsir

Ṭanāwī, Najwā, 'Rāʾida al-lugha al-Rūsiyya wa-mutarjima ʿAbd al-Nāṣir, Dr. Sumayya ʿAfīfī: Rawītu ẓamaʾan sabʿīna milyūnan', *al-Ittiḥād Dunyā*, 21 August 2003.

Turgenev, Ivan, *al-Aʿzab*, trans. by Sumayya ʿAfīfī (Kuwait: Ministry of Information, 1983).

Vampilov, Alexander, *Wadāʿ fi Yūniyū*, trans. by Sumayya ʿAfīfī (Kuwait: Ministry of Information, 1993).

PART II

STATE POLICIES AND QUR'AN TRANSLATIONS

4. The State, 'Official' *Ulamā'* and Tatar Qur'an Commentary-Translations in Russia

Elmira Akhmetova[1]

Introduction

During the launch of a new translation of the Qur'an into Tatar, *Kälam Shärif: Mäghnäwi Tärjemä* ('*Kalām Sharīf*: A Semantic Translation') on 18 October 2019 in Moscow, Kamil Samigullin—the Mufti of the Republic of Tatarstan—posed the rhetorical question: 'Why should the Arabs authorise our Qur'an?' He further elaborated: 'We do not wait for *fatwas*[2] from Turkey, Pakistan, Egypt, or Saudi Arabia. When a *fatwa* is necessary, we [Muslim scholars of Russia—in this case, Tatars] get together, debate it, and reach a consensus. Come, let the Arabs learn

---

1   This paper was written under the fund provided by the Alexander von Humboldt Foundation Award for Experienced Researchers (2021–23), entitled 'Tatar Translations and Commentaries on the Qur'an in Imperial Russia'.

2   By *fatwa*, Mufti Samigullin here refers to a special certification provided by Muslim institutions that authorises a specific Qur'an translation. To minimise the possibility of unconventional and different interpretations, al-Azhar University, the Saudi Ministry of Islamic Affairs and Endowments, and the King Fahd Complex for Printing the Holy Qur'an have each produced their own guidelines and standards for evaluating and approving new translation works.

from us. Why should they verify our Qur'an? How can I trust our book to some Arab who doesn't know a single word of Tatar?'[3]

Samigullin's statement exposes the realities concerning matters of representation, the contested nature of Islamic authority, and religious knowledge creation in contemporary Tatar society in Russia. When it comes to the Tatars, who represents Islam today? Who judges whether a particular Tatar translation of the Qur'an and interpretation of Islam is accurate? What are the primary motivations behind contemporary vernacular translations and interpretations of the Qur'an? Additionally, what role does the Russian state play in these readings?

Thijl Sunier has described the domestication of Islam that occurred in Europe during the second half of the twentieth century as having two primary targets: national integration and the securitisation of Islam.[4] The process of domesticating Islam in European countries has a political aspect that necessitates new vernacular readings and interpretations of the Qur'an which primarily serve the state's domestic and international policies, as well as national security and other interests. This implies the secular state's intervention in the actual content of Islamic systems and convictions, usually through the mechanism of state-sponsored, official Muslim religious bodies—a process which Hernandez Aguilar and Zubair Ahmad have referred to as the 'policing of the Qur'an' in the German context.[5] However, Russia appears to be quite a different case to Western European countries, in which Muslim populations are primarily composed of recent immigrants.

Russia's history of intervention in the affairs of its Muslim population extends over two centuries, beginning in the days of the empire and continuing through the Soviet era to the present time. In 1788, Catherine II (r. 1762–96) ordered the establishment of the first Islamic directorate (commonly known as a muftiate) in Russia: the Orenburg Muslim Spiritual Assembly (OMSA, Orenburgskoe Magometanskoe

---

3   Razim Sabirov and Elena Kolebakina-Usmanova, 'Kamil Samigullin: Pochemu araby dolzhny proveriat' nash Koran' [Why Should Arabs check our Qur'an], *Business Gazeta*, 18 October 2019, https://m.business-gazeta.ru/article/442980

4   Thijl Sunier, 'Toward a Common European Islamic Landscape?', in *Yearbook of Muslims in Europe*, vol. XII, ed. by Egdunas Racius et al. (Leiden: Brill, 2021), pp. 1–18 (p. 3).

5   Luis Manuel Hernández Aguilar and Zubair Ahmad, 'A Dangerous Text: Disciplining Deficient Readers and the Policing of the Qur'an in the German Islam Conference', *ReOrient*, 6:1 (2020), 86–107 (p. 88).

Dukhovnoe Sobranie), which became an essential component of the government and which oversaw and managed the empire's expanding Muslim populace.[6] Since then, as this chapter will explore, the Russian state has changed its form of governance significantly several times, yet this specific approach to 'managing' the Muslim population continues to dominate the relationship between the state and its Muslim subjects. The institution of the muftiate has repeatedly proven its indisputable authority to determine the guidelines and standards for Islamic beliefs and customs inside the boundaries of Russia. Thus, ongoing developments and debates around the Tatar interpretation and translations of the Qur'an should be understood in light of the influence of Russian colonial policy.

This chapter contributes to regional and historical perspectives on Qur'anic studies by discussing the Qur'an commentary (*tafsīr*) and translation (*tarjama*) traditions among Tatars in Russia from the nineteenth century to the present. Special emphasis is devoted to changes in the Tatar Qur'an commenting-translating patterns, priorities, and trends, by evaluating the topic through an analytical framework that explores the interactions between the institution of the muftiate and the Kremlin. The main focus of the discussion is vernacular commentaries (*tafsīr*s) and translations of the Qur'an among Kazan Tatars, also referred to as Volga Tatars ('Idel Buyï Tatarlarï' in Tatar): a Turkic-speaking ethnic group that resides in the Volga-Urals and central areas of contemporary Russia. They are descendants of the Volga Bulghars who ruled the region between the seventh and thirteenth centuries, and—from the tenth and eleventh centuries—founded an Islamic educational and civilisational system with advanced *madrasa*s and renowned scholars, as well as strong relations with the rest of the Muslim world. According to Edhem Tenishev, a few commentaries on the Qur'an in local Turkic dialects appeared during that time, particularly in the Bulghar and Karakhanid-Uygur dialects, such as a translation of the *Tafsīr al-Ṭabarī*

---

6   Renat Bekkin, 'People of Reliable Loyalty ... Muftiates and the State in Modern Russia' (unpublished doctoral thesis, Södertörn University, 2020), p. 71; Galina M. Yemilianova, 'Muslim-State Relations in Russia', in *Muslim Minority–State Relations: Violence, Integration, and Policy*, ed. by Robert Mason (New York: Palgrave Macmillan, 2016), pp. 107–32 (p. 108).

(d. 310/923).⁷ None of these manuscripts have survived, as some were burnt during the Russian colonial administration while others were lost or destroyed over time.

Up to nearly 1900, the Russian-ruled Volga-Ural region endured its importance as the Persianate world's northern frontier.⁸ From the seventeenth century onwards, the Persian language and tradition became crucial to Qur'anic exegesis among Tatars. Persian interpretations of the Qur'an remained popular until the October Revolution of 1917, as did Persian poetry and religious literature.⁹ What mechanisms then facilitated the significant shift from the dominant Persianate tradition to a modern interpretation of the Qur'an influenced by Tatar perspectives, as evidenced by Samigullin's statement? This chapter delineates the intellectual shift within the Tatar Qur'an translation tradition, highlighting it as a part of the decline of Persianate culture in the Volga region and the subsequent rise of modern Tatar models toward the Qur'an.

The first section of this chapter will explore several commentary-translations in vernacular Türki-Tatar produced during the period of Russian colonial rule, including ʿAbd al-Naṣīr Qurṣāwī's (1776–1812) *Haftiyak Sharīf*, Nuʿmān b. ʿĀmir b. ʿUthmān al-Samānī's *Tafsīr*, the *Tafsīr-i fawāʾid* of Ḥusayn b. Amīrkhān al-Talqishī (1816–93), Muḥammad Ṣādiq b. Shāḥ Aḥmad al-Imānqulī al-Qazānī's (1870–1932) *Tashīl al-bayān fī tafsīr al-Qurʾān*, and Asadullāh al-Ḥamīdī's (1869–1911) *al-Itqān fī tarjamat al-Qurʾān*. This section will highlight the historical background against which these commentaries emerged, the decline in the Persianate commentary culture in the region,¹⁰ and the gradual localisation of the *tafsīr* genre during the first half of the nineteenth century. In light of this review of the 'official' *ʿulamāʾ* 's undisputable historical privilege when

---

7   Edhem Tenishev, *Iazyki mira. Turkskiye iazyki* [World Languages: Turkic Languages] (Moscow: Russian Academy of Sciences RAN, 1997), pp. 35–47.
8   Gulnaz Sibgatullina and Gerard Wiegers, 'The European Qur'an: Towards an Inclusive Definition', *in European Muslims and the Qur'an: Practices of Translation, Interpretation, and Commodification*, ed. by Gulnaz Sibgatullina and Gerard Wiegers (Berlin: Walter de Gruyter GmbH, 2024), p. 10.
9   Nile Green, 'Introduction: The Frontiers of the Persianate World (ca. 800-1900)', in *The Persianate World: The Frontiers of a Eurasian Lingua Franca*, ed. by Nile Green (Oakland: University of California Press, 2019), p. 53.
10 On the impact of the Persianate world's decline on Turkic vernacular Qur'an translation traditions, see Gulnaz Sibgatullina, 'The Ecology of a Vernacular Qur'an: Rethinking Mūsā Bīgī's Translation into Türki-Tatar', *Journal of Qur'anic Studies*, 24:3 (2022), 46–69.

it comes to explaining the Qur'an to laypeople, the next section outlines debates that surfaced among Tatars in the 1910s regarding the necessity of translating the Qur'an into Tatar, the accuracy of the printed copies of the Arabic Qur'an in the Russian Empire, and the eligibility of new Türki-Tatar translations and translators. The final section elaborates on Tatar translations of the Qur'an in the post-Soviet sphere.

I would like to clarify two terms used in this chapter before moving on to the main discussion. I refer to the language of the vernacular commentary-translations written by Kazan Tatars before the October Revolution of 1917 as 'Türki-Tatar' despite the fact that grammatical and lexical variations between these works are evident.[11] Türki-Tatar was a written language that used Arabic and Persian words extensively, and was written in Arabic script. Thus, it was not the same as the Kazan Tatar spoken vernacular, but was rather a literary language that was comprehensible to a wide range of Turkic peoples from the Balkans to Central Asia, serving as the *lingua franca* of Muslims in imperial Russia.[12] The second term pertains to the classification of vernacular Türki-Tatar commentaries. Though the authors themselves mostly classified their works as *tafsīr* ('commentary', 'exegetics'), these texts are actually translations of the Qur'an into the vernacular Türki-Tatar, supplemented by lengthy commentary drawn from classical Arabic or Persian works of *tafsīr*. Therefore, I refer to them primarily as 'commentary-translations'—a term Nathan Spannaus has employed to describe the *Haftiyak Sharīf* of Qurṣāwī,[13] although other terms like '*tafsīr*', 'commentary', or 'interpretation of the Qur'an' are also used interchangeably with the same meaning.

---

11 Gulnaz Sibgatullina uses the same term, 'Türki-Tatar', to define the language of Jārullāh. See Gulnaz Sibgatullina, 'The Ecology of a Vernacular Qur'an: Rethinking Mūsā Bīgī's Translation into Türki-Tatar', *Journal of Qur'anic Studies*, 24:3 (2022), 46–69.

12 In fact, the term 'Tatar' did not imply the literary language of the Kazan Tatars until the twentieth century. At the beginning of the nineteenth century, for example, Nuᶜmānī described the language of Qurṣāwī's *Haftiyak Sharīf* simply as 'Türki'. See Nuᶜmān al-Samānī, *Tafsīr-i Nuᶜmānī*, vol. I (Kazan: Millet, 1911), p. 3.

13 Nathan Spannaus, 'Islamic Thought and Revivalism in the Russian Empire: An Intellectual Biography of Abū Naṣr Qūrṣāwī (1776–1812)' (doctoral thesis, McGill University, 2012), p. 70.

The Türki-Tatar Qur'an Commentary Tradition Prior to 1917

At the dawn of the nineteenth century, an intellectual dynamism arose among Kazan Tatars, who made conspicuous attempts to produce localised vernacular commentaries and interpretations of the Qur'an in Türki-Tatar. For about two hundred years, from the fall of the Kazan Khanate in 1552 until the reign of Empress Catherine II, the Kazan Tatars experienced a multidimensional intellectual and scholastic stagnation as a result of the severe anti-Islamic policies of the Russian empire; the number of learned individuals was severely limited, primarily to those few who had had a chance to travel to the major intellectual centres of the Persianate world, Central Asia, or the Caucasus, to pursue an advanced level of education. However, a series of religious, political, and economic reforms initiated by Catherine changed the imperial attitude towards its Muslim subjects. Prior to Catherine's rule, the empire conceived of itself as a religiously and ethnically homogeneous state, only recognising its Orthodox Christian and ethnic Slav citizens while completely denying the needs of other subjects with 'non-Russian' nationalities. The state's insistence on homogeneity in dealing with its multireligious and multiethnic population became unsustainable with the massive expansion of the empire's borders to the south and west that took place during Catherine's reign, during which the empire absorbed the northern parts of the Black Sea region, Ukraine, Crimea, the Northern Caucasus, Belarus, and Lithuania. In seeking effective ways to monitor and control the empire's growing Muslim population, Catherine opted for the legalisation of Islam.[14] As a result, in 1773 the Holy Synod issued a Toleration of All Faiths Edict which granted Muslim subjects of the empire the freedom to confess their faith openly, and religion-based persecution substantially decreased.[15] In Catherine's imperial vision, the Kazan Tatars were pictured as 'potential promoters of Russia's interests and as a civilising force among the culturally less developed Islamic regions within and outside the borders of the

---

14 Yemelianova, 'Muslim-State Relations', p. 108.
15 Alan Fisher, *The Crimean Tatars* (Stanford: Hoover Institution Press, 1978), p. 71; Mikhail Khudiakov, *Ocherki po istorii kazanskogo khanstva* [Essays on History of the Kazan Khanate], 3rd edn (Moscow: Insan, 1991), p. 154.

Russian empire.'¹⁶ Furthermore, to promote her project, Catherine went so far as to provide favourable conditions for Kazan Tatars to pursue economic and cultural development. Restrictions placed on Muslim trade and entrepreneurship were partially lifted, and the educational and intellectual activities of Tatars received a boost from the proceeds of international trade and manufacturing.

The creation of an Islamic religious administration for Eastern European and Western Siberian Muslims—the Orenburg Muslim Spiritual Assembly, in 1788¹⁷—was the next step in Catherine's project to create a formal relationship between the imperial government and Tatar ʿulamāʾ, and its head, the Mufti, became the highest Muslim religious authority in Russia.¹⁸ In her discussion of the function of the muftiate under Russian imperial rule, Danielle Ross has commented that, 'Whether Catherine meant it or not, the founding of the OMSA integrated the Kazan Tatar 'ulama into the imperial administrative structure.'¹⁹ In the nineteenth century, due to its further imperial expansion into other Muslim-populated areas, the empire opened two additional muftiates, one in the Caucasus in 1823 and the other in the Crimea in 1831.²⁰

The establishment of the muftiates in Russia gradually reduced Kazan Tatars' theological, educational, and intellectual dependence on Central Asian religious authorities and centres of learning, where Persian was a language of instruction. The muftiates were designed by the state to oversee local religious education structures, theological discourses, and mosque communities, and also their imams. Soon, dozens of local *madrasa*s emerged in the Muslim-populated towns and larger Tatar villages in the Volga-Urals region, mostly with generous financial assistance from manufacturers and merchants from the

---

16   Galina Yemelianova, 'Islam in Russia: An Historical Perspective', in *Islam in Post-Soviet Russia: Public and Private Faces*, ed. by Hillary Pilkington and Galina Yemelianova (New York: RoutledgeCurzon, 2003), p. 25.
17   The muftiate carried out operations in Ufa from 1789, until its headquarters was transferred to Orenburg in 1796. In 1802, the muftiate moved to Ufa back again. As a result of these moves, the institution went under different names at different times: the Orenburg Muslim Spiritual Assembly or the Ufa Spiritual Muslim Spiritual Assembly (Bekkin, 'People of Reliable Loyalty', p. 71).
18   Danielle Ross, *Tatar Empire: Kazan's Muslims and the Making of Imperial Russia* (Bloomington: Indiana University Press, 2020), pp. 43–44.
19   Ibid., p. 44.
20   Yemelianova, 'Muslim-State Relations', p. 108.

emerging Tatar middle-class.[21] By 1844, there were four *madrasa*s in Kazan alone,[22] although the most famous ones—such as the Estärlebash Madrasa in the Ufa province, the Kïshkar, Kargalï, and Tüntär Madrasas in the Kazan province, and the Bubi Madrasa in Viatka province—were located in rural areas. Alongside the localisation of religious education and theological discourse among Kazan Tatars, imperial restrictions on the publication of Islamic literature were gradually loosened in the 1800s, and the ensuing decades saw a surge in the printing of various types of religious works. The new religious, intellectual, and economic possibilities for Kazan Tatars—reinforced by the industrial revolution, which facilitated transportation and book printing—nourished Islamic discourse in the Volga-Urals region and imbued it with a fresh scholarly dynamism. Most of the issues subject to intellectual debate among Kazan Tatars in the nineteenth century were of local origin, and were derived as a reaction to the existing realities of their time and daily lives.

Alongside these scholarly and educational transformations, a Türki-Tatar vernacular Qur'an commentary genre developed progressively among Tatars throughout the nineteenth century—however, these commentaries were not all the result of a single, unified movement. The first such Qur'an commentary was undertaken by ʿAbd al-Naṣīr Qurṣāwī (1776–1812), a Tatar Muslim theologian and a graduate of the traditional educational system in Bukhara who later became a renowned scholar and *mudarris* ('teacher') at the Madrasa Qursa in the Kazan province, and who gained high esteem for his innovative thought and advanced teaching methods. The style, format, and methodological aspects of his approach were articulated in his interpretation of one seventh of the Qur'an in vernacular Türki-Tatar: *Haftiyak Sharīf* (or *Häftiiäk Täfsire* in Tatar—*haft* in Persian means 'seven' and *yak* means 'one', so the title literally means 'The Noble One-Seventh'). This partial Qur'an commentary, which was certainly an inspiration for later Tatar Qur'anic interpretations of the nineteenth century, consisted of an interpretation of *al-Fātiḥa* (Q 1), the first five verses of *al-Baqara* (Q 2), the entirety of *Yāsīn* (Q 36), and all of the *sūra*s from *al-Fatḥ* up to the end of the Qur'an (i.e. Q 48–114), and was intended for a lay readership.

---

21 Serge Zenkovsky, *Pan-Turkism and Islam in Russia* (Cambridge: Harvard University Press, 1967), pp. 21–22; Ross, *Tatar Empire*, pp. 77–78.
22 Gaiaz Ishaqi, *Idel-Ural* (Naberejniyi Chelny: KAMAZ, 1993), p. 32.

As Spannaus has commented, Qurṣāwī's aim was 'to make the Qur'an understandable to those who have no knowledge of Arabic.'[23] Qurṣāwī's method of commenting in his *Haftiyak* differed from that found in the traditional *tafsīr* works that were used as textbooks in Central Asian *madrasa*s, predominantly due to his cautious attitude towards excessive symbolic-allegorical interpretation (*taʾwīl*) of the Qur'an and the abstract polemics associated with God's attributes, which, Qurṣāwī deemed, often distorted the original meaning of the Qur'an.[24]

In addition to further works of the *haftiyak* genre, other attempts to interpret the entire Qur'anic text in vernacular Türki-Tatar were undertaken around the same period—firstly by Qurṣāwī's student, Nuʿmān b. ʿĀmir b. ʿUthmān al-Samānī, during the first half of the nineteenth century. Nuʿmān remained dedicated to his teacher's method and style of commenting in his two-volume exegesis, entitled *Tafsīr-i Nuʿmānī* ('The *tafsīr* of Nuʿmānī'). His dedication was such that, when interpreting those parts of the Qur'an that had been included in Qurṣāwī's *Haftiyak*, Nuʿmān simply replicated Qurṣāwī's text within his own *tafsīr* without substantial modifications.[25]

Tafsīr-i Nuʿmānī is notable because it also shows early signs of the localisation of Qur'an commentary among Kazan Tatars even though, as can be expected, Nuʿmān consulted numerous classical works of exegesis in his *tafsīr*, including Ibn al-Athīr's (d. 630/1233) *Jāmiʿ al-uṣūl fī aḥādīth al-rasūl* ('A Collection of Precepts in the Collected *Hadīth*s of the Messenger'); a compilation of six *ḥadīth* books, *al-Muwaṭṭaʾ*, *Saḥīḥ al-Bukhārī*, *Saḥīḥ Muslim*, *Sunan Abū Dāwūd*, *Sunan al-Tirmidhī*, and *Sunan al-Nasāʾī*; the *tafsīr* of al-Qurṭubī (d. 671/1273); and Abū'l-Layth al-Samarqandī's (d. 373/983) *Qurrat al-ʿuyūn wa-mufriḥ al-qalb al-maḥzūn* ('The Joy of the Eyes and the Heart in Sorrow').[26] *Tafsīr-i Nuʿmānī*, however—in its purpose, method, and style of commentary—represents much more than a simple translation of the existing *tafsīr* tradition into

---

23 Spannaus, 'Islamic Thought and Revivalism', p. 36.
24 Gulnara Idiiatullina, 'Vvedeniie' [Introduction], in Abū Naṣr ʿAbd al-Naṣīr al-Qurṣāwī, *al-Irshād lil-ʿibād* (Kazan: Tatarskoie Knizhnoie Izdatel'stvo, 2005), pp. 45–46.
25 al-Samānī, *Tafsīr-i Nuʿmānī*, vol. I, p. 266.
26 Arthur Azmukhanov, 'Kazan Bölgese Tefsir Çalışmalarından Tefsir-i Nu'mani Örneği' [*Tafsīr-i Nu'mani*: An Example of *Tafsīr* Studies in the Kazan Region] (master's thesis, University of Ankara, 2012), pp. 27–28.

Türki-Tatar. Rather, Nuʿmān expressed his rationalistic approach to interpreting Qur'anic concepts in a way that reflected the realities of his time and was relevant to the challenges and problems experienced by the Russian Tatar Muslim community. For instance, while commenting on Q 9:60, he interpreted the phrase *fī sabīlī llāh* ('in the way of Allah'), which references the legitimate use of alms, in the following, detailed manner: '[...] such as giving to those poor who struggle [make *jihād*] in the way of Allah, building mosques and *madrasa*s, assisting students who receive education, and spending for necessities of *madrasa*s.'[27] Azmukhanov has documented many other instances in which Nuʿmān attempts to use *ijtihād* and independent rational reasoning to construct a personal, opinion-oriented interpretation of the Qur'anic verses.[28] Such interpretations commonly emerge out of a regional public need to understand the Qur'anic message in the light of ongoing social changes, and scientific and technological developments, as well as specific local cultures. *Tafsīr-i Nuʿmānī* earned extensive popularity among laypeople and was initially transmitted through handwritten copies, in multiplying numbers. The first printed edition appeared in 1907 in Orenburg, and the Milliyet Electro-Printing House reprinted it in Kazan in 1911.

The advent of Muslim book publishing in the Russian Empire and, by extension, the opportunities for Muslim communities and individuals to publish religious works they deemed relevant to their socio-religious context, accelerated the process of vernacularisation of the Qur'an among Tatars throughout the nineteenth century. State restrictions on the publication of Islamic literature were greatly relaxed in 1800, and shortly thereafter a number of Tatar individuals were granted their first licences to print Islamic books. By 1802, about 14,300 copies of various Islamic works, including the Qur'an in its original Arabic,[29] had been printed in the empire.[30] The nineteenth century also witnessed the opening of new local *madrasa*s, reformed learning institutions with a renewed curriculum that was deemed more appropriate to the

---

27 al-Samānī, *Tafsīr-i Nuʿmānī*, vol. I, p. 272.
28 Azmukhanov, 'Kazan Bölgese Tefsir', p. 61.
29 The publication of the Qur'an in the Russian Empire started much earlier, in 1787, when the typography of the Academy of Sciences in St. Petersburg published the Qur'an in its original Arabic on royal orders. By 1798, five editions of this Qur'an copy had been published in St. Petersburg.
30 Zenkovsky, *Pan-Turkism and Islam*, p. 26.

Volga-Urals context, and which increasingly placed weight on the use of Türki-Tatar as their language of instruction and scholarship, both leading to and reflecting the waning authority of Persian and even Arabic. The predominant trend of localisation of Islamic education necessitated the production of more simplified Türki-Tatar vernacular Qur'an commentary-translations. One of the earliest printed Türki-Tatar full commentary-translations of the Qur'an—*Tafsīr-i fawāʾid* ('The Useful Commentary') by Ḥusayn b. Amīrkhān al-Talqishī (1816–93)—should thus be appraised within the context of this urgency for Türki-Tatar textbooks and religious literature.

Ḥusayn b. Amīrkhān served in Kazan as an imam of the Iske Tash ('Old Stone') Mosque between 1847 and 1889, and was a teacher at the famous Madrasa Amirkhaniia. Before *Tafsīr-i fawāʾid*, he had already authored several scholarly books and textbooks for the local curriculum. In the introduction of his *tafsīr*, Amīrkhān emphasised the fact that many ordinary inhabitants of the Volga-Urals region were not capable of understanding the sophisticated literary language of existing Qur'an commentaries in Arabic, Persian, or Ottoman Turkish. For that reason, he said, we should write 'a new *tafsīr* in a simple regional Türki-Tatar language which would be understandable to all its speakers and would lead them out of the darkness of ignorance and which would become a light of useful knowledge.'[31] The outcome of Amīrkhān's labours, *Tafsīr-i fawāʾid*, was first printed by the G. Viacheslav Printing House between 1885 and 1889 in four volumes at the expense of Amīrkhān's son, Muḥammad Ẓarīf Amīrkhān.[32] It was reprinted several times in the following years due to high demand, and gained broad popularity among Kazan Tatars because of its easy language and timely interpretation.

Two other analogous vernacular Türki-Tatar commentary-translations of the Qur'an that also earned extensive popularity in imperial Russia were *Tashīl al-bayān fī tafsīr al-Qurʾān* ('The Facilitation of Clarification in

---

31 Ḥusayn ibn Amīrkhān, *Tafsīr-i fawāʾid*, vol. I (Kazan: Typography of G Viacheslav, 1885), p. 2.

32 G. Nurgatina, '*Tafsir-i Fawaid* Husaina ibn Amirkhana i Tatarskaia Ekzegeticheskaia traditsiia kontsa XIX- nachala XX vekov' [The *Tafsīr-i fawāʾid* of Husain ibn Amirkhan and the Tatar Exegetic Tradition at the End of the Nineteenth and the Beginning of the Twentieth Centuries], in *Teologiia Tradisional'nikh Religiy v Nauchno-Obrazovatel'nom Prostranstve Sovremennoi Rossii: Sbornik Materialov* (Kazan: Brig, 2020), p. 109.

the Interpretation of the Qur'an') by Muḥammad Ṣādiq b. Shāḥ Aḥmad al-Imānqulī al-Qazānī (1870–1932), and *al-Itqān fī tarjamat al-Qurʾān* ('The Perfect Guide to the Translation of the Qur'an') by Asadullāh al-Ḥamīdī (1869–1911)—both published in 1911.

Both al-Imānqulī and al-Ḥamīdī served as imams at local mosques that functioned under the close supervision of the muftiate. Al-Imānqulī received his religious education in Bukhara and Samarkand, and later emerged as an eminent religious scholar, publicist, and poet. He also was an imam at the Sixth Mosque in Kazan. He completed his vernacular commentary-translation of the Qur'an, *Tashīl al-bayān*, in 1905 and published it in 1911 in two volumes. Al-Imānqulī described the language of *Tashīl al-bayān* as 'Qazan mämleketeneng ahle islamï lisanï' ('the language of the followers of Islam in the Kazan province').[33] Based on *Tashīl al-bayān*'s style of commentary and linguistic peculiarities, Saidbek Boltabayev has concluded that al-Imānqulī's work is nothing more than a translation of Ḥusayn Wāʿiẓ Kāshifī's (d. 910/1504–5) Persian *tafsīr*, *Mawāhib al-ʿAliyya* (also known as *Tafsīr-i Ḥusaynī*, completed in 899/1494), into vernacular Türki-Tatar.[34] Al-Imānqulī mentions al-Kāshifī in his introductory section, in which he wrote that he benefitted extensively from *Mawāhib al-ʿAliyya* as this classical work, especially in its translations into Turkic dialects, was widely accepted and highly respected and was used as the main *tafsīr* textbook at *madrasa*s in the Volga-Urals region, Central Asia, and Anatolia.[35] Its first translation into Ottoman Turkish, by Selânîklü ʿAlī bin Walī, appeared in 1543.[36] Another Turkic version of *Mawāhib al-ʿAliyya* that was widely read by Kazan Tatars in the nineteenth century was published by a Crimean Tatar, Ismāʿīl Ferrūkh Efendi (d. 1840).

Besides heavily depending on al-Kāshifī's *tafsīr*, al-Imānqulī also enriched his vernacular text with material gleaned from other classical *tafsīr*s such as *Tafsīr Qāḍī* (i.e. the *Anwār al-tanzīl wa-asrār al-taʾwīl* of Naṣr al-Dīn al-Bayḍāwī, d. 718/1319), *Tafsīr al-Kashshāf* (i.e. the *al-Kashshāf ʿan ḥaqāʾiq al-tanzīl* of al-Zamakhsharī, d. 538/1143), and *Tafsīr Madārik*

---

33 Muḥammad Ṣādiq b. Shāḥ Aḥmad al-Imānqulī al-Qazānī, *Tashīl al-bayān fī tafsīr al-Qurʾān* (Kazan: Ürnäk, 1911), p. 2.
34 Saidbek Boltabayev, 'Çağatayca Tefsir-i Hüseyni (Mevahib-i Alıyye) Tercümesi ve Farsça Dil Özellekleri Üzerine', *Journal of Old Turkic Studies*, 3:2 (2019), 287–309.
35 al-Imānqulī, *Tashīl al-bayān*, p. 2.
36 Boltabayev, 'Çağatayca Tefsir-i Hüseyni', p. 298.

(i.e. the *Madārik al-tanzīl wa-ḥaqāʾiq al-taʾwīl* of Abū l-Barakat al-Nasafī, d. 710/1310). In terms of its genre, *Tashīl al-bayān* can be classified as a continuation of the classical *tafsīr* genre in vernacular, rather than an independent direct translation of the Qur'an into Türki-Tatar. Al-Imānqulī follows the same paraphrastic method of commenting as Ḥusayn b. Amīrkhān before him. He first provides a small fragment from the Qur'anic verse in its original Arabic, within brackets, and then interprets it into Türki-Tatar. Yet al-Imānqulī's interpretation is more detailed than Amīrkhān's. Along with the main text of his interpretation, al-Imānqulī also provides relevant additional information in an annotation section in the margins of each page, mostly focusing on the *asbāb al-nuzūl* (the 'circumstances of revelation'), for which he relied on al-Suyūṭī's (d. 911/1505) *tafsīr*.[37]

Another significant commentary-translation of the Qur'an into Türki-Tatar was written by al-Ḥamīdī. Unlike preceding Tatar interpreters of the Qur'an, al-Ḥamīdī did not travel to study at the famous Central Asian *madrasa*s. Rather, he received his education at local *madrasa*s, such as Madrasa Marjaniia and Madrasa Muḥammadiia, both situated in Kazan, after which he was appointed as an imam in the village of Yakhshïbäy near the city of Minzälä in Ufa province. He also worked as a *mudarris* at the Madrasa Usmaniia in Ufa.[38] Al-Ḥamīdī completed his vernacular commentary-translation of the Qur'an, *al-Itqān fī tarjamat al-Qurʾān*, in December 1907 (as he states in the second volume).[39] The work was published in two volumes a few years later, in 1911, in Kazan.

In *al-Itqān*, al-Ḥamīdī frequently refers to other verses of the Qur'an, the *ḥadīth*s of the Prophet Muḥammad, and the sayings of the Companions in his interpretations of the Qur'anic verses. These are first cited in their original Arabic, separated from the Türki-Tatar text with brackets, followed by an extensive discussion of their meanings in vernacular. Many exegetical traditions and the opinions of authoritative classical exegetes are also incorporated into the main body of the text and smoothly integrated

---

37 al-Imānqulī, *Tashīl al-bayān*, p. 2.
38 G. Nurgatina, 'Traditsiia kommentirovaniia Korana u tatar' [The Commentary Tradition among Tatars], in *Teologiia traditsional'nikh Religii v Nauchno-Obrazovatel'nom Prostranstve Sovremennoi Rossii: Sbornik Materialov* (Kazan: Brig, 2020), pp. 115–116.
39 Shaykh al-Islām Asadullāh al-Ḥamīdī, *al-Itqān fī tarjamat al-Qurʾān*, vol. II (Kazan: Lito-Tipografiia Brat'ia Karimovy, 1911), p. 451.

with the vernacular Türki-Tatar interpretation. Unlike the earlier *Tashīl al-bayān* and *Tafsīr-i fawāʾid*, *Al-Itqān* does not provide supplementary clarifications in the margins of each page separated from the main text, except in some rare cases where al-Ḥamīdī felt it essential to provide additional information and explanation, or his own opinion on the relevant concepts. For example, on page 73, while interpreting the phrase 'do not throw [yourselves] with your [own] hands into destruction' in Q 2:195, al-Ḥamīdī provides an analogy in a footnote between this verse and the actions of some of his Tatar contemporaries who refrained from learning Russian. Al-Ḥamīdī underlines the potential threat of such an attitude to the well-being and resilience of the Kazan Tatars as a successful nation. Based on the lived realities of his Tatar compatriots, he labels it a 'sinful action for which Tatars are answerable in front of Allah.'[40] However, such attempts to relate the Qur'anic text to local occurrences and realities are rare in *al-Itqān*.

Overall, the authority of classical Arabic and Persian *tafsīr*s was pivotal for the authors of these early vernacular Türki-Tatar commentary-translations, and they adopted their conventions and techniques, selecting specific main sources through which to interpret specific terms and concepts. For example, the similarity between the titles of al-Ḥamīdī's *al-Itqān fī tarjamat al-Qurʾān* and al-Suyūṭī's *al-Itqān fī ʿulūm al-Qurʾān* ('The Perfect Guide to the Sciences of the Qur'an') signifies the importance of this specific authoritative work of *ʿulūm al-Qurʾān* for al-Ḥamīdī.

All of these Türki-Tatar vernacular works had Arabic titles: *Tafsīr-i fawāʾid* (Ḥusayn b. Amīrkhān), *Tashīl al-bayān fī tafsīr al-Qurʾān* (al-Imānqulī), and *al-Itqān fī tarjamat al-Qurʾān* (al-Ḥamīdī). Interestingly, for the first time among Kazan Tatars, al-Ḥamīdī used the word *tarjama* ('translation') in the title of his two-volume vernacular commentary-translation. Yet, on the cover page of his work he indicated that it was *Qur'ān täfsīre Qazan telendä* ('a *tafsīr* of the Qur'an in the Kazan language').[41] In conclusion, on the eve of the twentieth century, a new trend appeared among Kazan Tatars that aimed at interpreting the Qur'anic verses relevant to their localised context and realities.

---

40 al-Ḥamīdī, *al-Itqān*, vol. I, p. 73.
41 Ibid.

The Muftiate and the Qur'an Debates

The Türki-Tatar commentary-translations of the Qur'an that emerged during the nineteenth and the beginning of the twentieth centuries signified a gradual shift from Kazan Tatars' intellectual and educational dependency on Central Asian scholarship and centres of learning to the localisation of Islamic intellectual discourse, the *madrasa* curriculum, and Qur'anic interpretation generally in the Volga-Urals region. In addition, around the same period, the quantity of printed Islamic books produced in the empire multiplied. The number of Kazan Tatar readers also increased, leading to a social change that has been described by Brett Wilson in the Ottoman context as the 'rise of commoners.'[42] The expansion of the educated stratum of Tatar society necessitated the production of simplified commentary works and vernacular interpretations of the Qur'an for a broader audience. A new subgenre in the exegetical tradition—which Gunasti refers to as a 'vernacular paraphrastic commentary'[43]—emerged in nineteenth-century Russia and immediately established itself as a characteristic phenomenon of modern *tafsīr* studies.

Having said that, the Türki-Tatar commentary-translations of the Qur'an that were discussed earlier did not challenge the authority of classical Arabic and Persian *tafsīrs* in terms of their style, methodology, references, or main sources, and they continued to use traditionally accepted concepts while interpreting the verses in the vernacular. The main goal of those who had interpreted the Qur'an in Türki-Tatar seems to have been making the meaning of the Qur'anic message available for Tatar laypeople and conveying it in line with generally accepted religious views and well-established and widely accepted *tafsīr* traditions that they found worth mentioning.

The transformation in exegetical scholarship from the Persianate tradition towards regional vernacular interpretations was not limited to the Russian context alone. A dynamic intellectual atmosphere flourished throughout the entire Muslim world during this period and eventually

---

42 M. Brett Wilson, 'The Qur'an after Babel: Translating and Printing the Qur'an in Late Ottoman and Modern Turkey' (doctoral thesis, Duke University, 2009), p. 97.

43 Susan Gunasti, *The Qur'an between the Ottoman Empire and the Turkish Republic: An Exegetical Tradition* (London: Routledge, 2019), p. 53.

influenced approaches to the Qur'an. Issues related to *madhhab* boundaries, educational reforms, *madrasa* syllabuses, the questions of *ijtihād* and *taqlīd*, and the decline of the Islamic world in contrast to the progressively advancing West were all being vigorously debated, and this led to a new branch of intellectual discourse at the beginning of the twentieth century—known as the 'Qur'an debates'. The scope of these debates encompassed robust discussions regarding the legitimacy of printed copies of the Qur'an in the original Arabic, as well as that of specific exegetes, translations, translators, or critics. In the Ottoman context, Susan Gunasti has observed that participation in these debates took several forms, such as 'publishing anything related to the Qur'an, publishing an opinion piece about Qur'an-related works in the press, or direct intervention to resolve a hotly contested issue relating to the Qur'an.'[44] In Russia, too, the newly emerging Muslim periodicals of the post-1905 Revolution empire provided a perfect arena for such debates, along with other ongoing developments in intellectual rethinking and reformulation.

The first Qur'an debate took place in 1909, following claims put forward by Mūsā Jārullāh (1875–1949)—one of the most energetic and thought-provoking Tatar Muslim intellectuals of the beginning of the twentieth century in imperial Russia—that the copies of the Arabic Qur'an printed in the empire (i.e. the St. Petersburg and Kazan editions) contained errors, and that some spellings were different from those found in the codex owned by ʿUthmān b. ʿAffān: one of Muḥammad's closest Companions and the third caliph (r. 644–56).[45] This was particularly political because the printing of the Qur'an in Russia was a genuine imperial project rather than an initiative pursued by its Muslim subjects. In 1787, following a royal order issued by Catherine II,[46] the Academy of Sciences in St. Petersburg published the Qur'an in its original Arabic,

---

44 Ibid., p. 62.
45 Selcuk Altuntas, 'How to Be a Proper Muslim in the Russian Empire: An Intellectual Biography of Musa Jarullah Bigiyev (1875–1949)' (doctoral thesis, University of Wisconsin-Madison, 2018), p. 56.
46 This edition of the Qur'an was printed in a special Arabic typographic script based on the handwriting of one of the most renowned calligraphers in the Russian Empire, Mullah ʿUthmān Ismāʿīl. This script cast was later passed on to Kazan, to the newly opened publishing house of G. Burnashev, which in 1829 merged with the publishing house of the Kazan Imperial University. See: Ravil Bukharaev, *Islam in Russia: The Four Seasons* (London: Curzon Press, 2000), p. 310; Efim A. Rezvan,

to be distributed freely to Russian Muslim subjects.⁴⁷ This went hand in hand with another of Catherine's colonial projects—the construction of new mosques at the state's expenditure. Both of these policies were intended to create a positive image of the Russian state in adjoining Muslim lands as a 'protector of Islam' and a 'friend of Muslim peoples' during the decisive years of Russian colonial expansion into the Central Asian Steppes and the Caucasus.⁴⁸ By 1798, just before the Arabic script cast that had been designed for this imperial printing project was passed on to the city of Kazan, five editions of the Arabic Qur'an had appeared in St. Petersburg. In the following decades, the production of Arabic Qur'ans continued unabated: some half-century later, between 1853 and 1859 alone, Kazan Imperial University published 326,700 copies of what is now known as the Kazan edition of the Qur'an, along with other Islamic books in Arabic.⁴⁹

Jārullāh's criticisms of the print editions of the Arabic Qur'an primarily targeted Shihāb al-Dīn Marjānī (1818–89), one of the most prominent Kazan Tatar religious scholars and educational reformers of the nineteenth century, who had been appointed by the muftiate in 1857 to proofread the Kazan edition of the Qur'an before it went into print.⁵⁰ In an article published on 25 January 1909 in the periodical *al-Iṣlāḥ* ('The Reform'), Jārullāh asserted that a few typesetting errors still remained in the Kazan edition of the Qur'an after Marjānī's proofreading, and called upon the ʿulamāʾ of Kazan to gather to discuss the issue.⁵¹ Jārullāh's criticism of Marjānī—the leading intellectual and religious authority of the period—elicited a range of responses to the point that some of his

---

Koran i ego mir [The Qur'an and its World] (St. Petersburg: Russian Academy of Sciences, 2001), p. 399.

47 Imperial documents state that the beneficiaries of these free copies of the Qur'an were the Kyrgyz people, this being a general term used by the Russian state in that period for the Turkic-speaking peoples of the Central Asian Steppe.

48 The obscured colonialist agenda behind the printing of the Qur'an was documented in the diary of Alexander Khranovitskiy, the personal secretary to Catherine II, who noted on 17 December 1786 that Catherine explained the aim of this project as 'creating a fishing lure' (*'primanka na udu'*) rather than assisting the spread of Islam (Rezvan, *Koran i ego mir*, pp. 397–98).

49 Zenkovsky, *Pan-Turkism and Islam*, p. 26.

50 Mulla Kashshāf al-Dīn Tarjumānī, 'Tashīh al-Qur'ān Haqqïnda', *Yoldïz*, 362, 10 February 1909.

51 Musa Bigiyev, 'En Lazïm Bir İ'lan', *Al-Iṣlāḥ*, 58, 25 January 1909; Musa Bigiyev, 'Yine Muhim Bir Mäs'älä', *Waqt*, 569, 21 January 1910.

contemporaries, such as ᶜAbd al-Raḥmān Gumerov and Kashshāf al-Dīn Tarjumānī (two local religious scholars), considered his attitude to be blasphemous.⁵²

In the 1910s, Jārullāh initiated another Qur'an-related debate in the Tatar press, this time on the permissibility of translating the text of the Qur'an into vernacular languages. None of the Türki-Tatar commentaries on the Qur'an that had been published so far had claimed to be a 'translation', and the word *tarjama* (*tärjemä*) had never been used for the Qur'an at this time either. As mentioned earlier, the relevant Türki-Tatar works that had been published by this date can be classified as belonging to the sub-genre of 'commentary-translations'—a term used by Brett Wilson to refer to vernacular commentaries in Ottoman Turkish.⁵³ This meant that the issue of their 'permissibility' had never posed a problem. Conversely, Jārullāh publicised his intentions to *translate* the Qur'an into Türki-Tatar. The vernacular translation of the Qur'an, in addition to the production of timely and relevant commentaries of the Qur'an, was crucial, he argued, for the advancement of Muslim societies, going so far as to say that it was '[a] religious obligation of the time in order to explain and reveal its meanings to every member of society.'⁵⁴ Jārullāh was, however, not the first Kazan Tatar who wanted to translate the Qur'an into Türki-Tatar. An Azhar graduate, Ḍiyāʾ al-Dīn al-Kamālī (1873–1942), had also embarked on a similar translation project during the same period. Jārullāh's project, in contrast, attracted a great degree of attention from the Muslim press, both domestically and internationally, and several eminent Muslim periodicals in Cairo and the Ottoman capital published diverse reactions to it from their readers.⁵⁵

Making the meaning of the Qur'an accessible to every Kazan Tatar was the main emphasis of the Qur'an debates, which took place primarily in the pages of the most prominent post-1905 Tatar periodicals, such as *Din wä Maghïïshät* ('Religion and Life', 1906–18), *Waqt* ('Time', 1906–18),

---

52 'Abd al-Raḥmān Gumerov, 'Ulema Dikkatenä', *İdel*, 125, 3 February 1909; Tarjumānī, 'Taṣḥīḥ-i al-Qur'ān'; Altuntas, 'How to Be a Proper Muslim', p. 58.
53 M. Brett Wilson, *Translating the Qur'an in an Age of Nationalism: Print Culture and Modern Islam in Turkey* (Abingdon: Oxford University Press, 2014).
54 Mūsā Jārullāh, *Halïq Nazarïna Bernichä Mäs'älä* [A Few Issues for the Attention of the People] (Kazan: Elektro-Tipographiia Umid, 1912), p. 88.
55 See, for example, the Istanbul-based periodical, *Islam Dünyası*, 1:10 (1913), pp. 149–55; and 1:14 (1913), p. 217.

Yoldïz ('Star', 1906–18), *Idel* (the Tatar name for the River Volga), and *Shura* ('Consultation', which was likely a Tatar version of *Al-Manār* based in Orenburg, 1908–18).⁵⁶ For example, in the four months from January to April 1910, the relatively conservative Orenburg-based periodical *Din wä Maghüshät* published forty articles that sought to criticise Jārullāh's translation project by emphasising the prohibition against translating the Qur'an. In contrast, modernist and more reform-oriented periodicals such as *Shura* argued in favour of Qur'an translation as, for them, the ability to understand the Qur'an was vital. As Brett Wilson has observed, for Tatar modernists, increased access to the Qur'an was envisaged as 'an integral part of becoming modern and bringing about progress for the Muslim world.'⁵⁷

The disputes linked to Jārullāh's announcement that he would translate the Qur'an reverberated beyond the boundaries of the Tatar press. For example, in 1912, the Turkish writer Haşim Nahid (1880–1962) exclaimed with delight that 'the Luther of Islam has just emerged on the Asian horizon. This reformer of religion is Mūsā Jārullāh Bigiyev from Kazan. He is translating the Qur'an into Turkish at the moment.'⁵⁸ An Azerbaijani journalist, Muhammad Amin Resulzade (1884–1955), discerned some resemblances between Jārullāh and Martin Luther's translation efforts, stating that while Luther criticised the Pope's authority, Jārullāh challenged the *ʿulamāʾ*'s privileged authority as mediators in the interpretation of the Qur'an for the public. Resulzade suggested that, throughout the Muslim world, the *ʿulamāʾ* restricted intelligence and science, although they were not solely responsible for the fact that the masses were left in ignorance. Resulzade commented that in Christendom, the Catholic Church burned all who defied its teachings to death, whilst in the Muslim world, the *ʿulamāʾ* threatened those who opposed them with eternal fire.⁵⁹

Having said that, it would be an error to oversimplify the scope, nature, and driving forces of the Qur'an debates that took place in

---

56 Sibgatullina, 'The Ecology of a Vernacular Qur'an', pp. 51–52.
57 Wilson, *Translating the Qur'an*, p. 8.
58 Haşim Nahid, *Türkiye İçin Necat ve İtila Yolları* (Istanbul: Şems Matbaası, 1915), p. 213.
59 M. E. Resulzade, 'Bahadır ve Sona', *Ikbal*, 541, 29 December 1913 (quoted in Məhəmməd Əmin Rəsulzadə, *Əsərləri II Cilt (1909–1914)* (Bakı: Təhsil, 2014), pp. 287–89); and Altuntas, 'How to Be a Proper Muslim', pp. 58–59.

post-1905 Tatar society by interpreting them within the standard Qadimist (conservative and old-fashioned ʿulamāʾ) vs Jadidist (modernists and reform-minded Muslim Tatar intellectuals) binary paradigm. Selçuk Altuntaş, for example, has studied Jārullāh from a non-binary perspective using Talal Asad's discursive Islamic tradition model[60] to analyse 'where he stands within the intellectual history of Islam and what vision he has for the future of the Islamic community in Russia and beyond.'[61] Adopting this methodology, Altuntaş describes Türki-Tatar commentary-translations, including Jārullāh and Kamālī's projects, as 'a byproduct of internal Muslim affairs in Russia'[62] that emerged out of the domestic intellectual, social, political, and religious necessities of that historical environment. He consequently argued that disagreements and diversity in ideas are always central to the nature of a discursive tradition.[63]

I suggest approaching vernacular Türki-Tatar commentary-translations on the basis that they articulate their authors' critiques of the established privilege held by ʿulamāʾ when it comes to explaining the Qur'an to laypeople. Qurṣāwī's *Haftiyak Sharīf* shows the earliest indications of such tendencies toward breaking away from the intellectual and exegetical predominance of Central Asian scholars and centres of learning—which had been, perhaps, almost the only possible contacts that Tatar intellectuals could maintain within the Muslim *umma* for 300 years following the Russian invasion of the Volga-Urals region in the sixteenth century.[64] As explained earlier, towards the end of the nineteenth century, Türki-Tatar commentary-translations proliferated and the genre developed quickly, and these works were printed in large quantities. The availability of religious texts in vernacular undermined

---

60 Talal Asad suggested the 'discursive tradition' model in his conceptualisation of Islam. He defined the Islamic discursive tradition as 'a tradition of Muslim discourse that addresses itself to the conceptions of the Islamic past and future, with reference to a particular Islamic practice in the present.' See Talal Asad, *The Idea of an Anthropology of Islam* (Washington, D.C.: Centre for Contemporary Arab Studies, Georgetown University, 1986), p. 20.
61 Altuntas, 'How to Be a Proper Muslim', p. 44.
62 Ibid., p. 113.
63 Ibid., p. 45.
64 M. Kemper, 'Imperial Russia as Dar al-Islam? Nineteenth-Century Debates on Ijtihad and Taqlid among the Volga Tatars', *Encounters: An International Journal for the Study of Culture and Society*, 6 (2015), 95–124 (p. 97).

the official ʿulamāʾ 's monopoly over the interpretation and mediation of the Arabic text of the Qur'an for non-Arab believers.[65] However, in the case of the Kazan Tatars, the rank of the official ʿulamāʾ was also associated with imperial power, as the institution of the muftiate developed as an integral component of the colonial structure. As a result, the authority of the official ʿulamāʾ over the Muslim population in the Russian imperial context was unquestionable.

As Yemelianova has observed:

> By the end of the nineteenth century, St. Petersburg, via the *mufti*'s appointees, established its control over the Muslim inhabitants of substantial parts of present-day Poland, Lithuania, Belarus, Moldova, Russia, Crimea, Azerbaijan, Georgia, and Kazakhstan. The close ties between *mufti*s, who came to embody 'official' Islam, and the Russian Orthodox authorities undermined the moral and spiritual credentials of the former with their flock and enhanced the moral and political authority among ordinary Muslims of 'unofficial' *ulama* (Islamic scholars), Sufi *sheikh*s and other charismatic Islamic preachers.[66]

Thus, attempts to produce new interpretations or translations of the Qur'an were banned in Russia not merely because they challenged the ʿulamāʾ 's authority to interpret the sacred texts, but also because they were considered 'dangerous' for the colonial project and state interests. Whilst new and timely interpretations were still in demand, the question of who (or what group of people) had the authority to write such works became contentious.[67]

Jārullāh's groundbreaking ideas and personality were, it seems, sufficient for the muftiate to ban his translation of the Qur'an in 1912, before it had even appeared in print.[68] As Sibgatullina has discussed, Jārullāh's fundamental tenet was that the message contained in the Qur'an is fixed, and can and should be understood through independent reasoning.[69] As Jārullāh notes in his *Ozïn Künlärdä Ruza* ('Fasting During Long Days'), this crucial component of Qur'anic exegesis was largely disregarded for centuries, leading to a misinterpretation of the text's

---

65 Gunasti, *The Qur'an*, p. 68.
66 Yemilianova, 'Muslim-State Relations in Russia', p. 108.
67 Gunasti, *The Qur'an*, p. 63.
68 'Qur'ān Tärjemäse Haqïnda', *Yoldïz*, 810, 25 March 1912.
69 Sibgatullina, 'The Ecology of a Vernacular Qur'an', p. 57.

meaning and purpose that ultimately contributed to the decline of Islamic civilisation:

> If we refer to the *tafsīr*s such as *al-Bayḍāwī* and *al-Kashshāf*, which devoted all their efforts to the Arabic features of the Qur'an, and if we also take a look at the commentaries on the verses that have been compiled that cover all the verses that may refer to *sharʿī* laws, we will see that everything is included in these books, but that there is nothing related to the main purpose of the Qur'an and Islam. In such matters, it would be better if an individual would look at the expressions of the Qur'an with their own eyes and minds. Naturally, I did this.[70]

Hence, Jārullāh deemed the translation of the Qur'an into Türki-Tatar to be an initial step in his broader mission of establishing intellectual freedom and advancing reason and education in the Muslim world.[71] In a newspaper article published in 1912, Jārullāh asserted that translation becomes a Muslim's sacred duty (*farḍ*) when 'silly' and 'absurd' Tatar *tafsīr*s dominate the religious market.[72] It seems he called for a fresh method of interpreting the Qur'an into the local vernacular that is pertinent to contemporary, historical, political, and socio-cultural circumstances—which, he believed, was missing from the earlier Kazan Tatar *tafsīr* tradition.

In early 1912, Jārullāh signed a contract with the Umid Publishing House in Kazan to publish his Qur'an translation. However, on 1 March 1912, according to an article in the *Yoldïz* newspaper, an official notice issued by the Ufa muftiate was sent to the Umid Publishing House to halt printing immediately:

> On 25 February [1912], the Assembly received a telegram signed by fourteen Muslims from Kazan. It informed [us] that printing had begun on Jārullāh's translation of the Qur'an at the Umid Printing House and demanded the Assembly stop its publication. According to the applicable regulation, only the Assembly is eligible to issue permission to print any work related to the sacred book of Muslims, the Qur'an, and its parts, such as *haftiyak*s. Hence, without the consent of the Assembly, the Umid Printing House is not authorized to publish the Tatar translation of the

---

70 Mūsā Jārullāh, *Ozïn Künlärdä Ruza: Ijtihad Kitabï* [Fasting During Long Days: The Book of *Ijtihād*] (Kazan: Umid, 1911), p. 130.
71 Wilson, *Translating the Qur'an*, p. 143.
72 Jārullāh, 'Tatar Dünyasïnda Räzälät', *Waqt*, 19 April 1912, p. 2.

Qur'an. Therefore, the Assembly urges the Umid Printing House to cease printing.[73]

During that same period, other Kazan Tatars initiated similar projects with creative exegetical approaches. These included Ḍiyāʾ al-Dīn al-Kamālī (1873–1942), Burkhān Sharāf (1883–1942), Sunʿat Allāh Bikbulatov (1886–1954), Murād Ramzī (1854–1934), and ʿAbd Allah Gismatullin (1883–1938), all of whom aimed to interpret or translate the Qur'an so that it might provide solutions to the prevailing problems that plagued their society. As a result of their progressivism, some of these authors were accused of *kufr*, and the Spiritual Assembly and other regional muftiates barred their works from publication.

The Tatar Muslim intellectual Muḥammad Kāmil al-Muṭīʿī Tukhfatullin's (1883–1941) *Tatarcha Qurʾān Täfsire* ('A *tafsīr* of the Qur'an in Tatar') was destined for the same fate. Al-Muṭīʿī was born in the city of Uralsk and graduated from al-Azhar University in Cairo. His original plan was to publish his commentary-translation in 121 small-sized parts.[74] The first two volumes were published in 1914 by the Maʿārif Printing House, which was owned by ʿAbd Allah Kildishev and based in Kazan, and a few more volumes were published in 1915. At the end of the fifth volume, the author notifies his readers that the first two volumes had already sold out, which means we can assume that this new style of vernacular *tafsīr* gained immediate popularity among Kazan Tatars.[75] Nevertheless, production of the subsequent parts of *Tatarcha Qurʾān Täfsire* was halted, and the distribution of the earlier volumes was banned by the Muslim Spiritual Assembly in 1915.

The immediate fame of *Tatarcha Qurʾān Täfsire* could be attributed to its simplistic language and the fact that the interpretation of each verse was pertinent to the local realities of the author's specific time and place: on the back cover of the sixth volume, al-Muṭīʿī highlighted the lack of *tafsīr*s in Türki-Tatar that were of relevance to the twentieth

---

73 'Qurʾān Tärjumäse Haqïnda', *Yoldïz*, 810, 25 March 1912.
74 Muhammad Kāmil al-Muṭīʿī Tukhfatullin, *Tatarcha Qurʾān Täfsire*, vol. II (Kazan: Ma'ārif, 1914), p. 16. These volumes were small and cheap (each cost 15 Russian kopeck) and were affordable even for low-income Tatars. The second volume, for example, covers the interpretation of verses 1 to 43 of *Sūrat* al-Baqara in sixteen pages. The fifth volume consists of twenty-one pages, and the sixth of eighteen.
75 al-Muṭīʿī Tukhfatullin, *Tatarcha Qurʾān Täfsire*, vol. V, p. 21.

century.⁷⁶ Furthermore, his work includes only minimal references to classical *tafsīr*s. Rather, *Tatarcha Qur'ān Täfsire* appears to be more in line with the socio-literary exegetical approach that had been popularised by Muḥammad ʿAbduh towards the end of the nineteenth century, as he advocated for an updated interpretation of the Qur'an that was pertinent to contemporary cultural and socio-political realities. Numerous homegrown examples of this approach can be found in the *Tatarcha Qur'ān Täfsire*. In his commentary on Q 2:23–24, for example, which discusses how humans are incapable of producing a perfect copy of the Qur'an or altering its meaning, al-Muṭīʿī cites a very local example of an Arabic edition of the Qur'an which was printed with some technical mistakes in 1913 by the Kazan-based Kharitonov publishing house.⁷⁷

In another example drawn from his commentary on *Sūrat al-Baqara*—his description of the qualities of hypocrites (*munāfiqūn*) and non-Muslims (*kuffār*)—al-Muṭīʿī used the exemplar of a real-life swindler called Gromov who had hoodwinked Kazan Tatars by adopting an idealised Muslim appearance, shaving his head and donning a turban and *kaftan* (*chalma-chapan*): a look that was perceived by his contemporary Tatars as denoting piety.⁷⁸ In fact, al-Muṭīʿī frequently used the Tatar expression *chalma-chapan* to characterise the outlook of the official Kazan Tatar clergy, the muftis and their officials; and the *ishan*s, or Sufi religious aristocracy and clergy—the descendants of local Sufi family clans. Careful reading of his use of *chalma-chapan* gives the impression that al-Muṭīʿī is not simply criticising the erroneous belief that a person's religiosity is determined by their outward appearance and clothing. Al-Muṭīʿī also asserts that recent closures of *madrasa*s, *maktab*s, and consultative bodies (*majlis al-shūrā*) in the empire are not directly the fault of the Russian government, but rather of individuals who adopt 'pious' garb and hide their hypocrisy under religious titles.⁷⁹ Given his critique of the religious establishment, it should come as no surprise that the printing and distribution of *Tatarcha Qur'ān Täfsire* was banned by the Muslim Spiritual Assembly, a state-run regulatory religious body; or that its author, al-Muṭīʿī, was charged with *kufr*.

---

76   al-Muṭīʿī Tukhfatullin, *Tatarcha Qur'ān Täfsire*, vol. VI, p. 18.
77   al-Muṭīʿī Tukhfatullin, *Tatarcha Qur'ān*, vol. II, pp. 9–10.
78   Ibid., p. 6.
79   Ibid., p. 5.

In sum, although the imperial state did not interfere in regional Muslim-related affairs and scholarly developments directly, its colonial policies and mechanisms indirectly imposed stringent controls. When it came to vernacular *tafsīr*s and Qur'an translations, the state's intervention was implemented through the mechanism of the muftiates and the local imams recognised by these organisations. The main duty of the muftiates was to oversee religious discourse and debates among scholars, as well as the empire's mosque communities and their imams. Eventually, this imperial muftiate mechanism attempted to detach the intellectual and religious thought of Muslims in the Russian empire from the rest of the Muslim world. Thus, these institutions gradually brought the empire's Muslims under direct state control, not simply in terms of their political interests and ideas, but also in terms of the control of their thoughts, beliefs, interests, rituals, and their fundamental understanding of their religion.

The Role of the Qur'an in the Domesticisation of Islam in Russia

Following the Bolshevik revolution in 1917, militant atheism coupled with laicism provided the basis for the legal regulation of state-Muslim relations. Islamic scholarship and the ability of Kazan Tatars to access religious literature—especially the Qur'an and its commentaries and translations—were severely curtailed during the Soviet era due to state-regulated atheism and anti-religious persecution. However, a few attempts to translate the Qur'an into contemporary Soviet Tatar did begin to surface towards the end of Soviet rule. For instance, MuṭīʿAllāh Sungatullin (1891–?) from Nurlat, Tatarstan, made an abortive attempt to publish his Tatar translation of the Qur'an during the 1960s.[80] During the same period, ʿAbd al-Bārī Isaev (a Muslim authority of the late Soviet era, 1907–83), the imam of the mosque in Leningrad (St. Petersburg), and the Mufti of the Spiritual Board of Muslims in the European part of

---

80　In 1967, Sungatullin sent a letter to Alexei Kosygin, the Premier of the Soviet Union between 1964–1980, asking for his permission and assistance in publishing his newly completed Soviet version of the translation of the Qur'an into Tatar. His request was not successful. See Alfrid Bustanov, 'The Qur'an for Soviet Citizens: The Rhetoric of Progress in the Theological Works of 'Abd Bari Isaev', *Forum for Anthropology and Culture*, 37 (2018), 93–110 (pp. 95–96).

Russia and Siberia (1975–80), also endeavoured to translate the Qur'an into Tatar.[81] Broadly speaking, these isolated translation efforts—which were not published or disseminated to the public during the Soviet era—produced a version of the Qur'an that would be acceptable to Soviet citizens. They largely demonstrated an amalgamation of Soviet ideology into their understanding of Islam and the Qur'an.

As a consequence of centuries of state control, Kazan Tatars emerged from the ruins of the Soviet Union in the 1990s with extremely limited knowledge of their religious, cultural, and linguistic traditions, yet with a great zeal to discover all that set them apart from 'Russians'. Therefore, a more comprehensive understanding of the Qur'an—as the basis of their religion—was envisaged as an important part of the Tatar national identity-building process. Towards the end of the Soviet regime, during *perestroika* (1985–91), some international institutions began reprinting the earlier Türki-Tatar commentary-translations written before 1917 in Arabic letters. For example, Elif Ofset Tesisleri reprinted al- Ḥamīdī's *al-Itqān* in its original Türki-Tatar in Istanbul using an offset lithography method. Three years later, in 1987, the Istanbul version of *al-Itqān* was reprinted by the Mubārak b. Nāṣir al-ʿAlī Foundation in Doha, which classified it as a *tafsīr* of the Qur'an in Tatar.[82] In 1989, *Tafsīr Nuʿmāni* was reissued in Qatar on the private initiative of Ḥasan al-Maʾāyrijī. Al-Imānqulī's *Tashīl al-bayān* was reprinted in Doha in 1996, using Arabic letters in the original Türki-Tatar script. However, Tatars in the post-Soviet setting could not benefit much from these reprinted Qur'an commentaries as the state had changed the official Tatar script twice, from Arabic to Latin in 1927 and then to Cyrillic in 1937, and so the younger generations were unable to read the Arabic script.[83] Furthermore, modern Tatars were completely unfamiliar with the old version of Türki-Tatar used in these works because their language had undergone extensive lexical and grammatical changes throughout the Soviet era. Accordingly, to

---

81 Isaev was the student of Ḍiyāʾ Kamālī, the pre-revolutionary Tatar translator of the Qur'an whose translation has been described by Bustanov as a 'peculiar combination of a thorough study of the Quran and the Prophetic traditions on the one hand and a fascination with the success of Soviet cosmonautics and science on the other'. Bustanov, 'The Qur'an for Soviet Citizens', p. 92.

82 Shaykh al-Islām Asadullāh al-Ḥamīdī, *al-Itqān fī tarjamat al-Qurʾān* (Doha: Mubārak b. Nāṣir al-ʿAlī Foundation, 1987).

83 Yemelianova, 'Islam in Russia', p. 44.

satisfy the public desire to understand the Qur'an during the immediate post-Soviet era, Nurulla Arslani prepared and published a modernised version of *Tafsīr Nuʿmānī* in 1991. The Türki-Tatar text in Arabic script used in the original underwent a thorough revision to make it suitable for a modern readership: it was transferred into the modern Tatar language and Cyrillic alphabet, the interpretations were simplified, and the lengthy stories (including *riwayāt*) which characterised the classical *tafsīr* genre were either eliminated or substantially condensed. As a result, this classical work was reincarnated as a modernised vernacular text and was subsequently reprinted numerous times in Kazan.

A decade later, at the beginning of the twenty-first century, several local Muslim activists and clergy published their own vernacular partial or complete translations of the Qur'an, giving rise to another Tatar commentary-translation subgenre in post-Soviet times. For instance, the renowned Tatar playwriter and novelist Rabit Batulla brought out his *Qur'ān Aiatläreneng Tatarcha Mäghnäläre* ('The Meaning of the Qur'anic Verses in Tatar') in 2001.[84] Batulla's proficiency in Arabic was insufficient to enable him to translate the Qur'an from the original Arabic, and so he depended heavily on contemporary Turkish translations. Ramil Yunusov, a former student of the Islamic University of Madinah, was another contributor to this post-Soviet subgenre. After his return from Medina to Kazan in 1995, he started delivering *tafsīr* classes to the public at the recently restored Madrasa Muḥammadiia. His oratory prowess and solid grasp of Arabic and Tatar enabled him to quickly earn widespread recognition among laypeople when his interpretations were released as audio cassette recordings. Other noteworthy efforts to produce a modern Tatar vernacular Qur'an were made by Kamil Bikchantaev, an imam from Kazan and a candidate for the position of mufti of the Republic of Tatarstan in 2001; and Farit Salman, who held important positions at the Central Spiritual Board of Muslims of Russia and European Countries of the Commonwealth of Independent States (TsDUM, Tsentral'noe Dukhovnoe Upravlenie Musul'man Rossii i Evropeiskikh Stran SNG) based in Ufa, and was the Mufti of

---

84 R. Batulla, *Qur'ān Aiatläreneng Tatarcha Mäghnäläre* [The Meaning of the Qur'anic Verses in Tatar] (Kazan: Qul Sharif Nashriiate, 2001).

the Republic of Tatarstan from 1997 to 2001.[85] The popularity of these impromptu Tatar translations of the Qur'an—which emerged in the immediate post-Soviet space to bridge the religious and cultural gaps felt by both Tatar intelligentsia and laypeople—was contingent upon the translator's perceived legitimacy and proficiency in Arabic, in addition to their affiliation with recognised religious institutions. However, as with the official posts these translators held in these institutions, the majority of their translations had a short lifespan.

In 2019, the Huzur publishing house (based in Kazan) printed another contemporary translation of the Qur'an into Tatar in 760 pages, titled *Käläm Sharif: Mäghnäwi Tärjemä* ('*Kalām Sharīf*: A Semantic Translation'). A team of forty experts in Islamic studies, Arabic and Tatar linguistics and literature, and sociology had worked for seven years on this project, which was undertaken by the muftiate of the Republic of Tatarstan and led by Mufti Kamil Samigullin. The translation team consulted twenty-eight modern and classical Qur'an commentaries and translations, including those in Türki-Tatar (such as Nuʿmān's *Tafsīr*, al-Imānqulī's *Tashīl al-bayān*, al-Ḥamīdī's *al-Itqān*, and the modern Tatar translations of Isaev, Salman, and Batulla).[86] They also made extensive reference to classical *tafsīr*s, including the works of al-Ṭabarī, Abū Nafs ʿUmar al-Nasafī (d. 537/1142), al-Qurṭubī, and Abū al-Barakāt al-Nasafī (d. 710/1310).

The *Kalām Sharīf* gained immediate popularity among laypeople due to its simple language and accessibility: 45,000 copies of the Tatar version were produced in 2020 alone. In addition to a print edition, it is also available online and in audio format and, recently, a smartphone application has also been launched. The appearance of *Kalām Sharīf* was hailed by the media and the Tatar intelligentsia as one of the top ten achievements of modern Tatarstan,[87] and as the best alternative to the Salafi *tafsīr*s available in Russian translation (such as that by the Saudi

---

85 *Qur'ani Karim* (*Farit Hazrat Haydar Salman Qur'ān Karim Aiatläreneng Mäghnälärenä Tatarcha Anglatmalar Birüche*) [The Qur'an Karim: Farid Hazrat Haydar Salman as a Commentator on the Meanings of the Qur'anic Verses in Tatar] (Kazan: Rannur, 1999).

86 A. Mukhametrahimov, '*Umma* sovremennogo Tatarstana: Ot korana i rodnogo iaazyka do svoego TV i kol-tsentra' [The *Umma* of Modern Tatarstan: From the Qur'an and Native Language to its own TV and Call Centre], *Business Gazeta*, 20 August 2020, https://www.business-gazeta.ru/article/478266

87 Mukhametrahimov, 'Umma Sovremennogo Tatarstana'.

shaykh ʿAbd al-Raḥmān al-Saʿdī, 1889–1957, which was translated by Elmir Kuliev into Russian in 2014 and later banned as extremist literature in 2020).[88] Perhaps the most important reason for the appeal of this Tatar vernacular Qur'an is that it is the product of a collaborative effort, whereas other contemporary Tatar translations are generally regarded as reflecting the opinions of a single person—and, worse, someone without proficiency in Arabic.

However, despite its popularity, the interpretation of certain verses in the *Kalām Sharīf* instilled doubts about its legitimacy among many members of the Muslim community, including the Spiritual Board of Muslims in the Russian Federation: a state-sponsored central muftiate based in Moscow.[89] For instance, while interpreting the first five verses of *Sūrat al-Nāziʿāt* (Q 79), the translators included the ambiguous phrase 'seeking help from the grave-dwellers' ('qäber ähellarennän iärdäm sorau'); Salafi-oriented critics argued that this posed a serious threat to Islamic monotheism, as only Allah is worthy of being worshipped or called upon for help. The *Kalām Sharīf*'s heavy reliance on the Ismail Aga (*Ismailağa Cemaati*)[90] tradition explains the rationale behind such interpretations, as the *tafsīr* of Mahmut Ustaosmanoğlu al-Ufi (1929–2022)—the community's founder—is extensively cited as one of the primary sources.[91] *Kalām Sharīf*'s inclinations towards this ultra-conservative Turkish branch of the Naqshbandi Sufi order in interpreting the Qur'anic verses are not accidental. The head of the translators' team, Mufti Samigullin, received his theological education at the Madrasa *Ismailağa* in Fatih, Istanbul from 2003 to 2007. When Samigullin was voted to the position of Mufti of Tatarstan in 2013, the *Ismailağa* Sufi order strengthened its position in

---

88   Up to the present date, much Islamic literature has been banned in Russia on the basis that it is deemed to violate the 1996 Religion Law and the 2002 Law of Extremism, based on allegations of 'terrorism', 'violence', 'stirring up religious hatred', and 'missionary activity.' See Religiia Segodnia, 'Strasti Vokrug Tafsira Qur'ana *Kalām Sharīf*' [Heightened Emotions Surround the Qur'anic Exegesis *Kalām Sharīf*], *Religiia Segodnia*, 23 February 2021, https://reltoday.com/news/strasti-vokrug-tafsira-korana-kaljam-sharif

89   A. Mukhametrahimov and L. Farkhutdinov, 'Spor pro 'Obitateley mogil: Pochemu Gainutdin poslal Minnikhanovu donos na Samigullina?' [The Dispute about "Grave Dwellers": Why did Gainutdin Denounce Samigullin to Minnikhanov?], *Business Gazeta*, 8 April 2021, https://www.business-gazeta.ru/article/505238

90   The Ismail Aga is an ultra-conservative branch of the Naqshbandi Sufi order in Turkey.

91   https://www.business-gazeta.ru/article/505238

the republic.[92] Interestingly, various contemporary media sources feature the sharp increase of interest among Tatars in various Naqshbandi Sufi orders, including *Ismailağa Cemaati*.[93]

The current discourse around Qur'anic exegesis in the post-Soviet sphere is frequently framed in terms of a conflict between the 'Salafis' (the Salafi label in the Russian context is given to any stance which represents 'unofficial Islam,' primarily deemed to be inspired by foreign ideas) and the Sufis (who are deemed traditional in the region, and embody 'official Islam', which is thought to be 'more appropriate' to the Tatar environment). Accordingly, the Religiia Segodnia—a community of researchers who are monitoring the religious situation in Russia— have highlighted that 'the current crisis serves as a clear example of how the Muslim community in Russia is not ideologically cohesive but rather a patchwork of divergent currents, with long-running disagreements between Salafis and Sufis over how to interpret sacred scriptures.'[94]

In conclusion, three distinguishing characteristics of the development of the Tatar Qur'an commentary-translation tradition in the post-Soviet arena can be identified. First, the central or regional muftiates—with their priorities and principal interests—determine the future, reputation, and fate of Tatar Qur'an translations as they emerge onto the market. This is not only true for Tatar translations, but also holds for vernacular Qur'an versions in other languages in the Russian sphere. Currently there are about eighty central, ethno-national or regional muftiates in Russia with direct or indirect connections to the Kazan Tatars, Russia's second-largest ethnic group (which numbers 4,713,669 according to the 2021 Census, i.e. 3.61% of the total population) after ethnic Russians (who number 105,620,179, or 80.85% of the total population). Renat Bekkin describes the interactions between these Russian muftiates as 'firms competing in the Islamic segment of the religious market.'[95] He further asserts that the Islamic segment of the Russian religious market exhibits an oligopolistic

---

92 'Muftiia Tatarstana obvinili v popytke rassprostraneniia sektantskogo ucheniia' [Mufti of Tatarstan is Accused of Attempting to Spread Sectarian Teachings], *Information Agency TASS*, 8 April 2021, https://tass.ru/obschestvo/11100323
93 https://tass.ru/obschestvo/11100323; R. Suleimanov, 'Mufti Tatarstana i magnat iz Bashkirii' [Mufti of Tatarstan and Tycoon from Bashkiria], *MKRU*, 6 July 2020, https://kazan.mk.ru/social/2020/07/06/muftiy-tatarstana-i-magnat-iz-bashkirii-kogo-privlekayut-tureckie-sufiyskie-bratstva.html
94 https://reltoday.com/news/strasti-vokrug-tafsira-korana-kaljam-sharif
95 Bekkin, 'People of Reliable Loyalty', pp. 46–47.

4. The State, 'Official' ʿUlamāʾ and Tatar Qur'an Commentary-Translations   189

structure at the federal, regional, and local levels.⁹⁶ The direction and priorities of debates over Qur'an translation in Russia, especially the issue of the eligibility of a translator or the authenticity of a translation, have been used as a marketing tool by competing muftiates. The 'official Islam' of the Volga-Urals region, where the majority of Tatars reside, is primarily associated with Tatar-centred Hanafism, which is a synthesis of the Ḥanafī school of Islamic law and the Māturīdī school of theology. Accordingly, Mufti Gainutdin and his Spiritual Board of Muslims in the Russian Federation affirm their adherence to 'traditional' Islam, which is associated with Hanafism, and have consistently branded their opponents as Wahhabis and Salafis.⁹⁷ In the case of the debates regarding the *Kalām Sharīf*, its Turkish-style Sufi and Ismail Aga tendencies were likewise viewed as 'untraditional' for the region.

Second, the domestication of Islam through the muftiate in modern Russia has necessitated the production of new vernacular Qur'anic interpretations and debates that primarily serve the state's policies, and other interests such as national security. The muftiates' relations with the Kremlin have always been shaped by the latter's domestic and international agenda,⁹⁸ and Islam in Russia has undergone a long and gradual process of top-down institutionalisation since the establishment of the Orenburg Spiritual Assembly in 1788. In the post-Soviet period, the state's management of Muslim affairs has taken the form of a 'churchification' of Islam according to which, as Egdunas Racius observes, 'representative Muslim organisations are expected to model themselves after, and function like, Christian Churches, with their ecclesiastical hierarchical structures.'⁹⁹ In all the state's dealings with Islam, national security takes precedence. As a result, policies intended to securitise and domesticise Islam have been adopted, requiring the strict oversight and management of religion and, in the end, 'impl[ying] an intervention in the very content of Islamic practices and convictions.'¹⁰⁰ Although national integration is not a primary concern in modern Russia for indigenous Muslim minority groups such as Tatars, Chechens, Balkars, and Avars, the securitisation

---

96   Ibid., p. 55.
97   Yemelianova, 'Muslim-State Relations', p. 116.
98   Ibid., p. 118.
99   Egdunas Racius, 'Governance of Islam in Europe', in *Yearbook of Muslims in Europe*, vol. X, ed. by Oliver Scharbrodt et al. (Leiden: Brill, 2019), pp. 1–22 (p. 15).
100   Sunier, 'Toward a Common European Islamic Landscape?', p. 4.

of Islam has become one of the priorities of the federal state as a result of the Chechen Wars of 1994–96 and 1999–2009, and 9/11. The Russian state's efforts to regulate Islamic discourse, literature, and education are evident effects of their attempts to domesticise Islam. In 2002, the state passed the 'Law on Extremism', which permits the prohibition of any Islamic publications, speeches, or associations on the grounds that they are 'extremist' and 'contradictory to the traditional Ḥanafī *madhhab*.'[101] The process of domesticising Islam in Russia has been accomplished with the establishment of a model of 'traditional' Islam which has clear dimensions and a state-endorsed attitude. Because the Qur'an constitutes the fundamental source of Islamic religious thought and moral codes, muftiates were assigned the responsibility to interpret its message in ways that accord with Russian national interests and priorities. Attempts to decode the Islamic message in line with Russian state interests could be seen at work, for example, in Russian military aggression against Ukraine in 2022 and the subsequent war in Ukraine. Islamic concepts such as 'the greater *jihād*', 'fighting in the way of Allah' (*fī sabīlī llāh*), and martyrdom (*shahīd*) were often circulated by Muslim official institutions to justify Russia's war against Ukraine.

Thirdly, and finally, the domesticisation of Islam in Russia has gradually led to its 'Russification'. In the immediate post-Soviet era, contemporary Tatar translations of the Qur'an functioned as a component of the national awakening and identity construction of Kazan Tatars. These vernacular translations were a result of state democratisation policies of the late 1980s that assisted in reviving Russia's indigenous languages. In 1992, together with Russian, Tatar became the official language of the Republic of Tatarstan. However, as Tatarstan gradually lost the essentials of its illusory sovereignty over the next twenty-five years, the prestige of Tatar in the official and public spheres has also been significantly degraded. Since 2017, Tatar classes are no longer mandatory in schools—a fact which does not inspire much optimism about public demand for Qur'an translations in Tatar in the future, and the situation is similar when it comes to other indigenous minority languages in Russia. As in Soviet times,

---

101 Elmira Akhmetova and Ildus Rafikov, 'The Legacy of Islamic Education in Russia Since the Bulghar Kingdom', *Islam and Civilizational Renewal*, 13:2 (2022), 30–51 (pp. 42–43).

the Russian language has effectively remained the *lingua franca* for all of Russia's Muslims, who hail from over forty different ethnic groups. Muslim authors have eventually begun to use Russian more and more, which has facilitated the Russian Federation's multi-ethnic discourse on Islam.[102] At present, the Russian language is the major vehicle for Islamic knowledge and education in Russia. In the coming decades, if a similar policy of domesticisation of Islam is maintained at the federal level by the centralised state, with Russian serving as the primary medium of Islamic communication, there may be no more need, or demand, for Tatar vernacular translations of the Qur'an. Consequently, while the Soviet context facilitated a thorough divergence of vernacular Tatar Qur'an interpretations from the linguistic and conceptual dependency on Persianate and Arab models, the post-Soviet period has led to the marginalisation of Tatar and other minority languages.

Conclusion

This chapter has expounded the Kazan Tatar Qur'anic commentary and translation tradition from the nineteenth century to the present day, in the context of a critique of the 'official' ʿulamāʾ's privileged position when it comes to interpreting the Qur'an for laypeople. The role of the 'official' ʿulamāʾ, throughout Russia, has been performed by the institution of the muftiate—which emerged during Catherine II's reign and evolved as an integral component of the colonial structure that was designed to assist the state's agenda, at both domestic and international levels. Samigullin's rhetorical question cited in the introduction, 'why should the Arabs authorise our [Tatar] Qur'an?', thus perfectly encapsulates the whole picture of political maneuvering that surrounds Tatar Qur'an commentary and translation in modern Russia. The fundamental purpose of the earliest Türki-Tatar commentary-translations in the nineteenth century was to provide Tatar laypeople with an explanation of the meaning of the Qur'an that was in line with generally recognised religious perspectives and established and acknowledged *tafsīr* traditions.

---

102 Michael Kemper and Alfrid K. Bustanov, 'Introduction: Voices of Islam in Russian', in *Islamic Authority and the Russian Language: Studies on Texts from European Russia, The North Caucasus and West Siberia*, ed. by Michael Kemper and Alfrid K. Bustanov (Amsterdam: Uitgeverij Pegasus, 2012), pp. 7–6 (p. 7).

When interpreting the verses of the Qur'an, these vernacular works did not challenge the methodological or stylistic authority of classical Arabic and Persian *tafsīr*s, or their primary sources and references, or their approach to traditionally accepted concepts. These works were not deemed as a threat to the muftiate's power or the survival of the colonial government, so they were published and extensively circulated.

It was not until the advent of a new trend among Kazan Tatars in the 1910s that conflicts began, when a number of Tatar scholars such as Jārullāh, al-Muṭīʿī Tukhfatullin, and Ḍiyāʾ Kamālī produced modernist interpretations of the Qur'an which were intended to be pertinent to their time and socio-cultural and political context, and which, sometimes, had an anti-colonial approach. These translation efforts indicate a divergence from past conceptual and linguistic dependency on the Persianate domain.[103] The intellectual debates in the region at the time about the interpretation and understanding of the Qur'an, as described by Kemper, showed 'significant dynamism in responding to the colonial situation in Russia.'[104] In these new circumstances, the muftiate shouldered new duties, authorising new translations and vernacular commentaries and determining which groups of people had the authority to write such works.

The disputes over Tatar Qur'an translations in the post-Soviet context once again reveal the muftiate's prioritisation of upholding and promoting state policies when interpreting the Qur'an and Islamic teachings or dealing with Muslim affairs. Policies promoting the domesticisation of Islam in modern Russia through the mechanism of the muftiate have necessitated new, vernacular interpretations of the Qur'an that primarily serve the state's policies, national interests, and priorities. Consequently, this domesticisation has been characterised as 'an intervention in the very content of Islamic practices and convictions',[105] which is commonly actualised through the muftiate. At present, as Samigullin's rhetorical question indicates, the institution of the muftiate represents Islam in Russia, and its official *ʿulamāʾ* are the sole judges of whether a particular

---

103 Alfrid Bustanov, 'On Qur'anic Culture in Inner Russia between the Seventeenth and Twentieth Centuries', in *European Muslims and the Qur'an: Practices of Translation, Interpretation, and Commodification*, ed. by Gulnaz Sibgatullina and Gerard Wiegers (Berlin: Walter de Gruyter GmbH, 2024), p. 166.
104 Kemper, 'Imperial Russia as Dar al-Islam'.
105 Sunier, 'Toward a Common European Islamic Landscape?', p. 4.

Tatar translation of the Qur'an and interpretation of Islam is accurate or not. This situation virtually eliminates any prospect of individually authored Tatar Qur'an translation projects in modern Russia. Furthermore, the two-centuries-long tradition of Tatar Qur'an translations may vanish entirely in the next few decades, if the Russian state does not change its language policies and attitude towards ethnic minorities.

Bibliography

Aguilar, Luis Manuel Hernández, and Zubair Ahmad, 'A Dangerous Text: Disciplining Deficient Readers and the Policing of the Qur'an in the German Islam Conference', *ReOrient*, 6:1 (2020), https://doi.org/10.13169/reorient.6.1.0086

Akhmetova, Elmira, and Ildus Rafikov, 'The Legacy of Islamic Education in Russia Since the Bulghar Kingdom', *Islam and Civilisational Renewal*, 13:2 (2022), https://doi.org/10.52282/icr.v13i2.919

Altuntas, Selcuk, 'How to Be a Proper Muslim in the Russian Empire: An Intellectual Biography of Musa Jarullah Bigiyev (1875–1949)' (doctoral thesis, University of Wisconsin-Madison, 2018).

Anon., 'Qur'ān Tärjumäse Haqïnda', *Yoldïz*, 810, 25 March 1912.

Asad, Talal, *The Idea of an Anthropology of Islam* (Washington, D.C.: Centre for Contemporary Arab Studies, Georgetown University, 1986).

Azmukhanov, Arthur, 'Kazan Bölgese Tefsir Çalışmalarından Tefsir-i Nu'mani Örneği' (master's thesis, University of Ankara, 2012).

Batulla, R., *Qur'ān Aiatläreneng Tatarcha Mäghnäläre* (Kazan: Qul Sharif Nashriiate, 2001).

Bekkin, Renat, 'People of Reliable Loyalty ...: Muftiates and the State in Modern Russia' (unpublished doctoral dissertation, Södertörn University, 2020).

Bigiyev, Musa, 'En Lazïm Bir İ'lan', *Al-Iṣlāḥ*, 58, 25 January 1909.

——, 'Yine Muhim Bir Mäs'älä', *Waqt*, 569, 21 January 1910.

Boltabayev, Saidbek, 'Çağatayca Tefsir-i Hüseyni (Mevahib-i Alıyye) Tercümesi ve Farsça Dil Özellekleri Üzerine', *Journal of Old Turkic Studies*, 3:2 (2019), https://doi.org/10.35236/jots.560320

Bukharaev, Ravil, *Islam in Russia: The Four Seasons* (London: Curzon Press, 2000).

Bustanov, Alfrid, 'The Qur'an for Soviet Citizens: The Rhetoric of Progress in the Theological Works of 'Abd al-Bari Isaev', *Forum for Anthropology and Culture*, 37 (2018), https://doi.org/10.31250/1815-8927-2018-14-14-169-184

——, 'On Qur'anic Culture in Inner Russia between the Seventeenth and Twentieth Centuries', in *European Muslims and the Qur'an: Practices of Translation, Interpretation, and Commodification*, ed. by Gulnaz Sibgatullina and Gerard Wiegers (Berlin: Walter de Gruyter GmbH, 2024), pp. 165–188.

Fisher, Alan, *The Crimean Tatars* (Stanford: Hoover Institution Press, 1978).

Green, Nile, 'Introduction: The Frontiers of the Persianate World (ca. 800-1900)', in *The Persianate World: The Frontiers of a Eurasian Lingua Franca*, ed. by Nile Green (Oakland: University of California Press, 2019), pp. 1–74.

Gumerov, 'Abd al-Raḥmān, 'Ulema Dikkatenä', *İdel*, 125, 3 February 1909.

Gunasti, Susan, *The Qur'an between the Ottoman Empire and the Turkish Republic: An Exegetical Tradition* (London: Routledge, 2019).

al-Ḥamīdī, Shaykh al-Islām Asadullāh, *al-Itqān fī tarjamat al-Qurʾān* (Kazan: Lito-Tipografiia Brat'ia Karimovy, 1911).

Ibn Amīrkhān, Ḥusayn, *Tafsīr-i fawāʾid* (Kazan: Typography of G. Viacheslav, 1885).

Ishaqi, Gaiaz, *Idel-Ural* (Naberejniyi Chelny: KAMAZ, 1993).

al-Imānqulī al-Qazānī, Muḥammad Ṣādiq b. Shāh Aḥmad, *Tashīl al-bayān fī tafsīr al-Qurʾān* (Kazan: Ürnäk, 1911).

Jārullāh, Mūsā, *Halïq Nazarïna Bernichä Mäs'älä* (Kazan: Elektro-Tipographiya Umid, 1912).

——, *Ozïn Künlärdä Ruza: Ijtihad Kitabï* (Kazan: Umid, 1911).

——, 'Tatar Dünyasïnda Räzälät', *Waqt*, 19 April 1912, p. 2.

Kemper, Michael, 'Imperial Russia as Dar al-Islam? Nineteenth-Century Debates on Ijtihad and Taqlid among the Volga Tatars', *Encounters: An International Journal for the Study of Culture and Society*, 6 (2015).

——, and Alfrid K. Bustanov, 'Introduction: Voices of Islam in Russian', in *Islamic Authority and the Russian Language: Studies on Texts from European Russia, The North Caucasus and West Siberia*, ed. by Michael Kemper and Alfrid K. Bustanov (Amsterdam: Uitgeverij Pegasus, 2012), pp. 7–26.

Khudiakov, Mikhail, *Ocherki po istorii Kazanskogo khanstva*, 3rd edn (Moscow: Insan, 1991).

Mukhametrahimov, A., '*Umma* sovremennogo Tatarstana: Ot Korana i rodnogo yazyka do svoego TV i kol-tsentra', *Business Gazeta*, 20 August 2020, https://www.business-gazeta.ru/article/478266

——, and L. Farkhutdinov, 'Spor pro 'obitateley mogil: Pochemu Gainutdin poslal Minnikhanovu donos na Samigullina?', *Business Gazeta*, 8 April 2021, https://www.business-gazeta.ru/article/505238

Nahid, Haşim, *Türkiye İçin Necat ve İtila Yolları* (Istanbul: Şems Matbaası, 1915).

Nurgatina, G., '*Tafsir-i Fawaid* Husaina ibn Amirkhana i Tatarskaia ekzegeticheskaia traditsiia kontsa XIX- nachala XX vekov', in *Teologiia Tradisional'nikh religii v nauchno-obrazovatel'nom prostranstve sovremennoi Rossii: Sbornik Materialov*, ed. by R. Mukhametshin (Kazan: Brig, 2020).

——, 'Traditsiia kommentirovaniia Korana u Tatar', in *Teologiia Traditsional'nikh Religii v nauchno-obrazovatel'nom prostranstve sovremennoi Rossii: Sbornik materialov*, ed. by R. Mukhametshin (Kazan: Brig, 2020), pp. 114–118.

al-Qurṣāwī, Abū Naṣr ʿAbd al-Naṣīr, *al-Irshād lil-ʿibād* (Kazan: Tatarskoie Knizhnoie Izdatel'stvo, 2005).

Racius, Egdunas, 'Governance of Islam in Europe', in *Yearbook of Muslims in Europe*, vol. X, ed. by Oliver Scharbrodt et al. (Leiden: Brill, 2019), pp. 1–22.

Religiia Segodnia, 'Strasti Vokrug Tafsira Kurana *Kalam Sharif*', *Religiia Segodnia*, 23 February 2021, https://reltoday.com/news/strasti-vokrug-tafsira-korana-kaljam-sharif

Resulzade, M. E., 'Bahadır ve Sona', *Ikbal*, 541, 29 December 1913.

—— (Məhəmməd Əmin Rəsulzadə), *Əsərləri II Cilt (1909–1914)* (Bakı: Təhsil, 2014).

Rezvan, Efim A., *Koran i ego mir* (St. Petersburg: Russian Academy of Sciences, 2001).

Ross, Danielle, *Tatar Empire: Kazan's Muslims and the Making of Imperial Russia* (Bloomington: Indiana University Press, 2020).

Sabirov, Razim, and Elena Kolebakina-Usmanova, 'Kamil Samigullin: Pochemu araby dolzhny proveriat' nash Koran', *Business Gazeta*, 18 October 2019, https://m.business-gazeta.ru/article/442980

Salman, Farit, *Qur'ani Karim (Farit Hazrat Haydar Salman Qur'ān Karim Aiätläreneng Mäghnälärenä Tatarcha Anglatmalar Birŭche)* (Kazan: Rannur, 1999).

al-Samānī, Nuʿmān, *Tafsīr Nuʿmāni*, 2 vols (Kazan: Millet, 1911).

Sibgatullina, Gulnaz, 'The Ecology of a Vernacular Qur'an: Rethinking Mūsā Bīgī's Translation into Türki-Tatar', *Journal of Qur'anic Studies*, 24:3 (2022), https://doi.org/10.3366/jqs.2022.0515

——, and G. Wiegers, 'The European Qur'an: Towards an Inclusive Definition', in *European Muslims and the Qur'an: Practices of Translation, Interpretation, and Commodification*, ed. by Gulnaz Sibgatullina and Gerard Wiegers (Berlin: Walter de Gruyter GmbH, 2024), pp. 1–22.

Spannaus, Nathan, 'Islamic Thought and Revivalism in the Russian Empire: An Intellectual Biography of Abū Naṣr Qūrṣāwī (1776–1812)' (doctoral thesis, McGill University, 2012).

Suleimanov, R. 'Mufti Tatarstana i magnat iz Bashkirii' ('Mufti of Tatarstan and Tycoon from Bashkiria'), *MKRU*, 6 July 2020, https://kazan.mk.ru/social/2020/07/06/muftiy-tatarstana-i-magnat-iz-bashkirii-kogo-privlekayut-tureckie-sufiyskie-bratstva.html

Sunier, Thijl, 'Toward a Common European Islamic Landscape?', in *Yearbook of Muslims in Europe*, vol. XII, ed. by Egdunas Racius et al. (Leiden: Brill, 2021), pp. 1–18.

Tarjumānī, Kashshāf al-Dīn, 'Tashīḥ-i Qur'an Haqqïnda', *Yoldïz*, 362, 10 February 1909.

Tenishev, Edhem, *Yazyki mira. Turkskiye yaziki* (Moscow: Russian Academy of Sciences RAN, 1997), pp. 35–47.

Tukhfatullin, Muhammad Kāmil al-Muṭīʿī, *Tatarcha Qur'ān Täfsire* (Kazan: Maarif, 1914).

Wilson, M. Brett, 'The Qur'an after Babel: Translating and Printing the Qur'an in Late Ottoman and Modern Turkey' (PhD thesis: Duke University, 2009).

——, *Translating the Qur'an in an Age of Nationalism: Print Culture and Modern Islam in Turkey* (Abingdon: Oxford University Press, 2014).

Yemilianova, Galina M., 'Islam in Russia: An Historical Perspective', in *Islam in Post-Soviet Russia: Public and Private Faces*, ed. by Hillary Pilkington and Galina Yemelianova (New York: RoutledgeCurzon, 2003), pp. 15–61.

——, 'Muslim-State Relations in Russia', in *Muslim Minority-State Relations: Violence, Integration, and Policy*, ed. by Robert Mason (New York: Palgrave Macmillan, 2016), pp. 107–32, https://doi.org/10.1007/978-1-137-52605-2_5

Zenkovsky, Serge, *Pan-Turkism and Islam in Russia* (Cambridge: Harvard University Press, 1967).

5. A 'Qur'an Race' in the Cold War: Max Henning's Qur'an Translation in the German Democratic Republic

Johanna Pink

Introduction

In 1968,[1] the publishing house Philipp Reclam jun. in Leipzig, then part of the German Democratic Republic (GDR), published a new, revised edition of the Qur'an translation by Max Henning, which dated back to 1901.[2] This was not a minor event in the GDR publishing landscape, but was rather the result of four years of deliberation, political struggles, ideological arguments, and practical challenges, and the project may only have come to fruition due to the special situation of Germany during the Cold War. The division of Germany after World War Two had also brought about the division of Reclam, an important publisher of inexpensive, accessible literature for a mass readership. Reclam Stuttgart, the legally and administratively independent branch situated in the Federal Republic of Germany (FRG), had published a revised edition

---

1 This publication is the result of the project 'GloQur—The Global Qur'an', which has received funding from the European Research Council (ERC) under the European Union's Horizon 2020 research and innovation programme (grant agreement no. 863650).
2 Max Henning (trans.), *Der Koran* (Leipzig: Reclam, 1901).

of Henning's Qur'an translation in 1960,[3] and Reclam Leipzig—which liked to keep abreast of the publishing achievements of the Stuttgart branch—very much took notice of that fact. This was entirely in the spirit of the East-West competition that so deeply characterised the Cold War, from the arms race to the Olympic Games, and from the Space Race to (as this chapter shows) the publication of a Qur'an translation: a Cold War 'Qur'an race', so to speak. However, the political and economic realities of the GDR were very different from those of Western Germany. Publishing a religious text was ideologically fraught, risky, and required extensive justification. Reclam Leipzig commissioned the historian of religion Kurt Rudolph (1929–2020), a professor at the University of Leipzig, to revise Hennings's translation and notes, and they arranged for a new introduction to be written by Rudolph and socialist historian Ernst Werner (1920–1993)—his colleague at the University of Leipzig. The blurb on the back cover of the book advertised it by emphasising the 'eminently political significance' of 'the life and work of Muhammad', and described him 'as a model of a conscious, energetic, and responsible statesman who paved the way for racial equality and social justice' as well as 'Arab unity.'[4]

In this chapter, I will examine the history and ideological framing of the first and only Qur'an translation that was ever published in the German Democratic Republic, using the 1968 translation itself, and its subsequent editions, as well as archival sources from the publisher and the GDR Ministry of Culture.[5] I will first outline the features of

---

3   Max Henning (trans.) and Annemarie Schimmel (ed.), *Der Koran* (Stuttgart: Reclam, 1960).
4   Max Henning (trans.) and Kurt Rudolph (ed.), *Der Koran* (Leipzig: Reclam, 1968), back cover. Translations from German are my own throughout this chapter.
5   I would like to thank the Deutsches Literaturarchiv in Marbach for providing access to the Reclam Verlagsarchiv and the Federal Archive for the opportunity to inspect the file of the GDR Ministry of Culture regarding the printing application and authorisation for the GDR edition of Henning's translation of the Qur'an. I quote documents from the Reclam-Verlagsarchiv in the Deutsches Literaturarchiv with the permission of the Reclam-Verlag and the Deutsches Literaturarchiv. I have also endeavoured to obtain permission from the copyright holders of all persons quoted. I succeeded in doing so in the case of Annemarie Schimmel, Kurt Rudolph, and Ernst Werner. In the other cases, I was unable to locate any copyright holders. I am prepared to settle justified claims retrospectively. I have anonymised the names of employees of Reclam Verlag below the highest management level who were involved in the correspondence, as the identity of these persons is not essential to the chapter.

the original 1901 version, following which I will discuss the division of Reclam, and the 1960 edition of Reclam Leipzig's West German sister branch. After situating Reclam Leipzig in the publishing and censorship landscape of the GDR, I will move on to the main three sections of this chapter, in which I will tell the story of the debates, complications, and endeavour from which the GDR Qur'an translation was born. I will then describe the features of the edition resulting from competition with the FRG, and outline the image of Muḥammad and Islam that the GDR edition draws. In the final section, I will make some brief remarks on the intriguing fate of Henning's Qur'an translation in reunified Germany, which was characterised both by the aftershock of the partition of Germany and by demographic changes that led to a large Muslim population in Germany.

Henning's Original Qur'an Translation in its Wilhelminian Context

Max Henning (1861–1927) was a German writer known for his involvement in a movement of secularist 'free thinkers' (*freigeistige Bewegung*). He was an autodidact in Arabic and had already translated extracts from the 'Tales of a Thousand and One Nights' for the Reclam publishing house before he produced his translation of the Qur'an.[6] Both works were part of an established and widely popular series called 'Reclam's Universal-Bibliothek' ('Reclam's Universal Library'), which aimed to make literary works available to a mass readership in the form of small, inexpensive books. Philipp Reclam jun. endeavoured to equip the 'common people' with cultural capital, but inclusion in the series soon also became a source of prestige, or symbolic capital, for books and their authors or editors.[7] Both functions later translated very well into the realities of the GDR book market.

---

6   Brigitte Haberländer, 'Max Henning', in *Glaubensbuch und Weltliteratur. Koranübersetzungen in Deutschland von der Reformationszeit bis heute*, ed. by Hartmut Bobzin and Peter M. Kleine (Arnsberg: Stadt Arnsberg, 2007), p. 41.
7   York-Gothart Mix, 'Kulturelles Kapital für 20, 50 oder 80 Pfennige: Medialisierungsstrategien Leipziger Verleger in der frühen Moderne am Beispiel der „Universal-Bibliothek", der „Insel-Bücherei" und der Sammlung „Der Jüngste Tag"', *Archiv für Kulturgeschichte*, 82:1 (2000), 191–210 (pp. 200–203).

At the time Henning's translation of the Qur'an came out in 1901, the majority of German readers were unfamiliar with Islam, which was, in the public perception, mostly equated with the Ottoman Empire. While negative Orientalist stereotypes as well as Christian polemical tropes against Islam persisted, there was also a countercurrent, partly born out of political interests. The German Empire was, at the time, aiming to establish good relations with the Ottoman Empire and saw the Near East as strategically valuable for guaranteeing access to its recent colonial ventures. Palestine and Egypt were attractive destinations for affluent tourists, and Kaiser Wilhelm II had undertaken a trip to the 'Orient' in 1898 that had received much public attention.[8]

As a result of this context, the paratexts of Henning's translation—specifically, the introduction and the notes—reflect several conflicting tendencies.[9] Henning professes a desire to promote a better understanding of 'the Orient' due to the large number of Muslims worldwide and the vitality of Islam, which continues to gain new followers despite the fact that, according to Henning, Islam's political role has ceased to be relevant. He highlights the economic and intellectual relationship between Germany and the Muslim world, but, at the same time, clearly expects his target readership to consist exclusively of non-Muslims who perceive Islam as foreign and alien to their own culture and beliefs—a perception they ultimately share with the translator. Despite his secularist tendencies, his perspective on Islam is based in a notion of Christian superiority. Henning considers the Qur'an to be the work of Muḥammad who, in assembling it, drew extensively on Biblical material.[10] Therefore, his introduction to the Qur'an has a heavy focus on the life of Muḥammad, which he describes in a narrative style, elaborating on the physical features, emotions, and motives of the Prophet as if he were writing a novel. Henning attributes

---

8 Wolfgang G. Schwanitz, 'Paschas, Politiker und Paradigmen: Deutsche Politik im Nahen und Mittleren Orient 1871–1945', *Comparativ*, 14:1 (2004), pp. 22–45; Sabine Mangold-Will, *Eine 'weltbürgerliche Wissenschaft': die deutsche Orientalistik im 19. Jahrhundert* (Stuttgart: Steiner, 2004), p. 274.

9 For a more extensive analysis of Henning's original Qur'an translation than can be delivered in this chapter, see Johanna Pink, 'Eine Koranübersetzung im Kalten Krieg: Reclam, Max Henning und das Bild Muḥammads im geteilten Deutschland', *Welt des Islams*, pre-print publication (2025), 1–49.

10 See, for example, Henning, *Der Koran*, p. 81 and 322, including references to Abraham Geiger's *Was hat Mohammed aus dem Judenthume aufgenommen?* (1833).

Muḥammad's first revelatory experiences to a mental illness, as was commonplace in nineteenth-century Orientalism,[11] and the expansion of Islam is seen as the result of Muḥammad's command to wage war against all unbelievers in order to make Islam a world religion.[12] At times, Henning shows a certain sympathy towards Muḥammad, whom he credits with carrying out social reforms to the extent that he was able to—for example, with regard to polygyny.[13] Then again, he approvingly quotes a statement by the German Orientalist Gustav Weil (1808–1889), an assimilated Jew posing as a 'cultural Protestant', who contrasts Muḥammad unfavourably with Jesus. Weil criticises Muḥammad for his human weaknesses and lack of morals, for refusing to suffer the persecution he was facing, for resorting to violence, and for turning Islam into a law-giving religion, much like Judaism—which, according to Weil, resulted in both religions becoming anachronistic.[14]

All in all, Henning's view of the Qur'an was centred around Muḥammad, judging him from a position of perceived superiority and comparing him to Jesus as the ideal type of founder of a religion. In this model, efforts to enact social reforms to help the weak are considered acceptable, but political leadership, law-giving, or statesmanship are not. A Christian influence is also visible in the translation itself, which contains many stylistic borrowings from the Luther Bible, a religious text with which German readers were familiar. This included the use of the outdated, and by this time firmly pejorative, term 'Weiber' as a translation of the Arabic *al-nisāʾ* ('women'), while the neutral term in modern German would have been 'Frauen'.[15] That said, Henning generally took care to make the translation accessible. It was considered

---

11 See, for example, Henning, *Der Koran* pp. 10, 21. Cf., for example, Gustav Weil, *Mohammed der Prophet, sein Leben und seine Lehre* (Stuttgart: Metzler, 1843), pp. 42–45; A. Sprenger, *Mohammed und der Koran. Eine psychologische Studie* (Hamburg: A. G., 1889), pp. 8–9; Suzanne L. Marchand, *German Orientalism in the Age of Empire: Religion, Race, and Scholarship* (Cambridge: Cambridge University Press, 2010), pp. 174–76.

12 Henning, *Der Koran*, pp. 14–15, 21.

13 Ibid., pp. 16, 34–35.

14 Ibid., pp. 35–36; based on Gustav Weil, *Historisch-kritische Einleitung in den Koran* (Bielefeld: Velhagen & Klasing, 1844), pp. 114–116. On Weil, see Marchand, *German Orientalism*, p. 77.

15 In the Luther Bible, this was revised in 1984. On the pejoration of *Weib* during the emergence of New High German, see Werner König, *dtv-Atlas der deutschen Sprache*, 15th edn (Munich: dtv, 2005), p. 112.

fluent and easy to read, if not free from mistakes.[16] Unlike its competitors, it used individual verse numbers, based on the idiosyncratic number system used by Flügel in his edition of the Qur'an, which was dominant in European Oriental studies at the time.[17] Each verse was set in a separate paragraph which made the translation more easily digestible than a long running text would have been, especially when it came to the longer *sūras*.

The success of Henning's translation is difficult to assess since data regarding Reclam's sales before the Second World War seems to have been lost. The catalogue of the German National Library contains reference to a reprint dated 1919 'on war paper'.[18] There does not appear to have been a further reprint, but the fact that the first edition from 1901 is still readily available in antiquarian bookshops suggests that the edition was sizeable, even though there were some competitors on the German book market. The first complete translation of the Qur'an had been published by Lion Ullmann in 1840, and often reprinted during the nineteenth century, but fell out of fashion in the early twentieth century.[19] In the same year as Henning, Theodor Grigull published his own Qur'an translation, and in 1916, a translation by Lazarus Goldschmidt hit the market.[20] It is impossible to compare the relative success of these translations, but it is safe to say that none of the competitors' works markedly outperformed Henning's Reclam translation in terms of popularity and none of them received any critical acclaim either. Conversely, as late as 1963, the leading Qur'an scholar Rudi Paret (1901–83) described Henning's translation as the 'best German translation of the Qur'an'.[21] By this time, however, Germany had changed drastically, with massive consequences for all levels of society. This included the

---

16   Haberländer, 'Max Henning'.
17   Flügel, Gustav, *Corani textus arabicus* (Leibzig: Tauchnitz, 1834).
18   German National Library, Frankfurt/M., shelfmark SA 7 – 4206/4210 a,b.
19   L. Ullmann (trans.), *Der Koran. Aus dem Arabischen wortgetreu neu übersetzt und mit erläuternden Anmerkungen versehen*, 5th edn (Bielefeld: Velhagen & Klasing, 1865); see also Hartmut Bobzin and Peter M. Kleine (eds), *Glaubensbuch und Weltliteratur. Koranübersetzungen in Deutschland von der Reformationszeit bis heute* (Arnsberg: Stadt Arnsberg, 2007), p. 38.
20   Bobzin and Kleine, *Glaubensbuch und Weltliteratur*, pp. 40, 42.
21   Rudi Paret, '[Rezension von:] Der Koran. Aus dem Arabischen übertragen von Max Henning. Einleitung und Anmerkungen von Annemarie Schimmel', *Zeitschrift der deutschen morgenländischen Gesellschaft*, 113:2 (1963), 277–78.

fate of Reclam's publishing house, as well as that of Max Henning's Qur'an translation.

After the War: The German Division and the Division of Reclam

The Second World War ended, at least on European soil, in May 1945 with the defeat of Germany, resulting in the occupation of the country by the Soviet Union, the United States, the United Kingdom, and France. Germany was divided into four zones, each of which was ruled by one of the allied states. Increasing alienation between the Western Allies and the Soviet Union, in the wider context of the beginning of the Cold War, ultimately led to the foundation of two separate German states in 1949: the Federal Republic of Germany in the West and the German Democratic Republic in the East. From the beginning, the GDR was part of the Eastern Bloc, essentially a satellite state of the Soviet Union, and it became one of the founding members of the Warsaw Pact when that was established in 1955.

Even before the GDR was founded, companies located in the Soviet occupation zone were negatively impacted by the policy of reparations and socialist economic policies, as well as increasing harassment of 'capitalists' who were sometimes accused of involvement in the Nazi regime's crimes. For publishing houses, censorship was an additional problem. Reclam Leipzig, like most industries in the Soviet zone, fell victim to dismantling at the end of 1946 as a result of the reparations that had to be paid to the Soviet Union. This led the owner, Ernst Reclam, to establish a branch office in Stuttgart, which was part of the American occupation zone, in spring 1947. Following this, Reclam Stuttgart concluded a licence agreement with the Leipzig parent company for the production and distribution of the Universal-Bibliothek in the Western occupation zones. Ernst Reclam initially continued to run the Leipzig publishing house and reside there; he also restored the damage caused by the dismantling. But after he was arrested twice, he decided in 1950 to run the company from West Germany. With the company owner gone, the GDR authorities placed the publishing house under trustee administration. As a result, any co-operation between Reclam Leipzig and Reclam Stuttgart was terminated; titles from Reclam Stuttgart could not be distributed in the GDR and the importation of Reclam Leipzig's products into the FRG was prohibited by the Stuttgart publishing house. In 1953, Reclam Leipzig was declared a nationally-owned enterprise (Volkseigener Betrieb, abbr. VEB) by decree of the GDR Ministry of Light Industry—but this decree was reversed on legal grounds, as this form of expropriation was only permitted for companies whose owners could be proven to be 'Nazi activists' or war criminals. In 1958, Reclam Leipzig finally became a 'company with state participation'. Production was completely separated from the publishing house and taken over by a combine (Kombinat).[22]

The Stuttgart publishing house, on the other hand, was a private company in a market economy. As early as the late 1940s, it emerged as a pioneer in the production of inexpensive books for the mass market in Western occupied zones. Its success was boosted by the long and renown history of the Universal-Bibliothek. However, from 1950, the Universal-Bibliothek faced increasing competition from a new phenomenon on the German book market, namely paperback series. These became very successful, and more and more publishers jumped on the band wagon. By 1959, more than 3,500 paperbacks were available on the West German market. Among the most successful genres of this market segment were popular science books and literary 'classics': a Qur'an translation is positioned at the intersection of these trends. One of Reclam Stuttgart's competitors, Goldmann, is noteworthy in this context. Goldmann, too, was a company originally based in Leipzig whose owner, Wilhelm Goldmann, had relocated to West Germany after

---

22 Frank Rainer Max, *Der Reclam-Verlag: eine kurze Chronik*, Universal-Bibliothek 18280 (Stuttgart: Reclam, 2003), pp. 51–59; Anke Schüler, 'Ein Name, zwei Wege: Reclam Leipzig und Reclam Stuttgart. Hintergründe der Trennung der Verlagshäuser in den 1950er-Jahren', *Deutsch-deutscher Literaturaustausch 8+9 2012*, 20 September 2012, https://www.bpb.de/themen/deutschlandarchiv/139840/ein-name-zwei-wege-reclam-leipzig-und-reclam-stuttgart/; Karolin Schmahl, 'Kontinuitäten im Neubeginn. Der Reclam-Verlag zwischen Kapitulation und Lizenzierung unter der Leitung von Ernst Reclam und Gotthold Müller', in *An den Grenzen des Möglichen: Reclam-Leipzig 1945–1991*, ed. by Ingrid Sonntag (Berlin: Ch. Links Verlag, 2016), pp. 30–39; Carmen Laux, 'Ein schwerer Anfang. Von der Lizenzierung zur Demontage', in *An den Grenzen des Möglichen: Reclam-Leipzig 1945–1991*, ed. by Ingrid Sonntag (Berlin: Ch. Links Verlag, 2016), pp. 40–51; Carmen Laux and Ingrid Sonntag, 'Ein Name, zwei Verlage. Reclam Leipzig und Reclam Stuttgart', in *An den Grenzen des Möglichen: Reclam-Leipzig 1945–1991*, ed. by Ingrid Sonntag (Berlin: Ch. Links Verlag, 2016), pp. 52–72. A *Kombinat* was a large company which produced a variety of goods that were somewhat related.

harassment and arrests. In 1956, he started publishing mass editions of classic works—these were produced quickly and inexpensively, and were often of poor quality. Within three years, the series 'Goldmann's Yellow Pocketbooks' (*Goldmanns gelbe Taschenbücher*) comprised around 150 titles.[23] In 1959, Goldmann published the first German Qur'an translation to hit the post-World War Two mass market: a superficial adaptation of Lion Ullmann's 1840 translation, which was attributed to 'Ludwig' Ullmann,[24] despite the fact that it was stylistically outdated and riddled with mistakes.[25] Five years earlier, in 1954, the Ahmadiyya Movement had published a German Qur'an translation in Zürich[26] that was also available in West German bookstores but, since it was a hardcover edition that contained the Arabic text, it probably held less appeal for casually interested German readers.

Reclam Stuttgart's Henning-Schimmel Edition

When Goldmann published their low-quality Qur'an translation, they capitalised on the fact that Henning's Qur'an translation was out of print and completely unavailable.[27] This angered the Reclam Stuttgart management, who promptly commissioned the Orientalist Annemarie Schimmel (1922–2003), then based at the University of Marburg, to produce a revised edition. A simple reprint of the original edition was

---

23 Fetzer, Günther, *Das Taschenbuch. Geschichte – Verlage – Reihen* (Tübingen: Narr Francke Attempto, 2019), pp. 137–60.
24 This was probably an attempt to disguise the original translator's Jewish identity, in a slightly different manner than the nineteenth-century editions that had only carried the initial of Lion Ullmann's first name ('L. Ullmann').
25 L. Ullmann, *Der Koran. Das heilige Buch des Islam* (München: Goldmann, 1959).
26 Hazrat Mirza Bashir-ud-Din Mahmud Ahmad (ed.), *Der Heilige Koran* (Zürich: Der Islam, 1954). This is not to be confused with the earlier German Qur'an translation by the Lahore Ahmadiyya by Maulana Sadr-ud-Din, first published in 1939 (Maulana Sadr-ud-Din, *Der Koran: Arabisch-Deutsch*, 1st edn (Berlin: Verlag der moslemischen Revue, 1939)), which will be mentioned in the discussion of the GDR Qur'an publication project later in this chapter. Sadr-ud-Din's translation was reprinted in 1964, but was virtually unavailable before that.
27 Hartmut Bobzin, 'Max Henning – Annemarie Schimmel', in *Glaubensbuch und Weltliteratur. Koranübersetzungen in Deutschland von der Reformationszeit bis heute*, ed. by Hartmut Bobzin and Peter M. Kleine (Arnsberg: Stadt Arnsberg, 2007), p. 47. In 1960, Reclam Stuttgart only possessed a single, carefully guarded archive copy of Henning's translation. Cf. letter from K.N. to Annemarie Schimmel, 25 January 1960 (Reclam-Verlagsarchiv, Deutsches Literaturarchiv Marbach).

out of the question, if only due to the fact that it was set in Gothic type, which had not been taught in German schools since 1941 and had not been used by Reclam since 1947.[28] Reclam also aimed to replace the introduction with one that reflected the state of the art and thought it prudent to have a specialist revise Henning's notes. However, to compete with Goldmann, everything had to happen fast, and so Reclam Stuttgart explicitly asked Schimmel to dispense with revising the text of the translation itself. Accordingly, Reclam was able to publish Schimmel's revised edition of Henning's translation in October 1960, only ten months after they had initially reached out to Schimmel.

The translation was completely unchanged. Save for a single mistake that stuck out to Schimmel in Q 2:70, Reclam Stuttgart had merely modernised the typeface and spelling. Schimmel continued to use Flügel's verse numbering system, although it had already largely fallen out of use by 1960 in favour of the Kufan system used in Egyptian, Indian, or Turkish *muṣḥaf*s.[29] However, she made changes to the presentation of the text and to the paratexts. As requested by the publisher, she wrote a new introduction that replaced Henning's and slightly expanded the footnote section. The usability of the translation was significantly improved by headers containing *sūra* numbers and names. She also provided a four-page selective bibliography of German, English, and French scholarship on the Qur'an as well as a ten-page thematic index.

The paratexts introduced by Schimmel match the sympathies for Islam apparent in her life's work and reflect a phenomenological approach, centring the religious experiences of believers.[30] Her introduction focuses almost completely on the role of the Qur'an in Muslim piety and art. A very brief summary of Muḥammad's biography is included, merely because Reclam asked for it; it was not something that Schimmel considered relevant. In the notes section, she added references to the

---

28 Friedrich Forssmann, 'Zur Neugestaltung 2012', in *Die Welt in Gelb*, ed. by Karl-Heinz Fallbacher (Stuttgart: Reclam, 2012), pp. 17–22.

29 Cf. Anton Spitaler, *Die Verszählung des Koran nach islamischer Überlieferung* (München: Verlag der Bayerischen Akademie der Wissenschaften, 1935).

30 On Schimmel's life and works, see Stefan Wild, 'Der Friedenspreis und Annemarie Schimmel: Eine Nachlese', *Die Welt des Islams*, 36:1 (1996), 107–22; Stefan Wild, 'In Memoriam Annemarie Schimmel (7. April 1922–26. Januar 2003)', *Die Welt des Islams*, 43:2 (2003), 131–42; Stefan Wild, 'Annemarie Schimmel und der Islam', *Theologie der Gegenwart*, 57:3 (2014), 162–75; Anne Hofmann, *Islam in den Medien. Der publizistische Konflikt um Annemarie Schimmel* (Münster: LIT, 2004).

role of particular verses in Muslim piety, as well as some nods to South Asian modernism, especially Muhammad Iqbal (1877–1937), whom she greatly revered. While she does not speak with a Muslim voice and, like Henning, clearly addresses a non-Muslim readership, she is extremely respectful of Muslim views of the Qur'an and religious customs, to the point of using eulogies in some *sūra* titles when the name of a Prophet is mentioned. For example, Q 10 is entitled 'Jonas (Frieden sei auf ihm!)' or 'Jonah (peace be upon him!)'.[31] Her focus is almost exclusively on spirituality; she is fascinated with mysticism, disinterested in political Islam, and disdainful of modernist rationalism as it is represented, for example, in the Ahmadiyya movements. In her reading, all aspects of Islamic life are based on the Qur'an, but by this she does not mean politics or the organisation of society; she means piety, inner faith, and aesthetics. This is a far cry from Henning's position of superiority, his focus on the life of Muḥammad, and his criticism of the Prophet's political actions; but despite being sympathetic, it is judgemental in the way it defines 'true' Islam as spirituality, beauty, and mysticism, all of which are supposedly based on the Qur'an, at the expense of other approaches to Islam that have been embraced by Muslims before, during, and after Schimmel's lifetime.[32]

But in 1960, and for several decades after that, there were few, if any, readers of German who would have complained about this. The renowned Qur'an scholar Rudi Paret declared the edition far superior to both the Ahmadiyya and the Goldmann versions that had preceded it, despite the fact that he was working on his own Qur'an translation.[33] But his was geared towards academics, whereas Reclam's translation was meant to appeal to non-specialists. And it seems to have been successful. Reclam reprinted the edition as a paperback in 1962 and 1966, reflecting the publisher's general transition towards publishing paperbacks. In

---

31 This is a strange decision because it does not reflect the customary naming of sūras in Arabic *muṣḥaf*s. Schimmel adopted the practice from Flügel and used it precisely as selectively as Flügel did: for Jonas, Joseph, and Abraham, and with a different eulogy for Muḥammad, but not for Hūd, Noah, or Mary.

32 This is a brief summary of my far more extensive analysis of Annemarie Schimmel's edition in German in Pink, 'Eine Koranübersetzung', which is based on Schimmel's edition of Henning's translation as well as her correspondence with Reclam from the Reclam Verlagsarchiv in Deutsches Literaturarchiv. For a very brief overview, see also Bobzin, 'Max Henning – Annemarie Schimmel'.

33 Paret, '[Rezension von:] Der Koran'.

1973, the Schimmel edition was included in the enormously cheap and popular 'yellow series' and was subsequently reprinted numerous times, continuing well past German reunification and up until today.[34] It became a staple of the Reclam Stuttgart portfolio—part of their attempt to provide German readers with the world's 'classics', including the central religious and philosophical texts of the major 'civilisations'.[35]

East of the Iron Curtain: Reclam Leipzig in the GDR Book Market of the 1960s

Meanwhile, Reclam Leipzig—completely severed from its offshoot in Stuttgart—played a pioneering role in the paperback market in the GDR, particularly in the area of fiction, dominating the market to a much greater extent than Reclam Stuttgart did in the FRG. As early as 1946, the publishing house delivered its first titles under licence from the Soviet military administration. They switched to paperback editions in 1953, inspired by the success of the West German paperback publisher Rowohlt.[36] In 1963, in the course of the constant restructuring of the publishing industry during the foundational decades of the GDR, the fully state-run Aufbau-Verlag became a shareholder, reflecting the fact that Reclam Leipzig was now firmly anchored in the cultural policy of the GDR and, while still *de iure* a private company, considered to be in need of oversight.[37] The post-war Universal-Bibliothek Leipzig became the uncontested major paperback series of the GDR. By 1991, Reclam Leipzig had published over 2,000 titles. The closest competitors on the mass market, Aufbau-Verlag and Verlag Neues Leben, did not manage more than a few hundred.[38]

---

34 More on the post-reunification fate of the FRG and GDR editions will be said in the conclusion.

35 In 1960, this was very much in line with the zeitgeist. For example, Penguin Classics had published its own Qur'an translation: N. J. Dawood, *The Koran* (Harmondsworth: Penguin Books, 1956). The ambivalence and power dimension inherent in the inclusion of the Qur'an in a canon of 'world literature' defined in Europe is discussed in Pink, 'The Qur'an as World Literature'.

36 Ingrid Sonntag, 'Die C-Reihe und die Rekonstruktion der Universal-Bibliothek', in *An den Grenzen des Möglichen: Reclam-Leipzig 1945–1991*, ed. by Ingrid Sonntag (Berlin: Ch. Links Verlag, 2016), pp. 101–08.

37 Max, *Der Reclam-Verlag*, pp. 51–59; Schüler, 'Ein Name, zwei Wege'.

38 Fetzer, *Das Taschenbuch*, pp. 192–93, 240–42.

Under the management of Hans Marquardt (1920–2004)—chief editor from 1953, and publishing director from 1961—Reclam Leipzig developed its own profile and began to provide far more than cheap editions of school and university texts, as the GDR government had probably envisaged. The programme expanded beyond the conventional 'classics' and Reclam became known for exciting, artistically illustrated books as well as daring new literary works—provided it was allowed to print them.[39] Under Marquardt's leadership, the staff of the publishing house became experts at testing boundaries and making works publishable that seemed doomed to fall prey to censorship. Censorship did not officially exist but was, in fact, a defining feature of the cultural sector. Both the Hauptverwaltung Verlage (Department for Publishers) in the Ministry of Culture and the organs of the Socialist Unity Party (Sozialistische Einheitspartei, abbr. SED) had to be won over for every ambitious publishing project. This was often achieved through the solicitation of expert opinions that provided ideological justification and helped to frame texts as valuable academic sources, with extensive introductions that were supposed to guide readers towards the 'correct' understanding of the texts.[40] It was also achieved through conversations and deals with the State Security Service (Staatssicherheitsdienst, abbr. Stasi)[41] and the SED, which were unavoidable even though only a minority of the staff were party members.[42] The process of seeing a sensitive book to publication could often take years.

Reclam Leipzig had autonomy in shaping its programme, but it was always dependent on the approval of their shareholder, the

---

39   Juergen Seuss, 'H. M. – Grenzgänger', in *An den Grenzen des Möglichen: Reclam-Leipzig 1945–1991*, ed. by Ingrid Sonntag (Berlin: Ch. Links Verlag, 2016), pp. 109–19.
40   Wolfgang Thierse, 'Zwischen Anpassung und kontrollierter Aufmüpfigkeit', in *An den Grenzen des Möglichen: Reclam-Leipzig 1945–1991*, ed. by Ingrid Sonntag (Berlin: Ch. Links Verlag, 2016), pp. 112–14 (p. 13); for a wide variety of detailed case studies of successful and failed publication projects and their way through the censorship system, see Ingrid Sonntag (ed.), *An den Grenzen des Möglichen: Reclam-Leipzig 1945–1991* (Berlin: Ch. Links Verlag, 2016), pp. 378–501.
41   Ingrid Sonntag, 'Kommentar zu Hans Marquardts Stasiakte', in *An den Grenzen des Möglichen: Reclam-Leipzig 1945–1991*, ed. by Ingrid Sonntag (Berlin: Ch. Links Verlag, 2016), pp. 131–41.
42   Ingrid Sonntag, 'Geschichte als Verlagsgeschichte', in *An den Grenzen des Möglichen: Reclam-Leipzig 1945–1991*, ed. by Ingrid Sonntag (Berlin: Ch. Links Verlag, 2016), pp. 115–28 (p. 26).

Aufbau-Verlag, a publication permit from the Ministry of Culture, and the approval of the party organisations. Moreover, Reclam was dependent on the state-owned companies that typeset and printed the books; it needed to obtain slots in the schedule of the state-owned typesetting facilities, and to secure allotments of paper.[43] Many hurdles had to be overcome before a book could be distributed, and the situation was made even more complex by the unpredictability of censorship which had formal and informal components, changed over time, and was often dependent on the whim of the person making the decision: 'Every single book was an adventure, the centre of a story that was complicated, often nerve-wracking for those involved, and long.'[44]

Previous studies of Reclam's and other publishers' endeavours to navigate the GDR institutions and circumvent censorship have mostly focused on literary works, with some forays into philosophy.[45] The publication of a religious text, such as the Qur'an, was clearly no less sensitive in a state that was officially governed by an anti-religious ideology. Printing the Bible would have been out of the question, but it was clear that the Qur'an would not be perceived as equally dangerous, given that there were no Muslim minorities to speak of living in the GDR. Besides, even the Soviet Union had finally permitted the posthumous publication of the Russian Qur'an translation by the non-Muslim Orientalist Ignatii Krachkovskii (1883–1951) in 1963, during the Khrushchev Thaw.[46] It was shortly thereafter, in 1964, that the editorial team of Reclam Leipzig hatched the daring plan of printing a new edition of Henning's Qur'an translation. In the wake of Reclam Stuttgart's success with the Schimmel edition, and in light of the fact that even the USSR had seen the publication of a Qur'an translation, this scheme would have seemed feasible to the Reclam editors—but it was still a courageous decision,[47] and its implementation required considerable

---

43 Simone Barck, Martina Langermann, and Siegfried Lokatis, „Jedes Buch ein Abenteuer". Zensur-System und literarische Öffentlichkeiten in der DDR bis Ende der sechziger Jahre (Berlin: Akademie Verlag, 1997), p. 11.
44 Barck, Langermann, and Lokatis, „Jedes Buch ein Abenteuer", p. 15.
45 See especially Sonntag, An den Grenzen des Möglichen; Barck, Langermann, and Lokatis, „Jedes Buch ein Abenteuer".
46 Elvira Kulieva, 'Ignatii Krachkovskii', in Encyclopaedia of the Qur'ān Online (Brill: Leiden, 2024), https://doi.org/10.1163/1875-3922_q3_EQCOM_061331
I am grateful to Elvira Kulieva for this plausible suggestion.
47 Seuss, 'H. M. – Grenzgänger', p. 119.

ingenuity and tenacity. The history of the GDR Qur'an demonstrates the complexity of justifying its publication, and the particular framing that was instrumental in finally bringing the project to fruition.

Between Scholarship and Ideology: Preparing a Qur'an Edition for Socialist Readers

The existing correspondence relating to the Leipzig edition of Henning's Qur'an translation clearly reflects the sensitivity of this book, the protracted nature of the publishing process, and the multiple academic and political safeguards that had to be implemented in order to convince the censorship bodies. Some letters suggest that there were previous telephone conversations or personal meetings beyond the documented evidence; some documents give the impression that they are following a script that had been discussed in advance. The time period between the initial idea and the eventual printing of the GDR edition of Henning's translation stretched across at least four years.

The very first document relating to this project in the Reclam Leipzig archive is addressed to Herbert Melzig, an Orientalist specialising in Turkey.[48] It suggests that he brought up the idea of a Qur'an edition in a conversation with Reclam's editorial team, probably in late 1964. On 15 February 1965, 'E.P.' (the publisher's chief editor) sent him a letter asking whether the Henning translation, to which Reclam held the copyright, would be suitable for this purpose.[49] Melzig did not reply immediately. However, the Reclam team seemed to have already made up their minds because on 8 March, the editor in charge ('H.M.') wrote to Johann W. Fück, Professor Emeritus of Oriental Studies in Halle, on the matter of plans for a new edition of Henning's translation. He explicitly pointed to the

---

48 Melzig (1909–?), the author of a popular biography of Atatürk, had worked for the German Ministry of Propaganda during the Third Reich before emigrating from Germany to Turkey in 1938. He returned to the FRG after the Second World War but moved to the GDR in 1957, probably to escape prosecution for fraud, and worked as a translator and writer there before emigrating to Australia in 1976. See Stefan Ihrig, 'Nazi Leaks and Intrigues in Second World War Ankara: The Plot to Send Herbert Melzig to a Concentration Camp', *The International History Review*, 38:1 (2016), 109–25; Ömer Faruk Demirel, 'Ünlü Atatürk Biyografi Herbert Melzig Kimdir?', *Elektronik Siyaset Bilimi Araştırmaları Dergisi* 13:1 (2022), 41–57.
49 Letter from E.P. to Herbert Melzig, 15 February 1965, no. 1267 (Reclam-Verlagsarchiv).

Stuttgart edition of 1960 and explained that the historian of religion Kurt Rudolph, alongside the medievalist Ernst Werner, had agreed to oversee the production of a new revised edition, independent from Schimmel's. The reason he wrote to Fück about this was to ask for an expert opinion, for which he offered a fee.[50] Fück politely declined due to lack of time, but nevertheless outlined his opinion on the project. No translation of the Qur'an could be considered definitive, he wrote, because too much of the Qur'an was incomprehensible or open to multiple interpretations. Of all the German translations, however, he considered Henning's the most accessible for a general readership, despite some shortcomings. He therefore recommended making it available to the public again in an unaltered edition.[51]

This answer initially satisfied the editorial office,[52] especially as Reclam had already signed a contract with Rudolph and Werner.[53] However, shortly afterwards, Melzig replied belatedly and complicated the matter. He heavily criticised both of Henning's translations—the Qur'an and the Thousand and One Nights—as antiquated, and advised against reprinting them. Instead, he suggested adapting the Ahmadiyya Qur'an translation that had been printed 'many years ago' in Berlin. He was referring here to the translation by Maulana Sadr-ud-Din (1881–1981), written on behalf of the Lahore Ahmadiyya and first published in 1939. The introduction and notes to this had been written by the German convert Hugo Marcus (1880–1966) in keeping with the fascist zeitgeist, and this had led the Lahore Ahmadiyya to withdraw their support of the project and order the destruction of all printed copies; most of them fell victim to the World War Two bombings. A revised edition with new notes and a new introduction had been published in 1964, but Melzig was clearly unaware of this.[54] His main interest seems to have been in finding paid work for himself; he offered to undertake

---

50   Letter from H.M. to Johann W. Fück, 8 March 1965 (Reclam-Verlagsarchiv).
51   Letter from Johann W. Fück to H.M., 17 March 1965, no. 1349 (Reclam-Verlagsarchiv).
52   E.P. and H.M. attached Fück's statement to their application for a printing licence from the GDR Ministry of Culture, which they submitted in October 1966. Cf. BArch DR 1/2201, Image 285–286.
53   Cf. letter from Ernst Werner to Reclam-Verlag, 10 September 1965, no. 0304 (Reclam-Verlagsarchiv).
54   Cf. Gerdien Jonker, 'A Nietzschean *tafsīr* for Nazi Germany', *Journal of Qur'anic Studies*, 26:2 (2024), pp. 160–186. See also: Sadr-ud-Din, *Der Koran*, 1939;

the revision of the Ahmadiyya translation for Reclam, and to add an explanatory commentary. He argued that the Lahore Ahmadiyya would probably give Reclam permission to print their translation free of charge and promised to send some sections that he had already revised.[55] Melzig's hopes were somewhat delusional: first, because Reclam had already entrusted Rudolph and Werner with the project of revising Henning's translation; second, because there was little chance that Reclam would forego their own original translation in lieu of another one; and third, because the publication of a translation by an Islamic missionary movement would have been far more problematic in the GDR context than the re-publication of a work by a turn-of-the-century self-taught German Orientalist and free thinker. Ironically, Melzig was instead commissioned to revise Henning's translation of the Tales of a Thousand and One Nights, despite his harsh criticism of it.[56]

Melzig's intervention was nevertheless taken seriously. The statement he made about the Ahmadiyya in his letter was highlighted in red with an exclamation mark added, while a handwritten note asks the recipient to clarify the 'fee question' immediately. Moreover, E.P. and H.M. jointly wrote an apologetic letter to Rudolph—a professor of the history of religion and comparative religious studies at the University of Leipzig and an expert on Late Antique religions of the Near East, who was in charge of the project. They explained to Rudolph that Melzig had been asked for an opinion on Henning's translation at an earlier time and had now belatedly issued a negative judgement. While they hastened to assure Rudolph that they considered Melzig's objections unsubstantiated, and that they were not about to ignore Rudolph's and Fück's favourable opinion on Henning's translation, they nevertheless felt compelled to ask whether Rudolph could tell them more about the Ahmadiyya translation, which they had apparently been unable to obtain.[57]

Rudolph replied immediately with a long letter, which suggests that he, too, took the objections seriously. After all, given the extremely opaque

---

Maulana Sadr-ud-Din, *Der Koran: Arabisch-Deutsch*, 2nd edn (Berlin: Verlag der moslemischen Revue, 1964).

55 Letter from Herbert Melzig to E.P., 2 April 1965, no. 1404 (Reclam-Verlagsarchiv).
56 Max Henning (trans.), *Geschichten aus Tausendundeiner Nacht. Mit einem Nachwort von Herbert Melzig* (Leipzig: Reclam, 1966).
57 Letter from E.P. and H.M. to Kurt Rudolph, 8 April 1965 (Reclam-Verlagsarchiv).

nature of GDR censorship, any kind of criticism had the potential to endanger a publishing project. Rudolph argued that, while some aspects of Henning's translation were outdated, it was not wholly antiquated. When it came to the Ahmadiyya translation, he categorised this as the work of a particularistic modernist movement that had modernised the Qur'an in order to convert Germans to Islam. In his opinion, it was therefore unusable. Rudolph's emphasis on the missionary impetus of the Ahmadiyya movement was probably sufficient to blight the idea of publishing this work in the GDR. However, Rudolph went further, and brought in the state of play in the West German field. He mentioned that Rudi Paret was preparing his own translation that, according to Rudolph, was going to become the standard work for academics, whereas Henning's translation was sufficient for the general public. This was underlined, in his opinion, by the fact that Annemarie Schimmel—whom he considered an outstanding Orientalist—had prepared a Stuttgart edition of Henning's translation, which fact alone fully justified Reclam Leipzig's project.[58]

Thus, Rudolph refused to make a qualitative distinction between Western and Eastern scholarship, instead expressing his admiration for West German colleagues such as Rudi Paret and Annemarie Schimmel. This aligns with the description of Rudolph's classes by a former student as a breath of fresh, unideological air in the humanities programme at the University of Leipzig, since Rudolph was committed to the study of history rather than the promotion of socialism.[59] That he felt at liberty to express his unideological stance on West German scholarship in a letter to Reclam also tells us something about his relationship with the editor, H.M., who was known for his lacklustre attitude towards party doctrine.[60] But this attitude was probably a liability for the Qur'an project, even though Rudolph had obviously been selected for his academic merits. This was doubtless the reason why he had been paired with Ernst Werner for the composition of a joint introduction. Werner was a historian of the European Middle Ages, and thus neither

---

58 Letter from Kurt Rudolph to H.M., 13 April 1965, no. 1426 (Reclam-Verlagsarchiv).
59 Steffen Dietzsch, 'Als Herausgeber bei Reclam in Leipzig im „Freihafen der Philosophie"', in *An den Grenzen des Möglichen: Reclam-Leipzig 1945–1991*, ed. by Ingrid Sonntag (Berlin: Ch. Links Verlag, 2016), pp. 296–305 (p. 302).
60 Sonntag, 'Geschichte als Verlagsgeschichte', p. 26.

a specialist in the history of Islam nor in Late Antiquity; but he was extremely loyal to the party line, a member of the SED since 1946, and he even became Rector of the University of Leipzig in 1967, at which time the introduction had been written but the book not yet printed.

While Rudolph and Werner were working on the introduction, on 5 May 1965, Melzig sent the publisher a memorandum entitled 'Thoughts about a new QUR'AN EDITION in the Philipp Reclam publishing house' which offered such a hefty dose of ideological justification for the project that there are grounds for suspicion that it was staged—commissioned by Reclam for this exact purpose. Melzig talked about a spiritual transformation taking place in the 'Islamic Orient', where Arab scholars were developing entirely new interpretations of the Qur'an that served as a foundation for Arab socialism. This was at the height of the Cold War, and Gamal Abd al-Nasser—who was increasingly relying on an alliance with the Soviet Union—had sent troops to Yemen to lead a disastrous proxy war against the conservative Middle Eastern monarchies.[61] It was this situation that Melzig alluded to in his memorandum, bemoaning the fact that the common Arab people's faith in the Qur'an represented an obstacle to the spread of Marxism, but also evoking hope in the victory of dialectic materialism through contemporary Qur'an interpretations. He assured the editors that the Qur'an's contemporary role could be analysed in a neutral manner, without offending Muslims in the Near and Middle East, and then emphasised the idea that they had a duty to convey the 'REALITIES OF ISLAM' (in capital letters) to workers in the GDR by finally making the Qur'an accessible to them.[62]

The memorandum was apparently forwarded to Rudolph and Werner,[63] whose work on the introduction was hampered by their irreconcilable differences. On 15 September 1965, Werner informed the Reclam editors that writing a joint introduction with Rudolph had turned out to be impossible and that they had instead decided to write two

---

61 On the 'Arab Cold War' of the 1950s and 1960s, see the masterful study by Malcolm Kerr: Malcolm H. Kerr, *The Arab Cold War: Gamal ʿAbd al-Nasir and His Rivals, 1958–1970*, 3rd edn (London and New York: Royal Institute of International Affairs and Oxford University Press, 1971).
62 Enclosure to letter from Herbert Melzig to H.M., 5 May 1965 (Reclam-Verlagsarchiv).
63 Letter from E.P. to Herbert Melzig, 17 May 1965 (Reclam-Verlagsarchiv).

introductions, one of which focused on history in general and the other on the history of religion. Both were to be signed individually. Giving the publisher no chance to intervene, Werner submitted his introduction alongside his letter.[64] The joint reply of the editors gives the impression that they were not thrilled with this development but certainly did not want to mess with Werner, who was treated with extreme courtesy throughout the entire correspondence. They also commended him for allegedly emphasising two aspects of extraordinary importance to the current political situation in the Arab world: the idea of Arab unity and the 'relationship with Israel'—topics that they hoped would also feature in Rudolph's introduction.[65] Reading Werner's introduction, this commendation seems so far-fetched as to be absurd. While Werner could be seen as addressing the unification of the Arabs through Muḥammad and his message, the 'relationship with Israel' is not even mentioned. At best, this might be alluded to in a brief remark on Muḥammad's 'anti-Jewish policy', which Werner situates in the context of the war between the Persian and Byzantine Empires.[66] It is possible that the Reclam editors were writing less for Werner and more for the censors here, as the official political line of the GDR was hostile towards Israel[67] and sympathetic to pan-Arabism. As a matter of fact, the editorial staff of Reclam Stuttgart were also interested in the topic of Israel, although with quite different intentions. K.N., the editor of Reclam Stuttgart, had underlined the importance of the Qur'an for understanding 'the Arabic movement' and encouraged Schimmel to bring it up in her introduction, but to avoid an overly 'pro-Arab' note and to take Israeli sensitivities into consideration.[68]

By November 1965, Reclam had received both parts of the introduction, with Werner focusing on pre-Islamic Arabia and the biography of Muḥammad while Rudolph elaborated on the religion of Islam and the Qur'an. The editors, who were hoping to see the book printed in

---

64 Letter from Ernst Werner to Reclam-Verlag, 10 September 1965, no. 0304 (Reclam-Verlagsarchiv).
65 Letter from E.P. and H.M. to Ernst Werner, 15 September 1965 (Reclam-Verlagsarchiv).
66 Henning and Rudolph, *Der Koran*, p. 13.
67 Jeffrey Herf, '"At War with Israel": East Germany's Key Role in Soviet Policy in the Middle East', *Journal of Cold War Studies*, 16:3 (2014), 129–63.
68 Letter from K.N. to Annemarie Schimmel, 24 March 1960 (Reclam-Verlagsarchiv).

1966, now strove to obtain an expert opinion on these texts to further validate and safeguard the publication project, and once again, this was important enough to them that they offered to pay a fee. Walter Markov (1909–1993), a renowned historian with solid socialist credentials, was willing to take over the task. He was not a specialist in early Islam by any means but his involvement, just like Werner's, reflected the predominant Marxist view of history according to which it was more important to understand the principles and mechanisms guiding the development of societies than to have in-depth expert knowledge. In January 1966, Markov sent back a two-page list of queries and points of criticism. While his verdict was generally favourable, he expressed fairly explicit, even harsh, criticism of Werner's part of the introduction. Apparently, Werner had denied the importance of the pilgrimage for pre-Islamic Mecca and had described the city exclusively as a commercial hub.[69] Markov wrote that this was 'no masterpiece of dialectics', and pointed out that it was precisely the pilgrimage that attracted people to the area where they could then engage in trade, protected by the prohibition on fighting during the sacred months; and he made the point that without the Ka'ba, other Arabian cities might well have become commercial hubs instead of Mecca.[70] Werner implemented Markov's suggestions, albeit in a somewhat lacklustre fashion—sometimes he merely added them to his text verbatim, in brackets.[71]

H.M. now sent the introduction to Reclam's state-owned shareholder, the Aufbau-Verlag, requesting an assessment.[72] No written reaction is documented, but it seems quite possible that the verdict was sceptical because, apparently, another affirmative statement was needed. In March, the editors once again asked Fück for an expert opinion—and were turned down again for lack of time.[73] His obvious reluctance to engage with the project suggests that Fück was unwilling to be drawn into the ideological struggle for the publication of a Qur'an translation,

---

69   The draft manuscripts of the introductions are not part of the Reclam archive; this has to be inferred from Markov's criticism.
70   Expert opinion by Walter Markov for Reclam-Verlag, 31 January 1966, no. 0717 (Reclam-Verlagsarchiv).
71   See, for example, Henning and Rudolph, *Der Koran*, p. 7, about Mecca and the pilgrimage.
72   Letter from H.M. to Aufbau-Verlag, 16 February 1966 (Reclam-Verlagsarchiv).
73   Letter from E.P. and H.M. to Johann W. Fück, 17 March 1966; letter from Johann W. Fück to Reclam-Verlag, 21 March 1966 (Reclam-Verlagsarchiv).

or to provide the kind of political framing that Reclam needed. It appears that finding another expert reviewer was no easy task, but two months later the Reclam editors had managed to recruit the Semitist Heinrich Simon (1921–2010).[74] Simon delivered a report that consisted of no less than eight typewritten pages, in which he emphatically stressed the urgent need for a Qur'an translation in the GDR. The lack thereof, he wrote, was deplorable, given the importance of the Middle East and of good relations with Arab states. Therefore, he said, Reclam's project was timely. Moreover, the decision to use Henning's translation was the right one because of the translation's readability. However, Simon continues, Reclam Leipzig had a special responsibility towards GDR readers due to the existence of Reclam Stuttgart's Schimmel edition. Since Reclam Leipzig had obviously chosen not to obtain a licence to reprint that edition but instead to produce their own edition, 'then it would be a matter of proving that GDR scholarship, based on the principles of Marxism-Leninism, has something new and better to offer.'[75] In other words, when Reclam Leipzig had made the decision to revise Henning's translation, they had entered the Qur'an Race.

After these remarks, Simon, like Markov, offers some criticism and suggestions for improvement. The fact that Werner and Rudolph had written separate introductions had resulted in some redundancies and contradictions, in his opinion. As an example, he cites the respective authors' assessment of the Qur'anic *ḥanīfs*—who according to Werner were a sect, whereas according to Rudolph they were a group of religious individualists. Simon considered Rudolph's view the majority opinion, as a result of which Werner changed his description of the *ḥanīfs* as a sect and now spoke of them instead as 'peculiar syncretic enthusiasts'.[76] Much like Markov, Simon criticised Werner more thoroughly and extensively than Rudolph, and for quite similar reasons: 'In general, one would wish in many places that the author's judgements on the class structure were somewhat more cautious and at the same time give the reader more information, be it even by admitting to our lack of factual

---

74 Letter from E.P. and H.M. to Heinrich Simon, 18 May 1966 (Reclam-Verlagsarchiv).
75 Expert opinion by Heinrich Simon for Reclam-Verlag, 13 July 1966, no. 01244 (Reclam-Verlagsarchiv), p. 1.
76 Henning and Rudolph, *Der Koran*, p. 9.

knowledge.'[77] Once again, Werner was criticised for relying too much on ideology and too little on scholarship, despite the fact that Simon, like Markov, was a socialist.

While Simon thought that Rudolph's introduction was more reliable than Werner's, he considered it too verbose and full of details that went beyond the readers' needs. That Simon was specifically thinking of GDR readers here is clear from his criticism of a statement that Rudolph almost certainly adopted from Schimmel—according to which the first *sūra*, the *Fātiḥa*, can also be referred to as the 'Lord's Prayer of Islam'.[78] Simon considered this type of comparison entirely inappropriate. The only potential correspondence he sees between the *Fātiḥa* and the Lord's Prayer is with regard to the frequency with which the text is used, rather than the content. He also questioned whether non-Christian readers had a clear idea of what the Lord's Prayer is.[79] In doing so, he clearly acknowledged the high proportion of atheists among the GDR readership, besides writing from his own perspective as a person with a Jewish background. Rudolph subsequently changed the sentence to say that the *Fātiḥa* was 'somewhat infelicitously' called a kind of 'Lord's Prayer' of Islam due to its frequent use.[80] Generally, Werner and Rudolph once again seem to have implemented most of the criticisms contained in the expert statement. Simon had even pointed out transliteration errors, although he had not caught all of them.[81]

It follows that the expert opinions, besides convincing censors, also served to improve the academic quality of the work. But then, these two functions went hand in hand because it was precisely the academic quality of the work that was supposed to justify its publication. Only as an academic work, detached from any kind of religious sentiment or devotion, was its publication defensible. If Rudolph had displayed the same kind of sympathy for faith and piety as Annemarie Schimmel, the project would have been doomed.

---

77 Expert opinion by Heinrich Simon for Reclam-Verlag, 13 July 1966, no. 01244 (Reclam-Verlagsarchiv), p. 3.
78 Henning and Rudolph, *Der Koran*, p. 13.
79 Expert opinion by Heinrich Simon for Reclam-Verlag, 13 July 1966, no. 01244 (Reclam-Verlagsarchiv), p. 7.
80 Henning and Rudolph, *Der Koran*, p. 25.
81 Rudolph erroneously designated Friday as 'jaum adsch-dschum'a'; ibid., p. 20.

In October 1966, Reclam finally sent a formal application to the Ministry of Culture, asking for permission to print the Qur'an translation. They attached Fück's initial brief statement and the expert opinions of Markov and Simon, as well as a two-page memorandum by the Reclam editors which noted that all the comments made by the experts had been taken into account. The memorandum also contained a succinct justification of the importance of this work, presenting Reclam's carefully constructed argument for the publication of a sacred text in socialist Germany:

> For a better understanding of the situation and the developmental tendencies in the independent Arab states, a new edition of the Qur'an is undoubtedly still of great service. In order to characterise the significance of the Qur'an for 'Arab socialism,' we need only refer to the passage in the epilogue [sic] to our edition, where it is stated that Holy War (*jihād*) is today understood as a religious war against hunger and poverty. The connection between the religious sphere and the cultural and political sphere is a particular characteristic of Islam. Providing information about this phenomenon is a current necessity.[82]

Thus, the proposed Qur'an translation was connected to the official GDR policy of support for decolonising countries of the Global South on the 'non-capitalist path of development',[83] with Nasser's project of 'Arab socialism' looming large. Furthermore, Reclam argues that faith is closely linked with politics 'in Islam', which implies that knowledge about this religion is necessary not for the sake of religion itself but for understanding contemporary political realities. This argument was unheard of in Islamic studies in the FRG at the time, where the contemporary Middle East was perceived as moving towards secular modernity and discarding Islam along the way.

The memorandum also contains counterarguments against two potential objections, or possibly real objections that had previously

---

82 BArch DR 1/2201, Image 285. The explicit reference to an 'epilogue' suggests that the original idea might have been to have Rudolph's introduction, where the interpretation of *jihad* as the fight against underdevelopment is indeed mentioned, used as an epilogue.

83 Kai Hafez and Gerhard Höpp, 'Gegenwartsbezogene Orientwissenschaft in der DDR und in den neuen Bundesländern: Continuity or New Beginning?', in *Wissenschaft und Wiedervereinigung. Asien- und Afrikawissenschaften im Umbruch*, ed. by Wolf-Hagen Krauth and Ralf Wolz (Berlin: Akademie Verlag, 1998), pp. 95–163 (p. 100).

been presented to the editors in oral communication; either way, these objections are openly acknowledged because the editors assumed that they would not be overlooked by censorship. The first concerns Rudolph's frequent references to the Bible to explain Qur'anic text. 'In our opinion,' write the editors, 'this is fully justified in order to explain the relationship of Muslims to followers of other faiths and can hardly be understood as evidence of priority for any religion or as a restriction of the independence of Islam.'[84] Christianity was a far more sensitive subject than Islam in the GDR, and the editors obviously wanted to forestall the impression that the Qur'an translation was being used as a vehicle to promote it. The second alleged shortcoming of the translation related to the primacy of Marxist theory in historical analysis in the GDR. From this point of view, Rudolph's failure to provide a 'rational explanation [...] for the development of the Arab concept of God into the Islamic monotheistic God' is a problem. The editors argue that such an explanation would have exceeded the limited scope of the introduction.[85] All in all, Rudolph's approach to the topic as a historian of religion was an open flank, and the editors were well aware of this fact.

Permission to print the Qur'an translation was granted, at least for half of the 10,000 copies that Reclam had requested. Typesetting was planned for December 1966 and printing for 1967. However, a long sequence of supposedly technical delays ensued. Reclam did their best to reassure Rudolph and, especially, Werner, but this did little to mollify the authors of the introduction who, despite their differences, joined forces to express their anger and frustration. This seems to have had no effect whatsoever.[86] Only in February 1968 did the work reach the proofs stage,[87] and it was at this point that another conflict between Rudolph and Werner arose. This time it concerned the scope and content of the

---

[84] BArch DR 1/2201, Image 286.
[85] Ibid.
[86] BArch DR 1/2201, Image 284, 289; Letter from E.P. and H.M. to Kurt Rudolph, 23 November 1966; Letter from Kurt Rudolph to Reclam-Verlag, 27 January 1967, no. 07802; Letter from H.M. to Kurt Rudolph, 14 February 1966; Letter from H.M. to Kurt Rudolph, 26 May 1967; Letter from Hans Marquardt and E.P. to Ernst Werner, 2 August 1967; Letter from Hans Marquardt and E.P. to Kurt Rudolph, 3 August 1967; Letter from Ernst Werner and Kurt Rudolph to Hans Marquardt, 15 September 1967, no. 02416; Identical letters from Hans Marquardt to Ernst Werner and Kurt Rudolph, 13 October 1967 (Reclam-Verlagsarchiv).
[87] Letter from H.M. to Ernst Werner, 22 February 1968 (Reclam-Verlagsarchiv).

bibliography, for which Rudolph was solely responsible. Werner argued that they had agreed to only include titles that were accessible to readers in the GDR. Later, he wrote, a compromise had been reached to ensure that some titles published in the USSR could be added. But Rudolph, according to Werner, had blown the bibliography out of proportion. His displeasure was obviously aimed at the numerous titles from Western Europe, and especially the FRG, that Rudolph had included. After some haggling, Werner and Rudolph agreed on a shortened list that still referenced many titles which were not readily available in the GDR.[88]

The book was finally printed, and delivery started on 1 November 1968. Reclam's editor claimed that he had been able to double the print run,[89] and the 20,000 copies were sold out within a few weeks.[90] A reader from Dresden immediately took advantage of the event and sent a letter to the publisher in which he innocently asked whether there were any plans to publish the scriptures of other founding figures of great religions, such as Zarathustra and Jesus, 'e.g. the Old and New Testaments'.[91] However, the implied expectation—that the publication of the Qur'an translation would lead to state-sanctioned Bible production in the GDR—was not to be fulfilled. Reclam Leipzig's edition of the Qur'an was a success, though, and numerous subsequent editions were produced, all of which were sold out immediately: a reprint in 1970, a slightly updated edition in 1973, and another updated edition in 1980. Every time, the socialist economy caused production delays, and every time, the bookshops pre-ordered more copies than Reclam could deliver.[92] A fifth, sixth, and seventh edition were published in Leipzig in

---

88   Letter from Ernst Werner to the Reclam publishing house, 23 February 1968; Letter from H.M. to Ernst Werner, 26 February 1968; Letter from Ernst Werner to Reclam-Verlag, 28 February 1968, no. 148; Letter from E.P. and H.M. to Ernst Werner, 1 April 1968 (Reclam-Verlagsarchiv).
89   BArch DR 1/2201, Image 284, 288; Letter from H.M. to Ernst Werner, 13 January 1969 (Reclam-Verlagsarchiv).
90   Letter from H.M. to Ernst Werner, 13 January 1969; Letter from H.M. to Aufbau-Verlag, 1 November 1968, which emphasises the great demand that exceeded all expectations as well as the need for a second edition; Letter from Kurt Rudolph to H.M., 1 April 1969, no. 323 (Reclam-Verlagsarchiv).
91   Letter from R.S. (name anonymised), Dresden, to Reclam-Verlag, 29 November 1968 (Reclam-Verlagsarchiv).
92   Letter from H.M. to Johann W. Fück, 14 October 1969; Letter from Johann W. Fück to H.M., 16 October 1969, no. 1032; Letter from H.M. to Ernst Werner, 27 Jan. 1972; Letter from Ernst Werner to H.M., 1 Feb. 1972, no. 98; Letter from Kurt Rudolph to H.M., no. 1978, 16 Feb. 1972; Letter from H.M. to Kurt Rudolph, 9 July 1980.

1983, 1984, and 1989.[93] Moreover, from 1979, VMA-Verlag in Wiesbaden published a licensed edition for West German readers, which competed with the Reclam Stuttgart edition and was also reprinted several times. However, the correspondence on this project that is documented in the Reclam archive comes to a stop after 1982. This is because it was around this time that Rudolph was given the chance to take up a position as visiting professor in the United States—an opportunity he used to leave the GDR for good. He moved to West Germany in 1986 and spent the last years of his teaching career at the University of Marburg.[94] His pursuit of scholarship without subordination to the ideological demands of the GDR had obviously been untenable, especially in the stifling intellectual climate of the 1980s.[95]

A Better Qur'an from 'the Better Germany': Outdoing the FRG

The Leipzig Henning edition was, at least in part, a reaction to the Stuttgart Henning edition, and its publisher and editors were fully prepared to see it measured against Schimmel's work. This was in line with the competition that defined German-German relations. From the perspective of the GDR leadership and that of quite a few leftist idealists, whose numbers were still substantial in the 1960s, the GDR was the 'better Germany': a socialist project destined to overcome the legacy of German imperialism and fascism which lived on in the FRG.[96]

---

93 The 1983 edition was a reprint of the 1979 edition, with the addition of a table of contents. This version was published unchanged until 1989.
94 Marcell Saß, 'Nachruf Prof. Dr. theol. Dr. phil. habil. Dr. h. c. mult. Kurt Rudolph', *Universität Marburg*, May 2020, https://www.uni-marburg.de/de/fb05/aktuelles/news/nachruf-kurt-rudolph.pdf.
95 In November 1976, the singer-songwriter Wolf Biermann (b. 1936), who was a socialist but critical of the structures and policies of the GDR, was expatriated while he was performing in the FRG. After this event, many intellectuals and artists lost hope in the possibility of reforming the system from within, and a mass exodus ensued. The time between 1977 and 1989 is often described as a period of decline and frustration, marked by increasingly rigid policies. See Ralf Schnell, 'Literatur und Gesellschaft im Übergang (1977–1989)', in *Geschichte der deutschsprachigen Literatur seit 1945*, by Ralf Schnell (Stuttgart: J. B. Metzler, 1993), 207–37.
96 Wolfgang Bialas, 'Ostdeutsche Intellektuelle und der gesellschaftliche Umbruch der DDR', *Geschichte und Gesellschaft*, 33:2 (2007), 289–308 (p. 291).

Whether Reclam Leipzig actually wanted to prove the superiority of GDR scholarship—based on the principles of Marxism-Leninism, as the expert opinion by Heinrich Simon had implied—or whether this was just jargon meant to convince the censors is anyone's guess. But a comparison between the two editions shows that the Schimmel edition was constantly present in the minds of Rudolph and the Reclam Leipzig editors, and that their intention was to surpass it. This was quite feasible, because the hasty production of the Stuttgart edition meant that it left a lot of room for improvement.

In line with the general formats of their respective series, the Leipzig edition—unlike the Stuttgart edition—was published as a paperback from the start to ensure a low sale price. Much care was taken to design a visually appealing title page, however. The editors chose an image from a Qur'an manuscript owned by the Leipzig University Library as the cover image, which had a far more interesting look than the simple black-and-white geometric pattern that adorned the cover of the Stuttgart edition. When it came to typesetting and formal features, Rudolph followed Schimmel's decision to use page headers that indicated the *sūra* number, but he did not make an effort to adapt the *sūra* names to Muslim usage.[97] While Schimmel, like Henning, had arranged the text in single verse format, Rudolph organised it in paragraphs that formed coherent thematic units, which sometimes also served to highlight stylistic aspects such as parallelisms.[98] To the increasingly antiquated Flügel verse numbering system, Rudolph added in brackets the Kufan verse numbers that are common in Muslim editions of the Qur'an.

With regard to the text of the translation itself, the fact that Reclam Leipzig was willing to invest more time and effort than Reclam Stuttgart meant that Rudolph had the liberty to correct mistakes and improve the translation stylistically, which he did, even if not exhaustively so. For example, Henning had mistakenly identified the Qur'anic *ṣābiʾūn* as 'Sabäer' ('Sabaeans'), a term which denotes an ancient South Arabian

---

[97] For example, Schimmel had changed the title of Q 20 from 'T.H'. to 'Tâ-Hâ' but Rudolph did not, and he certainly did not include eulogies in the title of *sūras* that are named after prophets.

[98] For example, in Q 55, the verse *fa-bi-ayyi ālāʾi rabbikumā tukadhdhibāni* ('Which of the blessings of your Lord will you deny?') is repeated every two to three verses. Rudolph organises the sūra in paragraphs, each of which ends with this verse, to highlight this structure.

community that is not identical to the religious group referred to in Q 2:62 and Q 5:69 as ṣābiʾūn. Rudolph changed the translation to 'Sabier' ('Sabians'). Another example is the much-discussed verse Q 4:34, which contains the phrase *wa-hjurūhunna fī l-maḍājiʿi* addressed to husbands. This refers to the treatment of—according to Henning—potentially 'unruly' wives, and instructs men to refrain from sharing their bed (that is, having intercourse with them). Henning, however, understood the verse in an anachronistic way as an instruction to ground them, translating the segment as 'banish them to the bedchambers' ('Verbannet sie in die Schlafgemächer'). Rudolph changed this to say 'banish them *from* the bedchambers' ('Verbannt sie aus den Schlafgemächern'). He also modernised the old-fashioned Luther Bible style of the translation that would have seemed more outdated to GDR readers, many of whom were lacking familiarity with Christianity, than to West Germans. The most visible general revision concerns his decision to replace the derogatory 'Weiber' as a translation of *al-nisāʾ* with the neutral, standard German term 'Frauen' ('women') throughout. He missed numerous errors,[99] but compared to the Schimmel edition, Rudolph's edition nevertheless constituted an improvement.

The intent to outperform the Schimmel edition becomes even clearer when comparing the paratexts of the two editions. Just like the Stuttgart edition, the Leipzig edition replaced Henning's introduction with a new one, revised and expanded his notes, and added a thematic index as well as a bibliography of Qur'anic studies—and every single one of these paratexts is longer and more thorough in Rudolph's edition than in Schimmel's. The index is far more extensive and detailed than in the Stuttgart edition. The bibliography also contains more titles in more languages, especially Russian, and—in contrast to the Schimmel edition—a selection of Qur'an editions and translations is also listed. This is something that Schimmel had wanted to include but that the Reclam Stuttgart editor had discouraged out of reluctance to list the translation by Goldmann, their big competitor.[100] The footnotes were greatly expanded and supplemented with a wealth of helpful

---

[99] For example, in Henning's translation, some clauses are missing that he probably overlooked, e.g. in Q 7:158 and Q 5:18. See Haberländer, 'Max Henning'.

[100] Letter from K.N. to Annemarie Schimmel, 28 January 1960 (Reclam-Verlagsarchiv).

explanations, cross-references, and information on pre-Islamic reference texts, especially from Judaism and Christianity.

At the same time, both the index and the notes show the presence of Schimmel's edition in Rudolph's. This was not an independent revision of Henning's original edition that happened to be more thorough; rather, it specifically built on Schimmel's edition, improving and expanding it. For example, these are Schimmel's and Rudolph's index entries for the letter J, translated into English:

Schimmel[101]	Rudolph[102]
	Yaghūth, old Arabian deity
Jacob	Jacob (Yaʿqub)
	Yathrib (=Medina)
	Yaʿuq, old Arabian deity
	Hereafter, see Hell and Paradise
Jesus (Son of Mary)	Jesus (ʿIsa), the son of Mary
John (the Baptist)	John (the Baptist)
Jonah (Dhu l-Nun)	Jonah (Yunus), also called Dhu l-Nun 'Fish Man'
Joseph (son of Jacob)	Joseph (Yusuf, son of Jacob)
Jews (*see also* Children of Israel; People of the Book)	Jews (al-Yahud), *see also* Children of Israel, Moses
Judgment Day (*see also* Resurrection, 'Hour')	Judgment Day, *see also* Judgment, Resurrection, 'Hour'
Allah and Judgment Day (belief in)	

Also, compare Schimmel's and Rudolph's footnotes on Q 9:107—a verse in which a mosque built to cause harm or disbelief is mentioned, which Henning himself did not include a note on:

---

101 Henning and Schimmel, *Der Koran*, pp. 605–06.
102 Henning and Rudolph, *Der Koran*, p. 584.

Schimmel	Rudolph
According to tradition, twelve men had built a mosque near that of Kubâᶜ in order to cause division among the Muslims.[103]	According to tradition, it is the so-called 'rivalry mosque' which was built by some Medinans of the Banu Salim near the prayer place of Quba' at the instigation of the Hanif or monk Abu Amir, either to have their own place of worship or to harm Muhammad. He recognised the evil intentions and had it destroyed.[104]

Even in Rudolph's introduction, traces of Schimmel's influence can be found, as in the example of his comparison between the *Fātiḥa* and the Lord's Prayer mentioned above. However, the similarities are marginal here, partly because the Leipzig edition—unlike the one from Stuttgart—had a system of academic quality control in place, and the reviewers' suggestions were heeded. More importantly, the Leipzig edition had its own historical and political framing, and that was incompatible with Schimmel's vision. This is true for both Werner's and Rudolph's introductions, despite the major differences of opinion between them. They, as well as the Reclam editorial office, had distinctive ideas about why the Qur'an was relevant for a GDR readership.

A Prophet for GDR Readers: The Leipzig Edition's Framing of Islam

The entire project of introducing GDR readers to the Qur'an faced a big problem from the outset, and that is the fact that the Qur'an is a religious text. According to official Marxist ideology, religions were considered harmful. Therefore, one of the major paradigms of the edition was to move the focus away from matters of faith and piety towards more 'innocuous' fields such as social ethics, politics, and history. This is why Annemarie Schimmel's approach to the Qur'an was so badly suited to the GDR context, despite the respect that Rudolph obviously had for her.

---

103 Henning and Schimmel, *Der Koran*, p. 194.
104 Henning and Rudolph, *Der Koran*, p. 197.

One solution that Reclam found for this dilemma was to highlight the socio-political significance of Muḥammad's mission, which was emphasised not only with regard to his own times but especially for the present day. According to the blurb:

> The effects that emanate from this collection of Muhammad's proclamations up to the present day are immensely diverse [...] For today's Muslims in different parts of the world, the life and work of Muhammad have not only a religious but also an eminently political significance, inasmuch as he is regarded as a model of a conscious, energetic, and responsible statesman who paved the way for racial equality and social justice. For Arab nationalism, he paved the way for Arab unity.[105]

The perceived problems of this approach have already become apparent from Markov's expert statement, in which he criticised the fact that Werner had overlooked—or at least heavily downplayed—Mecca's role as a religious centre. But this approach also had its advantages. For example, it allowed a positive appraisal of Muḥammad's political role. While Henning, like many other European Orientalists, had bemoaned Muḥammad's turn to statesmanship after the *hijra*, this was decidedly seen as a redeeming quality in the GDR. In his introduction, Werner explains the emergence of Islam as a means to a political end—namely, the unification of Arabs—and he situates it in Marxist historiography, according to which feudalism was a necessary intermediate stage between slave-owning societies and capitalism that all societies go through.

> Muhammad not only charted the Arabs' path into the future through his religious foundation, he also gave them political maxims that his successors, the caliphs, sought to realise by all means. An early feudal state had emerged from the fragmented and disunited Arabia, which was held together by a uniform religious ideology and a minimum degree of centralization [...] Muhammad is one of the most important personalities in world history. He created a 'religion tailored to Orientals, especially Arabs, i.e. on the one hand to city dwellers engaged in trade and commerce, and on the other to nomadising Bedouins' (F. Engels). He thus gave Oriental society an ideology that corresponded to it, and in this way promoted its feudalization. More than almost any other religious founder, he merged politics and religion and orientated his

---

105 Ibid.

religious mission towards social conditions. In his later period, however, this also resulted in a remarkable lack of hesitation when using religious phraseology to achieve secular goals. Nevertheless, his work served a progressive development and significantly promoted the transition from slavery and kinship organization to feudalism.[106]

Rudolph, unsurprisingly, assumes a less ideological perspective on early Islamic history. For him, Muḥammad was the founder of a religion whose authentic statements are contained in the Qur'an. While acknowledging the role of politics in early Islamic history, he also stresses the 'internal, religious side' of Islam.[107] He has no doubt about Muḥammad's sincerity in this regard. However, his views of what it means to establish a new faith are very different from Schimmel's. They have a society-oriented component that leads him to reject the common distinction between the Meccan and Medinan Muḥammad. According to Rudolph, neither was the Meccan period a time of apolitical piety, nor did Muḥammad betray his religious ideals in favour of politics during the Medinan period. He was never an individualistic seeker of God, but always, from the outset, took responsibility for the community. What changed were the circumstances in which he did so and the amount of authority and agency he possessed, not the mission itself.

Rudolph also provides readers with an overview of the religion of Islam, in which he very much emphasises its present-day political role:

> When M. Henning wrote at the time that the political role of Islam was finished, he was (forgivably) mistaken. Islam is currently experiencing a renaissance (*nahda*) and has retained its dominant position in all Muslim countries liberated from the colonial yoke and imperialism, be it in Africa, the Middle East, India or Indonesia, or has regained it in a modern form. 'Islam promotes the ideals of freedom and liberation from the yoke of imperialism,' declared Gamal abd an-Nassir (Nasser) in 1964 at the 'Islamic Studies Congress' held in Cairo, which was attended by Muslim scholars from forty-two countries. The study of the Qur'an as the document that forms the basis of Islam is therefore only natural, especially for people who follow the struggle of these peoples with conscious involvement and sympathy.[108]

---

106 Ibid., p. 15.
107 Ibid., p. 16.
108 Ibid., p. 32.

230 *Qur'an Translations in the Eastern Bloc and Beyond*

However, it is quite obvious from Rudolph's extensive annotation that neither the liberation from the 'colonial yoke' nor Nasser's Arab socialism—which was firmly entrenched in the Eastern Bloc by 1968, after the catastrophic defeat in the Six-Day-War against Israel in 1967— were really among his areas of interest. Nor did he engage with the phenomenology of religion, as Schimmel had done; this is particularly visible in many instances where he built on Schimmel's notes but omitted her (often quite sweeping) statements about Muslim beliefs.[109] He also deleted her references to South Asian sources, including the exegesis of Muhammad Iqbal, in favour of pre-Islamic sources.[110] Overall, he had an academic interest in the history of Islam in the context of pre-Islamic religions and he strove to satisfy the ideological demands of the GDR publishing system to the smallest extent possible in order to carve out a space for the unideological pursuit of scholarship, with remarkable success. His annotation—in contrast to both the original edition and the Stuttgart edition—is extensive, providing readers with many useful explanations, a good overview of Qur'anic and Biblical parallels, references to other Late Antique sources, and information on the Arabian context of the Qur'anic revelation. Far from promoting the political agenda of the GDR, the annotation is instead successful at guiding readers through the text—a text that Rudolph had significantly improved by correcting mistakes, modernising the language, and arranging it in thematic units. Unfortunately, this achievement was not the decisive factor in determining the fate of the respective editions after the Berlin Wall came down and Germany was reunified.

The West has Won: Henning's Translation after Reunification

On 3 October 1990—less than a year after the GDR had opened its borders in a semi-accidental reaction to the mass exodus of its disillusioned citizens, which the crumbling Soviet Union refused to

---

109 See, for example, their respective notes on Q 6:60 where Rudolph disregarded Schimmel's reference to the importance that Muslims attach to dreams.
110 For example, in his note on Q 2:28, he replaced a reference to Muhammad Iqbal with one to Augustine; and he omits her mention in Q 21:85 of the identification of Dhū l-Kifl with the Buddha.

prevent—the 'better Germany' ceased to exist. Very little changed for West Germany but practically everything changed for the 'five new federal states', as the former territory of the GDR was now called. At this time, both Reclam Leipzig (1989) and Reclam Stuttgart (1990) were still publishing reprints of their respective versions of Henning's Qur'an translation. Moreover, Annemarie Schimmel was working on an update of her edition, which was published by Reclam Stuttgart in 1991. She now used the Kufan verse numbering system, with Flügel's numbers in brackets. She had also expanded the bibliography to include more recent titles and had minimally revised the annotations to be more considerate of the religious sensitivities of Muslim readers, in deference to the fact that the Germany of 1991 had a substantial and growing Muslim population.[111] By the 1980s, some of these German Muslims had also started to write their own translations of the Qur'an.[112]

However, Henning's translation remained relevant, first of all because Muslim translators into German frequently drew on it, and secondly because some Muslim individuals and institutions preferred it to translations that had not been produced by native speakers. Henning's translation seemed adequately respectful to them; among other things, his rendition of *Allāh* as 'Allah', rather than 'Gott', was cited as a reason for this.[113] Moreover, its copyright protection expired in 1997, and Reclam was willing to grant publishing rights even a few years before that date. For these reasons, no fewer than two Turkish editions of Henning's translation were published in the 1990s, both edited by converts. The first was prepared by H. Achmed Schmiede (1935–2010) on behalf of the Türkiye Diyanet Foundation in 1991. Targeting second- and third-generation

---

111 Max Henning (trans.) and Annemarie Schimmel (ed.), *Der Koran*, revised edn (Stuttgart: Reclam, 1991).

112 Hartmut Bobzin, 'Abu-r-Riḍā' Muḥammad Ibn Aḥmad Ibn Rassoul', in *Glaubensbuch und Weltliteratur. Koranübersetzungen in Deutschland von der Reformationszeit bis heute*, ed. by Hartmut Bobzin and Peter M. Kleine (Arnsberg: Stadt Arnsberg, 2007), p. 50; Hartmut Bobzin, 'Adel Theodor Khoury/Muhammad Salim Abdullah', in *Glaubensbuch und Weltliteratur. Koranübersetzungen in Deutschland von der Reformationszeit bis heute*, ed. by Hartmut Bobzin and Peter M. Kleine (Arnsberg: Stadt Arnsberg, 2007), p. 51; Ahmad von Denffer (ed.), *Der Koran: die Heilige Schrift des Islam in deutscher Übertragung; mit Erläuterungen nach den Kommentaren von Dschalalain, Tabari und anderen hervorragenden klassischen Koranauslegern*, 9th improved edn (München: Islamisches Zentrum, 2003).

113 Fatima Grimm, 'Review: Der Koran by Max Henning, Murad Wilfried Hofmann, Şaban Kurt', *Islamic Studies (Islamabad)*, 38:3 (1999), 465–68.

German-Turks, it contained Schimmel's edition without the paratexts, but with virtually no changes other than a complete adaptation to the Kufan verse numbering system, as well as the addition of the Arabic *muṣḥaf*. The second edition, published in 1998 by the *daʿwa*-oriented Turkish publisher Çağrı Yayınları, was prepared by the high-profile convert Murad Wilfried Hofmann (1931–2020) who had heavily revised it and turned it into a fairly polemical and apologetic text.[114]

Despite the growing competition, Reclam itself aimed to continue publishing a Qur'an translation, and due to the history of the Henning edition, it could choose from two options. This was because after the end of the GDR, the coexistence of Reclam Stuttgart and Reclam Leipzig was seen as untenable. Reclam Leipzig was heavily in debt and could not survive in the market economy conditions without radical reorganisation. Through the Treuhandanstalt—the privatisation trust agency that administered the restructuring, sale, or closure of GDR companies—the Stuttgart publishing house made a bid to take over the Leipzig branch. Their proposal, which allowed the Leipzig house to continue running its own programme, was favoured by a majority of the employees over a proposal by the Leipzig management to have Reclam Leipzig collectively owned and run by its employees. In 1992, the reprivatisation of Reclam Leipzig and its incorporation into the Stuttgart publishing house was completed.[115] In 2006, however, Reclam Leipzig was wound up, despite having a highly respected portfolio and large number of bestsellers. Many Germans in the 'five new federal states' considered this another case of the GDR legacy being sold off, regardless of profit or other value.[116]

---

114 Max Henning (trans.) and H. Achmed Schmiede (ed.), *Der gnadenreiche Koran* (Ankara: Türkiye Diyanet Vakfı, 1995); Max Henning (trans.) and Murad Wilfried Hofmann (ed.), *Der Koran: arabisch – deutsch*, 3rd edn (Istanbul: Çağrı Yayınları, 2002); Hartmut Bobzin, 'Max Henning – Hanspeter Achmed Schmiede', in *Glaubensbuch und Weltliteratur. Koranübersetzungen in Deutschland von der Reformationszeit bis heute*, ed. by Hartmut Bobzin and Peter M. Kleine (Arnsberg: Stadt Arnsberg, 2007), p. 52; Hartmut Bobzin, 'Max Henning – Murad Wilfried Hofmann', in *Glaubensbuch und Weltliteratur. Koranübersetzungen in Deutschland von der Reformationszeit bis heute*, ed. by Hartmut Bobzin and Peter M. Kleine (Arnsberg: Stadt Arnsberg, 2007), p. 55. For more details, see also Pink, 'Eine Koranübersetzung'.

115 Max, *Der Reclam-Verlag*, pp. 76–77.

116 Susanne Mack, 'Reclam Leipzig Ade', *Deutschlandfunk Kultur*, 29 March 2006, https://www.deutschlandfunkkultur.de/reclam-leipzig-ade-100.html

The fate of the two Cold War editions of Henning's translation of the Qur'an reflects a similar trajectory. Reclam reprinted Schimmel's 1991 edition several times, and it does not appear that the management in Stuttgart ever even considered swapping it for Rudolph's edition. 2022 saw a 'reviewed and updated' Schimmel edition, in which the main change appears to be that the term *Weiber* was replaced by *Frauen*—more than fifty years after Reclam Leipzig had done this.[117] Rudolph's edition, on the other hand, was no longer reprinted—at least not officially and under his name. To this day, online bookshops offer a print-on-demand title and ebook by a shady publisher called Nikol which contains Rudolph's version of Henning's translation without the paratexts but is marketed solely under Henning's name, with the blurb of the Schimmel edition: the ultimate rip-off, and a rather sad ending for an edition into which so much time and effort was invested under adverse circumstances.[118]

Bibliography

Ahmad, Hazrat Mirza Bashir-ud-Din Mahmud (ed.), *Der Heilige Koran* (Zürich: Der Islam, 1954).

Barck, Simone, Martina Langermann, and Siegfried Lokatis, *„Jedes Buch ein Abenteuer". Zensur-System und literarische Öffentlichkeiten in der DDR bis Ende der sechziger Jahre* (Berlin: Akademie Verlag, 1997).

Bialas, Wolfgang, 'Ostdeutsche Intellektuelle und der gesellschaftliche Umbruch der DDR', *Geschichte und Gesellschaft*, 33:2 (2007).

Bobzin, Hartmut, 'Abu-r-Riḍā' Muḥammad Ibn Aḥmad Ibn Rassoul', in *Glaubensbuch und Weltliteratur. Koranübersetzungen in Deutschland von der Reformationszeit bis heute*, ed. by Hartmut Bobzin and Peter M. Kleine (Arnsberg: Stadt Arnsberg, 2007), p. 50.

——, 'Adel Theodor Khoury/Muhammad Salim Abdullah', in *Glaubensbuch und Weltliteratur. Koranübersetzungen in Deutschland von der Reformationszeit*

---

117 It is possible that this has something to do with a blog post/Twitter thread by the author about the East-Western history of the Henning translation and the anachronism of the term *Weiber*, to which Reclam-Verlag responded at the time with a promise of an update. See https://twitter.com/ReclamVerlag/status/1353644131395002369, 25 January 2021.

118 See https://www.amazon.de/Koran-Vollständige-Ausgabe-Max-Henning/dp/3868200835/

bis heute, ed. by Hartmut Bobzin and Peter M. Kleine (Arnsberg: Stadt Arnsberg, 2007), p. 51.

——, 'Max Henning – Annemarie Schimmel', in *Glaubensbuch und Weltliteratur. Koranübersetzungen in Deutschland von der Reformationszeit bis heute*, ed. by Hartmut Bobzin and Peter M. Kleine (Arnsberg: Stadt Arnsberg, 2007), p. 47.

——, 'Max Henning – Hanspeter Achmed Schmiede', in *Glaubensbuch und Weltliteratur. Koranübersetzungen in Deutschland von der Reformationszeit bis heute*, ed. by Hartmut Bobzin and Peter M. Kleine (Arnsberg: Stadt Arnsberg, 2007), p. 52.

——, 'Max Henning – Murad Wilfried Hofmann', in *Glaubensbuch und Weltliteratur. Koranübersetzungen in Deutschland von der Reformationszeit bis heute*, ed. by Hartmut Bobzin and Peter M. Kleine (Arnsberg: Stadt Arnsberg, 2007), p. 55.

——, and Peter M. Kleine (eds), *Glaubensbuch und Weltliteratur. Koranübersetzungen in Deutschland von der Reformationszeit bis heute* (Arnsberg: Stadt Arnsberg, 2007).

Dawood, N. J., *The Koran* (Harmondsworth: Penguin Books, 1956).

Demirel, Ömer Faruk, 'Ünlü Atatürk Biyografı Herbert Melzig Kimdir?', *Elektronik Siyaset Bilimi Araştırmaları Dergisi* 13:1 (2022).

Denffer, Ahmad von (ed.), *Der Koran. Die Heilige Schrift des Islam in deutscher Übertragung; mit Erläuterungen nach den Kommentaren von Dschalalain, Tabari und anderen hervorragenden klassischen Koranauslegern*, 9th edn (München: Islamisches Zentrum, 2003).

Dietzsch, Steffen, 'Als Herausgeber bei Reclam in Leipzig im „Freihafen der Philosophie"', in *An den Grenzen des Möglichen: Reclam-Leipzig 1945-1991*, ed. by Ingrid Sonntag (Berlin: Ch. Links Verlag, 2016), pp. 296–305.

Fetzer, Günther, *Das Taschenbuch. Geschichte – Verlage – Reihen* (Tübingen: Narr Francke Attempto, 2019).

Flügel, Gustav, *Corani textus arabicus* (Leibzig: Tauchnitz, 1834).

Forssmann, Friedrich, 'Zur Neugestaltung 2012', in *Die Welt in Gelb*, ed. by Karl-Heinz Fallbacher (Stuttgart: Reclam, 2012), pp. 17–22.

Grimm, Fatima, 'Review: Der Koran by Max Henning, Murad Wilfried Hofmann, Şaban Kurt', *Islamic Studies (Islamabad)*, 38:3 (1999).

Haberländer, Brigitte, 'Max Henning', in *Glaubensbuch und Weltliteratur. Koranübersetzungen in Deutschland von der Reformationszeit bis heute*, ed. by Hartmut Bobzin and Peter M. Kleine (Arnsberg: Stadt Arnsberg, 2007), p. 41.

Hafez, Kai, and Gerhard Höpp, 'Gegenwartsbezogene Orientwissenschaft in der DDR und in den neuen Bundesländern: Continuity or New Beginning?', in *Wissenschaft und Wiedervereinigung. Asien- und*

Afrikawissenschaften im Umbruch, ed. by Wolf-Hagen Krauth and Ralf Wolz (Berlin: Akademie Verlag, 1998), pp. 95–163.

Henning, Max (trans.), *Der Koran* (Leipzig: Reclam, 1901).

——, (trans.), and Annemarie Schimmel (ed.), *Der Koran* (Stuttgart: Reclam, 1960).

——, (trans.), *Geschichten Aus Tausendundeiner Nacht. Mit Einem Nachwort von Herbert Melzig* (Leipzig: Reclam, 1966).

——, (trans.), and Kurt Rudolph (ed.), *Der Koran* (Leipzig: Reclam, 1968).

——, (trans.), and Annemarie Schimmel (ed.), *Der Koran*, revised edn (Stuttgart: Reclam, 1991).

——, (trans.), and H. Achmed Schmiede (ed.), *Der gnadenreiche Koran* (Ankara: Türkiye Diyanet Vakfı, 1995).

——, (trans.), and Murad Wilfried Hofmann (ed.), *Der Koran: arabisch – deutsch*, 3rd edn (Istanbul: Çağrı Yayınları, 2002).

Herf, Jeffrey,'"At War with Israel": East Germany's Key Role in Soviet Policy in the Middle East', *Journal of Cold War Studies*, 16:3 (2014).

Hofmann, Anne, *Islam in den Medien. Der publizistische Konflikt um Annemarie Schimmel* (Münster: LIT, 2004).

Ihrig, Stefan, 'Nazi Leaks and Intrigues in Second World War Ankara: The Plot to Send Herbert Melzig to a Concentration Camp', *The International History Review*, 38:1 (2016).

Jonker, Gerdien, 'A Nietzschean *tafsīr* for Nazi Germany', *Journal of Qur'anic Studies*, 26:2 (2024).

Kerr, Malcolm H., *The Arab Cold War: Gamal ʿAbd al-Nasir and His Rivals, 1958–1970*, 3rd edn (London and New York: Royal Institute of International Affairs and Oxford University Press, 1971).

König, Werner, *dtv-Atlas der deutschen Sprache*, 15th edn (Munich: dtv, 2005).

Kulieva, Elvira, 'Ignatii Krachkovskii', in *Encyclopaedia of the Qur'ān Online* (Brill: Leiden, 2024), https://doi.org/10.1163/1875-3922_q3_EQCOM_061331.

Laux, Carmen, 'Ein schwerer Anfang. Von der Lizenzierung zur Demontage', in *An den Grenzen des Möglichen: Reclam-Leipzig 1945–1991*, ed. by Ingrid Sonntag (Berlin: Ch. Links Verlag, 2016), pp. 40–51.

——, and Ingrid Sonntag, 'Ein Name, zwei Verlage. Reclam Leipzig und Reclam Stuttgart', in *An den Grenzen des Möglichen: Reclam-Leipzig 1945–1991*, ed. by Ingrid Sonntag (Berlin: Ch. Links Verlag, 2016), pp. 52–72.

Mack, Susanne, 'Reclam Leipzig Ade', *Deutschlandfunk Kultur*, 29 March 2006, https://www.deutschlandfunkkultur.de/reclam-leipzig-ade-100.html

Mangold-Will, Sabine, *Eine 'weltbürgerliche Wissenschaft'. Die deutsche Orientalistik im 19. Jahrhundert* (Stuttgart: Steiner, 2004).

Marchand, Suzanne L., *German Orientalism in the Age of Empire: Religion, Race, and Scholarship* (Cambridge: Cambridge University Press, 2010).

Max, Frank Rainer, *Der Reclam-Verlag. Eine kurze Chronik*, Universal-Bibliothek 18280 (Stuttgart: Reclam, 2003).

Mix, York-Gothart, 'Kulturelles Kapital für 20, 50 oder 80 Pfennige. Medialisierungsstrategien Leipziger Verleger in der frühen Moderne am Beispiel der „Universal-Bibliothek", der „Insel-Bücherei" und der Sammlung „Der Jüngste Tag"', *Archiv für Kulturgeschichte*, 82:1 (2000).

Paret, Rudi, '[Rezension von:] Der Koran. Aus dem Arabischen übertragen von Max Henning. Einleitung und Anmerkungen von Annemarie Schimmel', *Zeitschrift der deutschen morgenländischen Gesellschaft*, 113:2 (1963).

Pink, Johanna, 'Eine Koranübersetzung im Kalten Krieg. Reclam, Max Henning und das Bild Muḥammads im geteilten Deutschland', *Die Welt des Islams*, pre-print publication (2025), 1–49.

——, 'The Qurʾan as "World Literature" and the Residue of Empire: N. J. Dawood's English Qurʾan Translation', in *Literary Dimensions of the Qurʾan*, ed. by Shawkat Toorawa (Edinburgh: Edinburgh University Press), forthcoming.

Sadr-ud-Din, Maulana, *Der Koran: Arabisch-Deutsch*, 1st edn (Berlin: Verlag der moslemischen Revue, 1939).

——, *Der Koran: Arabisch-Deutsch*, 2nd edn (Berlin: Verlag der moslemischen Revue, 1964).

Saß, Marcell, 'Nachruf Prof. Dr. theol. Dr. phil. habil. Dr. h. c. mult. Kurt Rudolph', *Universität Marburg*, May 2020, https://www.uni-marburg.de/de/fb05/aktuelles/news/nachruf-kurt-rudolph.pdf

Schmahl, Karolin, 'Kontinuitäten im Neubeginn. Der Reclam-Verlag zwischen Kapitulation und Lizenzierung unter der Leitung von Ernst Reclam und Gotthold Müller', in *An den Grenzen des Möglichen: Reclam-Leipzig 1945-1991*, ed. by Ingrid Sonntag (Berlin: Ch. Links Verlag, 2016), pp. 30–39.

Schnell, Ralf, 'Literatur und Gesellschaft im Übergang (1977–1989)', in *Geschichte der deutschsprachigen Literatur seit 1945*, ed. by Ralf Schnell (Stuttgart: J. B. Metzler, 1993), pp. 207–37.

Schüler, Anke, 'Ein Name, zwei Wege: Reclam Leipzig und Reclam Stuttgart. Hintergründe der Trennung der Verlagshäuser in den 1950er-Jahren', *Deutsch-deutscher Literaturaustausch 8+9 2012*, 20 September 2012, https://www.bpb.de/themen/deutschlandarchiv/139840/ein-name-zwei-wege-reclam-leipzig-und-reclam-stuttgart/

Schwanitz, Wolfgang G., 'Paschas, Politiker und Paradigmen. Deutsche Politik im Nahen und Mittleren Orient 1871–1945', *Comparativ*, 14:1 (2004).

Seuss, Juergen, 'H. M. – Grenzgänger', in *An den Grenzen des Möglichen: Reclam-Leipzig 1945-1991*, ed. by Ingrid Sonntag (Berlin: Ch. Links Verlag, 2016), pp. 109–19.

Sonntag, Ingrid (ed.), *An den Grenzen des Möglichen: Reclam-Leipzig 1945–1991* (Berlin: Ch. Links Verlag, 2016).

——, 'Die C-Reihe und die Rekonstruktion der Universal-Bibliothek' in *An den Grenzen des Möglichen: Reclam-Leipzig 1945–1991*, ed. by Ingrid Sonntag (Berlin: Ch. Links Verlag, 2016), pp. 101–08.

——, 'Geschichte als Verlagsgeschichte', in *An den Grenzen des Möglichen: Reclam-Leipzig 1945–1991*, ed. by Ingrid Sonntag (Berlin: Ch. Links Verlag, 2016), pp. 115–28.

——, 'Kommentar zu Hans Marquardts Stasiakte', in *An den Grenzen des Möglichen: Reclam-Leipzig 1945–1991*, ed. by Ingrid Sonntag (Berlin: Ch. Links Verlag, 2016), pp. 131–41.

Spitaler, Anton, *Die Verszählung des Koran nach islamischer Überlieferung* (München: Verlag der Bayerischen Akademie der Wissenschaften, 1935).

Sprenger, A., *Mohammed und der Koran. Eine psychologische Studie* (Hamburg: A.G., 1889).

Thierse, Wolfgang, 'Zwischen Anpassung und kontrollierter Aufmüpfigkeit', in *An den Grenzen des Möglichen: Reclam-Leipzig 1945–1991*, ed. by Ingrid Sonntag (Berlin: Ch. Links Verlag, 2016), pp. 112–14.

Ullmann, L. (trans.), *Der Koran. Aus dem Arabischen wortgetreu neu übersetzt und mit erläuternden Anmerkungen versehen*, 5th edn (Bielefeld: Velhagen & Klasing, 1865).

——, *Der Koran. Das heilige Buch des Islam* (München: Goldmann, 1959).

Weil, Gustav, *Mohammed der Prophet, sein Leben und seine Lehre* (Stuttgart: Metzler, 1843).

——, *Historisch-kritische Einleitung in den Koran* (Bielefeld: Velhagen & Klasing, 1844).

Wild, Stefan, 'Der Friedenspreis und Annemarie Schimmel: Eine Nachlese', *Die Welt des Islams*, 36:1 (1996).

——, 'In Memoriam Annemarie Schimmel (7. April 1922–26. Januar 2003)', *Die Welt des Islams*, 43:2 (2003).

——, 'Annemarie Schimmel und der Islam', *Theologie der Gegenwart*, 57:3 (2014).

6. Constructing a Qur'an-Based *sīra* in Post-Soviet Azerbaijan: Denominational Approaches to the Prophet's Biography in Azerbaijani Qur'an Translations

Elnura Azizova

Introduction

Azerbaijan, the largest country in the South Caucasus in terms of both geographic area and population, is constitutionally a democratic, legal, secular, and unitary republic. Approximately 96.9% of the country's population is made up of Muslims, while 3% are Christians, and members of other religions such as Judaism make up the final 0.1%.[1] Because of its geopolitical situation, Azerbaijan has experienced the re-settlement and migration of many peoples throughout history. The process of Islamisation started in the middle of the seventh century, at which time

---

1 Pew Research Center, *The Global Religious Landscape: A Report on the Size and Distribution of the World's Major Religious Groups as of 2010* (Washington, D.C.: The Pew Research Center's Forum on Religion & Public Life, 2012), p. 45, https://www.pewresearch.org/religion/2012/12/18/global-religious-landscape-exec/

the population was a mixture of Zoroastrians, Christians, and Jews, and Muslims came to make up the majority in only a short time.

At the beginning of the nineteenth century, Azerbaijan was divided into two parts and split between the Qajar State and Tsarist Russia by the treaties of Gulistan (1813) and Turkmenchay (1828). Historically, the southern part of Azerbaijan fell within the borders of modern Iran. South Azerbaijani Turks make up 25–30% of the country's total population, forming the second-largest ethnic group in Iran today after Persians, and are concentrated in Tabriz, Ardabil, and Zandjan, although they are also present in other provinces. In Northern Azerbaijan, which remained under the rule of Tsarist Russia, efforts were made to assimilate the Muslim population, leading to the establishment of the Azerbaijan Democratic Republic in 1918—the first democratic republic of the Muslim world. However, after only two years of independence, the fledgling Republic was invaded by Soviet Russia in 1920. During the following seventy years of Soviet rule, the area was subject to the Soviet atheist agenda, and from the 1940s onwards a policy institutionally oppressing Muslims was implemented. After Azerbaijan regained its independence in 1991, the way was paved for the development of a new sense of national and religious identity. According to recent surveys, 90–99% of the population that identifies as Muslim describe themselves as believers, while the rate of practising Muslims is only 5–17%.[2] The Muslim population of Azerbaijan consists of Twelver Shiis and Sunnis, although there is no definitive statistic on their relative proportions from official or reliable sources. Furthermore, a survey conducted in thirty-nine mainly Muslim-majority countries found the highest degree of interdenominational tolerance between Sunnis and Shiis in Azerbaijan. The ratio of Azerbaijanians who accept Shiis as Muslims vs those who do not is 97% to 2%, and the ratio of those who accept Sunnis as Muslims and those who do not is 91% to 7%.[3]

---

[2] Elnurə Əzizova, 'Azərbaycan cəmiyyətindəki dindarlıq səviyyəsinin İslam dünyasındakı dindarlıq səviyyəsi ilə müqayisəsi', in *Azərbaycanda İslam*, ed. by Nahid Məmmədov (Baku: Nurlar, 2015), pp. 52–75; Asəf Qənbərov, *Azərbaycanda Dövlət-Din Münasibətləri: Dünyəviliyin nəzəri və hüquqi əsasları* (Baku: Nurlar, 2019), pp. 163–68.

[3] Pew Research Center, *The World's Muslims: Unity and Diversity* (Washington, D.C.: The Pew Research Center's Forum on Religion & Public Life, 2012), pp. 132–33, https://www.pewresearch.org/religion/2012/08/09/the-worlds-muslims-unity-and-diversity-executive-summary/

Over the last decade, Azerbaijan has initiated a policy of multiculturalism, with the officially declared goal of promoting harmonious coexistence among its diverse national, cultural, and religious groups, all built upon the principles of tolerance and mutual respect. For the purpose of showcasing and implementing this policy more effectively, the Baku International Multiculturalism Center was established by presidential decree in 2014, and the President also signed an order declaring 2016 the 'Year of Multiculturalism'. The continuation of the centuries-old peaceful relationship between Shiis and Sunnis is a crucial part of this policy. Within the framework of the Year of Multiculturalism, on 15 January 2016, Shii and Sunni believers jointly participated for the first time in the performance of the Unity Prayer (*vəhdət namazı*) at Haydar Mosque in Baku. Since then, the Unity Prayer has become a national tradition that symbolises interdenominational companionship, religious tolerance, and multiculturalism. Azerbaijan's model of interdenominational relations has been described as an example for many Muslim-majority countries.[4]

In 1997, the first issue of *Tarjūmān-e Waḥī*, a new journal dedicated to Qur'anic studies based in Iran, published an article on Qur'an translations in post-Soviet Azerbaijan. The author of the article, Rasūl Ismā'īlzāde Dūzāl—a theologian from South Azerbaijan and the author of a Qur'an translation into Azerbaijani—criticised the first Qur'an translation published in post-Soviet Azerbaijan, by Ziya Bünyadov and Vasim Mammedaliyev, for including some Sunni elements, on the basis that it had been 'influenced by the translations in Istanbul Turkish' (i.e. modern Turkish).[5] In direct contrast, ten years later, Dr Fethi Ahmet Polat—a theologian from the Republic of Türkiye—regretfully asserted that the very same translation reflected Shii denominational concerns in places.[6] Despite their particularistic approaches, these two studies

---

4   Qənbərov, *Azərbaycanda Dövlət-Din Münasibətləri*, pp. 192–95.
5   Rasūl Ismā'īlzāde Dūzāl, 'Negāhī be tarjama hāi Azerbāyjānī Qur'āni-Karīm', *Tarjūmān-e Waḥī*, 1 (1376/1997), 60–73 (pp. 71–72).
6   A number of studies instead deal with one particular Azerbaijani translation, or undertake a comparison between translations. See Ahmet Fethi Polat, 'Azerbaycan'da Yapılan Kur'an Tercümeleri ve Türkiye'de Neşredilen Meallerin Bu Tercümelere Etkileri—Memmedeliyev Tercümesi Örneği', *Uluslararası Türk Dünyasının İslamiyete Katkıları Sempozyumu Bildirileri*, ed. by İsmail Hakkı Göksoy and Nejdet Durak (Isparta: Süleyman Demirel Üniversitesi, 2007), pp. 441–57 (pp. 455–56).

demonstrate that the issue of Qur'an translation in Azerbaijan was of interest to the international academic community, and was on their radar. Since Dūzāl's 1997 article on Azerbaijani Qur'an translations, various other articles, master's theses, and book chapters on the subject have been produced. With some exceptions,[7] these studies tend to provide a bibliography of existing translations and draw a general picture of their methods and exegetical and linguistic characteristics.[8] However, many issues remain unexplored, such as the contextualisation of Azerbaijani Qur'an translation traditions and movements in relation to the wider Islamic world, their relationship with Qur'anic studies in the pre-Soviet and post-Soviet periods, the socio-political factors affecting the translation process, and the underlying reasons for editorial changes.

The biography of the Prophet—the *sīra nabawiyya*—promises to be a particularly fruitful subject of research in Azerbaijani Qur'an translations. Since the religious tradition of Azerbaijan has been interrupted by nearly seventy years of official atheist ideology, what perception of the Prophet Muḥammad might be reflected in religious texts? Translations of the Qur'an into Azerbaijani Turkish are among the most accessible and widely disseminated written sources presenting the life of the Prophet to the Azerbaijani-speaking local Muslim populace, and the use of the *sīra* as a methodological lens will enable a meaningful comparative assessment. In order to study the subject in detail, verses of the Qur'an related to the main events of the *sīra* will be highlighted, and comparisons will be made between the various translations, commentaries, and interpretations of the relevant verses. Particular attention will be paid to certain subjects, such as the Prophet's image in the context of ʿiṣma (infallibility), as well as how the differing depictions of the Prophet's Companions and his wives reflect specific denominational points of view.

---

7   Ibid.; Roya Aliyeva, 'Kur'an Tercüme Teknikleri Açısından Büniyatov-Mammedaliyev ve Guliyev Meallerinin Değerlendirilmesi' (unpublished master's thesis, Sakarya Üniversitesi, 2016).

8   Erdoğan Pazarbaşı, ''Azerbaycan'da Yaygın Kur'an Tercümeleri', *Erciyes Üniversitesi İlâhiyat Fakültesi Dergisi*, 10 (1998), 103–18; Mehman İsmayılov, '20. Yüzyılda Azerbaycan'da Yapılan Kur'an Tefsiri ve Meal Çalışmaları' (unpublished master's thesis, Marmara Üniversitesi, 2002), pp. 20–45; Ahmet Fethi Polat, 'Yirminci Yüzyıl Sonrasında Azerbaycan'da Yapılan Kur'an Tercümeleri—I', *Selçuk Üniversitesi İlahiyat Fakültesi Dergisi*, 16 (2003), 73–96; Ramiz Məmmədov and Abdurrəhman Nuruyev, *Təfsir Elmi* (Baku: İpəkyolu, 2016), pp. 105–8.

As of 2023, fourteen Azerbaijani Qur'an translations have been produced, and the publication history of these translations can be divided into three periods: (1) translations by Azerbaijani Arabists, from the late 1980s to the early 1990s; (2) institutional translations produced by foreign organisations from the late 1990s to the early 2000s; (3) a period of diversification from 2010 to the present day. In this chapter, I will briefly introduce translations from each of these periods, referring to the social-religious discourses affecting their production and analysing how this might be reflected in the various translations, with a focus on verses associated with the *sīra nabawiyya*.

Qur'an Translations by Azerbaijani Arabists: The Incorporation of the Classical *sīra* Tradition into the Framework of the Qur'an

The first complete translation of the Qur'an to be produced in the Republic of Azerbaijan was co-authored by an Arabist, Vasim Mammadaliyev, and a historian, Ziya Bünyadov, using the Cyrillic alphabet in 1992, with a print run of 100,000 copies.[9] Mammadaliyev's preface to the translation consists of an extensive article on the history of the Qur'an, which mainly focuses on the history of its translation.[10] The annotations that characterise this text as a commentary translation[11] were written by Ziya Bünyadov, who, as acknowledged in the preface,[12] makes great use of the Russian Qur'an translation by Ignatii Iul'ianovich Krachkovskii (d. 1951), one of the founders of the school of Soviet Arabic Studies. Mammadaliyev further explains that a sixty-six-page section covering the first three *suras* was translated by Ali Fahmi Alakbarov[13] in 1969

---

9   Ziya Bünyadov and Vasim Məmmədəliyev, *Qur'an* (Baku: Azərnəşr, 1992).
10 Ibid., pp. v–xxxii.
11 Ibid., pp. 651–711.
12 Ibid., p. xxxii.
13 Ali Fahmi was born in Baku in 1919, graduated from the Institute of Medicine in 1941, and worked as both a doctor and a school teacher in Sabirabad, a district of Azerbaijan, until 1949. He obtained a second degree in Azerbaijan Literature from Azerbaijan University between 1952 and 1957, following which he was admitted to their PhD programme, and worked as a lecturer in the Department of History of Azerbaijani Literature until his death in 1975. Yezqar Cəfərli, *Əli Fəhmi Dünyası* (Baku: Adiloğlu: 2011), pp. 17–19.

and 1970, and was proofread by Mammadaliyev at that time and then reviewed by him again before publication.[14]

The extensive use of commentary from Krachkovskii's translation on the one hand, and the inclusion of Ali Fahmi's Soviet-era translation of the first three *suras* on the other, raises the question of to what extent Bünyadov's and Mammadaliyev's translation can be seen as a continuation of the Soviet tradition of Qur'an translation.[15] While giving

---

14   Cəfərli, *Əli Fəhmi Dünyası*, p. xxxii. It is worth noting that Ahmad Hashimzade, a retired teacher from the Quba district, completed a hand-written four-volume commentary of the Qur'an titled *Tafsīru'l-Qur'āni'l-'Azîm*. For the latest comprehensive study on this manuscript, see Roya Kazımova, *Azerbaycanlı Müfessir Ahmed Hâşimzâde'nin Tefsîru'l-Kur'âni'l-Azîm İsimli Eserinde Kur'ân'ı Yorumlama Yöntemi* (unpublished doctoral thesis, Uludağ Üniversitesi, 2022) and submitted it to the Institute of Manuscripts, Azerbaijan National Academy of Sciences, in 1962. Was it a coincidence that Ali Fahmi, a former doctor who was proficient in Arabic and Persian, translated some part of the Qur'an shortly after the completion of a four-volume commentary by Ahmad Hashimzade in the Arabic alphabet in 1962? The question of the relationship between these two Qur'anic studies remains unaddressed. According to information conveyed by his family members, Ali Fahmi had a close friendship with Akhund Mirmöhsün Hekimzade (1882–1967), the ninth *shaykh al-Islām* (1954–1967) of Soviet Azerbaijan, from the 1940s until the latter's death, and Hekimzade provided Ali Fahmi with many copies of Islamic manuscripts and encouraged him to translate the Qur'an. Ali Fahmi translated 'seven' *juz*'s of the Qur'an (Cəfərli, *Əli Fəhmi Dünyası*, pp. 24–28; Mammadaliyev gives a differing opinion on the amount that Fahmi translated). According to available information, Ali Fahmi may have benefited from classical sources on the Qur'an while translating it. According to Cəfərli, Vali Akhundov, the First Secretary of the Azerbaijan Communist Party Central Committee between 1959 and 1969, wanted to appoint Ali Fahmi, his fellow student from the medical university, to the post of *shaykh al-Islām*, but Fahmi refused the post (Cəfərli, *Əli Fəhmi Dünyası*, pp. 78–79). Although it is not known whether this information is merely speculation, according to the information Pazarbaşı provides without specifying a source, the Central Committee of the Communist Party decided that the Qur'an should be translated into Azerbaijani, and the task was given to Ali Fahmi in 1968. He produced a partial translation, but this work remained unfinished (Erdoğan Pazarbaşı, 'Kur'an'ın Azerbaycan'da Yaygın Tefsir ve Tercümeleri', *Bilig*, 25 (2003), 73–97 (p. 86)). Davut Aydüz, the author of one of the first studies on Hashimzade's *tafsīr*, records that a number of researchers, together with Ali Fahmi—whom he cites wrongly as 'the Dean, the Professor of Baku State University', quoting from Hashimzade's family members—visited Hashimzade in his village to invite him to the university, but he did not accept this invitation (Davut Aydüz, 'Sovyet Döneminde Azerbaycan Türkçesi ve Arap Harfleriyle Yazılan Bir Tefsir', *Akademik Araştırmalar Dergisi*, 17 (2003), 99–104 (p. 100)).

15   Some studies on Azerbaijani translations of the Qur'an mention that the commentary section of Bünyadov's and Mammadaliyev's translation is influenced by I. Y. Krachkovskii's translation, based on the information in the preface of Bünyadov's and Mammadaliyev's translation. See: Polat, 'Yirminci Yüz Yıl

a definite answer to this question goes beyond the scope of this research, a certain level of clarity can be provided through comparison of their text with Krachkovskii's translation. This shows that the most important similarities between the two lie not in the text of the Qur'an translation but in their respective commentaries. Both translations contain similar supplementary information in terms of: (1) providing equivalent terms from the Hebrew Bible and New Testament for some terms found in the Qur'an; (2) explaining verses related to the history of the prophets; and (3) providing linguistic explanations. However, Bünyadov did not replicate the commentary from Krachovskii's translation verbatim, but rather chose to omit material and terminology that reflected an Orientalist point of view of the Qur'an's composition, which he may have found inappropriate for a Muslim audience or otherwise inconvenient for himself.[16]

While Bünyadov's and Mammadeliyev's translation contains elements that mirror the Soviet Orientalist tradition, and particularly Krachkovskii, the most important differences distinguishing it from its predecessor lie in the additional information given by in-text parentheses and the extensive and detailed commentary sections—which explain Islamic terms and provide historical information on the revelation of

---

Sonrasında Azerbaycan'da', p. 83; Fethi Ahmet Polat, 'Azerbaycan'da Yapılan Kur'an Tercümeleri ve Türkiye'de Neşredilen Meallerin Bu Tercümelere Etkileri— Memmedeliyev Tercümesi Örneği', in *Uluslararası Türk Dünyasının İslamiyete Katkıları Sempozyumu Bildirileri* (Isparta: Süleyman Demirel Üniversitesi, 2007), pp. 441–57 (p. 444); Pazarbaşı, 'Azerbaycan'da Yaygın Kur'an', p. 116.

16 For example, in the largest sura, *Sūrat al-Baqara*, there are 140 notes in the Bünyadov-Mammadaliyev translation, compared to Krachkovskii's 218 explanatory notes. Closer examination of notes that were omitted by Bünyadov, either completely or partially, reveals that although the majority of these notes are short notes on linguistic aspects of the text, the religious sensitivities of the audience were also taken into account in the selection process, to a relatively large extent. For example, statements included by Krachkovskii in his translation such as 'Muḥammad invented the legend' and 'It is a rare case that Muḥammad says "I" about himself' (Ignatii Yulianovich Krachkovskii, *Koran* (Mosow: İzdatelstvo vostochnoy literatury, 1963), pp. 509, 532) were not included by Bünyadov. However, some expressions that Krachkovskii quotes from European Orientalists, such as 'It is Uthman's addition', 'the expression is mistakenly repeated in verse [...]', 'Muḥammad probably combined these verses himself', 'the thirty-seventh to forty-first suras have been reworked' (Krachkovskii, *Koran*, pp. 510, 519, 533, 548) could be found in the first, 1992, edition of Bünyadov-Mammadaliyev's translation (see Bünyadov and Məmmədəliyev, *Qur'an*, pp. 656, 661, 668, 675) but were omitted from the new edition published in 2015.

suras and verses, as well as the biographies of leading figures of the Prophet's lifetime. Through these characteristics, this first complete translation of the Qur'an published in post-Soviet Azerbaijan contributed significantly to the restoration of the local religious language in the first years of independence. It also provided a useful combination of Qur'an translation and commentary, and effectively gave readers access to a 'biography' of the Prophet Muḥammad through the translators' use of the *sīra nabawiyya* in the commentary on their translation, as part of their goal was to give readers additional information about events at the time of the Qur'an's revelation. By prioritising narrative interpretation in explaining the Qur'an, they informed their readership about the events of the Prophet's life.

Subsequent translators of the Qur'an into Azerbaijani Turkish have often explicitly confirmed that Bünyadov's and Mammadaliyev's translation was an important influence, especially in terms of language and style.[17] The Bünyadov-Mammadaliyev translation includes material on the main topics that are addressed in the classical *sīra* literature[18]. Of all the Azerbaijani Qur'an translations of the first period studied in this chapter, it is the one containing the most *sīra* material, which provides information on subjects such as the first revelation to Muḥammad; his struggle against the polytheists;[19] migration to Medina;[20] important battles and military expeditions, especially those of Badr, Uḥud, Ahzab, Khaybar, Hunayn, and Tabūk, and the conquest of Mecca;[21] and the

---

17   Ələddin Sultanov, *Qurani-Kərim və Məalı* (Baku: İpəkyolu nəşriyyatı, 2021), preface; İlqar İsmayılzadə, *İlahi Sirlər: Qurani-Kərimin Azərbaycan dilində tərcüməsi və qısa təfsiri* (n.p.: Qurani-Kərim Elmi Araşdırmalar Mərkəzi, 2010), p. 7; Şıxbala Elcan, *Qurani-kərimin Anlamı: qafiyəli nəsrlə* (Baku: Elm və təhsil, 2015), p. 4.

18   None of the main *sīra* sources—including those by Ibn Isḥāq, Ibn Hishām, or al-Wāqidī—are explicitly mentioned by Bünyadov and Mammadaliyev, either in the parenthetical explanations included within the text or in their additional commentary. However, while citing their sources in the preface, the translators claim to have used *tafsīr*s by, among others, al-Ṭabarī, Abū Ḥayyān, and Ibn al-Kathīr, which can be regarded as 'narrative *tafsīr*s' in that they refer to *sīra* sources, including Ibn Isḥāq's *Sīra*, the earliest surviving Prophetic *sīra* (Sulaymān Ibrāhīm al-Lāhim, *Manhaj Ibn Kathīr fī al-Tafsīr* (Riyadh: Jāmiʿa al-Imām Muḥammad Ibn Saʿūd, 1401), pp. 155–62).

19   Bünyadov and Məmmədəliyev, *Qur'an*, pp. 540, 686, 701, 703, 705, 709, 711.

20   Ibid., pp. 162, 258–59, 686.

21   Ibid., pp. 44, 56, 58–60, 148–50, 153–54, 164, 166–69, 412–13, 522, 622, 670, 672, 677, 688, 699.

Treaty of Hudaybiyya;[22] Muslim relations with the Jewish tribes of Medina;[23] and the Prophet's familial relationships as well as the status of his household.[24] Ziya Bünyadov's identity as a historian undoubtedly had a significant impact on the level of attention given to historical events in the in-text parenthesis and the commentary,[25] and Bünyadov and Mammadaliyev usually explained the occasions of revelation of the verses from a historical point of view. Their translation has a strong reliance on *sīra* based on classical Islamic historical sources.

As stated in the introduction to this chapter, the Bünyadov-Mammadaliyev translation has been criticised for reflecting a denominational bias by both Rasūl Ismā'īlzāde Dūzāl from Iran (where Twelver Shiism is the official denomination) and Ahmet Fethi Polat from Türkiye (where the Sunni-Hanafī school is dominant). However, in arriving at their respective judgements, neither of these authors takes Azerbaijan's religious demographics into consideration, nor do they evaluate the translation from a holistic perspective. For example, the 'ablution verse' (Q 5:6) is translated differently by Sunnis and Shiis, reflecting a denominational difference with regard to the ritual of ablution. Contrary to what is claimed by Ismā'īlzāde, Bünyadov-Mammadaliyev's translation includes both explanations in its commentary on Q 5:6.[26] Another point that Ismā'īlzāde qualifies as a Sunni element is the lack of explanation in the commentary on Q 4:24 regarding *mutʿa* (temporary marriage), which is considered acceptable in Twelver Shii law but rejected by Sunnis who consider it abrogated. However, this alone is not sufficient evidence to classify Bünyadov's

---

22 Ibid., pp. 159, 518–23, 657, 661, 665, 694.
23 Ibid., pp. 563–66, 660, 663, 665, 671, 686, 688, 693, 699.
24 Ibid., pp. 416–17, 578–79, 683–84, 688, 700.
25 Contrary to Krachkovskii, in the commentary part of the translation, Bünyadov gives extensive information about Moses, Abraham, Isaac, Jonah, Joseph, and other prophets in accordance with their narratives as told in Islamic literature, quoting sources such as the *qiṣaṣ al-anbiyāʾ* of Abū Isḥāq al-Thaʿlabī (d. 427/1035) and Ibn al-Athīr's *al-Kāmil fī al-taʾrīkh* (d. 630/1233) (see Bünyadov and Məmmədəliyev, *Qur'an*, pp. 653, 655, 672–75).
26 Bünyadov and Məmmədəliyev, *Qur'an*, p. 89: 'Wipe your head [with your wet hand] and wash your feet up to both ankles [or: wipe your head or your feet up to both ankles].' In the later editions, the expressions in parenthesis were replaced. See Ziya Bünyadov and Vasim Məmmədəliyev, *Qurani-Kərim və Tərcüməsi* (Ankara: Diyanət İşləri Başqanlığı Nəşrləri, 2015), p. 107.

and Mammadaliyev's translation as 'Sunni',[27] because there are early Azerbaijani translations supported by Iranian organisations that do not interpret Q 4:24 as being related to the subject of *mutʿa* marriage either.[28]

As for Ahmet Fethi Polat's argument that the Bünyadov-Mammadaliyev translation is a Shii interpretation, this relates to their extensive use of Krachkovskii's commentary.[29] Krachkovskii emphasised Shii interpretations and clearly distinguished them from the Sunni position. His inclusion of Shii readings had a particular influence on the commentaries provided in the short *tafsīr*s of post-Soviet Azerbaijani Qur'an translation. However, a careful comparison shows that information in Krachkovskii's translation that was preceded by the phrase 'according to the Shiis [...]' was not adopted by Bünyadov verbatim, but only selectively. In other words, Bünyadov deliberately filtered Krachkovskii's statements about the Shii interpretation of the Qur'an, which often cited the Hungarian scholar Ignaz Goldziher (1850–1921). For instance, Bünyadov excluded a number of 'Shii' theological-political issues that had been explored by Krachkovskii, such as the concept of *rajʿa* (the return of the twelfth imam), 'the oppression of the rights of Āl-Muḥammad', or the claim that ʿAlī b. Abī Ṭālib was the leader of the *umma*. He also excluded some insulting statements that Krachkovskii had cited from other sources (mainly Goldziher), such as '*baqara* means ʿĀʾisha' and '*al-jibt* and *al-ṭāghūt* refer to Muʿāwiya and ʿAmr'.[30]

Bünyadov not only took a selective stance towards Krachkovskii's presentation of Shii views and beliefs, but also followed a conciliatory and balanced interdenominational translation policy by including positive information about, and even praise for, ʿUmar b. al-Khaṭṭāb[31] and

---

27 In the revised later editions of the Bünyadov-Mammadaliyev translation, changes have been made regarding *mutʿa* marriage (see Bünyadov and Məmmədəliyev, *Qurani-Kərim* (2015), p. 81).

28 In the translation commissioned by the Alhuda publishing house, *al-Quranu'l-Kərim* (Baku: Şərq-Qərb, 1999), the verse is translated without using the word *mutʿa* as: 'Faydalandığınız qadınların kəbinlərini verməyiniz vacibdir' ('You must marry (or give dowry to) the women you benefit from', *al-Quranu'l-Kərim*, p. 87).

29 For the parallelism between Krachkovskii's and Bünyadov-Mammadaliyev's translations regarding examples of the Shii interpretation of Q 2:31, 61, and 143, see Krachkovskii, *Koran*, pp. 505–6, 510; Bünyadov and Məmmədəliyev, *Qur'an*, pp. 652–53, 655.

30 Krachkovskii, *Koran*, pp. 506, 519, 523, 550, 573.

31 A narration about ʿUmar b. al-Khaṭṭāb's devotion to the Prophet is related to the reason for the revelation of Q 4:14, which is not the case in Krachkovskii's

ᶜĀʾisha bt Abī Bakr,³² the Companions who are most severely criticised in Shii polemics. Thus, Bünyadov and Mammadaliyev continue, at the end of the twentieth century, the tradition of a multicultural approach that in fact had its roots in pre-Soviet Azerbaijan.³³

The Bünyadov-Mammadaliyev translation is still the most accepted and authoritative Qur'an translation in Azerbaijan today. This is frequently attributed to the eloquence of their language,³⁴ their interpretive commitment to the classical exegetical tradition, and their inclusive, supra-denominational approach that does not favour one denomination over another. Another important point worth mentioning here is that the supra-denominational approach adopted by Bünyadov and Mammadaliyev preceded the doctrine of multiculturalism that has

---

translation (see Bünyadov and Məmmədəliyev, Qur'an, p. 663).

32 Krachkovskii provides a short note about events at Ifk: 'It is about 'Ā'isha's adventure, the necklace and Safwan' (Krackovsky, Koran, p. 569). In Bünyadov-Mammadaliyev's translation, brief biographical information is provided on 'Ā'isha, who is called 'the Prophet's lovely wife.' This recounts the process of their marriage, and how she won the Prophet's love shortly after their marriage. It also describes the events of Ifk, taking a stance of defending 'Ā'isha. They comment that ᶜAlī b. Abū Ṭālib advised the Prophet to divorce 'Ā'isha, and 'Ā'isha hated him for this, and also that Q 24:11 was revealed to absolve 'Ā'isha (Bünyadov and Məmmədəliyev, Qur'an, p. 684).

33 Mykhaylo Yakubovych, 'The First Vernacular Tafsīr in the Caucasus: The Legacy of Two 20th Century Azerbaijani Qur'ān Commentaries', Australian Journal of Islamic Studies, 7:1 (2022), 72–95 (p. 89). The journal Fuyuzat provides a good example of the multicultural approach common in Azerbaijan in the early 1900s. Published in Baku in 1906–7 with the sponsorship of Zeynalabdin Taghiyev, the sponsor of the first Azerbaijani Qur'an translation Kashf al-Haqāiq by Bākuwī, Fuyuzat represented a fairly tolerant environment that esteemed both the four Rightly Guided caliphs and the Twelver Shii Imams, and opposed the polemical use of these important political and religious figures. The articles that emerged from the Teachers' Second Congress that was held in Baku in 1907 under the chairmanship of Ali bey Huseynzade, the editor of Fuyuzat, promoted interdenominational tolerance in a number of ways. These included proposals for the removal from the school curriculum of issues that might contribute to divisions between Sunnis and Shiis; the use of a concise manual of Islamic faith in schools with students from both denominations; and the unification of the Omar and Ali schools in Tbilisi which were seen as deepening the gap between local Sunnis and Shiis. The journal also criticises Iran's Shii agenda and Arab Wahhabism for their extremes and fanaticism. See Elnurə Əzizova, 'Azərbaycanın Məzhəblərarası Tolerantlıq Tarixindən XX Əsrin Əvvəlinə Aid Bir Nümunə: Füyuzat Jurnalı', Bakı Dövlət Universitetinin İlahiyyat Fakültəsinin Elmi Məcmuəsi, 27 (2017), 205–15.

34 Subsequent translations of the Qur'an into Azerbaijani Turkish have often explicitly confirmed that Bünyadov's and Mammadaliyev's translation played an important role, especially in language and style (Sultanov, Qurani-Kərim və Məalı, preface; İsmayılzadə, İlahi Sirlər, p. 7; Elcan, Qurani-Kərimin Anlamı, p. 4).

been emphasised in the recent domestic and foreign policy of independent Azerbaijan. This suggests that the basis of this political strategy is not necessarily a top-down approach to Sunni-Shii relations. Rather, it has its roots in the foundational Muslim texts in the national language.

The second Qur'an translation in the Azerbaijani language that dates back to the early post-independence period is *Qur'an-i Kərim* by Nariman Gasimoghlu.[35] Gasimoghlu undertook this translation on the premise that the Qur'an would make an essential contribution to the national self-realisation of Azerbaijanis in the 1990s, serving as the holy book for its Muslim population. In his opinion, the Qur'an is important to 'understanding one's historical-civilizational heritage, repairing historical memory by investigating the sources of national reflection, and helping to solve national problems at the global level.'[36] Through his translation of the Qur'an, Gasimoghlu purports to defend not the 'traditionalist Islam'—which, according to him, was distorted over centuries—but rather what he views as the 'authentic Islam', which is necessary in the struggle for national freedom and for reviving Turkism. He sees this as 'the demand of the green colour based on the tricolour flag raised in the Parliament for the revival of statehood.'[37] In addition to highlighting this role of the Qur'an in the formation of a national-cultural identity in his introduction, Gasimoghlu advised readers to take advantage of the valuable principles outlined in the Qur'an in dealing with contemporary political and military difficulties facing Azerbaijan in a wide range of fields including administration, legislation, the politics of war, and international relations.[38]

However, despite these lofty ideological aims, Gasimoghlu states that he translated the Qur'an not as a theologian but as an Orientalist who knows Arabic and Azerbaijani Turkish at a reasonable level, and comments that he used the famous *Tafsīr al-Jalālayn* as a theological resource for his interpretation.[39] His dependence on *al-Jalālayn* aligns his translation with Sunni ideas in its treatment of legal and ethical

---

35 Nəriman Qasımoğlu, *Qur'an-i Kərim* (Baku: 'Azərbaycan' nəşriyyatı, 1993). This translation was partly printed in the *Khazar* journal between 1989 and 1992.
36 Ibid., pp. 355–56.
37 Ibid, p. 357.
38 Ibid., pp. 356–59.
39 Nəriman Qasımoğlu, 'Quranda adı keçən hicabın baş örtüyü mənası yoxdur', *AZPOST*, 20 November 2019, https://azpost.info/n%C9%99riman-qasimoglu/

verses.⁴⁰ When it comes to how Gasimoghlu structures his commentary, he sometimes briefly explains certain subjects that form the framework of the Prophet's biography in the main text of the translation;⁴¹ and although the section titled 'Some Explanations' at the end of the translation is shorter than the equivalent commentary section in Bünyadov-Mammadaliyev's translation, it has similar features.⁴²

The image of Muḥammad revealed in this translation—both in the text and the appended commentary section—is essentially in line with the basic information that forms the framework of the classic *sīra* literature.⁴³ The Prophet is described as a head of state and army commander on the one hand, and a husband who could be resentful of his wives (for example, with reference to the events described in Q 66:1–5) on the other; a prophet who performs a miracle by scattering soil into the eyes of the Qurayshi polytheists at the Battle of Badr on the one hand, and a fallible man reproved by Allah for his dismissal of a blind person (Q 80) on the other. Likewise, in accordance with the *sīra* narrative, Gasimoghlu identifies ᶜĀʾisha bt Abī Bakr (Həzrət Aişə) as the person being slandered in Q 24:11, and records—both in the actual text and in his commentary on the relevant verse—that the Qur'an here makes it clear that the slander about her is false. In describing the circle of close Companions around the Prophet he singles out Abū Bakr, the Prophet's companion during the Hijra, and ᶜAlī b. Abī Ṭālib, who ensured the Prophet's entrance to the Kaᶜba on the day of the conquest of Mecca.⁴⁴ The first edition of Gasimoghlu's translation contains information about events in Muḥammad's lifetime, since it follows the paradigm of interpretation by transmission (*tafsīr bi l-riwāya*). However, as I will discuss later, Gasimoghlu applied different translation methods, linguistic explanations, and approaches in the second edition of his translation.

The last of this first generation of Qur'an translations is *Qur'an-i Kərim* (*Azərbaycanca tərcüməsi ilə*), published as a co-authored translation by

---

40 For the verses related to *al-wuḍū* (ablution) prayer times, see Qasımoğlu, *Qur'an-i Kərim*, pp. 49, 111.
41 Qasımoğlu, *Qur'an-i Kərim*, pp. 89, 90, 91, 95, 174, 209, 292.
42 Ibid., pp. 332–51.
43 Ibid., pp. 89, 90, 91, 95, 174, 209, 292, 333–35, 337–38, 341, 348.
44 Ibid., pp. 91, 174, 292, 334–35, 337, 341, 348.

Mammadhasan Ganioghlu and Tariyel Bilaloghlu.[45] In the preface, the translators state that they had each undertaken separate translations of the Qur'an in 1984 and 1989 without being aware of each other's work, then they compared their versions of the text in 1990 and 1991 and merged them into a single copy by making use of classical and contemporary commentaries and translations into various languages.[46] The translators note that a number of Qur'an scholars from the Türkiye Diyanet Foundation (the TDF) played an essential role in the publication of this translation, which appeared approximately nine years after its completion.[47] It is not clearly specified how the Qur'an scholars of the TDF actually contributed to this translation, but expressions derived from Anatolian Turkish can be found in the translation of some verses.[48]

In Ganioghlu-Bilaloghu's translation, the information provided about the lifetime of the Prophet is not extensive enough to form a *sīra* framework. The authors sometimes record Mecca and Medina as the locus of the events taking place using parenthesis, and mention some historical events such as the battles of Badr and Uḥud, and the conquest of Mecca.[49] The information given about the Companions is also limited. ᶜĀʾisha bt Abī Bakr and Abū Bakr are the only Companions mentioned in the translation. Āʾisha is, as in Gasimoghlu's translation, referenced in connection with the affair of the necklace,[50] when Ganioghlu and Bilaloghlu translate Q 24:11 as 'They who spread the slander [against ᶜĀʾisha] are a gang among you.'[51] Abū Bakr is brought into their translation of the 'verse of the cave' (Q 9:40), which is understood as referring to the time when Muḥammad and one of his Companions hid from the Quraysh in a cave on Jabal Thawr for three days during

---

45 Məmmədhəsən Qəni oğlu and Tariyel Bilal oğlu, *Qur'ani-Kərim* (*Azərbaycan dilinə tərcüməsi ilə*) (Baku: Göytürk, 2000).
46 Ibid., p. 6.
47 Ibid., pp. 5–6. This translation was published by the 'Göytürk' printing house, run by the Türkiye Diyanet Foundation in Azerbaijan, with a print run of 3,000 (p. 607).
48 Ibid., pp. 36, 43, 47.
49 Ibid., pp. 66, 176, 179, 181, 259, 289, 384, 403, 418, 504, 537, 545, 593.
50 During the return journey from a raid on the Banū Muṣṭaliq, ᶜĀʾisha lost her necklace, and while she was looking for it the convoy moved on without her, not realising her absence. Aisha was found by Ṣafwān b. al-Muʿaṭṭal, one of the Companions, and brought to Medina. A rumour about the two of them having an illicit relationship emerged as a result of this event.
51 Qəni oğlu and Bilal oğlu, *Qur'ani-Kərim*, p. 350.

the Hijra, and is translated by Ganioghlu and Bilaloghlu as follows: '[...] still Allah helped him when those who disbelieve drove him forth [from Mecca], the second of two; when those two (Muḥammad and Abū Bakr) were in the cave when he said unto his comrade [...]'[52] This limited information is not sufficient to suggest that the translation was made with one specific denomination of target readership in mind. However, when their translation of the 'ablution verse' (Q 5:6)[53] is taken into account, it seems reasonable to infer that this translation does not incline towards Twelver Shiism, at least from the point of view of ritual practice. This is supported by the fact that the translators render the expression *ahl al-bayt* in Q 33:33 as simply 'ev əhli' (people of the household),[54] without any specific embellishment as would be expected from a Shii translation.

Although the translators from this period were Azerbaijani Arabists trained in the Soviet school of Orientalism, their views of the Qur'an were not the same as their traditionally Orientalist predecessors since they approached the Qur'an from a faith-based perspective, declaring their acceptance of Islam and their faith in the Qur'an in the prefaces of their translations. They also emphasised their view that it was necessary to translate the Qur'an due to its place in the religious thought of the Azerbaijani people. Another common feature of these translations is the fact that they do not advocate one particular denominational reading as the only correct interpretation of Islam. The same *Weltanschauung* behind these Qur'an translations could be seen at the beginning of the twentieth century, which was also a time of Azerbaijani nation-building and identity formation. Just as the Qur'an commentaries of al-Bākuwī and al-Shakawī—published in the last periods of Azerbaijan's subordination to Tsarist Russia at the beginning of the twentieth century—attempted to manifest a religious-national essence in religious writing,[55] the translations of the Qur'an that were written and published in the late 1980s and early 1990s were also the products of a similar process during the early period of Azerbaijan's independence from Soviet Russia.

---

52 Ibid., p. 192.
53 '[...] and also wipe your heads, and wash your feet up to the ankles.' Ibid., p. 107.
54 Ibid., p. 421.
55 Yakubovych, 'The First Vernacular *Tafsīr*', p. 75.

Institutional Translations Affiliated with Foreign Organisations: Competing Versions of the *sīra* with Different Companion Circles

Since the early 1990s, in conjunction with increased religious awareness in the general public, the activities of different foreign religious institutions in the region have included the publication of Qur'an translations tailored to the beliefs of specific communities. The target readership of the first period of Qur'an translations was the general Muslim Azerbaijani population who saw Islam as an essential aspect of their awakening sense of national identity, traditionally associated their culture with Islam, and had little knowledge of the ritual requirements of their religion. In contrast, the target readership of the second period of Qur'an translations had a more profound religious socialisation, with a much higher rate of practising believers[56] who considered religion the peak of civilisation, saw themselves as adherents to a particular interpretation of Islam, and even had a certain degree of affiliation with distinct religious communities.[57]

The translations published during this second period were mainly produced by foreign organisations affiliated with the Islamic Republic of Iran, the Republic of Türkiye, and the Kingdom of Saudi Arabia. In terms of the publication of religious literature aimed at an Azerbaijani audience, Iran has been notably more active than other foreign countries and has reached a considerably larger readership. This is partly because it is the only country to produce its publications in various alphabets—Cyrillic, Latin, and Arabic—which sets it apart. The first Qur'an translation in the Azerbaijani language to be published with the support of an Iran-affiliated institution was by Rasūl Ismā'īlzāde Dūzāl, a theologian from South Azerbaijan who received his religious education in Qom. Ismā'īlzāde's translation was published in the Arabic

---

[56] Available information indicates that between 5% and 17% of Muslims in Azerbaijan are practising believers (Əzizova, 'Azərbaycan cəmiyyətindəki', pp. 52–72; Qənbərov, *Azərbaycanda Dövlət -Din Münasibətləri* , pp. 163–68).

[57] For brief analyses on the change in religious situation in Azerbaijan after independence, see: Gündüz İsmayılov, *Azərbaycanda dini məsələ* (Baku: Tuna, 2020), pp. 256–61; Əzizova, 'Azərbaycan cəmiyyətindəki', pp. 52–75.

alphabet in 1999, and in the Cyrillic and Latin alphabets in 2000.⁵⁸ In 1999, a committee of the international Alhuda publishing house brought out another Iran-supported translation in the Cyrillic alphabet.⁵⁹ Thus, by 2000, with the support of Shii organisations affiliated with Iran, translations of the Qur'an into Azerbaijani had been published in three different alphabets, making them accessible to a wide readership that included the younger and older generations of the Azerbaijan Republic who were more familiar with the Cyrillic and Latin alphabets than they were with the Arabic script.

One of the most consistent features of these 'Iranian' translations is the fact that some verses reflect the Twelver Shii interpretation in terms of practical issues.⁶⁰ But, when it comes to the Prophetic *sīra*, the Alhuda translation does not contain any remarkable content. Although there is no commentary section, Rasūl Ismā'īlzāde uses parantheses to cite various battles as the reason behind the revelation of some Qur'anic verses.⁶¹ Most notably, although the translation does not provide detailed information about the events of the Prophet's life, it comments that the Prophet's wife mentioned in the 'affair of the necklace' was Maria, not ᶜĀ'isha.⁶² Another translation, by Ahmed Kavyanpūr,⁶³ which was published in Azerbaijani using the Arabic alphabet in Iran in 1992, takes a similar approach to explaining the Prophet's life.⁶⁴ While it does mention some relevant political and military events in parentheses,⁶⁵ it

---

58   Rasūl İsmāīlzāde Dūzāl, *Qurāni-Kərim: Azərbaycan Türkcəsilə tərcüməsi* (Qom: Qurâni-Kərimin bütün dillərə tərcüməsi mərkəzi, 1999). Since the translations printed in Cyrillic and Latin alphabets could not be found, the example printed in Arabic alphabet was used in researching this chapter.

59   Əlhuda, *əl-Quranu'l-Kərim* (Baku: Şərq-Qərb, 1999), henceforth referred to as 'Alhuda'.

60   For example, the translation of the ablution verse includes reference to 'anointing of the feet' (Alhuda, p. 113; Duzāl, *Qurāni-Kərim*, p. 108). Regarding Q 4:24, the word *mutᶜa* is used in the translation by Dūzāl (Dūzāl, *Qurāni-Kərim*, p. 82) but is not included in the Alhuda translation (Alhuda, p. 87).

61   Dūzāl, *Qurāni-Kərim*, pp. 69, 71–72, 152–53, 165, 177–78.

62   Ibid., pp. 351.

63   Ahmed Kavyānpūr, *al-Qur'āni'l-Karīm bā tercemeyi Türkī* (s.l.: İqbāl, 1372/199 2).

64   This translation was not discussed above because he should not be considered as one of the Qur'an translators whose target group is readers from post-Soviet Azerbaijan. The translation was published in the Arabic alphabet for a Southern Azerbaijanian readership and was thus largely inaccessible to a post-Soviet readership.

65   Kavyānpūr, *al-Qur'āni'l-Karīm*, pp. 69–70, 199–206, 511–14.

does not include the names of the Prophet's wives and Companions. For example, Kavyanpūr states that the person who spread the slander about the affair of the necklace was ᶜAbdallāh b. Ubayy,[66] but he does not mention ᶜĀʾisha by name and refers to the Prophet's migration to Medina in parenthesis without naming the second person who was in the cave with Muḥammad.[67] However, he states that the person described in Q 9:19 'who strives in the way of Allah by believing in Allah and the Day of Judgement' is 'ᶜAlī a.s.'[68] Thus, persons revered by the Shiis are highlighted, while those wives and Companions of the Prophet who have high status in Sunni Islam but who Shiis consider hostile to the *ahl al-bayt* are not named.

The most important example of Iran-affiliated translation activity in Azerbaijan is *Qurani-Kərim, tərcümə və transkripsiyası*, which was translated from Farsi in 2006 as a project financed by the Iranian Cultural Center affiliated with the Iranian Embassy in Baku.[69] As the title suggests, one unique feature of the translation is that on each page, the original Arabic text and its translation into Azerbaijani Turkish is presented alongside its transliteration in the Latin alphabet. The author of the original Persian work is Ayatollah Mirza ᶜAlī Meshkīnī Ardabīlī (d. 2007), who played an essential role in the Islamic revolution in Iran, was an influential supporter of the revolutionary leader Khomeini (d. 1989), and carried out essential tasks in terms of Iranian political Shiism such as leading the Friday prayer in Qom, among other religious duties. The first edition of the translation of this text into Azerbaijani was undertaken by Aghabala Mehdiyev and Durdana Jafarli and was published in 2006 when Meshkīnī was still alive, while the second edition came out in 2022. The author of the forewords of both editions is Sayyid ᶜAlī Akbar Ojag Nejad: the head of the Iranian Cultural Center, and a crucial figure in Iran's religious activities in Azerbaijan between 1991 and 2021. Ojag Nejad is on record as presenting a number of arguments for the necessity of translating the Qur'an into Azerbaijani, two of which are particularly noteworthy. Firstly, there was the fact that the Religious Branch of the Cultural Center of the Baku Embassy of Iran took responsibility for the

---

66   Ibid., p. 351.
67   Ibid., p. 193.
68   Ibid., p. 189.
69   Əli Meşkini Ərdəbili, *Qurani-Kərim, tərcümə və transkripsiyası* (Baku: Nurlar, 2022).

religious and cultural needs of Azerbaijani-speaking Muslims in the Republic of Azerbaijan and the Caucasus. Secondly, according to Ojag Nejad, a large number of Azerbaijani citizens had asked him to meet this particular need.[70] As an official religious representative of Iran in Azerbaijan, Ojag Nejad's claims about the unique responsibility of Iran to deliver Islamic education to the Azerbaijani Turkish-speaking people of the Caucasus, and a particular religious segment of Azerbaijan, is crucial. It shows special status of this translation compared to other Iranian-supported translations.

In discussing the need for an Azerbaijani translation of Ardabīlī's Persian translation, Ojag Nejad states that while some respected scholars produced admirable translations during Azerbaijan's first year of independence, these contained many flaws. Declaring these translations insufficient, Ojag Nejad also called into question the legitimacy of the earlier Azerbaijani Qur'an translations that came before them. According to him, the main reason why this new translation by the Centre under his presidency was more reliable than others available in Azerbaijani was because of the scholarly and religious authority of the translator, an ayatollah.[71]

The main difference between Meshkīnī's translation and earlier Iranian-supported translations is the fact that it embraces the political ideology of *nāʾib al-imām* (the deputy of the Imam) and is thus aligned with the official religious discourse of Iran. This aspect of the text is especially visible in its interpretation of verses related to the Prophet's message. Many of these verses are interpreted to state that the duty of the Prophet is only to convey the message, and that it is the duty of the Imams to carry out the sharia precepts preached by the Prophet[72]— which presents Imams as the only persons authorised to maintain the Islamic religion. After the Prophet and the Imams, the individuals appointed by 'infallible ones' (*maʿsūms*) are held the most responsible for managing society.[73] In asserting this, Meshkīnī invokes an essential doctrine of Shii political Islam by arguing that righteous servants will take the sovereignty of the Earth from the hands of usurpers and cruel

---

70   Ibid., preamble.
71   Ibid., preamble.
72   Ibid., pp. 123, 124, 293, 300, 357, 365, 398, 557.
73   Ibid., p. 84.

rulers and transfer it to the Imams of justice and their representatives.[74] According to Meshkīnī's translation, this system of administration will culminate in Mahdi's promised divine government—a period so sacred that it is sworn on in the Qur'an.[75]

Information given in Meshkīnī's translation about events in the Prophet's lifetime includes a variety of topics mentioned in the classical *sīra* sources, from battles to treaties, to the Prophet's family members, to his relations with non-Muslims. In interpretations of the Qur'anic verses, while describing the political-military events of the Prophet's period in lieu of other historical information such as chronology, persons, and places, Meshkīnī highlights the lessons to be learned from these events.[76] The attitude expressed towards the Companions in general, and the *ahl al-bayt* in particular, in the commentary of relevant verses is also worth noting. Meshkīnī makes no negative statements about the Companions in terms that could be faulted from a Sunni perspective, and he mentions Abū Bakr in the context of the Prophet's migration from Mecca to Medina.[77] On the other hand, it is noteworthy that Meshkīnī—whose general approach to the Prophet's wives is to 'respect them'[78]—uses the generic expression 'one of the Prophet's wives' rather than naming ᶜĀʾisha bt Abī Bakr in the affair of the necklace.[79] Additionally, the fact that Meshkīnī attributes the 'cursed tree' expression[80] to the Banū Umayya (Umayyads)—which, according to the traditional Sunni view, includes some of the Companions—further reveals his denominational views. Meshkīnī, who praises the Prophet's daughter Fāṭima and son-in-law ᶜAlī as belonging to the *ahl al-bayt* in his commentary on various verses,[81] reveals his denominational attitude overall by relating many expressions that are used in the Qur'an in a positive sense to refer to Muslims in general[82] to the *ahl al-bayt* specifically, thereby restricting the scope of their meaning.

---

74 Ibid., p. 331.
75 Ibid., p. 601.
76 For examples, see Meşkini, *Qurani-Kərim*, pp. 51, 66–67, 71, 177–79, 181–83, 185–86, 421, 512–13, 545–47.
77 Ibid., p. 193.
78 Ibid., p. 418.
79 Ibid., p. 351.
80 Ibid., p. 288.
81 Ibid., pp. 32, 57, 117, 602.
82 Ibid., pp. 5, 87, 156, 206, 341, 438, 473.

Although not officially published by any organisation affiliated with Iran, another essential translation of the Qur'an that falls into this category is *İlahi sirlər: Qurani-Kərimin Azərbaycan dilində tərcüməsi və qısa təfsiri*, by the Azerbaijani theologian Ilqar Ismayilzade, who pursued his higher religious education in Qom and obtained a PhD in comparative exegesis there.[83] My main reason for including Ismayilzade's translation in this category is that it was published with a preface by Dr Muḥammad Ḥasan Zamanī, a scholar from the Qom seminary (*hawza*), as are some of his other works. This suggests that the translation received academic support at least from Iran's most important religious centre.[84] Ismayilzade took Bünyadov's and Mammadaliyev's translation as a template for his own translation, but replaced Bünyadov's annotations with his own commentary.[85] He represents himself as the successor to al-Bākuwī and al-Shakawī, while noting that the short comments he added to the translation are drawn and summarised from his twelve-volume *Yeni Təfsir*—the first *tafsīr* written in Azerbaijani in the twenty-first century, after nearly 100 years since the last.[86] Ismayilzade provides some information about the social, political, and military events of the Prophet's lifetime, partly in the text of the translation but more broadly in the separate commentary section. In framing his account of the Prophet's *sīra*, Ismayilzade follows two premises that ground his approach in theology rather than biographical narrative, and uses historical information to support these premises. The first premise relates to the Prophet's attribute of ᶜ*iṣma* (immunity from sin), while the second relates to the real meaning and scope of the concept of the *aṣḥāb*, or 'Companions of the Prophet'. According to Ismayilzade's first premise, which reflects the basic Shii approach to the ᶜ*iṣma* of prophets[87] and Imams, Muḥammad was not reprimanded in the Qur'an for his actions.[88] Thus, Ismayilzade finds it incorrect to interpret some verses as reprimands directed against Muḥammad, arguing that

---

83   İlqar İsmayılzadə, *İlahi Sirlər: Qurani-Kərimin Azərbaycan dilində tərcüməsi və qısa təfsiri* (n.p.: Qurani-Kərim Elmi Araşdırmalar Mərkəzi, 2010).
84   It is unclear whether the work was published in Azerbaijan, as the place of publication is not provided.
85   İsmayılzadə, *İlahi Sirlər*, p. 7.
86   Ibid., p. 6.
87   The author defends his approach in the case of Abraham's father and Joseph. See İsmayılzadə, *İlahi Sirlər*, pp. 105, 166, 211, 224, 252.
88   İsmayılzadə, *İlahi Sirlər*, p. 407.

the actual addressee of such verses is not the Prophet himself, which he explains through an Azerbaijani proverb: 'I speak to my daughter, let my daughter-in-law hear'.⁸⁹ Criticising the interpretation that Muḥammad is reprimanded for disregarding a blind man in Q 80:1–7, Ismayilzade argues that the actual addressee of this reprimand is a wealthy Umayyad individual,⁹⁰ thereby revealing his opinion on the Umayyads' role in the political events of early Islamic history. Ismayilzade further reveals this opinion by asserting that the Qur'anic 'cursed tree' is a reference to the Umayyad dynasty.⁹¹

Ismayilzade's approach to the Companions, the prominent luminaries of the Prophet's lifetime, is similarly theological. When commenting on Qur'anic verses related to events involving the Companions, Ismayilzade repeatedly argues against the view that Muslims should respect them, because not all of them were just, reliable, and self-sacrificing.⁹² The 'notable' circle of Companions, according to Ismayilzade, consists of specific figures—those privileged among Shiis—such as ʿAlī b. Abī Ṭālib, Ḥamza, Salmān, Abū Dharr, Miqdād, ʿAmmār, Bilāl, and Zayd b. Thābit.⁹³ However, in his commentary on some verses that relate to historical events, Ismayilzade mentions other Companions. For instance, he records that the person who hid in the cave on Jabal Thawr with the Prophet during the Hijra was 'the first caliph, Abū Bakr b. Abī Quḥāfa, who was a Companion of the Prophet',⁹⁴ and that (regarding the affair of the necklace) 'the slander against ʿĀʾisha, the mother of the believers, is unfounded'.⁹⁵ He thus adopts a different approach to the Iran-affiliated translations discussed above; it appears that Ismayilzade's perspective on the status of the Companions is closely related to the interdenominational unity that he emphasises in other aspects of his translation.⁹⁶ Ismayilzade acknowledges both the standard views of Sunni Muslims, whom he calls 'our *ahl al-sunna* brothers', and his own sect, whom he refers to as 'those on the path of *ahl al-bayt*'. Among the

---

89   Ibid., pp. 153, 204, 280, 290, 351, 407, 411.
90   Ibid., p. 411.
91   Ibid., p. 197.
92   Ibid., pp. 63–64, 129, 140, 144, 240, 386, 415.
93   Ibid., pp. 189, 290, 415.
94   Ibid., p. 139.
95   Ibid., p. 240.
96   Ibid., p. 60.

instances where he explicitly refers to denominational positions, there are rare occasions when he presents a common, unified approach, such as the belief that the Qur'an has not been falsified. Still, in most cases, he refers to the *ahl al-sunna* sources as testimony to his own confessional view.[97] According to Ismayilzade, the Prophet's faithful followers and the true bearers of his Sunna are not all the Companions but rather the sinless members of the *ahl al-bayt*.[98] Limiting the category of *ahl al-bayt* to ʿAlī, Fāṭima, Ḥasan, Ḥusayn, and other sinless Imams from the Prophet's actual family,[99] Ismayilzade—like Meshkīnī—restricts the applicability of positive statements in the Qur'an to the *ahl al-bayt* rather than (as read by Sunnis) to Muslims in general.[100] According to Ismayilzade, as stated in the verse of *taṭhīr* (Q 33:33), the *ahl al-bayt* are the leaders of the Islamic *umma* whom Muslims should unconditionally obey,[101] as they are superior, virtuous, and sinless.[102] Ismayilzade's denominational view is also reflected in his translation and commentary when it comes to his treatment of religious practices, as he defends these views as the only correct interpretation with an exclusivist approach that reveals his theological approach to the events of the Prophet's time.[103]

During the period of institutional Qur'an translation, the Republic of Türkiye also played an important role in the publication of Azerbaijani Qur'an translations. Turkish involvement began with the publication of two Qur'an translations authored by Azerbaijani translators.[104] Following this, *Kur'ân-ı Kerim ve Açıklamalı Meali* was translated into Azerbaijani Turkish by Fazil Qaraoğlu under the same name (*Qur'ani-Kərim və açıqlamalı məali*) with the approval of the Supreme Council of Religious Affairs, and published in Ankara in 2003.[105] The original text was a Turkish Qur'an translation first published in Ankara in 1993 and

---

97 Ibid., pp. 38, 87, 93–94, 256
98 Ibid., p. 75.
99 Ibid., pp. 56, 220, 289, 396, 406, 429.
100 Ibid., pp. 50, 145, 176, 187–88, 406.
101 Ibid., p. 145.
102 Ibid., p. 289.
103 For the author's discussion of *mutʿa*, ablution, and *khums*, see İsmayılzade, *İlahi Sirlər*, pp. 71–72, 88, 132, 190.
104 The PRA and TDF published several editions of Bünyadov's and Məmmədəliyev's translation, and one of Ganioğlu-Bilaloğlu's (in 2000).
105 Fazil Qaraoğlu, *QUR'ANİ-KƏRİM və Açıqlamalı Məali* (Ankara: s.n., 2003). The same translation was published in Baku by Qanun publishing house in 2021, without any significant changes and with notes referring to the first edition. See

produced by a committee the TDF had set up for this purpose, which included prominent Turkish theologians such as Ali Özek, Hayreddin Karaman, Ali Turgut, Mustafa Çağrıcı, Ibrahim Kafi Dönmez, and Sadreddin Gümüş.

The committee's original Turkish translation includes biographical information about the Prophet mainly in the additional commentary provided in parentheses at the end of some verses. Using the method of narrative exegesis, Qaraoğlu inserted additional information about the Prophet's life and early Muslim society to construct the perception of an ideal Islamic society. Although he adds new commentary that mentions the conquest of Mecca and Khaybar,[106] and interprets some verses as being related to the Muslim victory in the Battle of Badr with the help of divine aid,[107] there is no mention in his translation of the Uḥud and Tabūk battles where, according to traditional exegesis, some Companions were condemned for their mistakes.[108] There is a similar omission of any kind of wrongdoing from verses related to the Prophet's family life. In the event described in *Sūrat al-Taḥrīm* (Q 66) in which the Prophet was offended by his wives, there is no mention of any reprimand addressed to the Prophet's wives. Instead, the translation takes a positive stance, saying of Q 66:5 that 'This verse is proof that the Prophet did not divorce any of his wives.'[109] Likewise, Qaraoğlu is reluctant to bring up other accounts of events that have caused rumours and further polemics about the Prophet's wives. For example, there is no mention of Zaynab bt Jaḥsh and her divorce from Zayd b. Thābit and subsequent marriage to the Prophet (Q 33:37), or of ʿĀʾisha bt Abī Bakr and the affair of the necklace (Q 24:11–22), as it is approached in other translations. Only one of the Prophet's wives is referred to in the entire translation: Khadīja, who is mentioned as a consoler of the Prophet in the early stage of the revelation.[110]

Fazil Qaraoğlu, *Qurani-Kərim və Açıqlamalı Məalı* (Baku: Qanun Nəşriyyatı, 2021). The latter edition is used here.
106 Qaraoğlu, *Qurani-Kərim* (2021), pp. 89, 289, 513.
107 Ibid., pp. 177–78, 181.
108 For example, one can look at *Sūrat Āl ʿImrān* for the battle of Uḥud, and *Sūrat al-Tawba* for the battle of Tabūk, compared with other translations.
109 Qaraoğlu, *Qurani-Kərim* (2021), p. 559.
110 Ibid., p. 573.

In both the committee's Turkish and Qaraoğlu's Azerbaijani Turkish translations, the first two caliphs—usually privileged as *shaykhān* in the orthodox Sunni tradition—are attributed with a unique position within the circle of the Prophet's close Companions. Abū Bakr is mentioned in two contexts: as the Prophet's companion during his emigration[111] and as a *ḥadīth* transmitter,[112] while the information provided about ʿUmar b. al-Khaṭṭāb does not relate to the interpretation of a verse but instead serves to emphasise the virtue of ʿUmar himself.[113] In this translation, which does not even include historical narration for the revelation of many verses, it seems as though the translators deliberately chose to emphasise the reasons why ʿUmar b. al-Khaṭṭāb became a Muslim.

Unlike the first two caliphs, ʿAlī b. Abū Ṭālib is not mentioned individually by Qaraoğlu in the text, but he is listed as one of the Companions who is inclined to asceticism.[114] The author narrates that ʿAlī and his friends decided to lead an ascetic life, which they took to such extremes that they decided they wished to be castrated, but this was forbidden by the Prophet. On the one hand, this anecdote emphasises their religious commitment, but on the other, it criticises them for their misinterpretation of Islamic ideas. A genuinely negative point that is made about ʿAlī in this translation is its replication of the narration that his father died as a polytheist. The translators compare Muḥammad, who prayed for God's forgiveness for Abū Ṭālib, to Abraham, who prayed similarly for his father. The narration states that both prophets realised their mistakes and gave up, which suggests that Abū Ṭālib died as a polytheist. This firm stance on the faith of Abū Ṭālib, whose acceptance of Islam is the subject of disagreement between Sunnis and the Twelver Shii, reveals the translators' Sunni approach. In the context of the *sīra*, the translation includes other material that opposes the views of Shii translators, such as its interpretation of the phrase 'dream and cursed tree' in Q 17:60, as well as its stance on the legitimate ownership of properties and lands conquered peacefully (*fay*) by Muslims addressed

---

111 Ibid., p. 192.
112 Ibid., p. 124.
113 Ibid., p. 311.
114 Ibid., p. 121.

in Q 59:6—both of which are polemical subjects in terms of Twelver Shii and Sunni interpretations.[115]

The final, most recent example of a Turkish-affiliated translation is *Kur'ân-ı Kerîm Meali*. This was produced by two Turkish theologians, Halil Altuntash and Muzaffer Shahin, published by the Turkish Presidency of Religious Affairs, and translated under the name *Qur'ani-Kərim və məalı* by Kovsar Taghiyev: an Azerbaijani theologian with a PhD in *tafsīr* from a Turkish university. As will be seen in the examples discussed in the following paragraphs, this translation also generally reflects Sunni (Māturidī/Hanafī) ideas in its interpretation of practical theological issues[116] and is therefore intrinsically different from the Iran-affiliated translations. Thus, while this translation perceives the prophets as sinless, it also expresses that their ʿiṣma does not protect them from being mistaken.[117] In contrast, the Twelver Shii doctrine of 'iṣma holds that *ma'ṣūm*s ('infallible ones', i.e. prophets and imams) are protected from even the smallest of sins or mistakes. Above and beyond this, Muḥammad is presented as a prophet who performed miracles, such as splitting the moon (Q 54:1) and undertaking the Night Journey (Q 17:1). This challenges his characterisation in contemporary debates as an 'ordinary human prophet'.

Altuntash and Shahin's translation mentions some of the Prophet's wives in the following contexts: Khadīja is mentioned in their commentary on the early periods of revelation; Zaynab bt Jaḥsh is mentioned in relation to the marriage prohibitions of the *jāhiliyya*; and ʿĀʾisha's role in the affair of the necklace is described in detail.[118] While Qāsim, one of the Prophet's sons, is mentioned with regard to the polytheists who ridiculed his death,[119] Altuntash and Shahin include no information about the Prophet's daughter Fāṭima and her family, in contrast to some

---

115 Ibid., pp. 176, 287. For a similar parallel, see Kövsər Tağıyev, *Qurani-Kərim və məalı* (Ankara: Türkiye Diyanet Vakfı, 2020), pp. 287, 545.
116 Tağıyev, *Qurani-Kərim*, pp. 37, 233, 289, 420, 423, 519, 545. For parallelism related to the transdenominational differences reflected in Qur'an translations on the subject that loot belongs to the Islamic state, and the meaning of 'dream' and 'cursed tree', see: Ibid., pp. 287, 545; Qaraoğlu, *Qurani-Kərim*, pp. 176, 287.
117 Tağıyev, *Qurani-Kərim*, pp. 281, 527.
118 Ibid., pp. 350, 422, 573.
119 Ibid., p. 602.

other translations which provide this through extensive commentary on the *mubāhala* verse (Q 3:61).[120]

Altuntash and Shahin also include striking narration about the Banū Hāshim, the Prophet's tribe, in the scope of the Prophet's relatives (*al-qurbā*) as mentioned in Q 42:23, in the broader sense. According to this narration, which relates to the distribution of booty after the Battle of Badr, ʿAbbās b. ʿAbd al-Muṭṭalib and ʿAqīl b. Abī Ṭālib were captured as prisoners by the Muslim side during the battle and, on the Prophet's instructions and the advice of Abū Bakr, they were released in return for a ransom. However, ʿUmar b. al-Khaṭṭāb had made a different proposal, which the Qur'an would later approve, that they should be sentenced to death.[121]

As with other translations from this period discussed earlier, the translator's choices clearly have a significant influence on the overall plot line of the *sīra*. In these texts, the translators base their 'axis of virtue' not on the reputations of the Prophet's relatives, but rather his Companions. This reflects the general theological view of the target audience about the importance of the Companions, who are presented by Altuntash and Shahin as 'people who should be remembered for their good deeds, against whom it is forbidden to speak ill words or to be hostile', and it is stated that their views can be used as evidence in legal judgements.[122] However, the Companions are not idealised in this translation. They are in fact criticised and reproved for their behaviour in many verses for various reasons, in particular for their pursuit of worldly possessions.[123]

When the information in Altuntash and Shahin's translation about the Companions' innermost circle is evaluated, it becomes clear that Abū Bakr occupies a unique position and is portrayed as superior to the others. Altuntash and Shahin point out that he was chosen by the Prophet to accompany him during his emigration, and that Muḥammad cites Abū Bakr's views on important issues, and praises him in verse for his virtues.[124] However, the translators single out other Companions in their commentary on historical events related to the revelation of verses:

---

120 Ibid., p. 56.
121 Ibid., p. 184.
122 Ibid., pp. 546, 582.
123 Ibid., pp. 65, 68, 93, 176, 178, 189, 205, 552.
124 Ibid., pp. 179, 184, 595.

ʿUmar is presented as the Companion with whom the Prophet consulted the most, and whose opinion was confirmed by the Qur'an'; while ʿAlī is mentioned because he lay down in the Prophet's bed during the Hijra, impersonating him so that he could flee to safety.[125]

Although Altuntash and Shahin devote special attention to the subject of war during the Prophet's lifetime, they usually highlight the role of divine intervention in a given battle, or remind their readers of the negative consequences of various personal weaknesses, rather than actually explaining historical events.[126] This translation has a particular focus on the Islamic attitude towards war, which is a central issue in modern discussions of Islam, and Altuntash and Shahin state that the priority is 'peace', which is the meaning of 'Islam'. They recommend peaceful relations with non-Muslims, as long as they do not pose a threat to Muslim lives. To the translators, this view is supported by Qur'anic verses about the battles undertaken during the Prophet's life, and their historical background.[127] In their translation, they show that during the Prophet's life, conflicts between Muslims and non-Muslims arose from the breakdown of agreements made to facilitate their peaceful coexistence.[128]

Compared with the Islamic Republic of Iran and the Republic of Türkiye, the Kingdom of Saudi Arabia has been less active when it comes to the institutional production of Azerbaijani Qur'an translations. Work on a translation of the full text of the Qur'an into Azerbaijani at the King Fahd Glorious Qur'an Printing Complex in Saudi Arabia began relatively late, after the 2000s.[129] This translation, first published in 2013, was authored by Alikhan Musayev: an Azerbaijani theologian who

---

125 Ibid., pp. 57, 63, 84, 310.
126 Ibid., pp. 33, 50, 65, 68, 73, 108, 176–78, 184, 189, 193, 205, 350, 418, 510–13, 549.
127 Ibid., pp. 29, 506.
128 Ibid., pp. 544–45. It can be considered that the political stance developed by the Turkish Presidency of Religious Affairs in the face of challenges such as interreligious dialogue since the end of the 1990s, had a significant impact on this translation. The establishment of the 'Interreligious Dialogue Branch Directorate' in 1999 as a unit carrying out the secretariat of interreligious dialogue work can be seen as the reflection of this process in institutional structure. For the historical development of discourse on interfaith dialogue by the Presidency of Religious Affairs, see Olgun, Hakan, 'Diyanet'in Dinlerarası Diyalog Algısı', *Milel ve Nihal: inanç, kültür ve mitoloji araştırmaları dergisi*, 4:1 (2009), 265–286.
129 A translation of the Qur'an into Russian by Elmir Quliyev, an Azerbaijani theologian, was published with the support of this translation centre. Since the scope of study is limited to translations in the Azerbaijani language, Quliyev's translation has not been analysed in this chapter.

pursued his higher religious education in Medina.¹³⁰ In this translation, Musayev gives precedence to a literal approach to the Qur'an, reflecting the Salafi view, which is not part of the traditional religious mosaic of Azerbaijan. He also avoids the use of explanatory expressions and commentary as much as possible. Despite this lack of paratextual additions, the representation of the Companions might constitute a *sīra nabawiyya* in Musayev's translation. Zayd b. Ḥāritha is the only Companion mentioned by name in the Qur'an, so he naturally features in this translation. Two further Companions mentioned in Musayev's commentary on the translation are Abū Bakr—who, the reader is told, emigrated with the Prophet to Medina—and ᶜĀʾisha bt Abī Bakr—who is depicted as the victim of slander in the affair of the necklace.¹³¹ Although the fragmentary information provided about the Companions is far from sufficient to construct a *sīra* framework, it does notably reveal a Salafi bias. The selective picture of the Companions' circle is critical to this translation, because Musayev renders the expression *al-kitāb wa'l-ḥikma* (literally, 'the Qur'an and the wisdom') in various verses of the Qur'an as 'the Qur'an and the Sunna'—highlighting the importance of Prophetic *ḥadīth*s and, by extension, the Companions as the first transmitters of this material.¹³²

Diversification in Translation: Varying Approaches to the Inclusion of *sīra* in Translations of the Qur'an

The most crucial translation example from this third time period, characterised by nontraditional translations, is the second edition of Nariman Gasimoghlu's translation—which was published in 2018 under a new name, *OXU: Quran açıqlaması* ('A READING: The Qur'anic Explanation'), with new content.¹³³ This new translation is the fruit

---

130 Əlixan Musayev, *Qurani Kərim və Azərbaycan dilində mənaca tərcüməsi* (Medina: King Fahd Glorious Qur'an Printing Complex, 1434/2013).
131 Ibid., pp. 245, 466 (Abdullah b. Ubayy b. Salūl is also mentioned due to the event of Ifk).
132 Ibid., p. 119. Unlike the edition used here, the verses of the Qur'an including the phrase 'book and wisdom' are explained as 'Qur'an and Sunna' (Q 2:231; Q 3:164; Q 4:113) in the online version of Musayev's translation. www.quran.az
133 Nəriman Qasımoğlu, *OXU: Quran açıqlaması* (Baku: Təhsil, 2018).

of Gasimoghlu's theological research over the last twenty-five years, intended to propagate the 'correct' Islam, which has never lost its relevance; to help cleanse Islam from historical superstitions; and to aid in the development of a new religious way of thinking in contemporary Azerbaijan.[134]

There are fundamental differences between the two editions of Gasimoghlu's translation in terms of the methodology, the theological interpretation of verses, and the religious language used. Following a new method for the second edition, Gasimoghlu refuses to use 'outdated commentaries (*tafsīrs*) that subordinate religious consciousness in particular and human thought in general to superstition and prevent them from receiving their share of the divine light.'[135] Gasimoghlu's translation is thus an example of the modernist trend in Qur'an interpretation, which began with Jamāl al-Dīn al-Afghānī (d. 1897) and was primarily pioneered by Muḥammad ʿAbduh (d. 1905) at the end of the nineteenth century. He argues that the views of classical commentators and their explanations about grammatical rules detach their Qur'anic interpretations from the spirit of their time. Gasimoghlu's tendency to interpret certain verses on the basis of scientific fact further characterises the new edition of this translation as modernist.[136]

However, what makes this edition unique among post-Soviet Azerbaijani translations, and significantly different from the first edition, is the lexical choice of Azerbaijani Turkish terms for basic religious concepts. In this translation, fundamental words relating to worship—such as *namaz* (prayer), *oruc* (fasting), *zəkat* (alms), *həcc* (pilgrimage)—and other concepts such as *cənnət* (heaven) and *cəhənnəm* (hell), have been rendered using centuries-old terminology that has long been used in Azerbaijani religious literature. However, for some other established terms and notions—such as *Allah, İslam, müsəlman, kafir, küfr, müşrik,* and *ibadət etmək*—the author uses unusual translations such as *Tanrı, təslimolma, təslimolan, danan, danma, riyacıl,* and *qulluq qılmaq*. The most striking difference is his translation of the name of the Qur'an as 'OXU' ('READING'). In the same way, the author uses various innovative terminology and syntax that is completely new to the Azerbaijani Qur'an

---

134 Ibid., p. 345.
135 Ibid., p. 347.
136 On the translation of verses Q 25:48–50 and Q 84:19, see Ibid., pp. 200, 333.

translation tradition, for example in his use of 'Tanrı eşidəyən, biləyən' ('God hearing, knowing'). In this respect, Gasimoghlu's second edition reminds the reader of translations that defended ideas of nationalism and Turkism, at the centre of discussions on the Turkisation of the Qur'an in the Republic of Türkiye.[137] On the other hand, the removal of all explanatory commentary from this edition excludes supplementary information about the Prophet's life and times. Unlike the previous edition, the second edition contains no additional information about events at the time of the Qur'an's revelation, and it underemphasises the importance of historical context to readers' understanding of the Qur'anic message.

Another translation of the Qur'an published during this period is *Qurani-Kərim və sözbəsöz tərcüməsi*[138] ('The Holy Qur'an and its Word-by-Word Translation'), an interlinear translation by Aladdin Sultanov: an Azerbaijani theologian with a PhD in *tafsīr* from a Turkish university. Its publication under the joint editorship of Allahshukur Pashazade—the head of the Caucasus Muslim Board—and Vasim Mammadaliyev—the most famous Azerbaijani translator of the Qur'an—has granted prestige to this translation among the religious community in Azerbaijan. This word-by-word translation in Azerbaijani is the first of its kind, and it is designed to help Azerbaijani readers with some knowledge of Arabic grammar to read the Qur'an from Arabic.[139] It does not contain any

---

137 Since the Tanzimat period, the translation of the Qur'an into Turkish has become a part of Ottoman modernisation in general, as well as the ideology of nationalism and therefore Turkism in particular. The issues of the call to prayer in Turkish, the Turkish prayer, and worship in the mother tongue, which have been discussed since the Second Constitutional Era and continued in the first years of the Republic, have completely politicised the issue of Qur'an translation in the context of the ideal of Turkifying Islam, and the issue has generally been discussed on two extreme axes: support for the idea of Turkism under the guise of serving the Qur'an or Islam, and betrayal of the Qur'an. Although many Turkish Qur'an translations were made in the process, the language in these translations made until the beginning of the twenty-first century was considered deficient in two respects: (1) it was not compatible with contemporary Turkish, or (2) it was not pure Turkish. The latter criticism can be seen as an extension of the ideology of nationalism (Turkism). In some of these translations, many Qur'anic words and concepts that had become Turkish over the centuries were completely changed in the name of pure Turkish. Mustafa Öztürk, 'II. Meşrutiyet'ten Günümüze Kur'an Mealleri', *Türkiye Araştırmaları Literatür Dergisi*, 9:18 (2011), 174–82.
138 Ələddin Sultanov, *Qurani-Kərim və Sözbəsöz Tərcüməsi* (Baku, Şərq-Qərb, 2012).
139 Ibid., p. vii.

annotation in the form of footnotes or endnotes, but there are some additions inserted as in-text parentheses to form a complete sentence in the Azerbaijani translation. Since explanatory information is limited, this translation does not contain much data on the *sīra nabawiyya*. In an exceptional instance, Sultanov mentions Abū Bakr in a parenthesis regarding migration, in the context of Q 9:40.[140] This could reflect the traditional Sunni view that praises Abū Bakr as the most virtuous of Muḥammad's Companions, but this factor alone is not sufficient to cast this text as a Sunni translation. It is worth noting that, in the ablution verse (Q 5:6)—which is commonly seen as determining the text's denomination—Sultanov prefers to remain neutral, harmonising the Sunni and Shii interpretations by specifying both possible meanings in parenthesis as 'yuyun/məsh edin' ('wash/anoint').[141]

In 2021, Sultanov published another translation of the Qur'an, entitled *Qurani-Kərim və Məalı*, as a continuation of his earlier *Qurani-Kərim və Sözbəsöz Tərcüməsi*.[142] Although it was published with the same editorial team and presented as a second edition of his previous translation, this edition includes the translator's commentary on the verses. In his new translation, Sultanov replicates both his own earlier text and Bünyadov's and Mammadaliyev's line on the ablution verse (Q 5:6), thereby including both Sunni and Twelver Shii views.[143] However, the fact that the citations he uses, although not numerous, usually refer to the revered *ḥadīth* collections of al-Bukhārī indicates a preference for Sunni sources.[144]

Sultanov reflects on the issue of the Prophet's fallibility in his discussion on *ʿiṣma* in the commentary section, giving examples of his reproval by God for some small mistakes.[145] Other features of the Prophet's image that Sultanov brings to the fore include his reliability and promotion of the *shūrā* (council) while ruling.[146] Sultanov also

---

140 Ibid., p. 194. Although it is not an example for this chapter, a similar exception is the name of 'Züleyxa' given within parentheses, related to the story of Joseph. Ibid., pp. 239, 240, 242.
141 Ibid., p. 109.
142 Ələddin Sultanov, *Qurani-Kərim və Məalı* (Baku: İpəkyolu nəşriyyatı, 2021).
143 For a broad explanation of interdenominational differences regarding the interpretation of Q 5:6, known as the ablution verse, see Ibid., p. 107.
144 Ibid., pp. 65, 92, 121, 123, 293.
145 Ibid., pp. 132, 280, 337, 584.
146 Ibid., pp. 70, 130.

includes some information about the Prophet's family life, and mentions his wife Khadīja in relation to Muḥammad's first experience of revelation, as well as Zaynab bt Jahsh in the context of her divorce from Zayd b. Hāritha, and he reaffirms ᶜĀʾisha's innocence in the affair of the necklace. He writes that ᶜĀʾisha and Ḥafṣa, whom he refers to as 'analarımız' (our mothers), gave false information to the Prophet out of 'jealousy', and cites this as a factor in the revelation of the relevant verse of *Sūrat al-Taḥrīm* (Q 66).[147] In this regard, Sultanov's translation bears a striking similarity to some of the institutional translations of the Qur'an originating from Turkey.[148]

Sultanov's translation also contains some information about the Companions, attributing Abū Bakr and ᶜAlī b. Abī Ṭālib with unique positions. His translation praises Abū Bakr as the Prophet's Companion during the Hijra, and as a person whose virtues are extolled in the Qur'an.[149] At the same time, in reference to Q 9:19, he confirms that ᶜAlī b. Abū Ṭālib boasted that he had begun to practise prayer and *jihād* earlier than the other Companions.[150] Sultanov also mentions the story that the Prophet should not ask for forgiveness for Abū Ṭālib, ᶜAlī's father, since he was in Hell,[151] which is also found in some translations based on works from the Turkish Republic. Sultanov likewise incorporates information on political events such as battles and treaties.[152] However, on close inspection, there is little detail about the underlying historical circumstances. For the most part, Sultanov instead draws attention to divine intervention in these events, and the lessons that Muslims should learn from them.

The final example in this category is Shıkhbala Elcan's versified translation, *Quran-i Kərimin anlamı (qafiyəli nəsrlə)* ('The Meaning of the Noble Qur'an in Rhymed Prose').[153] In this work, Shikhbala Elcan (Şıxbala Nəsrəddin oğlu Bayramov)—a retired civil engineer with no official religious education—has not translated the Qur'an

---

147 Ibid., pp. 350–51, 422, 559, 573.
148 Halil Altuntaş and Muzaffer Şahin, *Kur'an-i Kerim Meâli* (Ankara: DİB yayınları, 2008), pp. 350–51, 422, 572; Tağıyev, *Qurani-Kərim*, pp. 350, 422, 573.
149 Sultanov, *Qurani-Kərim*, pp. 192, 351.
150 Ibid., p. 188.
151 Ibid., p. 204.
152 Ibid., pp. 29, 65–67, 70, 176–81, 189, 194, 196, 204, 280, 420, 511–13, 537, 549, 551, 554, 572.
153 Şıxbala Elcan, *Quran-i Kərimin anlamı: qafiyəli nəsrlə* (Bakı: Elm və təhsil, 2015).

from its original Arabic but has instead transformed Bünyadov's and Mammadaliyev's Qur'an translation into rhymed prose. His primary purpose in doing so was 'to make this knowledge [which was revealed by Allah] understandable to those whose thoughts are as simple as myself.'[154] However, Elcan's translation is somewhat restricted in the sense that it remains as faithful to the source text as possible, and tries to maintain the same level of sensitivity when it comes to some essential religious practices.[155]

In addition to relying on Bünyadov's and Mammadaliyev's translation for his own text, Elcan also included their in-text explanations for events that occurred during the Prophet's lifetime. When dealing with military history, the names of battles are usually given without parentheses, which might mislead readers into thinking that these are explicitly identified in the Qur'an.[156] In some cases, Elcan not only inserts the name of the event in question, but also incorporates further historical context given by Bünyandov and Mammadaliyev within the translation without any indication that it is an addition to the text, thereby giving the impression that the Qur'an itself provides this information on these issues.

A similar situation arises in verses associated with the Prophet's family life, such that the author presents some of the Prophet's children and wives as being explicitly mentioned in the Qur'an when they are not.[157] In his efforts to match the rhyme of the original Arabic text, Elcan makes some mistakes when incorporating historical context.[158] He also removes the verse numbers, simplifies the text, and adapts it to the spoken language—all of which is understandable given that he aimed to create a legible translation that would be accessible to the wider masses. However, because the author has included so much parenthetical additional information from Bünyadov's and Mammadaliyev's translation in his own text without parentheses to distinguish it, *Quran-i Kərimin anlamı* (*qafiyəli nəsrlə*) should be considered a literary text rather than a translation of the holy book.

---

154 Ibid., pp. 4, 461.
155 On the ablution verse, see Ibid., p. 73.
156 Ibid., pp. 38, 48, 49, 121, 127, 132, 135–37, 140, 195, 247, 269, 313.
157 Ibid., pp. 157–58, 426, 459.
158 For example ʿAbdallāh b. Umm Maktūm was recorded as 'Um Maktum'. Ibid., p. 445.

Conclusion

Work on the first generation of Qur'an translations covered in this chapter began towards the end of the Soviet period, and they were published as complete editions in the early years of Azerbaijani independence. Although the translators of this first period were Azerbaijani Orientalists who graduated from the Soviet Oriental School, they approached the Qur'an from a faith-based perspective and argued that Qur'an translation was necessary due to the scripture's importance in the religious thought of the Azerbaijani people. Another defining characteristic of these translations is that they do not defend any particular denominational doctrine as the only correct interpretation of Islam. Rather, they approach the views of both the Sunni and Twelver Shii denominations with sensitivity, as evidenced in material relating to the Prophet's biography. Beyond that, what distinguishes Bünyadov's and Mammadaliyev's translation in terms of its use of the Prophetic *sīra* is that it focuses on providing historical (as opposed to theological) information about the events of the Prophet's life. In other words, this translation places more emphasis on the context of the revelation and the *sīra nabawiyya* than its contemporaries. Bünyadov's and Mammadaliyev's translation also reflects some elements of the Soviet-era Oriental tradition as manifested in Krachkovskii's translation, to which it is indebted. The inclusion of Shii readings in the mid-twentieth century Soviet Orientalist tradition (at least in the case of Krachkovskii) has clearly influenced post-Soviet Azerbaijani Qur'an translations. The format of these translations has also been influenced by the Soviet Orientalist tradition to include a separate commentary section which acts as a short *tafsīr*. However, Bünyadov did not adopt additional information verbatim from Krachkovskii's translation. It seems that he deliberately filtered Krachkovskii's statements about the Shii interpretation of the Qur'an, reflecting his own specific preferences. Not only was Bünyadov selective in his inclusion of parts of Krachkovskii's commentary that reflected Shii views, he also followed an intersectoral, conciliatory translation policy by adding positive, even laudatory information about the Companions who are most severely criticised in Shii polemics, adding balance to his translatorial approach.

One of the main differences between the first two generations of Qur'an translators—firstly Azerbaijani Arabists, and secondly foreign organisations—is that the first generation engaged in Islamic studies only after they had translated the Qur'an. After the 1990s, religious and theological aspects, rather than Arabic philology, came to the fore in the approaches of translators such as Mammadaliyev and Gasimoghlu. Since the translators of the second period worked on their Qur'an translations after graduating from higher religious institutions in Iran, Turkey, and Saudi Arabia, they tend to adhere to the classical exegetical narrative in large part, much like translations from the first generation.

The main common feature of the second generation of translations is that they contain interpretations which reflect the official or widespread denominational view of the state which sponsored or produced them. This is apparent in biographical information, especially in the treatment of the Prophet's family members and close relatives, the emphasis on the virtue of specific Companions, and the overall characterisation of the Prophet. The Iran-affiliated Qur'an translations present the Prophet as infallible; exhortations and reprimands are never addressed to him, but to others instead, and the real Companions around him are members of the *ahl al-bayt*, his close relatives. These translations present the Imams and the current rulers—their representatives—as the successors to the Prophet's religious-political administration. According to these translations, the appointed and wise deputies of the infallible ones (*maʿṣūms*) will continue the holy administration initiated by the Prophet until the appearance of the Mahdi.

In Turkish-affiliated translations, the image of the Prophet is based on a different interpretation of ʿiṣma. He is portrayed as a prophet who is not immune to making mistakes, but who always receives a divine admonition to ensure he will set things right. These translations interpret the Qur'an as respecting the Prophet's Companions, but they also imply that the Qur'an sometimes criticises the Companions for their human weaknesses and mistakes. They include the Prophet's children and wives within the concept of *ahl al-bayt* and argue that the Qur'an mandates respects for Muḥammad's wives. However, in some cases, the wives are depicted as the subjects of divine reprimand for their human weaknesses. In these translations, the purpose of supplementary information about the battles that took place during the Prophet's life is not to inform the reader about the politico-military history of the period, but to draw spiritual lessons from them.

The Qur'an translations from these first two generations feature significant confessional differences in matters of creed—such as different understandings of ʿiṣma and the doctrine of imāma—and practice—such as temporary marriage and ablution. Although there are some exceptions, these translations largely avoid extreme interpretations that would lead to religious and sectarian separatism.

The third generation is marked by diversification, and it is notable that almost all of the translations that have been discussed from this time constitute the first of their kind in Azerbaijani Turkish, with the exception of the second edition of Sultanov's translation. In line with their authorial purpose, some of the authors of this period did not provide any explanation for the reasons behind the revelation of the Qur'anic verses, and consequently they do not include any biographical information about the Prophet in their translations. On the other hand, one author, Elcan, does include extra-Qur'anic sīra material in his translation, and its presentation makes it seem integral to the original text. This diversification in translation reflects diverging approaches to the Qur'anic source text, and changes in the perception of the translation process over a quarter of a century. It also indicates that a number of the issues in Qur'an translation that have been discussed in the wider Islamic world for more than a century have finally come to the fore in Azerbaijan, in one way or another.

It seems likely that more Qur'an translations will be published, reflecting a variety of methodologies and perspectives, in the near future. Considering the historical presence of different denominations in Azerbaijan, in addition to the state policy of multiculturalism, one of these new Qur'an translations may well be commissioned from the new generation of Azerbaijani theologians that has emerged in recent years.

Bibliography

Aliyeva, Roya, 'Kur'an Tercüme Teknikleri Açısından Büniyatov-Mammedaliyev ve Guliyev Meallerinin Değerlendirilmesi' (unpublished master's thesis, Sakarya Üniversitesi, 2016).

Altuntaş, Halil, and Muzaffer Şahin, *Kur'an-i Kerim Meâli* (Ankara: DİB yayınları, 2008).

Aydüz, Davut, 'Sovyet Döneminde Azerbaycan Türkçesi ve Arap Harfleriyle Yazılan Bir Tefsir', *Akademik Araştırmalar Dergisi*, 17 (2003).

Bünyadov, Ziya, and Vasim Məmmədəliyev, *Qur'an* (Baku: Azərnəşr, 1992).

——, *Qurani-Kərim və Tərcüməsi* (Ankara: Diyanət İşləri Başqanlığı Nəşrləri, 2015).

Cəfərli, Yezqar, *Əli Fəhmi Dünyası* (Baku: Adiloğlu: 2011).

Dūzāl, Rasūl Ismāʿīlzāde, 'Negāhī be tarjama hāi Azerbāyjānī Qurʾāni-Karīm', *Tarjūmān-e Waḥī*, 1 (1376/1997).

——, *Qurāni-Kərim: Azərbaycan Türkcəsilə tərcüməsi* (Qom: Qurâni-Kərimin bütün dillərə tərcüməsi mərkəzi, 1999).

Elcan, Şıxbala, *Quran-i Kərimin anlamı: qafiyəli nəsrlə* (Baku: Elm və təhsil, 2015).

Əlhuda, *əl-Quranu'l-Kərim* (Baku: Şərq-Qərb, 1999).

Əzizova, Elnurə, 'Azərbaycan cəmiyyətindəki dindarlıq səviyyəsinin İslam dünyasındakı dindarlıq səviyyəsi ilə müqayisəsi', in *Azərbaycanda İslam*, ed. by Nahid Məmmədov (Baku: Nurlar, 2015), pp. 52–75.

——, 'Azərbaycanın Məzhəblərarası Tolerantlıq Tarixindən XX Əsrin Əvvəlinə Aid Bir Nümunə: Füyuzat Jurnalı', *Bakı Dövlət Universitetinin İlahiyyat Fakültəsinin Elmi Məcmuəsi*, 27 (2017), 205–15.

İsmayılov, Gündüz, *Azərbaycanda dini məsələ* (Baku: Tuna, 2020).

İsmayılov, Mehman, '20. Yüyzılda Azerbaycan'da Yapılan Kur'an Tefsiri ve Meal Çalışmaları' (unpublished master's thesis, Marmara Üniversitesi, 2002).

İsmayılzadə, İlqar, *İlahi Sirlər: Qurani-Kərimin Azərbaycan dilində tərcüməsi və qısa təfsiri* (n.p.: Qurani-Kərim Elmi Araşdırmalar Mərkəzi, 2010).

Kavyānpūr, Ahmed, *al-Qurʾāni'l-Karīm bā tercemeyi Türkī* (n.p.: İqbāl, 1372/1992).

Kazımova, Roya, 'Azerbaycanlı Müfessir Ahmed Hâşimzâde'nin Tefsîru'l-Kur'âni'l-Azîm İsimli Eserinde Kur'ân'ı Yorumlama Yöntemi' (unpublished PhD thesis, Uludağ Üniversitesi, 2022).

Krachkovskii, Ignatii Yulianovich, *Koran* (Moscow: İzdatelstvo vostochnoy literatury, 1963).

al-Lāhim, Sulaymān Ibrāhīm, *Manhaj Ibn Kathīr fī al-tafsīr* (Riyadh: Jāmiʿa al-Imām Muḥammad Ibn Saʿūd, 1401).

Məmmədov, Ramiz, and Abdurrəhman Nuruyev, *Təfsir Elmi* (Baku: İpəkyolu, 2016).

Meşkini, Əli Ərdəbili, *Qurani-Kərim, tərcümə və transkripsiyası* (Baku: Nurlar, 2022).

Musayev, Əlixan, *Qurani Kərim və Azərbaycan dilində mənaca tərcüməsi* (Medina: King Fahd Glorious Qur'an Printing Complex, 1434/2013).

Olgun, Hakan, 'Diyanet'in Dinlerarası Diyalog Algısı', *Milel ve Nihal: inanç, kültür ve mitoloji araştırmaları dergisi*, 4:1 (2009), 265–286.

Öztürk, Mustafa, 'II. Meşrutiyet'ten Günümüze Kur'an Mealleri', *Türkiye Araştırmaları Literatür Dergisi*, 9:18 (2011).

Pazarbaşı, Erdoğan, 'Azerbaycan'da Yaygın Kur'an Tercümeleri', *Erciyes Üniversitesi İlâhiyat Fakültesi Dergisi*, 10 (1998).

——, 'Kur'an'ın Azerbaycan'da Yaygın Tefsir ve Tercümeleri', *Bilig*, 25 (2003).

Pew Research Center, *The Global Religious Landscape: A Report on the Size and Distribution of the World's Major Religious Groups as of 2010* (Washington, D.C.: The Pew Research Center's Forum on Religion & Public Life, 2012), https://www.pewresearch.org/religion/2012/12/18/global-religious-landscape-exec/

——, *The World's Muslims: Unity and Diversity* (Washington, D.C.: The Pew Research Center's Forum on Religion & Public Life, 2012), https://www.pewresearch.org/religion/2012/08/09/the-worlds-muslims-unity-and-diversity-executive-summary/

Polat, Fethi Ahmet, 'Yirminci Yüzyıl Sonrasında Azerbaycan'da Yapılan Kur'an Tercümeleri-I', *Selçuk Üniversitesi İlahiyat Fakültesi Dergisi*, 16 (2003).

——, 'Azerbaycan'da Yapılan Kur'an Tercümeleri ve Türkiye'de Neşredilen Meallerin Bu Tercümelere Etkileri—Memmedeliyev Tercümesi Örneği', in *Uluslararası Türk Dünyasının İslamiyete Katkıları Sempozyumu Bildirileri*, ed. by İsmail Hakkı Göksoy and Nejdet Durak (Isparta: Süleyman Demirel Üniversitesi, 2007), pp. 441–57.

Qaraoğlu, Fazil, *QURʾANİ-KƏRİM və Açıqlamalı Məalı* (n.p.: Ankara, 2003).

——, *Qurani-Kərim və Açıqlamalı Məalı* (Baku: Qanun Nəşriyyatı, 2021).

Qasımoğlu, Nəriman, *Qur'an-i Kərim* (Baku: 'Azərbaycan' nəşriyyatı, 1993).

——, *OXU: Quran açıqlaması* (Baku: Təhsil, 2018).

——, 'Quranda adı keçən hicabın baş örtüyü mənası yoxdur', *AZPOST*, 20 November 2019, https://azpost.info/n%C9%99riman-qasimoglu/

Qənbərov, Asəf, *Azərbaycanda Dövlət-Din Münasibətləri: Dünyəviliyin nəzəri və hüquqi əsasları* (Baku: Nurlar, 2019).

Qəni oğlu, Məmmədhəsən, and Tariyel Bilal oğlu, *Qur'ani-Kərim (Azərbaycan dilinə tərcüməsi ilə)* (Baku: Göytürk, 2000).

əl-Quranu'l-Kərim (Baku: Şərq-Qərb, 1999).

Sultanov, Ələddin, *Qurani-Kərim və Məalı* (Baku: İpəkyolu nəşriyyatı, 2021).

——, *Qurani-Kərim və Sözbəsöz Tərcüməsi* (Baku: Şərq-Qərb, 2012).

Tağıyev, Kövsər, *Qurani-Kərim və məalı* (Ankara: Türkiye Diyanet Vakfı, 2020).

Yakubovych, Mykhaylo, 'The First Vernacular *Tafsīr* in the Caucasus: The Legacy of Two 20th Century Azerbaijani Qur'an Commentaries', *Australian Journal of Islamic Studies*, 7:1 (2022), https://doi.org/10.55831/ajis.v7i1.457

7. Implications of Theological Diversity in Shii-Authored Translations of the Qur'an and *tafsīr*s into Russian

Akif Tahiiev

To date, there has been very little academic study of either Shii-authored translations of the Qur'an into Russian, or Russian translations of Shii *tafsīr*s. In general, if we compare the number of Sunni translations of the Qur'an and *tafsīr*s into Russian with Shii ones, we will see that there are many more of the former. The Soviet regime imposed constraints on the printing of religious texts, and, during that time, Shii *tafsīr*s were not officially translated into Russian at all. Religious life was controlled by the state through bodies such as the Spiritual Administration of Muslims. Of these, only the Spiritual Administration of Muslims of Transcaucasia—renamed to the Religious Council of the Caucasus in 1992—had several Shii religious figures. Since there were no Shii Islamic universities, aspiring Shii clerics were forced to study in Sunni institutions.[1] Additionally, only a limited number of state-approved individuals were permitted to undertake pilgrimages to holy cities

---

1   Akif Tahiiev, 'Prospects for Higher Shia Religious Education in Post-Soviet Countries', *Religions*, 1:7 (2023), 822.

such as Mecca, Karbala, and Mashhad. With the revival of Islam in the region that has taken place in the post-Soviet era, the lack of accessible religious literature became a general problem for all Russian-speaking Muslim communities, but this was especially pertinent for Russian Shiis: since the fall of the Soviet Union the number of Russian-speaking Shiis gradually increased, so there was a corresponding need for Russian-language Shii *tafsīrs* and/or translations of the Qur'an.

Although the authors of new Russian translations of the Qur'an have not tended to classify their translations or interpretations as 'Sunni', the specifics of the translation/interpretation of certain verses of the Qur'an are understood by Sunni and Shii theologians in different ways, and the treatment of these verses makes their theological leanings very clear. The fact that more Sunni translations have been produced is primarily because Sunnis represent the majority of the Muslim population in the post-Soviet region, and especially in Russia itself. Furthermore, the Russians, Ukrainians, and Belarusians who convert to Islam more often convert to Sunni Islam rather than Shii Islam. There are a number of other post-Soviet ethnicities who tend to convert to Shii Islam, but Shiis form the majority of the Muslim population only in Azerbaijan, and Azerbaijani diasporas most often form the core for Shii communities elsewhere in the post-Soviet region.[2] It is impossible to quantify the number of Russian-speaking Shiis with any exactness, since difficulties arise even when it comes to determining the number of Shiis in the post-Soviet region as a whole. However, some rough figures have been determined for Russia, where it is estimated that Shiis make up only 3% of the total Muslim population.[3] Based on approximate statistics about the numbers of Azerbaijanis living in Russia, and the Shii activist Taras Cherniyenko's assertion that there are 600,000 Shiis in St. Petersburg and 1.5 million in Moscow, Paul Goble tentatively calculated in 2010 that there were more than 2.1 million followers of Shii Islam in Russia at that

---

2   Ibid.; Akif Tahiiev, 'Studying Shiʿism in Ukraine: The State of the Field at the Crossroads of the Geopolitics of Knowledge Production', *International Journal of Middle East Studies*, 57:1 (2025); Akif Tahiiev, 'Minority within a minority: Shia community in Ukraine', *International Journal of Islamic Thought*, 19:2 (2021).

3   'Bol'shinstvo moskovskikh musul'man—shiity', *Iran*, 8 February 2005, https://iran.ru/news/politics/27472/Bolshinstvo_moskovskih_musulman_shiity

time.⁴ However, as an activist, Chernienko can hardly be considered an objective source: it is quite common for both Sunni and Shii activists to exaggerate the number of followers of their respective denominations. This tendency can be observed even in statements issued by some state institutions. For example, the government of Azerbaijan is currently pushing the narrative of an ongoing political trend of Sunnitisation in Azerbaijan,⁵ reflecting the local geopolitical situation (specifically in terms of pro-Turkish and anti-Iranian sentiments). There are some speculative claims that this narrative underestimates the size of the Shii population. The Administrative Department of the President of the Republic of Azerbaijan states that the Muslim population of Azerbaijan is approximately 85% Shii and 15% Sunni⁶ but, according to information provided by the State Committee on Religious Associations of the Republic of Azerbaijan (Dini Qurumlarla İş üzrə Dövlət Komitəsinin), only 65% of the Muslim population are Shiis, while 35% are Sunnis.⁷ In Chapter 6 of this book, Azizova implies an even smaller proportion of Shiis, suggesting that Shiis and Sunnis each constitute approximately half of the Muslim population in Azerbaijan. The general lack of clarity regarding the numbers of Shii Muslims is also tied to the fact that, historically, population censuses conducted in post-Soviet countries have only considered ethnic criteria which does not necessarily correspond to religious denomination. For example, simply counting all members of Azerbaijani diasporas as Shii will not necessarily reflect the true extent of the Shii population, as some of them may identify as Sunnis or follow other religions/beliefs, or they may be atheists. Hence, it is quite difficult to work out the exact number of Shiis in Azerbaijan and Russia, or indeed any other post-Soviet country—especially since no census takes any change of religious identity into account, which excludes religious converts.

---

4   Paul Goble, 'Who Will Manage the 2 Million Shiites of Russia?', *The Moscow Times*, 9 Feb 2010, https://www.themoscowtimes.com/2010/02/09/who-will-manage-the-2-million-shiites-of-russia-a35088
5   Zahiraddin Ibragimi, 'Azerbaijan: neob"iavlennaia voina protiv shiitov', *Informatsionnoe agentstvo REX*, 25 May 2017, https://iarex.ru/articles/54019.html
6   'Religion in Azerbaijan' (n.p.: Administrative Department of the President of the Republic of Azerbaijan, Presidential Library, n.d.), https://files.preslib.az/projects/remz/pdf_en/atr_din.pdf
7   'Dini demoqrafiya', https://2009-2017.state.gov/documents/organization/134425.pdf

Sunni communities are also often more visible in that they tend to be more institutionalised, and the majority of them operate under the administrative remit of clerical boards (*Duhovnoe upravlenie musul'man*), also known as muftiates, while Shii communities do not have such structures and usually exist as independent, self-governed communities. The exception to this is the aforementioned Religious Council of the Caucasus (*Upravlenie musul'man Kavkaza*), which is located in Baku and comprises both Shii and Sunni clerics, but this organisation did not participate in the production of Qur'an-related literature in Russian.

In the early 1990s, there was practically no Russian-language religious literature tailored specifically to Shiis. However, Russian-speaking graduates of Iranian universities eventually began to fill this gap. First of all, they translated books containing general information about Shiism to introduce people to the basics, as well as collections of *fatwas* that set out to explain the practical aspects of Shiism.[8] Over time, more diverse literature began to appear, related to subjects such as the Qur'an, *ḥadīth*, Islamic philosophy and jurisprudence, and history. Some of the pioneers in this translation movement will be discussed later, as they were actively involved in the translation of Qur'anic literature.

I theorise that the lack of governance and institutionalisation of local Shii communities guaranteed more freedom for authors and/or translators in their choice of primary sources and literature, leading to the diversification of Russian Shii Qur'anic literature. The main goal of this chapter is to study the available Shii literature on the Qur'an in Russian in order to determine the main actors in this field, and the reasons behind some of their specific translatorial choices. There is little existing scholarship on this topic, although a number of more general studies on Russian Qur'an translations have touched on Shii interpretations.[9] The only previous works specifically on Shiism in the

---

8   For example: Ali Sistani, *Prakticheskie zapovedi Islama*, trans. by Nazim Zeinalov (Moscow: Organizatsiia Imam Ali, 1999).

9   For example, see the following studies about differences in Sunni and Shii Qur'anic interpretations in Russian and in Azeri respectively: Damir Mukhetdinov, 'The Russian Qur'an Translations in the Early 21th Century: An Analytical Review', *Islam in the Modern World*, 18:2 (2022), 47–74 (pp. 63–64); Mykhaylo Yakubovych, 'The First Vernacular *Tafsīr* in the Caucasus: The Legacy of Two 20th Century Azerbaijani Qurʾān Commentaries', *Australian Journal of Islamic Studies*, 7:1 (2022), 72–95.

Russian context have been a number of studies devoted to individual Shii communities in the post-Soviet region.[10]

The following section will introduce the field and outline the main genres of religious literature that relate to Shii interpretation of the Qur'an in Russian. The rest of this chapter will go into more detail, analysing existing Russian works devoted to Shii interpretations and/or translations of the Qur'an. The conclusion will briefly summarise these sources and show how they correspond to the unsystematised nature of local Shii communities and the diversity of Shii Islamic thought among local actors.

Russian-Language Qur'anic Literature

Shii Qur'anic translations into Russian can be divided into three groups, according to their authorship by: (1) Russian-speaking academics, (2) Iranian scholars, and (3) local Shii scholars and activists. In this section, I introduce each group with reference to various sources, while in the following sections I will move on to the main focus of this chapter: works devoted entirely to Shii interpretations and/or translations of the Qur'an.

Russian and other post-Soviet academics have paid little attention to Shii works on Qur'an exegesis, which means that academic translations and papers constitute the smallest of the existing literature. Some information about the Shii interpretation of the Qur'an can be found in the works of non-Shii Qur'an translators—for example, Magomed-Nuri Osmanov sometimes refers to Shii *tafsīrs* in his own translation.[11] There are also textbooks and other works devoted to the general characteristics of Shiism or Islam in general. In the textbook *Shiitskii islam* ('Shii Islam'), for example, Knysh and Matochkina provide some information about the specific Shii interpretation of the Qur'an. They write that certain Qur'anic words and phrases, which Sunni scholars perceive as referring to abstract concepts and personalities, have been interpreted by Shii exegetes as referring to ʿAlī and the Shii Imams. In a similar vein, they note that some negative statements made in the Qur'an about a particular group of people were interpreted by Shii exegetes as referring

---

10   For example, see Tahiiev, 'Prospects'.
11   Magomed-Nuri Osmanov (trans.), *Koran. Perevod s arabskogo i kommentarii* (St. Petersburg: Dilia, 2011).

to the opponents of ʿAlī and his family.¹² In terms of academic works devoted entirely to Shii interpretations of the Qur'an, Russian Islamicist S. Prozorov's translation of the preface and first chapter of *Tafsīr al-Mīzān* by Muḥammad Ḥusayn Ṭabāṭabāʾī should be singled out.¹³ This text will be discussed in more detail later in this chapter.

Iranian state institutions and individuals have also been active in promoting the production of Shii literature in Russian since the 1990s. In addition to funding local academics and Shii scholars, they have translated and published the works of Iranian scholars in various fields, including the Qur'anic sciences. For example, there was a Russian translation of Bakha ad-Din Khurramshakhi's (Bahāʾ al-Dīn Khurramshāhī) *Koranovedenie (ocherki o Korane i ego roli v formirovanii kul'tury)*—'Qur'anic Studies (Essays on the Qur'an and its Role in the Formation of Culture)'.¹⁴ Various *tafsīr*s were also translated, such as Khusein Seiidi Saravi's commentary on *Sūrat Yūsuf* in his *Samoe prekrasnoe povestvovanie* ('The Most Beautiful Narration').¹⁵ In his discussion of the *sura*, Saravi provides general information such as the fact that this is the twelfth *sura* of the Qur'an and consists of 113 verses, that it is half a *juzʾ* long, and that was revealed in Mecca (although Ibn ʿAbbās believed that four of its verses were revealed in Medina). He writes that no other *sura* of the Qur'an contains such a lengthy narrative, and points out that the *sura* is dedicated specifically to the prophet Yūsuf. Saravi goes on to provide an overview of each verse, and in some cases considers their aesthetic (in terms of linguistics and the beauty of the narration) and educational aspects. His exegesis has a neutral, non-denominational style of narration, which may well be one of the reasons for its relative popularity with Sunni readers. Other factors in its popularity are undoubtedly its educational aspects and the contemporary character of Saravi's interpretation, in which he uses Qur'anic examples to mentor readers.

---

12 Alexander Knysh and Anna Matochkina, *Shiitskii islam* (St. Petersburg: St. Petersburg State University, 2016), pp. 67–68.

13 S. M. Prozorov, '*Al-Allama as-Sayyid* Muhammad Husayn al-Ṭabāṭabāʾī (d. in 1402/1981) "The Balance (of Equity) in the Commentary of the Qur'ān": Translation from Arabic with Commentaries by S. M. Prozorov', *Written Monuments of the Orient*, 1:4 (2006), 82–107.

14 Bakha ad-Din Khurramshakhi, *Koranovedenie (ocherki o Korane i ego roli v formirovanii kul'tury)*, trans. by B. V. Norik (Moscow: Sadra, 2016).

15 Khusein Seiidi Saravi, *Samoe prekrasnoe povestvovanie* (Moscow: Nauchnaia kniga, 2020).

It is quite interesting that in the majority of books written by Iranian authors, specifically Shii theological issues are not directly mentioned, and the authors do not acknowledge their personal Shii leanings or beliefs—quite probably because they are aiming to attract non-Shii readers as well as Shii readers. This can be seen, for example, in Sayyed Abbas Sadr Ameli's *Svet Sviashchennogo Korana. Raz"iasneniia i tolkovaniia* translation of Faqih Imani's *Nūr al-Qurʾān fī tafsīr al-Qurʾān* ('The Light of the Holy Qur'an'), which was popular among Russian Sunnis as well as Shiis. This will be discussed later in this chapter.[16]

Earlier, I mentioned that Shii Muslims gained access to religious literature in Russian mainly as a result of local activists, many of whom were graduates of Iranian universities. These works form the largest resource pool of Russian Shii Qur'anic literature; not all of them were formally published, and many of them only exist online, but these works are still accessible to anyone wishing to read them. They include translations of *ḥadīth* collections, works of 'classical' scholars who defined the foundations of Shiism, and exegetical works that contain thematic interpretations of individual verses and/or groups of verses that convey Shii ideas. For example, in Airat Baeshev's online translation of al-Nuʿmānī's (d. 360/970–1) *al-Ghayba*, the following *ḥadīth* is provided: 'According to Fudayl: Imam Sadiq, peace be upon him, said about the words of Allāh "You are only a warner, and there is a guide for every people" (Q 13:7): "Each Imam is a guide for the era in which he resides."'[17] This is an example of an exegetical *ḥadīth*, which aims to emphasise the role of the Shii Imams and Imamate, reflecting the Shii exegetical tradition. Some other examples from this source will be discussed later in this chapter.

Shii interpretations are also expressed in exegetical works written by local Shii Islamic scholars. For example, in Amin Ramin's untitled

---

16   Seied Kamal Fakikh Imani, *Svet Sviashchennogo Korana. Raz"iasneniia i tolkovaniia*, Vol. 1, trans. by Sayyed Abbas Sadr Ameli (St. Petersburg: Peterburgskoe Vostokovedenie, 2011).

17   Abū ʿAbd Allāh Muḥammad b. Ibrāhīm b. Jaʿfar al-Nuʿmānī, *al-Ghayba*, trans. by Airat Baeshev, p. 42, https://arsh313.com/al-gajba-numani/; the translation of the Qur'anic verses here, and elsewhere (unless otherwise indicated) is from the phrase-by-phrase English translation by Ali Quli Qara'i: *The Qur'an with a Phrase-by-Phrase English Translation* (London: Islamic College for Advanced Studies Press, 2005).

tafsīr[18], as well as his translation of volumes 1, 2, and 8 of Hashim al-Baḥrānī's (~1050/1640–1 to 1107/1695–6 or 1109/1697–8) *al-Burhān fī tafsīr al-Qurʾān*.[19] More specifically, Nazim Zeinalov in his *Sorok rasskazov Sviashchennogo Korana o semeistve Proroka* ('Forty Stories of the Holy Qur'an about the Family of the Prophet') collected stories and references from the Qur'an about the family of the Prophet which, in his opinion, are edifying for the faithful, who need to know them so that they can use them as exemplars for their own behaviour, and learn lessons from them.[20] In this work, he not only cites the Qur'anic verses but also draws on dozens of books on the history of Islam and the interpretation of the Qur'an, as well as *ḥadīth* collections, drawing on the Prophetic Sunna as well as the Qur'an itself. Zeinalov is also notable for being the author of the first Shii translation of the Qur'an into Russian.

Academic Translations: Prozorov's Translation of *Tafsīr al-Mīzān*

Al-Mīzān fī tafsīr al-Qurʾān, better known as *Tafsīr al-Mīzān*, was written by a famous theologian and philosopher of the twentieth century, Muḥammad Ḥusayn Ṭabāṭabāʾī (1321/1904–1402/1981), and is used by Shii and Sunni Muslims alike—partly because Ṭabāṭabāʾī used the Qur'an itself as the primary source for interpretation,[21] but also because he drew on a diverse range of both Shii and non-Shii sources in his interpretation of individual verses.[22] A partial translation of this *tafsīr* into Russian, specifically its preface and *Sūrat al-Fātiḥa*, has been produced by Prozorov under the Russian title *Vesy (spravedlivosti) v tolkovanii Korana* ('The Balance (of Equity) in Commentary on the Qur'an').

---

18 Amin Ramin, Tafsir Sviashchennogo Korana, *Arsh313*, 7 April 2022, https://arsh313.com/tafsir-svyashhennogo-korana-tom-1-amin-ramin/
19 Bakhrani, Seiid Khashim, *Tafsir "Burkhan"*, trans. by Amin Ramin, https://arsh313.com/tafsir-Burhan-tom-8/
20 Nazim Zeinalov, *Sorok rasskazov Svyashchennogo Korana o semeistve Proroka* (Moscow: Istok, 2009).
21 See, for example, Sohaib Saeed Bhutta 'Intraquranic Hermeneutics: Theories and Methods in Tafsīr of the Qurʾān through the Qurʾān' (doctoral thesis, SOAS University of London, 2017).
22 Abdul Wahid and Mazlan Ibrahim, 'The Characteristics of Tafsir al-Mīzān by Thabathaba'iy', *Jurnal Ilmiah Al-Mu'ashirah: Media Kajian Al-Qur'an dan Hadis Multi Perspektif*, 20:1 (2023), 27–38.

Prozorov was an academic who already had experience in translating Shii classical literature from Arabic into Russian, having authored an annotated translation of the *Kitāb Firaq al-Shīʿa* of Abū Muḥammad al-Ḥasan b. Mūsā al-Nawbakhtī (d. after 300/912), published under the title *Shiitskie sekty* ('The Shiite Sects').[23] In his translator's preface to his partial translation of *al-Mīzān fī tafsīr al-Qurʾān*, Prozorov highlights the fact that this constituted the first attempt in Russian Islamic studies to convey a Shii scholar's interpretation of the Qur'an, and states that he had chosen this particular *tafsīr* due to its significance and popularity. This translation was undertaken with the financial support of the Cultural Centre at the Embassy of the Islamic Republic of Iran in the Russian Federation, and it used two pre-existing Russian translations authored by non-Muslims—I. Y. Krachkovskii's *Koran* and G. S. Sablukov's *Koran perevod smyslov*—for all its Qur'anic quotations. This is quite demonstrative of the gap in the literature at that time, because a Qur'an translation with an explicitly Shii affiliation would have been more relevant for this project, but no such translations were available to use.

Ṭabāṭabāʾī's preface to *al-Mīzān* gives a brief history of the interpretation of the Qur'an, starting with a discussion on the Companions and *tābiʿūn*, and elucidates the exegetical 'mistakes' made by some interpreters of the Qur'an. Ṭabāṭabāʾī points out that exegetes parted ways after the branching of the different schools (*madhhabs*), and they lost the connection between personal opinion (*al-raʾy*) and (speculative) reasoning (*al-nazar*). And, he says, they disagreed about details such as the meaning of the divine names, God's attributes, predestination (*al-qadar*), rewards and punishments, death, the period between death and resurrection (*al-barzakh*), the Resurrection itself, and Paradise and Hell. The *muḥaddithūn* (transmitters of traditions) limited themselves to 'interpretation' through oral transmission of the words of the pious ancestors among the Companions and *tābiʿūn*. Ṭabāṭabāʾī writes that they were mistaken in this, because God in His Scripture did not declare the use of reason to be false. He goes on to say that scholastic theologians lost themselves in the abyss of grammatical 'exercises' and allegorical interpretations of verses in ways that contradicted their obvious (*ẓāhir*) meaning.

---

23   al-Khasan ibn Musa an-Naubakhti, *Shiitskie sekty*, trans. and ed. by S. M. Prozorova (Moscow: Nauka, 1973).

After criticising his predecessors, Ṭabāṭabāʾī moved on to outline and justify his own methodological approach, according to which he interpreted the Qur'an by means of the Qur'an, extracting the meaning from its original verses. In doing so, he appealed to the Qur'an itself, citing Q 16:89, 'We have sent down the Book to you as a clarification of all things and as a guidance and mercy [...]', commenting that not only does the Qur'an explain everything, it also explains itself.[24] Ṭabāṭabāʾī also justified his approach on the basis that his 'new' method of exegesis was in reality a continuation of the oldest, original method—the method used by the Prophet and the Imams. He also explains that this is why his *tafsīr* incorporates *ḥadīths* from these sources that were transmitted by both Shii and Sunni narrators. Ṭabāṭabāʾī's inclusion of Sunni material reflects his desire to engage non-Shii readers, as well as the fact that his *tafsīr* addresses various philosophical, social, and ethical topics that could incidentally attract a wider readership. Unfortunately, since Prozorov translated only the preface and first *sura*, the majority of the work is not accessible to Russian readers.

Prozorov notes that Ṭabāṭabāʾī, who preached the principle of the Qur'an's self-sufficiency, divided his interpretation of the Qur'an into several types.[25] First of all, he especially emphasises the concept of Qur'anic interpretation in accordance with the principle of *tafsīr al-Qurʾān biʾl-Qurʾān* ('the interpretation of the Qur'an through the Qur'an'), calling such interpretation 'clarification'. He also uses *ḥadīth*; religious, philosophical, and moral argumentation; historical material; or combinations of these types of interpretation. Al-Ṭabāṭabāʾī discusses each selected fragment of the Qur'an using a different combination of these types of interpretation, but the only type of interpretation that permeates the entire text of the work is the *tafsīr al-Qurʾān biʾl-Qurʾān* approach, which provides the basis for the rest of his exposition. He considers all other types of interpretation acceptable, but secondary, and suggests that they do not give a complete and deep understanding of the content of the divine revelation.[26]

Prior to *Tafsīr al-Mīzān*, it was unusual for exegetes to compare Qur'anic verses on the same subject in order to reach a definite conclusion

---

24 Prozorov, 'The Balance (of Equity)', pp. 84–85.
25 Ibid., p. 82.
26 Ibid.

regarding a given concept, as Ṭabāṭabāʾī did in this innovative work. For example, in his treatment of the stories of the prophets in the Qur'an, he collated all the verses from different *suras* concerning the history of a specific prophet, and then provided a comprehensive account of this prophet's life. Another distinctive feature of his *tafsīr* is the fact that, on the one hand, it deals with his opponents' objections to his approach, and on the other hand, it tries to present an understanding of religious beliefs that is compatible with the society of his time, and which engages with new scientific, philosophical, and theological ideas.[27]

In order to better understand the peculiarities of this interpretation, and to better appreciate Ṭabāṭabāʾī's insistence on *tafsīr al-Qurʾān bi'l-Qurʾān*, let us consider a small passage from his *tafsīr*, namely the interpretation of two words used to describe God in the first verse of *Sūrat al-Fātiḥa*, occurring in a phrase that is used at the beginning of every subsequent *sura* of the Qur'an: *bi-smi l-raḥmāni l-raḥīm*. Both words, *al-raḥmān* and *al-raḥīm*, are derived from the word *raḥmā* ('mercy'). According to Ṭabāṭabāʾī, *al-raḥmān* indicates the abundant divine mercy directed at both the believer and the unbeliever, and is often used in this sense in the Qur'an. He provides a number of examples of this usage, citing Q 20:5, 'the All-beneficent (*al-raḥmān*) settled on the Throne', and Q 19:75, 'Say, "Whoever abides in error, the All-beneficent (*al-raḥmān*) shall prolong his respite until they sight what they have been promised".' In contrast, Ṭabāṭabāʾī writes, *al-raḥīm* indicates the constant beneficence and the unceasing, eternal divine mercy directed at the believer, as indicated in the following verses: '[...] and He is most merciful (*raḥīm*) to the faithful' (Q 33:43), and '[...] indeed He is most kind and merciful (*raḥīm*) to them' (Q 9:117). Thus, he asserts that *al-raḥmān* is common to the believer and unbeliever, while *al-raḥīm* refers to divine mercy that is reserved exclusively for the believer.[28]

Prozorov's translation was aimed primarily at an academic readership, since it was published in an academic journal and focused on the translation of the preface and first *sura*, in which Ṭabāṭabāʾī sets out his methodological apparatus and agenda. The preface, outlining the general features of Ṭabāṭabāʾī's interpretive method, cannot be useful to lay Muslims in their understanding of the Qur'an for everyday life.

---

27 Rida Ustadi, *Ashnayi ba tafasir* (Tehran: Nashr-i Quds, 1963), pp. 228–231.
28 Prozorov, 'The Balance (of Equity)', pp. 95–96.

In addition to Prozorov's translation, two volumes of this *tafsīr* were also translated by Taras Chernienko in the early 2010s, by order of the representative office of the Al-Mustafa International University (Qom) in Russia, but, unfortunately, these were never published. Chernienko is an active Russian convert to Shiism who speaks Arabic and Farsi, and a graduate of the Faculty of Arabic Language and Literature at Kuwait State University. Previously, he had translated *Nahj al-balāgha* ('The Path of Eloquence') into Russian—this is a collection of sermons, letters, and sayings of great importance to Shii Muslims, attributed to ʿAlī b. Abī Ṭālib.[29]

Iranian-Authored Translations: *Svet Sviashchennogo Korana: Raz'iasneniia i tolkovaniia*

Svet Sviashchennogo Korana: Raz'iasneniia i tolkovaniia ('The Light of the Holy Qur'an: Explanations and Interpretations')[30] is the translation of a Persian *tafsīr* titled *Nūr al-Qurʾān fī tafsīr al-Qurʾān*, which was prepared by a group of authoritative Muslim theologians under the leadership of Saied Kamal Fakikh Imani (Sayyid Kamāl Faqīh Imānī): an Iranian cleric at the Islamic Centre for Scientific Research in the Islamic Republic of Iran. In addition to Russian, *Nūr al-Qurʾān* has been translated into many other languages. Also, Imani has authored numerous other works; for instance, to an English-speaking audience, he is known for *A Bundle of Flowers from the Garden of Traditions of the Prophet (S) & Ahlul Bayt (A)*,[31] but his *tafsīr* is widely considered to be his main achievement. Work on the Russian translation began in 1991, and this involved preparing a complete set of interpretations and commentary

---

29 Imam Ali, *Put' krasnorechiia*, trans. by Taras Chernienko (Moscow: Vostochnaia Literatura, 2007). This is a translation with commentary from Arabic discourses, attributed to Alī b. Abī Ṭālib from *Nahj al-balāgha*.

30 Seied Kamal Fakikh Imani, *Svet Sviashchennogo Korana. Raz"iasneniia i tolkovaniia*, trans. by Sayyed Abbas Sadr Ameli (St. Petersburg: Peterburgskoe Vostokovedenie, 2011).

31 Sayyid Kamal Faqih Imani, *A Bundle of Flowers from the Garden of Traditions of the Prophet [S] & Ahlul Bayt [A]*, trans. by Sayyid Abbas Sadr-'ameli and Celeste Smith (Isfahan: Amir ul-Mu'mineen Ali Library, 1998), https://www.al-islam.org/bundle-flowers-garden-traditions-prophet-ahlul-bayt

7. Implications of Theological Diversity in Shii-Authored Translations 291

on the Qur'an, then translating this into various languages.[32] In the early 2000s, a Russian translation was published in eight volumes, translated by Sayyed Abbas Sadr Ameli and edited by Nazim Zeinalov. The team relied on various different existing Russian translations of the Qur'an for the actual Qur'anic verses, selected on the basis that they offered the best style and, in their view, the most accurate meaning. However, in some cases, Ameli and Zeinalov also amended the wording of existing translations to more closely reflect the original Qur'anic text and allow for a specifically Shii interpretation.

The original preface by Imani and his translation team explains the need for interpretations of the Qur'an and the methodological particularities of this specific *tafsīr*. The authors state that an accurate, theologically and linguistically correct translation of the Qur'an is certainly necessary, but point out that sometimes this is not enough for the reader to fully understand all the explicit and implicit meanings of its verses. There is almost always a need for additional information. For example, sometimes, in order to understand a verse, it is necessary to know the circumstances of its revelation. It may also be useful to know what semantic changes a specific word has undergone over time, which meaning was in circulation at the time of the Qur'an's revelation, and what it means in modern Arabic. A typical Shii perspective is also presented on the Prophet's and the *ahl al-bayt*'s exclusive knowledge of and competence in interpreting the Qur'an (drawing on the *ḥadīth al-thaqalayn*, for example, which states that the Qur'an is inextricably linked with members of Prophet's family and that Muslims, in order not to go astray, must follow both the teachings of the Qur'an and the *sunna* of the *ahl al-bayt*). According to this view, interpreting the Qur'an allows us to find out the specific circumstances under which a verse or group of verses were revealed to the Prophet, but these verses still have their own general meanings. A particular event might belong to the past, but its generalised meaning remains relevant at all times, illuminating the

---

32 An English translation has been published under the title *An Enlightening Commentary into the Light of the Holy Qur'an* (Isfahan: Amir-ul-Mu'menen Ali Library, 1994).

world with the 'light of truth': 'This is one of the miracles of the Qur'an, which each new generation rediscovers through interpretation.'³³

In many ways, this *tafsīr* has a 'contemporary' character, as it tries to interpret verses of the Qur'an in the light of contemporaneous events. For example, the authors of this *tafsīr* often refer to achievements in modern sciences such as advancements in embryology, the doctrine of evolution, and scientific discoveries about space, as well as to the problems that plague contemporary society such as perceived increases in corruption, oppression, injustice, and war, drawing attention to the ways the Qur'an teaches us to react to these problems.

The exegesis follows a standardised structure: it begins by presenting the name of the *sura* in transliteration and in Russian translation, followed by information about the number of verses, the place of revelation (Mecca or Medina), the benefits of reading the *sura* (in a religious context), and the content of the *sura*. This then leads into commentary on each verse or group of verses, citing selected *ḥadīth*s on the topics raised in the specific verse(s).

The translation proved to be significant for the Russian speaking audience as it was published by various different publishers, which tells us that there was a strong interest in this particular book. While the different printed editions were practically identical reprints of the same translation, some of the publishers encountered significant problems with Russian censorship, in particular the Iran-based Tsentr islamovedcheskikh issledovanii Imam Amir al'-muminin Ali and the Russian Sadra publishing house.³⁴ In 2011, the fourth volume of the book published by the Iran-based organisation was included in the Federal List of Extremist Materials, and in 2020 it was re-recognised as such by court decision which also opted to censor the same translation published by the Sadra publishing house.³⁵ This means that the entire

---

33   Seied Kamal Fakikh Imani, *Svet Sviashchennogo Korana. Raz"iasneniia i tolkovaniia, Vol. 1*, trans. by Sayyed Abbas Sadr Ameli (St. Petersburg: Peterburgskoe Vostokovedenie, 2011), p. 4.

34   For more information about these publishers' censorship problems, see 'Povtorno priznan ekstremistskim chetvertyi tom tafsira sovremennykh iranskikh bogoslovov', *SOVA*, https://www.sova-center.ru/misuse/news/persecution/2020/08/d42769/

35   The decision to ban the work was taken by the Sovetskii District Court of Astrakhan in 2019, and approved by the Astrakhan Regional Court a year later, when they rejected the publisher's appeal against the decision.

Russian translation of the *tafsīr* is prohibited, except for the original Arabic verses and the actual translation of the Qur'anic text. The underlying issue that led to the ban seems to lie in the commentaries on *Sūrat al-Tawba* (as well as a few other chapters) which discuss the concept of *jihād*—which is either presented as a transliterated word or as 'sviashchennaia voina' ('the holy war'). These commentaries also use the word *mujāhidūn*, which the court interpreted to be extremist. It seems the court missed the exegetical explanation in this same chapter, which clearly states that *jihād* should be understood as 'a collective duty of Muslims, not a personal matter for everyone. Therefore, under the conditions of an Islamic regime, participation or non-participation in it requires the permission of the leader of the Muslim community.'[36]

The court's decision to include this title in the Federal List of Extremist Materials prohibits its distribution, production, or storage for the purpose of distribution on the territory of the Russian Federation.[37] This reflects a hardline policy of censorship that is applied to all kinds of Islamic literature.

It should be emphasised that, due to the modern[38] and non-denominational nature of *Svet Sviashchennogo Korana*, it was popular among both Shiis and Sunnis, and could even be found in Sunni mosques. In 2015, the Sadra publishing house published another translation based on *Svet Sviashchennogo Korana*, titled *Koran. Prochtenie smyslov* ('Qur'an: Reading the Meanings'). This was primarily a phrase-by-phrase translation, although in some cases the translators presented a specifically Shii interpretation inserted in square brackets. For example, they include an interpolation on Q 4:24 that indicates the permissibility of temporary marriage: 'Compensate them for the pleasure you receive from them [in a temporary marriage] according to the established terms'.[39]

---

36 Seied Kamal Fakikh Imani, *Svet Sviashchennogo Korana. Raz"iasneniia i tolkovaniia*, Vol. IV, trans. by Sayyed Abbas Sadr Ameli (St. Petersburg: Peterburgskoe Vostokovedenie, 2008), p. 166.

37 'Ekstremistskii material №1070 - Kniga "Svet sviashchennogo Korana (raz"iasneniia i tolkovaniia)" tom IV', *Lidrekon*, https://lidrekon.ru/1070

38 For more on modern Shii interpretations of the Qur'an, see: Akif Tahiiev, 'Understanding the 'Spirit' of Qurᵓānic Laws in Contemporary Shīʿī Islamic Thought', *Interdisciplinary Journal for Religion and Transformation in Contemporary Society*, (published online ahead of print, 2024).

39 Mukhetdinov, 'The Russian Qur'ān Translations', pp. 63–64.

Translations by Local Shii Scholars

Amin Ramin's *tafsīr* and Translation of al-Sayyid Hāshim al-Baḥrānī's *al-Burhān fī tafsīr al-Qurʾān*

In January 2017, Amin Ramin uploaded his translation of the eighth and final volume of Seiid Khashim Bakhrani's (al-Sayyid Hāshim al-Baḥrānī, c. 1050/1640 to 1107/1696 or 1109/1698) *al-Burhān fī tafsīr al-Qurʾān* to his portal *Arsh313*.[40] By the end of the same year, his translation of the first volume of this *tafsīr* had also been uploaded, followed by the second volume in 2020. At the time of writing, he is working on translating the third volume of this work, and chapters are being uploaded as they are translated. *Arsh313* is known for publishing translations of classical Shii works and sermons in Russian. It provides access to articles, videos, podcasts, prayers (*duʿāʾ and ziyāra*), *ḥadīth*s, and a library of books in Russian. One of its main features is the provision of a large number of translations of classical Shii religious literature, including works such as al-Kulaynī's *al-Kāfī*, al-Ṣadūq's *al-Tawḥīd* and *Kamāl al-dīn wa-tamām al-niʿma*, and, last but not least, Hāshim Baḥrānī's *al-Burhān fī tafsīr al-Qurʾān*.[41] The founder and main author of the project, Amin Ramin, is an independent researcher and convert to Shii Islam. He earned a PhD in philosophy from a Russian university, and later received a religious education at the seminaries of Qom and Najaf.[42]

According to Amin Ramin, *al-Burhān* is the best and most complete Shii *tafsīr*, consisting entirely of *ḥadīth* passed down from the *ahl al-bayt*. This feature is noteworthy because al-Baḥrānī was writing during the seventeenth century, an era which has been defined by a struggle between rationalists and traditionalists regarding Shii jurisprudence.[43] This was due to the new presence of Akhbārīs and their conflict with the Uṣūlis, named after their adherence to *ʿilm al-uṣūl* ('the principles

---

40   https://arsh313.com/
41   Akif Tahiiev, 'Shiizm na postsovetskom prostranstve: vliianie novykh media', in *Virtual Islam: Identity, Authorities and Religious Practices of Muslims in the Digital Age*, ed. by Z. Khabibullina and E. Muratova (Baku: Idrak, 2023) p. 100.
42   Amin Ramin, 'About me', https://aminramin.net/about/
43   Heinz Halm, *Shia Islam: From Religion to Revolution*, trans. by Allison Brown (Princeton: Markus Wiener Publishers, 1997), p. 112.

of jurisprudence', or 'the science of the sources of law'). The Uṣūlīs legitimised the use of *ijtihād* in Shii Islamic thought, but in a particular way—that is, in terms of the deductive derivation of legal norms from primary sources. The Akhbārīs, in contrast, held the opposite position and believed that during the major occultation of the 'hidden Imam', Shii theologians could not formulate new legal norms, citing as an example the negative attitude of Shii imams towards *ijtihād* and *qiyās*. In their opinion, Shii theologians should be like the *muḥaddithūn*, who engaged exclusively in collecting *ḥadīth*. In addition, the Akhbārīs believed that almost all Shii *ḥadīth*s are trustworthy and the science of *rijāl* (verifying the identities of *ḥadīth* transmitters) is unnecessary. Historically, the Akhbārīs lost the debate because they were unable to offer answers to the new challenges that arose within the Shii community, and they currently have a much smaller number of followers than the Uṣūlīs. But, in the seventeenth and eighteenth centuries, the Akhbārī movement set a trend, so Shii scholars returned to *ḥadīth* studies after a long break.[44] Mukhammad Bakir al-Sadr (Muḥammad Bāqir al-Ṣadr, 1353/1934 or 1935–1400/1980) noted that this trend came about for various reasons, the most important being the discovery of new *ḥadīth* materials at that time. Accordingly, new collections had to be complied to include these.[45] Thus, some of the largest *ḥadīth* collections came into being, such as the *Wasāʾil al-Shīʿa* by al-Ḥurr al-ʿĀmilī and *Biḥār al-anwār* by Muḥammad Bāqir al-Majlisī, and *tafsīr*s were written that drew exclusively on *ḥadīth* attributed to the Prophet and Imams, most famously Mullā Muḥsin Fayḍ Kāshānī's *al-Ṣāfīʾ*, ʿAbd ʿAlī al-ʿArūsī Ḥuwayzī's *Nūr al-thaqalayn*, and al-Baḥrānī's *al-Burhān*. Since the authors of the aforementioned *tafsīr* were mostly Akhbārīs, their works contained only the texts of the *ḥadīth*s they cited with almost no additional commentary, because the Akhbārīs denied the competence of anyone other than the Prophet and the Imams to interpret the Qur'an.

In *al-Burhān*, al-Baḥrānī uses the following structure: he first mentions the name of the *sura* he is discussing, then the place in which it was revealed, the merits of the *sura*, and its number of verses. He goes on

---

44 Akif Tahiiev 'Islams'ke pravo: osoblivosti shiits'koï doktrini' (doctoral thesis, Yaroslav Mudryi National Law University, 2021), pp. 35–36.
45 Mukhammad Bakir al-Sadr, *Kratkaia istoriia ilm al'-usul*, trans by A. A. Ezhova (Moscow: Sadra, 2009), p. 54.

to refer to the verses with special *ḥadīth*s, explaining their content and discussing them. Some scholars note that the main drawbacks of this work were the inclusion of unreliable *ḥadīth*s and the general lack of analysis. For example, Muḥammad Mahdī al-Āṣifī (1356/1937 or 1938–1436/2015) wrote that despite the author's considerable efforts, there are some unauthentic and distorted *ḥadīth*s in *al-Burhān*. He explains that the author most likely did not have the clarification of unreliable *ḥadīth* in mind, or did not prioritise it enough. Al-Baḥrānī included material transmitted by sources who stand accused of distorting *ḥadīth*s, and some *ḥadīth*s that have unreliable *isnād*s ('chains of narrators') and incoherent content. Hence, al-Āṣifī concludes that *al-Burhān* is a useful source for scholars who are familiar with the primary sources and aware of reliable and consistent *ḥadīth*s and can thus distinguish between authentic and unauthentic material, but not necessarily for the average lay Muslim. Although this *tafsīr* has been the subject of criticism by some scholars, it still remains important, simply because it is the largest *ḥadīth* collection dedicated to the interpretation of the Qur'an.[46] According to Amin Ramin, this was the main reason he chose to translate this particular *tafsīr*. Overall, the work is undeniably a major and important contribution to the Shii library.

In April 2022, Ramin uploaded the first volume of his own untitled *tafsīr* to the portal *Arsh313*. His *tafsīr* contains all the same *ḥadīth*s that are found in *al-Burhān* but with his own, more detailed explanation and commentaries. His comments allow the reader to analyse and understand the intended meaning of the *ḥadīth*s from *al-Burhān* on the basis that, according to Ramin himself, something important can be gleaned from each *ḥadīth* (although it must be noted here that Ramin is not an Akhbārī, as he has repeatedly made clear).[47]

Amin Ramin writes that *Sūrat al-Fātiḥa* can be translated as 'Otkryvaiushchaia' ('Opening') and is the first *sura*, which opens the Qur'an, and so the entire Qur'an is contained within it, as it were, 'v svernutom vide' (in a 'folded up' form, condensed). Then he goes on to

---

46 Baḥrānī, Hāshim. *al-Burhān fī tafsīr al-Qurʾān*. Introduction by Muḥammad Mahdī Āṣifī. (Tehran: Muʾassasa-yi Baʿthat, 1334 Sh./1955).
47 For bibliographical information about Amin Ramin, see Amin Ramin, 'Amin Ramin rasskazyvaet o sebe, svoei deiatel'nosti i nauchnoi kompetentsii', *Arsh313*, 24 October 2022, https://arsh313.com/amin-ramin-rasskazyvaet-o-sebe/

say that *Sūrat al-Fātiḥa* is also the 'sredotochie' ('focus', 'centre') of the Qur'an; the entire Qur'an is 'zashifrovan' ('encoded') in it, he argues, citing Muḥammad's saying 'There is no prayer, except with *al-Fātiḥa*', and commenting that every believer reads it at least ten times a day (i.e. during the five obligatory prayers). Ramin goes on to say that this *sura* begins by mentioning *tawḥīd* ('monotheism') and praising the Almighty, then he describes the *ahl al-bayt* and the path of the believer. He asserts that the 'straight path' in *Sūrat al-Fātiḥa* is nothing other than the *wilāya* of the *ahl al-bayt*, and that the number of letters in *Sūrat al-Fātiḥa* is significant—140, which corresponds to the number of Infallibles (who, according to Shii Twelvers, are the Prophet Muḥammad, his daughter Fāṭima, and the twelve Imams). This *sura*, he says, has several names: *al-Fātiḥa* ('The Opening'), *Ḥamd* ('Praise'), and *Umm al-kitāb* ('The Mother of the Book'). Finally, Ramin concludes that all *ḥadīth*s indicate that the 'straight path' in *Sūrat al-Fātiḥa* refers to ʿAlī, citing Q 4:34:

> The expression 'Mother of the Book' is used both in *ḥadīth*s and in the Qur'an itself: 'Indeed, it is in the Mother of the Book, with Us—ʿAlī is the wise one' (Q 43:4). And this is [a reference to] the leader of the faithful [i.e. Ali] in the Mother of the Book (i.e. *Sūrat al-Fātiḥa*), namely, in the words 'straight path.'[48]

Of particular interest are the fragments of Ramin's translations of the Qur'an, such as Q 43:4 cited above (*wa-innahu fī umma l-kitābi ladaynā la-ʿaliyun ḥakīmun*). This is usually translated along the lines of 'and indeed it is with Us, in the Mother of the Book [and it is] surely sublime and wise'—without any reference to ʿAlī. Almost all translators of the Qur'an (even Zeinalov in his Shii translation, which will be discussed in the following section) translate the word ʿ*alī* in Q 4:34 along the lines of 'wise', 'exalted', or 'esteemed', rather than translating it as the name. Since Ramin has only provided his reading of the first and second *suras* so far, it is not yet possible to see how often he translates the verses of the Qur'an in such a specific way. However, we can presume that he is likely to do so relatively frequently since the whole *tafsīr* is presented in

---

48 Amin Ramin, 'Tafsir Sviashchennogo Korana', *Arsh313*, 7 April 2022, https://arsh313.com/tafsir-svyashhennogo-korana-tom-1-amin-ramin/
The translation of Q 4:34 given here is an English rendering of the Russian translation by Amin Ramin from his *tafsīr*.

a consistent fashion, and the interpretations of most verses elaborate on the merits of the *ahl al-bayt*.

Nazim Zeinalov's *Sviashchennyi Koran. Perevod i kommentarii*[49]

The translators of the various works explored above, as well as other Islamic works, have often referred to the absence of a Shii translation of the Qur'an into Russian. One attempt to rectify this was made in 2015 when the academic publishing house Peterburgskoe vostokovedenie (Petersburg Oriental Studies), with the support and assistance of the Ministry of Culture and Islamic Education of the Islamic Republic of Iran, published the first ever Russian Shii translation of the Qur'an.[50] The translator of this work was Nazim Zeinalov, who was previously involved in editorial work on the *tafsīr Svet Sviashchennogo Korana: Raz'iasneniia i tolkovaniia* mentioned earlier. He is also the author and translator of a large quantity of Russian Shii literature. Zeinalov began to translate books on Islamic law, theology, morality, and related topics at the beginning of the 2000s while studying in Qom, driven by his concern that there were very few books on these topics in Russian at that time, and his belief that society needed more knowledge (especially Shii knowledge). He was also the first person to translate works on Shii *fiqh* into Russian, including *Prakticheskie zapovedi Islama (dlya molodezhi)* ('The Practical Commandments of Islam (for the Youth)').[51] Since 1999, he has begun to publish translations of a variety of Islamic materials, in addition to articles on Islamic topics, on various websites.[52] Zeinalov began working on the translation of specific Qur'anic verses in the late 1990s and early 2000s, when he translated books on various religious topics. For example, he translated numerous verses during the preparation of his aforementioned *Sorok rasskazov Sviashchennogo Korana o semeistve Proroka*. Independently, he also began to translate the

---

49 Nazim. A. Zeinalov (trans.), *Sviashchennyi Koran. Perevod i kommentarii* (St. Petersburg: Peterburgskoe vostokovedenie, 2016).
50 Mukhetdinov, 'The Russian Qur'ān Translations', p. 62.
51 Seiid Ali Sistani, *Prakticheskie zapovedi Islama (dlia molodezhi)*, trans. by Nazim Zeinalov (Moscow: Organizatsiia Imam Ali, 1999).
52 For example, on the multilingual site *al-Shia.com*, which later changed its domain name to *al-Shia.org* and was the first site to publish Shii materials in Russian.

entire Qur'an in 2011 while he was living in Derbent, a city in Dagestan which is one of the oldest historical centres of Shiism in Russia. There, Zeinalov translated approximately twelve *juzʾ*s of the Qur'an. After moving to Moscow, he spent over two years working at the offices of the Iranian al-Mustafa International University, during which time he translated several more *juzʾ*s. He finally completed the work in Istanbul, then decided to edit the entire text. Returning to Qom, he was immersed in the scholarly environment, where he benefited from the expertise of local scholars. The editorial process spanned six months, and the translation was finally published in 2015.[53] Zeinalov emphasised that his work marked the first 'theological' Russian translation of the Qur'an, pointing out that previous translations were either undertaken by non-Muslims or by Sunni Muslims lacking a specialised Islamic religious education.[54] In fact, there were other Russian translators of the Qur'an with a theological background and education, but Zeinalov was the first with specifically Shii theological training.

Zeinalov's translation contains both his Russian translation of the verses and the parallel Arabic text. In terms of translation methodology, Zeinalov states that he combined two main methods of translation—literal (phrase-by-phrase) and semantic—because, in his opinion, it would be wrong to use only one of these two methods since misinterpretations are usually introduced by either excessive literalism, or, conversely, excessive freedom of translation. He takes the position that phrase-by-phrase translation should be adopted as the basis for the target text, while semantics should be used to facilitate understanding. Each language has its own set of set expressions that carry a certain meaning—for example, the idiom 'to follow in someone's footsteps' does not literally mean stepping where another person has trodden but instead indicates copying another person's figurative path in life. A literal translation of such a phrase into another language may be incomprehensible to the reader, as it might completely lose the original meaning. In such cases, Zeinalov advocates the use of semantic translation, whereby

---

53   This information was derived from an interview conducted by Reza Kerbelai with Nazim Zeinalov, titled 'Nazim Zeinalov mnogoletnii put' k perevodu Sviashchennogo Korana', and published on the currently unavailable Russian internet portal *shia.world*.
54   Ibid.

an expression is used to convey the meaning of an idiom as a whole rather than the literal meaning of its individual words. When it comes to grammatical aspects of the Qur'anic text, he tried to convey its verses in a form that mirrors the Arabic constructions as accurately as possible, aiming to replicate the same particles, prepositions, and word forms found in the original. His translation also paid close attention to the etymology and semantics of both languages, especially in the preservation of verb roots. In addition to this combination of translation methods, he also added commentary in the form of notes, which contain information about such aspects as the circumstances of revelation of the verses, the merits of reading a particular *sura*, relevant historical events or personalities, and numerous references to the Bible. More than a thousand *ḥadīth*s commenting on the Qur'anic verses were cited, all of which were originally transmitted from the *ahl al-bayt*. He also provides readers with a glossary of Qur'anic expressions located at the end of his translation, after the text itself.

Zeinalov's approach is also characterised by his focus on the considerable distance between the seventh and twenty-first centuries, which leaves a huge mark on the semantic aspect of the text. According to him, nowadays even native speakers of Arabic have difficulty understanding the Qur'anic text due to its specific structure and language, which is very different from modern literary Arabic. He writes that he wanted to convey this experience of Arabic native speakers when reading the Qur'an, so that Russian-speaking readers of the translation could experience the same stylistic novelty.[55] In general, he achieved this through lexical and syntactic archaisms. As an example of this style of narration, as well as one of the distinguishing differences between Sunni and Shii translations and exegetical traditions[56], consider the interpretation of Q 5:55. Sunni translators usually translate the second part of this verse (*alladhīna āmanū lladhīna yuqiymūna l-ṣalāta wa-yuʾtūna l-zakāta wa-hum rākiʿūna*) as referring to 'those who keep up the prayer, pay the prescribed

---

55   Ibid.
56   For more on the reasons behind differences between Sunni and Shii translations and exegetical traditions, see: Akif Tahiiev, 'Impact of the Events of Saqifa on the Formation of Differences between the Islamic Sunni and Shia Tradition', *Journal of Al-Tamaddun*, 18:1 (2023).

alms, and bow down in worship.'⁵⁷ However Zeinalov—like almost all other Shii translators—instead translates this as 'those who believe, who pray, and give cleansing [alms], while they bow.'⁵⁸ This reading is based on the Shii reliance on a specific *ḥadīth* considered to be reliable. According to this, during the revelation of this verse to the Prophet, ᶜAlī was in the mosque praying and, during his 'belt-low bowing' (*rukūᶜ*), he took off his ring and gave it to the poor as alms.

Zeinalov's translation is available on the websites quranonline.ru and quranica.info. The former also provides transliteration of each verse into Russian, and, in addition to Zeinalov's Russian translation, it also provides Mirza ᶜAlī Meshkini Ardabili's Azerbaijani translation and ᶜAlī Quli Qarai's English translation, all of which align with the Shii interpretative approach. Quranonline.ru also offers Russian translations of various *ḥadīth*s from Ramin's translation of volumes 1, 2, and 8 of al-Baḥrānī's *al-Burhān*. Quranica.info provides only Zeinalov's translations of the Qur'an, as well as commentary and additional interpretations prepared by him. In order to facilitate the understanding of the text of every *sura*, and to inform readers about the historical events and personalities mentioned in the Qur'an, he supplements his translation with *ḥadīth*s about the merits of reading each *sura*, as well as *asbāb al-nuzūl* mostly cited from Sharīf al-Raḍī's *Nahj al-balāgha*, al-Kulaynī's *al-Kāfī*, al-Kāshānī's *al-Ṣāfī*, al-Qummī's *Safīnat al-biḥār*, al-Majlisī's *Biḥār al-anwār*, al-Ṭabrisī's *Majmaᶜ al-bayān*, Ṭabāṭabāʾī's *al-Mīzān*, al-Baḥrānī's *al-Burhān*, al-Ḥuwayzī's *Nūr al-thaqalayn*, and Fakih Imani's *Nūr al-Qurʾān*.

In 2016, Zeinalov was awarded the Iranian 'Book of the Year' award for his Qur'an translation. This international award is one of the most prestigious awards for Islamic and Iranian scholars.⁵⁹ However, while in Shii circles Zeinalov's translation received quite positive reviews, Sunni theologians and other Islamic scholars were explicitly critical in their assessment of this translation. Some local Russian muftiates, especially in Dagestan and Chechnya, stated that his translation was 'not recommended for reading by believers, since it distorts the meaning of

---

57 The translation of the second part of Q 5:55 is taken from M. A. S. Abdel Haleem's translation, which is available at: https://quran.com/5?startingVerse=55
58 This is my translation of Zeinalov's rendering from Russian into English.
59 'Nazvany pobediteli regional'noi premii', *Parstoday*, 8 December 2016, https://parstoday.ir/ru/news/russia-i52648

the Qur'an and gives interpretations according to Shiism, and reading it can adversely affect a person's beliefs.'[60] These muftiates are under state control and often adhere to state-supported narratives of 'traditional Islam', which exclude Shii Islam. Hence, on the website of the Spiritual Administration of Muslims of the Chechen Republic, Zeinalov was accused of methodologically 'hiding his beliefs in order to spread Shii delusions' and distorting Qur'anic verses.[61] Taking a somewhat different approach, the theologian and author of a literary translation of the Qur'an into Azerbaijani, Nariman Gasimoglu, commented that the publication of a new translation of the Qur'an into Russian was of no importance, since there were already many Russian translations and Zeinalov's new version did not change anything.[62] Last but not least, Igor Alexeev, a Russian Islamicist, wondered why Zeinalov's translation was published by an academic publishing house rather than a Shii missionary centre. His view is that Shii interpretations of the Qur'an have not been sufficiently studied in Russia, but such studies require a strictly academic approach grounded in serious comparative analysis with other approaches to the interpretation of the Qur'anic text. In his opinion, Zeinalov has failed to do this and, accordingly, his translation is narrowly confessional and of no academic value, and should not be taken seriously by academics.[63] Alexeev also criticised Zeinalov's prioritisation of the preservation of the meanings of Arabic roots in derivatives of the same root forms in Russian. According to him, this mission is utopian and meaningless and not only does it harm the style of the target language, it also harms the meaning of the original text. He comments that

> [...] in a variety of ways (from the abuse of interpolations in brackets to the falsification of Arabic grammar for the sake of his own doctrinal preferences) [Zeinalov] reads into the Qur'anic text the meanings predetermined by the tradition of text interpretation, for which he is an apologist.[64]

---

60 'Kavkazovedy sochli maloveroyatnymi presledovaniia chitatelei Korana v perevode Zeinalova', *Kavkazskii Uzel*, 25 November 2016, https://www.kavkaz-uzel.eu/articles/293214/
61 Ibid.
62 'Teologi usomnilis'' v akademicheskoi tsennosti shiitskogo perevoda Korana', *Kavkazskij Uzel*, 11 May 2016, https://www.kavkaz-uzel.media/articles/280146/
63 'Teologi usomnilis''.
64 'Nauchnaia recenziia na pervyi shiitskii perevod Korana', *Islamoved*, 13 March 2016, http://islamoved.ru/2016/nauchnaya-retsenziya-na-pervyj-shiitskij-perevod-korana/

7. *Implications of Theological Diversity in Shii-Authored Translations*   303

Analysing the reviews of Zeinalov's translation, it is clear that the only objective criticism can be found in Alexeev's views on Zeinalov's attempt to preserve the roots of Arabic words; the primary critique directed at *Sviashchennyi Koran* was aimed at its clear association with Shii theology and beliefs. Generally, its alignment with Shii Islamic thought was viewed negatively in the Russian context where Sunni theologians find a more welcome reception. The same biased attitude can be traced in reviews across the board, and is expressed not only by Sunni clerics and theologians, but also by 'secular' scholars of Islam such as Alexeev, who expressed bewilderment that a Shii translation should be published by an academic publishing house.

Conclusion

This discussion has brought to light many characteristic features of Shii translations, and has identified the main actors in this field. Among the latter, there are academics (such as Prozorov), theologians who hail from the local ethnic Muslim population (Zeinalov), and Shii converts both with and without a religious education (Ramin and Chernienko, respectively). The active role of Iran and Iranian theologians and institutions should also be noted, since not only do they provide funding for 'local' figures such as Prozorov and Zeinalov, they also produce their own translations of the Qur'an and other Islamic texts, such as the *tafsīr Svet Sviashchennogo Korana: Raz"iasneniia i tolkovaniia*. Significantly, the non-denominational nature of this translation has allowed it to attract non-Shii readers and has given it more popularity than other Shii *tafsīr*s and translations. In contrast, local actors have always tended to actively emphasise their Shii affiliation, which has sometimes led to a negative reception of their works. This was the case with Zeinalov's translation, which was criticised by some Russian Sunni clerics solely on the basis of anti-Shii prejudice. It is also clear that just as the methodological approaches taken in these works differ, the perception of these *tafsīr*s and/or translations also largely depends on the approach taken by the author/translator.

It has also become apparent that texts are chosen for translation on an unsystematised basis, and that various genres and types of Qur'anic literature have been translated. For example, when it comes to *tafsīr* works, *al-Mīzān* is predominantly predicated on the methodology of 'interpreting the Qur'an through the Qur'an'. In contrast, *al-Burhān* consists exclusively of *ḥadīth*s with almost no additional commentary, since its author was an Akhbārī. Amin Ramin's *tafsīr* contains the same *ḥadīth*s found in *al-Burhān*, but with additional commentary, which concentrates mainly on the significance of the Imamate and the virtues of the *ahl al-bayt*. In general, though, Amin Ramin's intellectual interests and aims are rather different from those of other local theologians and Shii figures, since he is mainly engaged in the translation of classical Shii literature. His web portal is an independent project, and its sole source of funding is voluntary donations from readers, in contrast to some other actors who may receive funding from official bodies in Iran, for example.

There is a similar diversity among the main publishers of Shii material in Russian, which include both secular academic publishers such as Peterburgskoe vostokovedenie (St. Petersburg Oriental Studies) and Nauchnaia kniga (the Science Book Publishing House), and local confessional publishers such as Sadra (formerly known as Istok), which was founded by Zeinalov. Iranian publishers have also played a part, publishing translations of works by both Iranian and local scholars.

All of this demonstrates the presence of various independent actors with different views on what kind of literature is more relevant to or more interesting for local Shiis. There is also cooperation between some of these translators—for example, Zeinalov acknowledges that he received help from Ramin during the editing of his Qur'an translation. It is also important to note that, apart from the problem of censorship, these authors have enjoyed a significant degree of freedom in their translation activities, mainly because there was a perceived need for this kind of literature in Russian, and there are no state controlled (or state funded) institutions to fill this gap.

Finally, one of the most important objectives of this chapter was to draw attention to the large and practically unexplored corpus of texts—most of which are available to read in various languages, including Russian, at www.alhassanain.org and www.quran.al-shia.org. This discussion has also highlighted the important issue of anti-Shii bias which exists not only among local, Russian-speaking, Sunni theologians but also some academics, leading Shii-authored works to be overlooked or neglected. Further research on the primary sources written by local Shii scholars from this area is also important, because it will advance a better understanding of the culture and characteristics of Russian-speaking Shiis.

Bibliography

Alekseev, Igor, 'Nauchnaia retsenziia na pervyi shiitskii perevod Korana', *Islamoved*, 13 March 2016, http://islamoved.ru/2016/nauchnaya-retsenziya-na-pervyj-shiitskij-perevod-korana/

Baḥrānī, Hāshim, *al-Burhān fī tafsīr al-Qurʾān*, Introduction by Muḥammad Mahdī Āṣifī (Tehran: Muʾassasa-yi Baʿthāt, . 1334 Sh./1955).

Bakhrani, Seiid Khashim, Tafsir "Burkhan", trans. by Amin Ramin, https://arsh313.com/tafsir-Burhan-tom-8/

Bhutta, Sohaib Saeed, 'Intraquranic Hermeneutics: Theories and Methods in Tafsīr of the Qurʾān through the Qurʾān' (doctoral thesis, SOAS University of London, 2017). https://doi.org/10.25501/SOAS.00030286

'Bol'shinstvo moskovskikh musul'man – shiity' [The majority of Moscow›s Muslims are Shii], *Iran*, 8 February 2005, https://iran.ru/news/politics/27472/Bolshinstvo_moskovskih_musulman_shiity.

'Ekstremistskii material №1070 - Kniga "Svet sviashchennogo Korana (raz"iasneniia i tolkovaniia)" tom 4', *Lidrekon.ru*, https://lidrekon.ru/1070

'Dini demoqrafiya', https://2009-2017.state.gov/documents/organization/134425.pdf

Goble, Paul, 'Who Will Manage the 2 Million Shiites of Russia?', *The Moscow Times*, 9 Feb 2010, https://www.themoscowtimes.com/2010/02/09/who-will-manage-the-2-million-shiites-of-russia-a35088

Halm, Heinz, *Shia Islam: From Religion to Revolution*, trans. by Allison Brown (Princeton: Markus Wiener Publishers, 1997).

Ibragimi, Zahiraddin, 'Azerbajdzhan: neob"iavlennaia voina protiv shiitov', *informatsionnoe agentstvo REX*, 25 May 2017, https://iarex.ru/articles/54019.html

Imani, Seied Kamal Fakikh [Sayyid Kamal Faqih Imani], *An Enlightening Commentary into the Light of the Holy Qur'an* (Isfahan: Amir-ul-Mu'mineen Ali Library, 1994).

——, *A Bundle of Flowers from the Garden of Traditions of the Prophet [S] & Ahlul Bayt [A]*, trans. by Sayyid Abbas Sadr-'ameli and Celeste Smith (Isfahan: Amir-ul-Mu'mineen Ali Library, 1997), https://www.al-islam.org/bundle-flowers-garden-traditions-prophet-ahlul-bayt.

———, *Nūr al-Qur'ān fī tafsīr al-Qur'ān* (Isfahan: Amir-ul-Mu'mineen Ali Library, 1998).

———, *Svet Sviashchennogo Korana. Raz"iasneniia i tolkovaniia*, trans. by Sayyed Abbas Sadr Ameli (St. Petersburg: Peterburgskoe Vostokovedenie, 2011).

'Kavkazovedy sochli maloveroiatnymi presledovaniia chitatelei Korana v perevode Zeinalova', *Kavkazskii Uzel*, 25 November 2016, https://www.kavkaz-uzel.eu/articles/293214/

Khurramshakhi, Bakha ad-Din, *Koranovedenie (ocherki o Korane i ego roli v formirovanii kul'tury)*, trans. by B. V. Norik (Moscow: Sadra, 2016).

Knysh, A., and A. Matochkina, *Shiitskii islam* (St. Petersburg: St. Petersburg State University, 2016).

Krachkovskii, Ignatii Yulianovich, *Koran* (Rostov: Feniks 2003).

Mukhetdinov, Damir, 'The Russian Qur'an Translations in the Early 21th Century: An Analytical Review', *Islam in the Modern World*, 18:2 (2022).

an-Naubakhti, al-Khasan ibn Musa, *Shiitskie sekty*, trans. and ed. by S. M. Prozorov (Moscow: Nauka, 1973).

'Nazvany pobediteli regional'noi premii', *Parstoday*, 8 December 2016, https://parstoday.ir/ru/news/russia-i52648

Nu'mani, Abu Abdulla Mukhammad ibn Ibragim ibn Dzhafar Katib, *Al'-Gaiba*, trans. by Airat Baeshev, https://arsh313.com/al-gajba-numani/

Osmanov, Magomed-Nuri (trans.), *Koran. Perevod s arabskogo i kommentarii* (St. Petersburg: Dilia, 2011).

'Povtorno priznan ekstremistskim chetvertyi tom tafsira sovremennykh iranskikh bogoslovov', *SOVA*, 13 August 2020, https://www.sova-center.ru/misuse/news/persecution/2020/08/d42769/

Prozorov S. M., '*Al-Allāma as-sayyid* Muhammad Husayn al-Ṭabātabā'i (d. 1402/1981) "The Balance (of Equity) in the Commentary of the Qur'an" (*Al-Mīzān fī tafsīr al-Qur'ān*): Translation from Arabic with Commentaries by S. M. Prozorov', *Written Monuments of the Orient*, 1:4 (2006). https://www.orientalstudies.ru/rus/images/pdf/a_prozorov_ppv_2006.pdf

Qara'i, 'Ali Quli (trans.), *The Qur'an with a Phrase-by-Phrase English Translation* (London: Islamic College for Advanced Studies Press, 2005).

al-Raḍī, al-Sharīf, *Put› krasnorechiia*, trans. by Taras Chernienko (Moscow: Vostochnaia Literatura, 2007).

Ramin, Amin, 'About me', 2020, https://aminramin.net/about/

———, 'Tafsir Sviashchennogo Korana', *Arsh313*, 7 April 2022, https://arsh313.com/tafsir-svyashhennogo-korana-tom-1-amin-ramin/

——, 'Amin Ramin rasskazyvaet o sebe, svoei deiatel'nosti i nauchnoi kompetentsii', *Arsh313*, 24 October 2022, https://arsh313.com/amin-ramin-rasskazyvaet-o-sebe/

'Religion in Azerbaijan' (n.p.: Administrative Department of the President of the Republic of Azerbaijan, Presidential Library, n.d.), https://files.preslib.az/projects/remz/pdf_en/atr_din.pdf

Sablukov, Gordii, *Koran* (Moscow: Dom Biruni, 1990).

al-Sadr, Mukhammad Bakir, *Kratkaia istoriia ilm alʾ-usul*, trans. by A. A. Ezhova (Moscow: Sadra, 2009).

Saravi, Khussein Seiidi, *Samoe prekrasnoe povestvovanie* (Moscow: Nauchnaia Kniga, 2020).

Sistani, Seiid Ali, *Prakticheskie zapovedi Islama (dlia molodezhi)* (Moscow: Organizatsiia Imam Ali, 1999).

Tahiiev, Akif, 'Impact of the Events of Saqifa on the Formation of Differences between the Islamic Sunni and Shia Tradition', *Journal of Al-Tamaddun*, 18: (2023), 161–167. https://doi.org/10.22452/JAT.vol18no1.13

——, 'Islams'ke pravo: osoblivosti shiits'koï doktrini' (doctoral thesis, Yaroslav Mudryi National Law University, 2021). https://dspace.nlu.edu.ua/jspui/handle/123456789/20476

——, 'Minority within a minority: Shia community in Ukraine', *International Journal of Islamic Thought*, 19: 1 (2021): 14–20. https://doi.org/10.24035/ijit.19.2021.191

——, 'Prospects for Higher Shia Religious Education in Post-Soviet Countries', *Religions*, 14:7 (2023), https://doi.org/10.3390/rel14070822

——, 'Shiizm na postsovetskom prostranstve: vliianie novyh media', in *Virtual Islam: Identity, Authorities and Religious Practices of Muslims in the Digital Age*, ed. by Z. Khabibullina and E. Muratova (Baku: Idrak, 2023), 80–108.

——, 'Studying Shiʿism in Ukraine: The State of the Field at the Crossroads of the Geopolitics of Knowledge Production', *International Journal of Middle East Studies*, 57:1 (2025).

——, 'Understanding the 'Spirit' of Qurʾānic Laws in Contemporary Shīʿī Islamic Thought', *Interdisciplinary Journal for Religion and Transformation in Contemporary Society*, (published online ahead of print 2024). https://doi.org/10.30965/23642807-bja10104

'Teologi usomnilis' v akademicheskoi tsennosti shiitskogo perevoda Korana', *Kavkazskii Uzel*, 11 May 2016, https://www.kavkaz-uzel.media/articles/280146/

Ustadi, Rida, *Ashnayī bā tafāsīr* (Tehran: Nashr-i Quds, 1963).

Wahid, Abdul, and Mazlan Ibrahim, 'The Characteristics of Tafsīr al-Mīzān by Thabathaba'iy', *Jurnal Ilmiah Al-Mu'ashirah: Media Kajian Al-Qur'an dan*

Al-Hadits Multi Perspektif, 20:1 (2023), http://dx.doi.org/10.22373/jim.v20i1.16432

Yakubovych, Mykhaylo, 'The First Vernacular *Tafsīr* in the Caucasus: The Legacy of Two 20th Century Azerbaijani Qurʾān Commentaries', *Australian Journal of Islamic Studies*, 7:1 (2022), https://doi.org/10.55831/ajis.v7i1.457

Zeinalov, Nazim. A., *Sorok rasskazov Sviaashchennogo Korana o semeistve Proroka* (Moscow: Istok, 2009).

—— (trans.), *Sviashchennyi Koran. Perevod i kommentarii* (St. Petersburg: Peterburgskoe vostokovedenie, 2016).

Index

'Abd al-'Azīz (son of Mīr 'Ābid Bāy) 36
ᶜAbduh, Muḥammad 130, 182, 268
Abdullayev, Ismatulla 87–89, 94–97, 99–100
Abū Jahl 56
adab (etiquette) 46, 121
Afghanistan 69, 82, 90
ᶜAfīfī, Sumayya 18–19, 109, 111–121, 123–130, 132–135, 138–149, 152
Africa 56–57, 117, 229
Ain Shams University, Cairo 113, 115, 120, 134, 150
Akhbārī 294–296, 304
Akhmad Abu Yahya (Kirill Ivanovich Ivaniugo) 151
ᶜĀlamgīr, Aurangzeb 75
Alexeev, Igor 302–303
dāmlā al-Hindustānī (Muhammadjon Rustamov) 83, 97
Aliautdinov, Shamil 151
ᶜAlī b. Ḥusayn al-Kāshifī 33, 170
ᶜAlī bin Walī, Selâniklü 170
Alimov, Usmonxon ('Uthmān-*khān*) 100
al-Alkadarī, Ḥasan 44
Almas Khan 57
Almat 30
alphabet 31, 89, 98, 185, 243–244, 254–256
Altay, Halifa 1–4, 101
Āltūn-*khān-tūra* 72. See also al-Ṭarāzī, al-Sayyid Maḥmūd
ambiguity 54, 139, 187
Ameli, Sayyed Abbas Sadr 285, 291
American University in Cairo (AUC) 118
al-ᶜĀmilī, al-Ḥurr 295
Anarbaev, Nurlan Sai'lay'uly 3
anthropomorphism 138, 140

anti-Christian polemics 43
anti-colonial interpretations 21, 192
anti-imperialism 51, 114
anti-religious policies 18, 69
anti-Soviet discourse 80, 83–84, 89
anti-Western orientation 63, 118
apologetic text 142, 213, 232
Arabic (language) 1, 31, 40, 60, 73, 76, 84, 93, 100, 118, 133, 145, 163, 169, 175, 184–187, 199, 207, 244, 255, 269, 287, 290
  script 1, 5, 84, 93–94, 96–98, 102, 163, 175, 184–185, 255
Arabic media 111
Arab nationalism 126, 228
Arab socialism 120, 132, 215, 220, 230
Arab students 114, 116, 118
Arnold, Thomas Walker 51–52, 57
ᶜ*arsh* ([God's] Throne) 138
asbāb al-nuzūl (circumstances of revelation) 75, 136, 171, 301
Ashᶜarism 128, 137–140, 150
Asia 7, 12, 13, 14, 18, 31, 32, 33, 36, 43, 49, 52, 54, 69, 70, 71, 72, 74, 76, 77, 78, 81, 83, 90, 97, 98, 99, 101, 149, 163, 164, 165, 167, 170, 171, 173, 175, 177, 178, 207, 230. See also Central Asia
al-Āṣifī, Muḥammad Mahdī 296
al-ᶜAsqalānī, Ibn Ḥajar 75
autobiography 46
Azerbaijani (language) 21, 239, 241–242, 244, 246, 249–250, 254–257, 259, 261, 263, 266, 268–269, 275, 302
al-Azhar 3, 6, 109–111, 121, 127, 130–132, 135, 137, 140, 142–144, 148–151, 159, 181

Babakhanov, Shamsuddin (Shams al-Dīn) 80

Baeshev, Airat 285
al-Baghawī, Abū Muḥammad al-Ḥusayn 75
al-Baghinī, Shuʿayb 33
Baḥrānī, al-Sayyid Hāshim 286, 294–296, 301
Bāqir al-Ṣadr 295
al-Baṣrī, Abū al-Ḥusayn 42
al-Baṣrī, al-Ḥasan 42
Batulla, Rabit 185–186
al-Bayḍāwī, Nāṣir al-Dīn 42, 44, 170, 180
Bedouins 58, 228
Berke Khan 57
Bigeev, Musa (Mūsā Bīgī) 41–42, 48
al-Biruni Institute of Oriental Studies, Tashkent 79, 82–83, 90, 92
Bolshevik revolution 17, 32, 162–163, 183
Bolsheviks 15–17, 32, 38, 43, 183
Bombay. See Mumbai
Boyko'cha Street, Tashkent 90
British India 3, 52
Bukhara 2, 32, 79, 90, 93, 166, 170
al-Bukhārī, Manṣūr 70–71, 167, 270
Bünyadov, Ziya 241, 243–249, 251, 259, 261, 270, 272–273

Cairo 112–113, 118–119, 129, 131, 134, 147, 176, 181, 229
calendar 35–36
Catherine II (Catherine the Great) 160, 164, 174–175, 191
Caucasus 44, 164–165, 175, 239, 249, 257, 269, 279, 282
censorship 10, 20, 21, 22, 89, 199, 203, 209, 210, 211, 214, 216, 219, 221, 224, 292, 293, 304. See also self-censorship
Central Asia 12–14, 18, 31–33, 36, 43, 49, 52, 54, 69–72, 74, 76–78, 81, 83, 90, 97, 99, 101, 149, 163–165, 167, 170–171, 173, 175, 178
Central Asian Muftiate (SADUM, 1943–92) 76–77, 80, 84–85, 90

Central Asian Turki 18, 72, 74, 78, 97, 101
Chaghatay 31, 48–49, 51
Cherniyenko, Taras 280
Chighatay, Abdulla 90
China, Chinese 1, 15, 17, 29, 36, 44, 51, 56–57
Chingis Khan 56–57
al-Chochakī, ʿImād al-Dīn b. Muḥammad ʿArīf Abū Bakrī 36
Cho'lpon (publisher) 86
Christianity 47, 221, 225–226
Christians 43, 239–240
Chuguchak, East Turkestan 30, 32, 35–36, 39, 42, 47–48
Chuguchak (Tacheng, Chawchak), West China 15, 17, 29
Cold War 11, 14–15, 18, 21, 70, 111, 197–198, 203, 215, 233
   paradigm 11
colophons 30, 35–39, 47, 51
commentary 4, 10, 18, 20, 21, 31, 40, 41, 43, 44, 45, 46, 47, 48, 49, 50, 54, 62, 72, 75, 81, 85, 86, 88, 89, 100, 130, 134, 136, 142, 151, 161, 162, 163, 164, 166, 167, 169, 170, 171, 172, 173, 176, 178, 180, 181, 182, 183, 184, 185, 186, 188, 191, 192, 213, 242, 243, 244, 245, 246, 247, 248, 251, 252, 253, 255, 258, 259, 260, 261, 262, 264, 265, 267, 268, 269, 270, 273, 284, 290, 292, 293, 295, 296, 300, 301, 304. See also exegesis
communism xiv, 7, 8, 9, 10, 12, 13, 14, 15, 16, 18, 110, 111, 116, 117, 118. See also Marxism-Leninism; See also Arab socialism
conservativism 19, 43, 112, 116, 177–178, 187, 215
(religious) converts 57–58, 231, 280–281, 290, 294, 303
copyists 37–38, 40, 47, 51
Crimean Tatars 86, 170
Cyrillic 1, 5, 30, 71, 79, 84, 88–89, 94–95, 98, 184–185, 243, 254–255

Daghestan 33, 38, 44
Dāmullāh, Shāmī 42
Dār al-Iᶜtiṣām 140
Darband / Derbent 44, 299
daᶜwa 5, 110–114, 126–128, 130, 135, 137, 142–144, 146–148, 151–152, 232
Deoband 96
Dhū l-Qarnayn 44
diaspora 1–2, 7, 12, 31, 70, 75, 102, 280–281
Din wä Maghïishät ('Religion and Life') 176–177
Doha 76, 91–92, 184
Duhovnoe upravlenie musul'man (Islamic administration) 282
duty (farḍ) 55, 180

East and West Germany. See German Democratic Republic (GDR); See Federal Republic of Germany (FRG); See also German reunification
Eastern Europe 13–14, 165
East Turkestan 1, 31–33, 42, 49, 51
education 2, 5, 32, 97, 110, 111, 112, 113, 114, 115, 116, 117, 118, 120, 140, 149, 164, 165, 166, 168, 169, 170, 171, 173, 180, 187, 190, 191, 254, 257, 259, 267, 271, 294, 299, 303. See also Arab students; See also Egyptian students
Egypt 2–3, 6, 15, 18–19, 70, 110–114, 116, 118–123, 129, 131, 133–135, 142–145, 148–149, 151, 159, 200
Egyptian Ministry of Religious Affairs 110
Egyptian-Soviet collaboration 18, 116
Egyptian students 18, 116–118
emigration 12, 17–18, 32, 69–72, 74, 76, 89–90, 97, 100–102, 211, 263, 265, 267
Engels, Friedrich 118, 228
English (language) 3, 7, 16, 57, 112–113, 119, 127–129, 134, 206, 226, 285, 290–291, 297, 301

Estärlebash Madrasa 166
ethics 46, 62, 136, 147, 227, 250, 288
Ethiopia 58
Europe 4, 9, 13–14, 34–35, 39, 50–52, 55–57, 63, 84, 112, 139, 160, 165, 183, 185, 202–203, 208, 214, 222, 228, 245
exegesis 4–6, 31, 42, 53–55, 72, 74–75, 79, 82, 84, 111, 143, 148, 162–163, 167, 171, 173, 178–179, 181–182, 188, 230, 242, 249, 259, 262, 274, 283–285, 287–288, 292–293, 300

Fan (publisher) 95
Fan va turmush ('Science and Life') 86, 88, 101
Faqīh Imānī, Sayyid Kamāl 290
fatwa 159, 282
Federal Republic of Germany (FRG) 15, 21, 197, 199, 203–205, 208, 211, 214, 220, 222–223, 225, 231
female dāᶜiya 120, 142
feminism 111, 114, 115, 120, 121, 127, 141, 147. See also gender; See also patriarchy
Fergana Valley 84, 93
Ferrūkh Efendi, Ismāᶜīl 170
al-Fiqh al-akbar 92
Firishta, Muḥammad-Qāsim 75
Flügel, Gustav 202, 206–207, 224, 231
footnotes 10, 136, 141, 225–226, 270
French (language) 3, 57, 112, 127–128, 134, 206
Friday markets (jumᶜa-bazaars) 77, 83–84, 89, 92–93

gardens 49–50, 52
Gasprinskii, Ismail 9
gender 18, 19, 20, 55, 58, 59, 110, 111, 112, 113, 115, 116, 120, 121, 122, 123, 124, 125, 126, 127, 130, 134, 135, 141, 142, 143, 145, 146, 147, 148, 149, 201, 225, 248. See also patriarchy; See also societal roles

German Democratic Republic (GDR) 15, 21, 197–199, 203–205, 208–216, 218–225, 227–228, 230–232
German (language) 231
German reunification 15, 21, 199, 208, 230
Gladstone, William Ewart 56
Global South 113–114, 116, 220
glossary 31, 35, 39–42, 46, 49, 51, 54, 95, 300

hagiography 44–45, 53, 55, 63
Hajj 70, 76, 93
al-Ḥamīdī, Asadullāh 162, 170–172, 186
Hamid Sulaymanov Institute of Manuscripts, Tashkent 81
Hamidullah, Muhammad 3
Ḥanafī 75, 77, 92, 99, 148–149, 189–190
Hanafi school of law 75, 99. See also madhhab
Ḥanīfa, Abū 92
Ḥast-i Imām (Ḥaḍrat-i Imām) 84, 93
Hausa 3
Hell 41–42, 44, 58, 226, 268, 271, 287
Henning, Max 21, 197–203, 205–207, 210–214, 218, 223–233
hermeneutics 13, 111, 138–142, 147
Hikmatullaev, Hamidulla 82
holy war 31, 55, 220, 293. See also jihadism
Hoshimov, Utkir 85
Hosni Mubarak 18
human rights 52, 55, 59
Ḥuwayzī, ʿAbd ʿAlī al-ʿArūsī 295, 301
hybridity 9–10, 17, 31, 34, 40, 42, 45, 48, 53–55

Ibn Bāz 140
Ibn Hāshim 58
Ibn Kathīr 75
Ibn Mujāhid 42
Ibn Taymiyya 43
Ibn ʿAbbās 284

Ibrāhīm-ḥaḍrat (Ibrahimjon Mamatqulov) 77, 81
Idel 177
ijtihād 168, 174, 295
Imam al-Bukhari Tashkent Islamic Institute 76, 79
Imamate 249, 257–259, 261, 274, 283, 285, 288, 295, 297, 304
al-Imānqulī al-Qazānī, Muḥammad Ṣādiq b. Shāh Aḥmad 162, 170
India 3, 52, 70, 76, 229
indoctrination 116–118, 149
Indonesian (language) 3
Inner Asia 14
institutionalisation 22, 189, 282
institutional translations 21, 243, 248, 254, 271
institutions 4–8, 13, 18, 20–22, 77–79, 85, 89, 91, 109–112, 114–115, 121–122, 126–127, 130, 135, 137, 142, 144, 148–152, 159, 161, 165, 168, 179, 183–184, 186, 190–192, 210, 231, 243, 254, 261, 266, 271, 274, 279, 281, 284, 303–304
intelligentsia 10, 186
interlinear translation 72, 269
Iqbal, Muhammad 207, 230
Iran 1, 21, 240–241, 247–249, 254–257, 259–260, 264, 266, 274, 281–285, 287, 290, 292, 298–299, 301, 303–304
ʿĪsā 56, 58
Isaev, Gabdelbari (ʿAbd al-Bārī) 9–10, 183–184, 186
al-Isbahānī, Abū Muslim 43
ISIS 137, 141
al-Iṣlāḥ ('The Reform') 175
Islamic reformism. See reformism
islamizdat 10–11
Israel 113, 120, 216, 226, 230
Istanbul 62, 76, 176, 184, 187, 241, 299

Jāhiz (al-Jāḥiẓ, Abū ʿUthmān ʿAmr) 42
Jeddah 76, 91–92

jihadism 31, 50, 51, 52, 53, 55, 59, 60, 63, 140, 168, 190, 220, 271, 293. *See also* holy war
Jīwan, Mullā 75
Judaism 59, 201, 205, 216, 219, 226, 239–240, 247
justice 4, 20, 38, 52, 60–61, 140, 198, 228, 258
juzʾ 30, 83, 284

Kabardino-Balkarian Republic 150
al-Kamālī, Diyyā al-Dīn 41, 176, 181
Karachi 76
Karīmān, Ḥamza 142–143
Karimov, Islam 86, 99
Kashgar 74
al-Kāshgharī, Muḥammad-Ẓarīf 74
Kazakh diaspora 1–2
Kazakh (language) 1, 101
Kazakh Muftiate 2
Kazakh SSR 2, 31
Kazakhstan 1–2, 72, 77, 90, 149–150, 179
Kazan 20, 30–32, 150, 161, 163–177, 179–186, 188, 190–192
Kazan Tatars 20, 161, 163–167, 169–170, 172–173, 179, 181–184, 188, 190, 192
Khan, Sultan Ahmad 57
Khodzhaeva, Rano Umarovna 134, 146, 150
Khrushchev, Nikita 126, 210
Khudāyār, Muḥammad 93
Khurramshakhi, Bakha ad-Din 284
King Fahd Glorious Qur'an Printing Complex (KFGQPC) 1, 6
King Farouk 112
King Fuʾād (edition of the Qur'an) 131
Kokand 77, 81, 83, 93
Kosygin, Alexei 126, 183
Krachkovskii, Ignatii 85–86, 138, 140, 243–245, 247–249, 273, 287
Kufan verse numbering system 206, 224, 231–232
Kuyuk Khan (Güyük Khan) 56

Kyrgyzstan 149–150

laqab 72
Latin (script) 5, 31, 71, 98, 184, 254–256
law, Islamic 54, 189, 298
Leipzig 197–199, 203–204, 208–211, 213–215, 218, 222–225, 227, 231–233
Leninism 116–117, 218, 224
Lenin, Vladimir 118
linguistics 2, 3, 17, 31, 47, 48, 90, 97, 98, 102, 117, 136, 170, 184, 186, 191, 192, 242, 245, 251, 284. *See also* vocabulary
literal translation 138–140, 267, 299–300
lithography 184
London University (University of London) 57
Luther Bible 201, 225
Luther, Martin 177, 201, 225

madhhab 75, 148–149, 174, 190
madrasas 2, 5, 32, 46, 76, 79, 83, 90–93, 149, 161, 165–171, 173–174, 182, 185, 187
al-Maḥjūb, Muḥammad Alī 127–128
Mahjuri, Muhammadxon (Muḥammad-*khān*) 83
Maktūbāt 17, 33, 62–63
male-dominated fields 111, 115, 142. *See also* patriarchy
Mali 3
Mammedaliyev, Vasim 241
al-Mansī, ʿAbd al-Salām 118, 134, 149
Mansur, Abdulaziz (ʿAbd al-ʿAzīz) 78, 98–101
Mansur, Alouddin (ʿAlāʾ al-Dīn) 78, 85–87, 98–99, 101
al-Manzalawī, Muḥammad Murād 32
al-Marāghī, Muṣṭafā 131
Marcus, Hugo 212
al-Marjānī, Shihāb al-Dīn 32
Marxism-Leninism 117, 218, 224
Marxist Orientalist tradition 12

Maryam 56
Matochkina, Anna 283
Māturīdism 138, 189
Mawdūdī, Abū l-Aʿlā 10
Mecca 32, 58–61, 70, 80, 89, 217, 228, 246, 251–253, 258, 262, 280, 284, 292
Medina 1, 58–59, 70–72, 76, 80, 89, 93, 185, 226, 246–247, 252, 256, 258, 267, 284, 292
Melzig, Herbert 211–213, 215
Meshkini Ardabili, Mirza ʿAlī 301
metaphysical concepts 46
methodology 42, 75, 166, 173, 178, 192, 242, 268, 288–289, 291, 299, 303–304
middle class 112, 115, 121, 166
Midhat Pāshā, Aḥmad 45
Mir-i ʿArab Madrasa, Bukhara 76, 79, 83, 90–91
Mīr ʿĀbid Bāy 39
al-Mīzān 284, 286–288, 301, 304
mobility 3, 17–18
modernisation 4, 18–19, 112, 114, 120–121, 185, 206, 214, 225, 230, 269
modernist interpretations 21, 62–63, 102, 177, 192, 207, 214, 268
Moscow 79, 111, 113, 117, 120, 151, 159, 187, 280, 299
Moscow State University 117
mosques 40, 71, 84–85, 90, 147, 165, 168, 170, 175, 183, 226–227, 293, 301
mudarris 93, 166, 171
mufti 2, 9, 61–62, 179, 182, 185
muftiates 2–3, 12–13, 20, 22, 76, 160–161, 165, 170, 175, 179–181, 183, 186–192, 282, 301–302
muḥaddithūn 287, 295
Muhammadiev, Fazliddin 70
Muhammad (Prophet) 21, 41, 55, 57–60, 75, 92, 171, 200, 207, 227, 239, 242, 246–249, 251–252, 255–267, 269–275, 286, 288, 290–291, 295, 297, 301

Muhammad Yusuf, Muhammad Sodiq (Muḥammad-Ṣādiq Muḥammad-Yūsuf) 77–78, 85, 98, 100
mujaddidī 62
mukhtaṣar 91
multiculturalism 241, 249, 275
Mumbai 74, 76, 82
al-Muntakhab 18–19, 109–112, 114, 118, 124, 128, 130–151
murāqaba 45
Muslim Board of Uzbekistan, Tashkent 77, 79, 98–100
Muslim Brotherhood 110, 121, 130, 137, 139
al-Muṣṭafā (Islamic University) 299
Mutazilites 42
mysticism 33, 207

Nahid, Haşim 177
Nahj al-balāgha 290, 301
Namangan 87, 92–93
Naqshbandī 33, 35, 53
Naqshbandiyya 30, 33, 46, 81
Naqshbandiyya-Ḥusayniyya 81
al-Nasafī, Abū al-Barakāt 42, 171, 186
Nasser, Gamal Abdel 19, 112–113, 115–116, 118–120, 126–127, 132, 215, 220, 229–230
Nasserism 15, 18, 111–112, 114–115, 120–121, 132
Nasserist socialism 18
national heroes 111, 125
al-Nawawī, Muḥyī l-Dīn 92
Nawbakhtī, Abū Muḥammad al-Ḥasan b. Mūsā 287
Nawfal, ʿAbd al-Razzāq 130
Nazarbayev, Nursultan 149
Non-Aligned Movement (NAM) 15
numeric miracles 130
Nūr al-baṣar 92
Nur-Mubarak University 149
Nysanbai'uly, Ra'tbek 2

October Revolution of 1917. *See* Bolshevik revolution

On'g'arov, Ers'at Ag'ybai'uly 2–3
Orenburg 32, 160, 165, 168, 177, 189
Orientalism 8, 12, 21, 38, 51–52, 55,
    62–63, 200–201, 205, 210–211,
    213–214, 228, 245, 250, 253, 273
Osmanov, Magomed-Nuri 283
Ottoman 33, 47–48, 52, 54, 169–170,
    173–174, 176, 200, 269
Ottoman Turkish 52, 169–170, 176

Pakistan 76, 82, 159
pan-Arabism 132, 216
Paradise 36, 42, 49–50, 58, 226, 287
paratext 10, 267
patriarchy 115, 142, 147. See
    also male-dominated fields
peace 56–57, 59–60, 137, 207, 241, 266,
    285
Pentateuch 43
perestroika 8, 11, 184
periodicals 33, 174–177
persecution 30, 72, 116, 164, 183, 201
Persian 33, 36, 47, 49, 69, 73–74,
    93, 162–163, 165–166, 169–170,
    172–173, 192, 216, 244, 256–257,
    290
Porokhova, Iman Valeriia 114
post-Soviet region 133, 148, 280, 283
Prophet. See Muhammad (Prophet)
Prozorov, Stanislav 77, 284, 286–290,
    303

al-Qaraḍāwī, Yūsuf 110
Qasımoğlu, Nəriman 277
Qatar 76, 91, 184
Qosimxonov, Boboxon 81
Quli Qarai, ʿAlī 301
Qur'an-centrism 12–13
quranica.info (Islamic website) 301
quranonline.ru (Islamic website) 301
Qursāwī, ʿAbd al-Naṣīr 162–163,
    166–167, 178
al-Qurṭubī, Muḥammad 167, 186
Qurʾān rabbī ('The Qur'an of My
    Lord') 142
Quṭb, Sayyid 10, 140

Ramin, Amin 285, 294, 296–297, 301,
    303–304
Ramzī, Muḥammad Murād 17–18,
    29–55, 61–63, 181
rationalism 47, 50, 207, 294
al-Rāzī, Fakhr al-Dīn 43
readership 1, 33, 72, 77, 97, 101, 110,
    166, 185, 197, 199–200, 207, 212,
    219, 227, 246, 253–255, 288–289
Reclam (publisher) 21, 197–199,
    202–225, 227–228, 231–233
reformism 10, 31, 34, 41–44, 47, 52,
    54, 63
Religious Administration 72
Religious Council of the Caucasus
    279, 282
Renan, Ernest 51
reprints 33, 76, 86, 110, 148–150,
    168–169, 184–185, 202, 205,
    207–208, 218, 222–223, 231, 233,
    292
Republic of Tatarstan 20, 30, 61,
    151–152, 159, 183, 185–187, 190
Republic of Uzbekistan 18, 20, 69–72,
    76–80, 83–86, 89, 93, 95, 97–102,
    150
resistance 10–11, 17–18, 111, 123, 141
(religious) revival 2–3, 8, 71, 121
revolution 9, 10, 112, 117, 184, 256.
    See also Bolshevik revolution
Riḍā, Rashīd 110
Riyāḍ al-ṣāliḥīn 92
Rudolph, Kurt 198, 212–216, 218–227,
    229–230, 233
Russia 8–9, 13–15, 17–18, 20–22,
    32–34, 38, 41, 43, 50, 54, 149–151,
    159–161, 163–165, 169, 173–174,
    178–179, 183–185, 187–193, 240,
    253, 280–281, 290, 299, 302
    Empire 13, 33, 163, 168, 174
Russian (language) 18, 22, 50, 85,
    109, 111, 112, 113, 117, 123, 124,
    125, 126, 127, 129, 130, 133, 134,
    145, 148, 151, 152, 187, 191, 266,
    279, 280, 282, 283, 286, 287, 290,

298, 300, 301, 302, 304, 305. *See also* Cyrillic
Russian literature 134

Sablukov, Gordii 287
Sadat, Anwar 113, 122, 127, 132
Sadr-ud-Din, Maulana 205, 212
al-Ṣaḥwa al-Islāmiyya (the 'Islamic revival') 8, 18–19, 71, 76, 111–112, 120–121, 127, 142–143
Salafi interpretations 20, 137, 140, 148
Salafis 62–63, 121, 128, 137–138, 151, 188–189
Salimov, Marif 90
al-Samānī's, Nuʿmān b. ʿĀmir b. ʿUthmān 162, 167
al-Samarqandī, Abū'l-Layth 43, 167
Samigullin, Kamil 61–63, 159–160, 162, 186–187, 191–192
samizdat 10, 84
Saravi, Khusein Seiidi 284
Saudi Arabia 2, 6, 18, 43, 70, 72, 76, 79, 89–90, 93, 127–128, 131, 137, 140, 148, 159, 186, 254, 266, 274
al-Saʿdī, ʿAbd al-Raḥmān 187
Schimmel, Annemarie 198, 205–208, 210, 212, 214, 216, 218–219, 223–227, 229–233
sectarianism 128, 137–139, 151, 275
secularisation 19, 31
secularity 5, 17–19, 30, 52, 62–63, 71, 76–77, 81, 111, 113, 115, 119–120, 143, 160, 220, 229, 239, 303–304
self-censorship 89
seven sleepers 43
Shāfiʿī legal school 148
Sharq yulduzi ('Star of the East') 85–86, 101
Shaykh 77–78, 81, 98, 100, 110, 135, 144
Shiism 13, 21–22, 240–241, 247–250, 253, 255–257, 259–260, 263–264, 270, 273, 279–288, 290–291, 293–305
shrines 34, 46
Shura ('Consultation') 177

Siberia. *See* Western Siberia
Ṣiddiqa (bint Muḥammad Murād al-Ramzī) 29
sīra 21, 75, 239, 242–243, 246–247, 251–252, 254–255, 258–259, 263, 265, 267, 270, 273, 275
Sirhindī, Aḥmad 17, 33, 62–63
SKD Bavaria (Islamic publisher) 139–140
Slavic department (of Ayn Shams University) 134
Socialist Unity Party (Sozialistische Einheitspartei, abbr. SED) 209, 215
social justice 140, 198, 228. *See also* feminism
societal roles 112, 115. *See also* gender
Soviet Union xiv, 2, 3, 4, 8, 11, 12, 15, 16, 18, 70, 71, 76, 77, 80, 81, 83, 84, 93, 100, 102, 109, 111, 112, 113, 114, 116, 117, 118, 119, 120, 123, 129, 130, 133, 134, 146, 147, 151, 183, 184, 203, 210, 215, 222, 230, 280. *See also* Kazakh SSR; *See also* anti-Soviet discourse
    era 2, 4, 10, 13, 18, 21, 50, 71–72, 84, 89, 93, 97–98, 101–102, 146, 160, 183–185, 189–191, 273, 280
    Islam 9–11, 70, 77, 84
    Orientalist tradition 21, 245, 273
    policy 15, 18, 116
    Russia 18, 38, 54, 240, 253
    state 31, 80, 83–84
    Uzbekistan 18, 69, 71, 72, 79, 80, 89, 97, 99, 101, 102. *See also* Uzbek SSR
Spiritual Administration of Muslims and Tatarstan (Muftiate DUMRT) 20, 151
Spiritual Administration of Muslims, Russia 20, 110, 151, 279, 302
Spiritual Board of Muslims 77, 183, 185, 187, 189
Stalinism 8–9, 12, 119
Stalin, Joseph 93
State Archive of the Russian Federation, Moscow 79

Stuttgart 197–198, 203–206, 208, 210, 212, 214, 216, 218, 223–225, 227, 230–233
Sufism 17, 29–30, 32–34, 38–39, 43–47, 51–52, 54–56, 61–63, 77, 81, 179, 182, 187–189
Sunni Islam 13, 21–22, 75, 141–143, 240–241, 247–250, 256, 258, 260–261, 263–264, 270, 273, 279–286, 288, 293, 299–301, 303–304
Sunnitisation 281
Supreme Council for Islamic Affairs, Egypt 110, 127, 129–130, 140
al-Suyūṭī, Jalāl al-Dīn 75, 171

al-Ṭabarī, Muḥammad 43, 161, 186, 246
Ṭabāṭabāʾī, Muḥammad Ḥusayn 284, 286–289, 301
Tajikistan 11, 84
Tāk-i Sarrafān (traditional covered bazaar in Bukhara) 93
Talfīq al-akhbār 33, 56
al-Talqishī, Ḥusayn b. Amīrkhān 162, 169
Ṭanṭāwī, Muḥammad Sayyid 135, 144
al-Ṭarāzī, al-Sayyid Maḥmūd 18, 72, 73, 74, 75, 76, 77, 78, 79, 80, 81, 82, 83, 84, 88, 89, 90, 91, 92, 93, 94, 95, 96, 97, 98, 100, 101, 102. *See also* Āltūn-*khān-tūra*
target language 111, 133, 137, 149, 302
Tashkent 2, 32, 71, 76–77, 79, 81–84, 90, 92–94, 96, 99–100
Tatar Congress 30
Tatar Islam 17, 54, 166, 168, 174, 181
Tatar press 50, 176–177
Tatar Qur'an 21, 159, 161–162, 164, 166, 188, 191–193
Tatars 20, 30, 159, 160, 161, 162, 163, 164, 165, 166, 167, 168, 169, 170, 172, 173, 179, 181, 182, 183, 184, 188, 189, 190, 192. *See also* Volga Tatars; *See also* Crimean Tatars; *See also* Kazan Tatars

Tatarstan. *See* Republic of Tatarstan
technical language 62, 136
theology 19, 43, 45, 52, 54, 74–75, 128, 135, 137–140, 165–166, 187, 189, 248, 250, 259–261, 264–265, 268, 273–274, 280, 285, 289, 298–299, 303
Timur Khan, Tughluq 57
Tokyo 39, 50
transgression 116, 124
Troitsk 32
Tsqaltubo, Georgia 126
Tukhfatullin, Muhammad Kāmil al-Muṭīʿī 181–182, 192
Turgenev, Ivan 118
Turkestan 1, 31, 32, 33, 42, 49, 51, 69, 71, 72, 102. *See also* East Turkestan
Turkestani emigrants 18, 70–72, 76, 89–90, 101–102
Turkestani language 74
Turkestani Muslim communities 74
Turkey 1, 21, 33, 70, 76, 90, 159, 187, 211, 271, 274
Turkic languages 17, 29, 35, 36, 39, 46, 47, 86, 91, 95, 102, 148, 161, 162, 163, 170, 175. *See also* Turkish (language); *See also* Azerbaijani (language); *See also* Uzbek (language)
Turkish Diyanet 6
Turkish (language) 52, 57, 73, 169, 170, 176, 177, 185, 241, 242, 246, 249, 250, 252, 256, 257, 261, 262, 263, 268, 269, 275. *See also* Ottoman Turkish
Turks 44, 54, 69, 232, 240

ʿUbaydallāh-makhdūm, Khwādja 93
Ubaydulloh, Ahmad 92–93
Ufa 165–166, 171, 180, 185
Ugedey Khan (Ögedei Khan) 56
Ukraine 14, 149, 164, 190, 280
ʿulamāʾ 5, 33, 43, 48, 70, 74, 81, 162, 165, 175, 177–179, 191–192
United Arab Emirates (UAE) 125
United Arab Republic 119

United States of America 4, 89–90, 203, 223
unpublished works 29, 31, 38, 184, 244, 290
Urdu 74
Urumchi 40
USSR. *See* Soviet Union
Uṣūlīs 295
ʿUthmānī, Shabbīr Aḥmad 75, 96
Uzbekistan. *See* Republic of Uzbekistan
Uzbekistan Academy of Sciences 95
Uzbek Khan 57
Uzbek (language) 73–74, 78, 80, 83, 95, 98, 102
  Cyrillic alphabet 89
  modern 71, 85–86, 97–98
Uzbek SSR 2, 18, 71, 76, 83, 84, 85, 100. *See also* Soviet Union: Uzbekistan

Vampilov, Aleksandr 118
veil 115, 121
vernacular 18, 47–48, 71–72, 76, 78–79, 101–102, 160–164, 166–167, 169–173, 176, 178, 180–181, 183, 185, 187–192
verses (of the Qur'an)
  Q 2:25 49
  Q 2:28 230
  Q 2:31 248
  Q 2:70 206
  Q 2:198 46
  Q 2:231 267
  Q 3:61 265
  Q 3:136 49
  Q 3:164 267
  Q 3:169–71 49
  Q 3:195 49
  Q 3:198 49
  Q 4:14 248
  Q 4:24 247–248, 255, 293
  Q 4:34 141, 297
  Q 4:113 267
  Q 5:6 247, 253, 270
  Q 5:18 225
  Q 5:55 300–301
  Q 5:69 225
  Q 6:60 230
  Q 6:71 42
  Q 7:158 225
  Q 9:19 256, 271
  Q 9:40 252, 270
  Q 9:117 289
  Q 10 37, 139
  Q 10:3 139
  Q 13:2 139
  Q 13:7 285
  Q 16:8 45
  Q 16:89 288
  Q 17:1 50, 264
  Q 17:5 49
  Q 17:60 263
  Q 19:75 289
  Q 20 138, 224, 289
  Q 20:5 138, 289
  Q 21:85 230
  Q 24:11–22 262
  Q 25:48–50 268
  Q 33:33 253, 261
  Q 33:37 262
  Q 33:43 289
  Q 42:23 265
  Q 54:1 264
  Q 55 224
  Q 59:6 264
  Q 66 251, 262, 271
  Q 66:1–5 251
  Q 79 187
  Q 80 251, 260
  Q 80:1–7 260
  Q 84:19 268
vocabulary 31–32, 48, 56, 89, 97–98
Volga Tatars 161
Volga-Ural region 33, 46, 161–162, 165–166, 169–170, 173, 178, 189

Wahhabis 42–43, 189
Waqt ('Time') 176

wasaṭiyya 137
Werner, Ernst 198, 212–219, 221–222, 227–228
Western Europe 9, 160, 222
Western Siberia 52, 165
wilāya 297
word-by-word translation 48, 269

Xinjiang 1, 17, 31, 38, 69

Yājūj and Mājūj 44
Yasawī 53
Yoldïz ('Star') 177, 180
Yusuf Ali, Abdullah 3

al-Zamakhsharī, Maḥmūd 43, 170
Zamalek, Cairo 112
Zaqzūq, Hamdi 128, 135, 144
Zeinalov, Nazim 286, 291, 297–304

About the Team

Alessandra Tosi was the managing editor for this book.

Hannah Bergin and Annie Hine proof-read this manuscript. Annie Hine compiled the index.

Jeevanjot Kaur Nagpal designed the cover. The cover was produced in InDesign using the Fontin font.

Annie typeset the book in InDesign and produced the paperback and hardback editions. The main text font is Tex Gyre Pagella and the heading font is Noto Serif.

Jeremy Bowman produced the EPUB and PDF edition.

The conversion to the HTML edition was performed with epublius, an open-source software which is freely available on our GitHub page at https://github.com/OpenBookPublishers

Raegan Allen was in charge of marketing.

This book was peer-reviewed by Prof. Gulnaz Sibgatullina and Prof. Michele Petrone. Experts in their field, our readers give their time freely to help ensure the academic rigour of our books. We are grateful for their generous and invaluable contributions.

This book need not end here...

Share

All our books — including the one you have just read — are free to access online so that students, researchers and members of the public who can't afford a printed edition will have access to the same ideas. This title will be accessed online by hundreds of readers each month across the globe: why not share the link so that someone you know is one of them?

This book and additional content is available at
https://doi.org/10.11647/OBP.0444

Donate

Open Book Publishers is an award-winning, scholar-led, not-for-profit press making knowledge freely available one book at a time. We don't charge authors to publish with us: instead, our work is supported by our library members and by donations from people who believe that research shouldn't be locked behind paywalls.

Join the effort to free knowledge by supporting us at
https://www.openbookpublishers.com/support-us

We invite you to connect with us on our socials!

BLUESKY
@openbookpublish
.bsky.social

MASTODON
@OpenBookPublish
@hcommons.social

LINKEDIN
open-book-publishers

Read more at the Open Book Publishers Blog
https://blogs.openbookpublishers.com

You may also be interested in:

The Official Indonesian Qurʾān Translation
The History and Politics of Al-Qur'an dan Terjemahnya
Fadhli Lukman

https://doi.org/10.11647/OBP.0289

The Kingdom and the Qur'an
Translating the Holy Book of Islam in Saudi Arabia
Mykhaylo Yakubovych

https://doi.org/10.11647/OBP.0381

Points of Contact
The Shared Intellectual History of Vocalisation in Syriac, Arabic, and Hebrew
Nick Posegay

https://doi.org/10.11647/OBP.0271

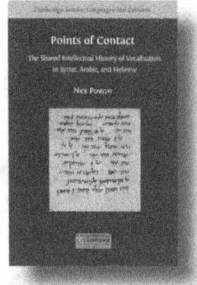

www.ingramcontent.com/pod-product-compliance
Lightning Source LLC
Chambersburg PA
CBHW050202240426
43671CB00013B/2213